We British

We British

The Poetry of a People

Andrew Marr

FOURTH ESTATE • London

First published in Great Britain in 2015 by
Fourth Estate
An imprint of HarperCollins*Publishers*
1 London Bridge Street
London SE1 9GF
www.4thestate.co.uk

1

A catalogue record for this book is
available from the British Library

ISBN 978-0-00-813089-3

Printed and bound in Great Britain by
Clays Ltd, St Ives plc

MIX
Paper from
responsible sources
FSC™ C007454

FSC
www.fsc.org

Find out more about HarperCollins and the environment at
www.harpercollins.co.uk/green

For Emily, a poetry reader

*I would also like to thank Gwyneth Williams,
Controller of Radio 4, who believed in this project;
and James Cook, who led the 'takeover' of the channel
for National Poetry Day, 8 October 2015*

Contents

Introduction   ix

1   The Earliest English Poetry   1
2   Knights in Green Satin   16
3   Fanatics and Courtiers   56
4   England's Miracle   88
5   Beyond the Nymphs and Swains:
     Renaissance Realities   112
6   Nothing Left But Laughter? Britain's Mullahs
     Confront the Problem of Pleasure   143
7   The Restoration of What? Satire, Science and
     Cynicism, as Political Britain is Born   170
8   The Age of Reason. And Slavery, and Filth,
     and So On   196
9   The Revolution   243
10 Romantic Agonies   278
11 The British Age   314
12 Plush, Mush and a Handful of Titans   350
13 The Poets of More Than One War   396
14 How Modern Were the Modernists?   438
15 Lefties and Righties: Outrage and Laughter
     in Britain Between the Wars   462

16 Revolt Against the Metropolis:
   Britain in the 1940s and 50s   488
17 The Age of Larkin   516
18 Fresh Freshness   537
19 Celts, Britons and Their Friends: Modern
   British Poetry Furth of England   562
20 Here Comes Everybody: The British
   and Poetry Now   605

   Acknowledgements   641
   Index of Poets   647

Introduction

Beyond the village, there's some marshy ground. There, on a warm evening, a horny, lonely man is making rhythmic noises and shuffling his feet. Inside his head there's a kind of music, and what he's doing is trying to fit words to it, words that express his feelings for a woman – too good for him – living in the village.

A few centuries later there's another man, who feels he has let down God and is facing eternal hellfire. Yet he's a kindly man, of gentle disposition, and somehow feels that God can't be as pitiless as the Church elders suggest. So, with a goose quill and a sheaf of rough paper, he is dipping into ink and writing down a kind of private, rather bouncy, prayer. He too is humming.

Then there is the woman in a foul dungeon, throbbing with pain from her torture, dictating to a shabby priest her defiant poem against the authorities.

There will be many more women – rich, in chambers coloured with stained glass, protected against the cold by animal skins; and poor, living in twentieth-century London, struggling with wailing children and an absent man. And many, many more men, too – Irish mystics, Scottish farmers, West Country priests, a Warwickshire actor – all doing the same thing, setting the words to rhythm, tightening them together like the ropes on a fast-moving yacht, trying to build a compact, thrumming little engine of meaning out of the sprawling magic of the English language.

Palaeo-archaeologists, who study early man, tell us that the rhythm and the music came first. Dances, perhaps led by tribal shamans, would be used to bind the people together and to express defiance of the surrounding dark and danger. To keep the beat, it was natural to hum, sing or shout. And at some point it seemed a good idea to add words. The earliest Greek tragedies, with their choruses, music and masks, give us some notion of where poetry came from.

The first poets that we know were read and discussed on the archipelago of islands we call British would have been the Latin poets of the Roman Empire. It's most unlikely that the Bronze Age tribes – technically competent people, farmers and metalworkers, miners and traders – didn't have their own poetry. But we know nothing about it. The Romano-British, however, would have had their Virgil and their Martial, and indeed their Greeks as well; there would have been poetry recitals in the villas of Sussex, and dirty, clever ditties murmured along Hadrian's Wall.

Eventually, with the scouring of invasion and the countersweep of resistance, with defeats and victories, the ethnic make-up of the British changes, and we begin to see a new language emerging from the clash of the Germanic tongues of invaders, and the Celtic speech, by now mingled with Latin, of the resisters. Like a perpetual bubbling broth, new ingredients will be added again and again through the centuries – Norse Viking, French, Italian and Spanish, Indian and Arabic. This linguistic paella will become the world's most extensive and flexible human tongue, used by generations of British people to express their strongest innermost feelings, their delight in the world, their loves and their terrors. Most human cultures seem to have specialities, for which they are particularly admired. What would Germany be without its music, or Italy without its painters and architects? The British have never had a musical tradition to rival that of Russia or Germany; or the gloriously exuberant architecture of Paris or Rome; or the coherent worldview of classical China. What they have had is the richest and most remarkable tradition of poetry of any major culture. The 'nest of singing birds' remains at the heart of the British achievement –

more important, I'd say, than empire or even the extraordinary British leaps forward in science.

What follows is an attempt to use British poetry as the framework for a kind of alternative epic, the story of what it was like to be British, told through poetry, and sometimes through the stories of the poets.

Hundreds of thousands of Britons have left traces of what it was like to be 'me in particular' – letters, drawings, works of art of all kinds, text messages, emails and social-network exhibitionism. Yet poetry is special. It's the most intimate and direct communication mankind has so far discovered. When it works – and quite often it doesn't – it can have an intensity and an interiority unmatched by anything else. When Shakespeare describes the accumulated guilt and despair of the murderer Macbeth, we see and hear a mind working in a way that seizes us still in the twenty-first century. We can read about the catastrophe of the First World War; but to feel what it was like to be there, even now, we don't turn first to the film-makers but to the poets. Those are rather obvious examples. But unlike texts, emails or television, poetry allows people from distant times to talk directly to us, with nobody else getting in the way: a medieval ploughman, a Tudor drunk or a jilted Georgian woman can look us straight in the eyes.

Writing this in 2015, I'm acutely conscious that the very word 'British' has become controversial. Many of my fellow Scots would far prefer an epic of the Scots in verse – and they can indeed find that. England, happily or otherwise, seems to be beginning to find its own voice again: many contemporary historians now focus unashamedly on the story of England, when perhaps even a decade or two ago they would have automatically reached for Britain.

If I restricted what follows to poetry written in English, however, I'd be in a quandary. The 'Inglis' tongue was established across much of southern Scotland by the early medieval period – even the patriotic epic about Robert the Bruce is written in a language which owes much more to the Saxon–French mangling we call English than to Gaelic. Scotland's greatest poets – Dunbar, Henryson,

Douglas, Fergusson, Burns, Scott and MacDiarmid – wrote at least sometimes in English; and when there was a determined attempt to return to the older Scottish versions of English in the twentieth century, the prickly 'Scots' that emerged was still a cousin of English. The same is true of the other Celtic nations: how could a survey of English poetry ignore Swift, Yeats and Dylan Thomas?

There is no political agenda in this book, though many of the experiences of the people across the archipelago have been similar. The Vikings arrived on the coasts of all of Britain, and settled in the Orkney and Shetland Islands, Dublin, the Isle of Man and the Gower Peninsula, as well as York and most of eastern England. The rage of the Reformation arrived in full force in Scotland, as well as England; plagues did not discriminate; nor changes in agriculture; nor many of the wars. So a lot of the British experience has been common, and I aim to reflect that. I also hope to include much that is specific to different parts of these islands.

And I have deliberately called this a 'British', not an 'English', epic, because I'm well aware that so much great poetry has been composed in other languages on these islands. There is a tradition of Gaelic poetry in Scotland, and Irish poetry in Ireland, and the work of the great Welsh bards. The fact that so much of this was transmitted orally, and lacks clarity about its authorship, doesn't mean it should be excluded. So where I can, I'm going to use non-English British poetry in translation. I wish there was more of it; but that's the fault of the rot and the rain, not mine. It also means that I will use translations where otherwise modern readers would struggle – thus, of Anglo-Saxon poetry, poetry in dialects from Cheshire to Northumbria, and a little Latin poetry too.

Some say poetry today, in the twenty-first century, is going through a revival; others insist that it's in terminal decline. I suppose that has always been the case. But the very source of the problem is how we hear and absorb poetry. These days most of us come across poetry on the printed page, though many of us were brought up with nursery rhymes recited to us. The story of poetry and the story of writing are closely connected, but historically poetry has more often been an oral art, heard rather than read. Even today some poets refuse to print their work, but insist that it can only be enjoyed properly at a live reading. So radio, as the prime spoken-word medium, even today, is the obvious place for this epic. What you are reading is the longer, book-length version of the takeover of BBC Radio 4 for a whole day. Poetry is going to elbow itself into programmes like *Today*, refusing to take no for an answer. It's going to lounge and sprawl between news and weather bulletins, with readings from around the whole country, and poems going back well over a thousand years in time.

This book includes some of the greatest of our poetry, including much that is far too little-known. I hope that it adds up to a new way of thinking about who we have been, and who we are now. I hope, as you come on the journey with me, you will find it surprising, uplifting, and at least a little disorientating.

1
The Earliest English Poetry

It begins in Yorkshire, on the coast by Whitby, in the year 657. Peat-smoke, the sound of waves and gulls, and winding through them the music of a harp, and words chanted in a language and a dialect so far-away we can barely understand one of them.

Nu sculon herigean heofonrices Weard,
Meotodes meahte on his modgeðanc,
weorc Wuldorfæder, swa he wundra gehwæs,
ece Drihten, or onstealde.
He ærest sceop eorþan bearnum
heofon to hrofe, halig Scyppend;
þa middangeard moncynnes Weard,
ece Drihten, æfter teode
firum foldan, Frea ælmihtig.

It's a very simple little hymn, and the traditional starting point for English poetry. Later on, we're going to hear a lot from the educated and self-confident elite of the British countries, poets from the great cities and the courts of barons and kings. But we start with a middle-aged man, Caedmon, whose name isn't English – it might be Celtic – and who was a herdsman looking after bullocks and heifers before he joined the great monastery of Abbess Hild as a farm labourer.

He was too shy to take his turn singing poems with the other labourers and monks, and retired to a stable where he fell asleep and had a vision in which he was told to sing about God. His story was told to the abbess, who commanded him to sing, with wonderful results.

We know about all of this because of the great chronicler Bede, who was working in Jarrow just fifty years after it all happened. Bede insists, again and again, on the remarkable nature of what Caedmon did. Why? In modern translation his hymn sounds pious but almost blandly straightforward:

Now we must praise the Guardian of Heaven,
the might of the Lord and his purpose of mind,
the work of the Glorious Father; for he,
God Eternal, established each wonder,
he, Holy Creator, first fashioned
heaven as a roof for the sons of men.
Then a Guardian of Mankind adorned
this middle earth below, the world for men,
Everlasting Lord, Almighty King.

This hardly seems like the beginning of the great story of English poetry. But almost everything about it should unsettle our sense of who we are, right at the beginning.

Let's start with the obvious, the Christian theme of the poem. Caedmon's world had been, until relatively recently, a pagan one. Christianity had arrived in Britain long before, towards the end of the Roman era; and it was strongly established in Wales, Ireland and western Scotland, in the Celtic Church whose rites went back to early Rome. Since then, however, the waves of Germanic invaders – Angles from Denmark and northern Germany, the Saxons and the Jutes – had pushed the old Romano-British and Celtic inhabitants to the west, re-establishing paganism as they slaughtered, and then settled.

Now, Northumbria, one of the new and powerful Germanic kingdoms of Britain, was being reintroduced to the religion of

Christ by missionaries from the Scottish island of Iona, themselves originally Irish. In modern times, we often assume that new ideas bubble up from the south and move north – and for centuries the Celts and the Irish were regarded by the southern English as barbarians. All wrong: right here at the beginning of the story, the new Christian religion had been brought southwards and eastwards from the north and west. Caedmon's monastery itself had been founded by Irish monks.

Eventually, a different form of Christianity would push up across the Channel, and establish a new base at Canterbury, after Pope Gregory I sent Bishop Augustine to the court of King Aethelbert of Kent in 596. But when our ploughman made his poetry he was living in the Celtic religious world, not the English one. Caedmon's Northumbria, with its monasteries at Lindisfarne, Whitby and Jarrow, was a great European centre of learning until it fell to the Vikings. And if many today think of Canterbury as the natural home of 'English Christianity', let's remember that Canterbury's power owed much to the arrival of a Greek, Theodore, and a North African monk, Hadrian.

Caedmon's Britain was differently shaped from today's state. After the withdrawal of the Roman Empire, the islands were a hodge-podge of tiny warring statelets: warlords passed power to their children and established royal dynasties. These slowly congealed into larger kingdoms. The great ethnic division was between the Celtic or British people still surviving in the west and north, and their enemies, the immigrant Germanic tribes of the south and east. Today 'Welsh' describes the land and the people to the west of Offa's Dyke, the smallest of the nations of Britain. But around the time Caedmon was writing, the 'Welsh' were every-where. There was for instance a kingdom of Welsh-speaking people to the north, centred on Edinburgh, fighting for their survival against the Saxons of Northumbria.

The tragic war poem about their failure and slaughter, Y Goddodin, is considered one of the earliest Welsh poems; it's classic, heroic-battle-against-the-odds stuff, though it perhaps didn't help its three hundred heroes that they had spent a year getting drunk on mead before they finally went into battle. Although the Anglo-Saxons and the Scandinavians were pushing the British or Celtic people back, there was no sense that one side was more cultured than the other. The heroes of Goddodin seem, as it happens, to have been Christians fighting pagans.

Does any of this matter much? Only because we need to shake up our ideas about what the very words 'British', 'English' or 'Welsh' mean. This was a harried, violent and marginal archipelago in which the offer of Christianity spread remarkably fast because it promised a happy and tranquil life after death – a great alternative to the cold, dangerous and relatively short experience of life in Northumbria, or anywhere else.

But it would also be a mistake to think of Caedmon's Britain as simply a wilderness of macho warlords. Note, for a start, that he answered not to a man, but to a woman – the abbess. For much of the Anglo-Saxon period, religious institutions for men and women existed side by side, with female religious leaders highly literate and, in their own way, powerful. Very little writing by them has survived, but we know enough to understand that in the world of the Church, at least, women could be as powerful as princesses. Second, from artworks that have survived, in gold hoards or the glorious illuminated manuscripts, we know that the Britain of Caedmon's time had a highly developed artistic sense; its people valued intricacy, complexity and show-off display. Although in translation his hymn may seem simple enough to us, in the original Anglo-Saxon it was a dazzling weave of assonance and rhythm, as carefully wrought as a letter colourfully inscribed in the Lindisfarne Gospels.

So, what of the language itself? I've called it Anglo-Saxon, and that's the term most scholars would use; but that's a very loose description of something that was in fact written in a specific Northumbrian dialect.

The marvel of Caedmon, according to Bede, was that he could pour out poetry while being, by the standards of the day, an uneducated man. In other words, he didn't speak Latin. Today we are used to thinking of Latin as the dry, dead, elite language of scholars and priests. Back then it was still the left-behind language of the Roman Empire, heard all over the place. In fact, it seems to have been more used in the west and the north than in the south.

Bede said Britain had five languages: English, by which he meant the Germanic dialects of Anglo-Saxon; British, close to what we would call Welsh; Irish; Pictish – another ancient British language from Scotland, now vanished; and Latin, which he said 'is in general use among them all'.

Latin was the language of the monasteries; yet it is only thanks to the monasteries that we have any early English surviving at all. In fact a single book, presented to Exeter monastery around 1070, contains the single greatest trove of Anglo-Saxon poetry, in a mish-mash of Germanic dialects. This is a language which takes root for just long enough that it can't be torn up again by the next wave of invaders, the Scandinavian Vikings; and it's still buried inside the mouths of everyone who speaks modern English today.

Caedmon's world, the great, humane monasteries of the north-east, would soon be obliterated. In the *Anglo-Saxon Chronicle* the record for the year 793 reads:

> Dire portents appeared over Northumbria and sorely frightened the people. They consisted of immense whirlwinds and flashes of lightning, and fiery dragons were seen flying into the air. A great famine immediately followed those signs, and a little after that in the same year, on 8 June, the ravages of heathen men miserably destroyed God's church on Lindisfarne, with plunder and slaughter.

Eventually Caedmon's tongue found its defender in the Anglo-Saxon kingdom of Wessex. Meanwhile, the thread of human thought and communication ran mainly in Latin. Even the old British scripts used for cutting language into stone and onto slate, runes and ogam were simplified versions of Latin letters. So having no Latin in a monastery was, even for a cowherd, a huge disability.

What was miraculous to Caedmon's contemporaries was that he used the earthy, rhythmic old German way of making poetry and applied it directly to a religious subject.

I hope it's obvious by now that Caedmon wouldn't have thought of himself as English – England as a country name didn't yet exist. His very name is probably Celtic, and alongside the Irish he'd have known in his monastery there were almost certainly Scandinavians too. It wasn't at all obvious that the west Saxons and their language would eventually triumph, or that the people of the biggest bit of the archipelago would one day call themselves English. Politically, everything was still up for grabs. We know this by looking at other early poems. For instance, 'The Battle of Maldon' is about a defeat of the English by the Danes, while 'The Battle of Brunanburg' describes a close-run-thing victory by Aethelstan, the ruler of Wessex, often described as the first King of England, over an alliance between the Viking King of Dublin, the King of the Picts and the Scots.

As the relentless warfare went on, almost everywhere Christianity was gaining ground. But outside the monasteries, almost everywhere, the older beliefs remained potent. This was a world still confused about the contradictions between the old Norse warrior culture, which was pagan and toughly pessimistic, and Christianity. The enormous poem *Beowulf* – not even set, by the way, in Britain but in Denmark – is famously confused between its Christian vision and its pagan funerals. *Beowulf* is famous but it's not much fun, except in the modern translation and rewriting by Seamus Heaney. Instead, here's something from the wonderful ecstatic poem 'The Dream of the Rood', in which the anguish of daily life is confronted by God Almighty, who seems to be something like a young Saxon chieftain:

then the young warrior, God Almighty,
stripped himself, firm and unflinching. He climbed
upon the cross, brave before many, to redeem mankind.
I quivered when the hero clasped me ...

... now I look day by day
for that time when the cross of the Lord,
which once I saw in a dream here on earth,
will fetch me away from this fleeting life
and listening to the home of joy and happiness
where people of God are seated at the feast
in eternal bliss ...

Here is a Warrior Christ, more like a Viking than a Hebrew figure, sitting down for a good old-fashioned feast – the early British didn't have much to compare things to, beyond their own lives and culture.

What sustained them? Apart from the hope of heaven, the answer is the security of their extended families or clans: thirty-five distinct tribes were recorded around the time of Caedmon's hymn. The most heavily populated areas were still the lowland farming territories, whose forests had been felled, and land ploughed, in prehistoric times. The Anglo-Saxon landscape was already old and heavily marked by the huge expansion of farming in the Bronze Age, and the burial mounds, castles and henges of earlier Britons. Caedmon's people lived in a haunted landscape. Much of the infrastructure of Romano-British culture remained semi-intact. The new Saxon settlement of Lundenwic, just to the west of the walls of Roman Londinium, had well-built-up river embankments and trade facilities. To the north, towns such as Newcastle kept their Roman names well into the 400s; York was a well-established Christian centre from Roman times.

People lived in their local tribal polities, but they travelled widely. Saxon roads, unmetalled, have rarely survived, but Roman roads were still being heavily used, and archaeology confirms that there was a vigorous shipping economy and trade with the Continent. Whether trading, raiding or fishing, the Anglo-Saxon British were at least as much a seafaring race as the British of the time of Raleigh, or Nelson. Hardly any of their boats survive, for obvious reasons, but there are two substantial ships, one from the famous Sutton Hoo burial, and the other from Graveney in Kent. Modern reconstructions of these clinker-built vessels (that is, overlapping planks, pinned together) suggest that they could travel long distances at around ten knots, a considerable speed, using a coarse cotton sail. Though very different from the sleeker Viking longships, these Saxon vessels could also be rowed at speed up rivers and along coasts, and beached very easily. Large numbers of finds by archaeologists and amateurs using metal detectors show that Anglo-Saxon Britain traded extensively across the North Sea and the Channel. Discoveries of French and German pottery and glass, and Continental coins, confirm that this was a well-connected culture. In a famous poem, 'The Seafarer', here translated by the modern poet Ezra Pound, we get a vivid sense of what this really meant. Addressing the soft-living, wine-drinking landlubbers, the poet reminds them:

> ... how I in harsh days
> Hardship endured oft.
> Bitter breast-cares have I abided,
> Known on my keel many a care's hold,
> And dire sea-surge, and there I oft spent
> Narrow nightwatch nigh the ship's head
> While she tossed close to cliffs. Coldly afflicted,
> My feet were by frost benumbed.
> Chill its chains are; chafing sighs
> Hew my heart round and hunger begot
> Mere-weary mood. Lest man know not
> That he on dry land loveliest liveth,
> List how I, care-wretched, on ice-cold sea,
> Weathered the winter, wretched outcast
> Deprived of my kinsmen;
> Hung with hard ice-flakes, where hail-scur flew,
> There I heard naught save the harsh sea
> And ice-cold wave, at whiles the swan cries,
> Did for my games the gannet's clamour,
> Sea-fowls' loudness was for me laughter,

The mews' singing all my mead-drink.
Storms, on the stone-cliffs beaten, fell on the stern
In icy feathers; full oft the eagle screamed
With spray on his pinion.

Bringing luxuries from the Rhine and the Seine was hard and dangerous work. And through most of the Anglo-Saxon era, Scandinavian raiders and pirates were an ever-present threat. Even on dry land, what mattered most in this dangerous world was what matters most still in today's colonised and harried societies, such as Iraq or Syria: a tight local network of kith and kin, to provide and sustain. Few things were scarier than exile, or losing your overlord. In 'The Wanderer', one of the great surviving poems of the period, it's being excluded that really hurts:

... I had to bind my feelings in fetters,
often sad at heart, cut off from my country,
far from my kinsmen, after, long ago,
dark clothes of earth covered my gold-friend;
I left that place in wretchedness,
ploughed the icy waves with winter in my heart;
in the sadness I sought far and wide
for a treasure-giver, for a man
who would welcome me into his mead-hall,
give me good cheer (for I boasted no friends),
entertain me with delights.

Anglo-Saxon poetry harps (literally) again and again on the loss of warrior-comrades as if it's the worst possible thing that could happen. There is remarkably little from a woman's point of view. Anglo-Saxon women had greater property and legal rights than medieval women enjoyed, and some exercised considerable power, in monasteries and in the courts. The random destruction of litera-ture means that we have only a single poem in a woman's voice: it complains about the disappearance of a husband – apparently after some misbehaviour – leaving his wife to the brutal mercies of his family.

> Early and late, I must undergo hardship
> because of the feud of my own dearest loved one.
> Men forced me to live in a forest grove,
> under an oak tree in the earth-cave.
> This cavern is age-old; I am choked with longings.
> Gloomy are the valleys, too high the hills,
> harsh strongholds overgrown with briars;
> a joyless abode. The journey of my Lord so often
> cruelly seizes me. There are lovers on earth,
> lovers alive who lie in bed,
> when I pass through this earth-cave alone
> and out under the oak tree at dawn;
> there I must sit through the long summer's day
> and there I mourn my miseries …

Along with the misery and mourning, the poet, then, understands that there are good married lives to be had. She has been forced out of her community, into the woods. We used to think of Anglo-Saxon Britain as being very heavily wooded. In fact, modern historians of the landscape tell us, much of the country had been opened up for farming for a thousand years or more.

There's a strong sense in this poem of life being literally close to the earth, and surrounded by foliage. That's an obvious separation from our lives today. Back then, even impressive towns were tiny and dangerous. Here is a fragment of an anonymous Anglo-Saxon poem about Durham, rare in being written after the Norman Conquest:

> All Britain knows of this noble city,
> its breathtaking sight: buildings backed
> by rocky slopes appear over a precipice.

(And, particularly if you pass through by train, Durham is pretty much like that today. But hang on:)

> Weirs hem and madden a headstrong river,
> diverse fish dance in the foam.
> Sprawling, tangled thicket has sprung up
> there; those deep dales are the haunt
> of many animals, countless wild beasts.

Archaeologists tell us that Anglo-Saxon Britain was studded with trading towns and urban centres huddled around churches, even if most of them, being made of wood and straw, have long disappeared. Durham, like York, got its sense of itself through the saints and missionaries buried there.

But what about the rest of the people? What sense of history did they have? Who did they think they were? We know we live in the twenty-first century. But by seven or eight centuries after the Roman legions had left, most British had no real sense of how their own history connected to that of the rest of mankind. There's a wonderful eighth-century poem in which an Anglo-Saxon wanders through the ruins of Bath:

> Wondrous is this stone-wall, wrecked by fate;
> the city-buildings crumble; the works of the Giants decay.
> Roofs have caved in, towers collapsed,
> barred gates are broken, hoar frost clings to mortar,
> houses are gaping, tottering and fallen,
> undermined by age. The Earth's embrace,
> its fierce grip, holds the mighty craftsmen;
> they are perished and gone.

So who were these craftsmen, who used techniques no longer understood, and built such walls? Wrongly, the Anglo-Saxon poet, himself a representative of the people who destroyed the Romano-British world, thinks they must have been destroyed by the plague, a contemporary problem; and he imagines them as being like bigger Anglo-Saxons – warriors bestriding courts where

> ... Once many a man
> joyous and gold-bright, dressed in splendour,
> proud and flushed with wine, gleamed in his armour ...

Interesting, isn't it, that passing reference to wine? But this Anglo-Saxon tourist is most impressed that these extraordinary people washed themselves, a pleasure which he almost salivates over:

> Stone houses stood here; a hot spring
> gushed in a wide stream; a stone wall
> enclosed the bright interior; the baths
> were there, the heated water; that was convenient.
> They allowed the scalding water to pour
> over the grey stone into the circular pool ...

And in 'The Seafarer', the poem quoted earlier, we get a similar strong sense that the world has decayed since the great days of – presumably – the Romans. That poet speaks of:

> Days little durable,
> And all arrogance of earthen riches,
> There come now no kings nor Cæsars
> Nor gold-giving lords like those gone.
> Howe'er in mirth most magnified,
> Whoe'er lived in life most lordliest,
> Drear all this excellence, delights undurable!
> Waneth the watch, but the world holdeth.
> Tomb hideth trouble. The blade is layed low.

This pessimism, so different from the Christian celebration of Caedmon, is something we should take with a pinch of salt. Anglo-Saxon Britain was full of advanced and sophisticated craftsmanship, from ornate goldwork to well-built ships and fine vellum books. No serious historian of the age now regards it simply as a time of anarchy and disaster. But if there is pessimism it is surely driven by politics – the restless, bloody tribal struggles that convulsed all of Britain, from the Picts in northern Scotland to the lands of the Jutes in southern England. Local warlordism isn't much fun even for the warlords. It isn't until the 800s, as the kingdom of the west Saxons pushed back against its Mercian, Northumbrian and Viking enemies, that the possibility of a dominant nation, an 'England', begins to emerge. Alfred the Great first managed to unite Wessex with Mercia, and then reached out until he could call himself the king of all the Anglo-Saxons. We know from a life written by the Welsh cleric Asser that Alfred was brought up on English poetry, though we don't know what that was. As a ruler he was much more than a warlord, a highly ambitious and cultured figure, in touch with the latest developments on the Continent. Alfred personally oversaw the translation of key European Christian texts from Latin into English. He imported French and German men of letters. He began – almost, it seems, single-handedly – to forge a coherent English culture.

Despite the devastating effects of the Norse raids on monasteries, with their books, we might from this point have expected a steady growth and flowering of English poetry.

It didn't happen. At least, it didn't happen for another three centuries, again because of dynastic politics, in this case the unwanted arrival of those transplanted Vikings with their strange foreign tongue, the Normans. Eventually, the violent collision between Anglo-Saxon English and Norman French would produce a supple, flexible new language. But the hugely disruptive collision of the Conquest meant that there is a long gap after 1066 before we hear again the authentic voice of ordinary British people expressed in verse in their own language. No doubt it once existed. But it's gone, and gone forever.

If the prose of the *Anglo-Saxon Chronicle* is to be believed, it would have been a poetry of lamentation. The *Chronicle* ends by describing the coronation of the man it calls simply Count William, who despite earlier promises 'laid taxes on people very severely'. He and Bishop Odo then 'built castles far and wide throughout this country, and distressed the wretched folk, and always after that it grew much worse. May the end be good when God wills!'

But there was more to this than the clash of Anglo-Saxons and Normans. Recent scholarly work points out that the pre-Norman Conquest court of Cnut, king of most of Scandinavia as well as England (and the Canute who mocked himself by ordering back the waves) and the court of Edward the Confessor were open to Danish, German, French and Latin learning. English queens were notable early sponsors of what became French literature. Britain in this period was very much part of Europe, and its dynasties were interlinked with those of France, Sweden and Hungary. The cowherds spoke Anglo-Saxon; but on the coasts and in the towns you would have heard a chatter of Norse, Latin, French – and Welsh too. For the people speaking the old British or Celtic languages hadn't gone away. What was their poetry like? Mostly oral, of course, and therefore mostly lost, of course. We have infuriatingly few fragments to go on, but there is an Irish poem about a fair in County Wexford, around the time of the Norman Conquest, which gives some idea of early non-English poetry in these islands:

There are the Fair's great privileges:
trumpets, harps, hollow-throated horns,
Pipers, timpanists unwearied,
poets and meet musicians.

Tales of Find and the Fianna, a matter inexhaustible,
sackings, forays, wooings,
tablets, and books of lore,
satires, keen riddles:

Proverbs, maxims …
… The Chronicle of women, tales of armies, conflicts,
hostels, tabus, captures …
Pipes, fiddles, gleemen,
bone-players and bag-pipers,
a crowd hideous, noisy, profane
shriekers and shouters.

They exert all their efforts
for the king of seething Berba:
the King, noble and honoured,
pays for each art its proper honour.

That's a translation, of course, by Professor Thomas Owen Clancy
of Glasgow University. He makes it sound great fun – like a modern
literary festival on acid. Not everybody in the so-called dark ages
was having a miserable time.

2
Knights in
Green Satin

It took hundreds of years for the elite language of Norman French to begin to mingle with the tongues of the Anglo-Saxons. For a long time, looking for English poetry we have to rely on very short lyrics, which nonetheless can remind us that Britain was a multi-ethnic place:

Ich am of Irlande
And of the holy lande
Of Irlande

Gode sire, pray Ich thee
For of saynte charite
Come and daunce with me
In Irlande

Oh, all right then. The lyrics of early medieval Britain are full of music and dancing, celebrations of spring and love. It's as if the shuddering, ice-bound, rainy islands of so many Anglo-Saxon manuscripts had been transformed. Up to a point, they had been. Historians talk about the early-medieval warm period, when the world's climate was more temperate. In Britain it lasted very roughly from 900 to 1300. Monks grew vines in Yorkshire; the Black Death hadn't been heard of.

16

Sumer is icumen in,
Llude sing cuccu!
Groweth sed, and bloweth med,
And springeth the wude nu –
Sing cuccu!

Close to nature, the medieval lyrics brim with references to flowers – primroses, roses, blossom of all kinds – and to the incessant sound of birdsong.

For more than a century after the Norman Conquest, Britain was riven by conflict – Saxon rebellions, wars between the Normans and the Welsh or the Normans and the Scots, and the bloody civil disputes between rivals for the crown. Although a lot of massive building of castles and some cathedrals was done, very little survives in English poetry, and that's hardly surprising. Henry II, who reigned from 1154 to 1189, is generally remembered these days as the man who ordered the killing of Thomas Becket in Canterbury Cathedral. He won the throne with his sword, and later fought long wars against his children and rebel barons – it was the Plantagenet way – but his reign brought great cultural advances and long periods of peace. He famously reformed and civilised English law. Henry was, like his predecessors and immediate successors, more French than English, Count of Anjou and Normandy, Duke of Aquitaine and so forth, whose empire covered rather more than half of modern France. This matters because France was the centre of European civilisation, going through its glorious twelfth-century renaissance. French literature, with its romances, its new ideology of courtly love and its reworkings of the Arthurian myths, had a huge influence.

Henry's death is referred to in a very rare survivor of English poetry from this period. It's a long, difficult poem, mostly read by students these days, which is nevertheless full of the sounds of medieval England – the arguments of peasants, the noise of birds – as well as the authentic stink and prejudice of the time.

It's called *The Owl and the Nightingale*, and it was probably written in the late 1100s, somewhere in southern England. There are teasing references to a Nicolas of Guildford, a priest living in the village of Portesham in Dorset. He may have been its author. The poem is a long argument between a nightingale, whose song represents love, lechery and frivolity, and a gloomy, croaking owl. As they argue, the nightingale stands on a sprig of foliage, and the owl on a dreary, ivy-encrusted stump.

At times we might imagine that the nightingale stands for the free English people and the owl for the oppressive Norman ruling class; more likely, the nightingale is an airy French troubadour, and the owl the moralistic representative of religious poetry and attitudes. Certainly, a lot of the argument is about the nature of love – is it mere sexual lust, and who may love whom properly? The early Middle English the poem is written in is too hard to be enjoyed without translation, so here is a modern version, by the former soldier and one-legged champion of Middle English verse, the late Brian Stone. The owl is having a go at the nightingale over her merely physical view of sex, and its effect on the common people:

> In summer peasants lose their sense
> And jerk in mad concupiscence:
> Theirs is not love's enthusiasm,
> But some ignoble, churlish spasm,
> Which having achieved its chosen aim,
> Leaves their spirits gorged and tame.
> The poke beneath the skirt is ended,
> And with the act, all love's expended.

Much of the fun in the poem comes from the side-swipes: the infuriated nightingale attacks the owl for choosing to sing at night in the very place where country people go to defecate, giving us a rare insight into medieval toilet habits:

Perceiving man's enclosure place,
Where thorns and branches interlace
To form a thickly hedged retreat
For man to bide his privy seat,
There you go, and there you stay;
From clean resorts you keep away.
When nightly I pursue the mouse,
I catch you by the privy house
With weeds and nettles overgrown –
Perched at song behind the throne.
Indeed you're likely to appear
Wherever humans do a rear.

As to the charge that the nightingale, representing the saucy Continental troubadour and courtly love tradition, is spreading immorality amongst the English people, the songbird first responds that she isn't to blame for the brutal behaviour of some husbands, who drive their wives to desperate straits:

The husband got the final blame.
He was so jealous of his wife
He could not bear, to save his life,
To see her with a man converse,
For that would break his heart, or worse.
He therefore locked her in a room –
A harsh and savage kind of doom.

This chauvinist husband gets what he deserves. Next, the nightingale goes on to champion the rights of girls to love whom they want. In a culture where the man of the house claimed rights over the women around him, this would have caused a lively chatter of argument among the listeners:

A girl may take what man she chooses
And doing so, no honour loses,
Because she did true love confer
On him who lies on top of her.
Such love as this I recommend:
To it, my songs and teaching tend.
But if a wife be weak of will –
And women are softhearted still –
And through some jester's crafty lies,
Some chap who begs and sadly sighs,
She once perform an act of shame,
Shall I for that be held to blame
If women will be so unchaste,
Why should the slur on me be placed?

The poem is a self-conscious literary confection, harking back to a long tradition of debate-poetry in Latin and French literature, and using many of the legal tricks and twists of the contemporary law. It doesn't refer only to the recently deceased Henry II, but to the Pope and a papal embassy to Scandinavia; it's very much a poem of its time. But for us, it's perhaps most interesting for the way it illuminates, almost by accident, changing attitudes. By the late 1100s, thanks to the Plantagenets, southern England was firmly part of the wider European culture dominated by the French. One strongly gets the sense in the poem that the other British, to the north and west, are no longer regarded as 'one of us' but as incomprehensible and threatening barbarians. As today, a divide is opening up across the archipelago. The owl, who is of course heard all over the place, attacks the nightingale for sticking to the soft southern landscape:

You never sing in Irish lands
Nor ever visit Scottish lands.
Why can't the Norsemen hear your lay,
Or even men of Galloway?
Of singing skill those men have none

For any song beneath the sun.
Why don't you sing to priests up there
And teach them how to trill the air?

To this, the nightingale replies with a ferocious description of the other British:

The land is poor, a barren place,
A wilderness devoid of grace,
Where crags and rocks pierce heaven's air,
And snow and hail are everywhere –
A grisly and uncanny part
Where men are wild and grim of heart,
Security and peace are rare,
And how they live they do not care.
The flesh and fish they eat are raw;
Like wolves, they tear it with the paw.
They take both milk and whey for drink;
Of other things they cannot think,
Possessing neither wine nor beer.
They live like wild beasts all the year
And wander clad in shaggy fell
As if they'd just come out of hell.

This is a poem still encrusted with the letters and spellings, as well as much of the archaic language, of an English we can no longer understand. That's terribly sad, because in its energy, humour and eye for detail it stands up well to Chaucer himself. It's interesting too because it ignores what was rapidly becoming the central story the British were telling about themselves.

At some point after the Norman Conquest, the people of Britain begin to spin new and more ambitious theories about their origins. The tales of the ancient Greeks and Romans had never quite disappeared, so along with the Bible there were ideas about the origins of humanity and civilisation preserved in the monasteries and courts. But the world of the ancient heroes and the Jews of the Bible must have been worryingly disconnected from the here-and-now of medieval Britain: did 'we British' emerge merely from barbarian tribes, or was there a more noble and respectable descent? Presumably this didn't much worry the fishermen of the east coast or the peasants of Wiltshire, but it certainly concerned baronial and royal courts.

So now we get chronicles which connect Britain to the earliest times of all. The Welsh monk Geoffrey of Monmouth wrote a Latin history of the kings of Britain. It begins with the Trojan wars, and claims that the British Isles were settled by the descendants of Virgil's hero Aeneas – his great-grandson Brutus arrived via the Devon settlement of Totnes, giving his name to Britain, and so on. Geoffrey, writing in around 1136, was regarded as a terrible liar by some of his contemporaries, but this notion of a connection reaching back to the Trojans proved long-lasting and popular. It probably began in Welsh and other oral literatures now lost to us. There is also a long tradition of romances and stories based on Danish or German originals, which linger in the oral tradition until they pop up as popular ballad-like poems, stanzaic or metrical romances, in the 1300s. These are 'Horn', 'Guy of Warwick', 'Bevis of Hampton' and the like. They were well-known in Chaucer's time, and in Shakespeare's, and in the case of 'Bevis', well into the early modern age. But they are little-known now, and perhaps for good reason. They tend to be all action, with the slaying of numerous foreign enemies – Saracens or Muslims above all – flesh-eating boars and dragons, and treacherous emperors and knights. Blood, gore, the ravishing or saving of maidens, sudden and unlikely reversals of fortune, and a hero with almost supernatural powers … They tell us, at least, that the British have always loved a good story, and have never been keen on foreigners.

The opening of a north-western poem, *Gawain and the Green Knight*, written 250 years after Geoffrey of Monmouth, tells us that as soon as Troy had been reduced to ashes, Aeneas and his descendants spread across the west, with Romulus founding Rome and

Brutus, charging across from France, founding Britain: his dynasty eventually produced King Arthur. Many of the popular romances, translated into English from Norman French, are about the doings of Arthurian knights. Arthur also features in the *Original Chronicle* of a Scottish priest, Andrew of Wyntoun. He says that it was Brutus who first cleared Britain of giants and founded its human story: his three sons then divided the islands between them. Wyntoun, with impressive ambition, tries to write a history of modern Scotland that connects it without a break to the creation of the world by God. It's important to him that the Scots arrived in Britain before the English. So he tells a complicated tale about a hero, Gedyl-Glays, who marries the daughter of a pharaoh, Scota, and settles in Spain. Their descendants occupy Ireland and thence arrive in Scotland, clutching the Stone of Destiny.

All of this stitching together of biblical history, the ancient myths, Arthur and the modern story of the British may not matter much to us today, but it was incredibly important to the medieval mind. It gave people in the rainy northern isles a sense of belonging to the wider human story, an essential dignity. And whether it was the Scottish priest in his tiny monastery by the edge of a loch, or the anonymous, magically gifted northern English poet who wrote *Gawain*, or Geoffrey of Monmouth, writing in Oxford with his tongue in his cheek, these zigzagging genealogies always seemed to foreground one single name, the man who became the ultimate British hero – and perhaps still is.

Sir Gawain, who slew the green knight, was a member of King Arthur's court, a Knight of the Round Table. Andrew of Wyntoun says that at the time of the first Pope Leo in Rome, when Lucius was Roman emperor, the 'King of Brettane than wes Arthour' ... And not of Britain alone. Rather than a misty, romantic figure hanging around Avalon, King Arthur was regarded as the ultimate military overlord – Andrew reckons that his conquests included France, Lombardy, Flanders, Holland, Brabant, Switzerland, Sweden, Norway, Denmark, Ireland, Orkney 'and all the isles in the sea'. He made Britain all one realm, free from foreign claims.

It's clear that the first references to Arthur come not from English, but from early Welsh sources. If Arthur ever existed as a historic figure – and it's a big 'if' – he was probably a Romano-British knight, leading campaigns against the Anglo-Saxon invaders. Between 800 and 900 he is described as a leader of the 'British' – i.e. not the Saxons. In the poem *Y Goddodin*, mentioned earlier, there is a glancing reference. It's clear that the retreating British people kept his name alive as a symbol of heroic resistance.

To begin with, the Norman chroniclers regarded him as a ridiculous fantasy of the people they were busily oppressing. William of Malmesbury wrote around 1125 of 'Arthur, about whom the foolish tales of the Britons rave even today; one who is clearly worthy to be told about in truthful histories rather than to be dreamed about in deceitful fables'; and seventy years later William of Newburgh attacked his rival Geoffrey of Monmouth as 'a writer … who, in order to expiate the faults of these Britons, weaves the most ridiculous figments of imagination around them, extolling them with the most impudent vanity above the virtues of the Macedonians and the Romans.'

Norman hostility to Arthur is interesting. It suggests that by the time of the Conquest the Saxons (against whom this Welsh hero fought) had already taken him over as one of their own, and saw him as their symbol of resistance to the latest, French-speaking, invaders. But Arthur proves a prize for almost everyone: almost immediately, French poets are appropriating him in turn, and he will flower as a Europe-wide hero and an enduring symbol of chivalry. During the medieval period he is steadily transformed and reshaped into the very image of Christian, knightly behaviour, a hero for all the new British – Welsh-speaking, Saxons and Norman French as well. He becomes, to all intents and purposes, the symbol of Britishness as the country coagulates.

If we want to understand how the medieval British understood themselves, the Arthur poems can't be ignored. One of the greatest, written around 1400, is the so-called *Alliterative Morte Arthure*, beautifully translated for modern times by the contemporary poet

Simon Armitage. This King Arthur, like Andrew of Wyntoun's, is an expansive military conqueror. His realm covers France, Germany and Scandinavia, as well as all of Britain; and he claims lordship over Rome itself, as well as all of northern Italy. The enemy is a combination of the Roman emperor Lucius with his Mediterranean allies, who, unhistorically, include Muslim warlords 'from Babylon and Baghdad', alongside Greek and Egyptian kings and Roman senators. No doubt this reflects the patriotic mood of England after the great victories against France of the early phase of the Hundred Years War, as well as the effect of centuries of crusading against 'Saracens'. The result is a medieval world war epic, extremely gory. Consider the unhappy but typical fate of a certain Sir Kay:

> Then keen Sir Kay made ready and rode,
> went challenging on his charger to chase down a king,
> and landed his lance from Lithuania in his side
> so that spleen and lungs were skewered on the spear;
> with a shudder the shaft pierced the shining knight,
> shooting through his shield, shoving through his body.
> But as Kay drove forward, he was caught unfairly
> by a lily-livered knight of royal lands;
> as he tried to turn the traitor hit him,
> first in the loins, then further through the flank;
> the brutal lance buried into his bowels,
> burst them in the brawl, then broke in the middle.

It's a poem probably based on much earlier oral sources, but by 1400 it's a modern poem too. It tells us a lot about the truth of medieval combat. In 1996, for instance, workmen at a site by the town of Towton in Yorkshire uncovered a mass grave of men killed during the battle there in 1461, just sixty years after this poem. The skeletons, stripped of their armour, showed horrific injuries. One had had the front of his skull bisected and then a second deep slash across the face splitting the bone, followed by another horizontal cut from the back. It is estimated that 3 per cent of the entire adult population of England took part in the battle, in which 28,000 people died. The corpses of the dead were said to have been mutilated, and evidence from the skeletons suggests that ears and tongues and noses were hacked off.

The audience for this poem, clearly made to be read aloud on long winter nights, well understood what a bloody butchery contemporary warfare was; but they also seem to have had an almost modern enthusiasm for the grotesque. They had been brought up on the stories of Bevis and Guy of Warwick, and our poet knows what they want. At times he sounds like a scriptwriter for a horror movie, as for instance when Arthur comes across a French cannibal giant who has just had his wicked way with an unfortunate princess:

> How disgusting he was, guzzling and gorging
> lying there lengthways, loathsome and unlordly,
> with the haunch of a human thigh in his hand.
> His back and his buttocks and his broad limbs
> he toasted by the blaze, and his backside was bare.
> Appalling and repellent pieces of flesh
> of beasts and our brothers were braising there together,
> and a cook-pot was crammed with Christian children,
> some spiked on a spit ...

Poems reflect the politics of their time. By 1400, when the English and the Scots were at war again and the great Welsh rebellion of Owen Glendower was at its height, King Arthur, once a Welsh hero who fought for Edinburgh, can no longer represent all the people of Britain. In this English poem, when he returns to confront his great enemy Mordred, he meets an army of all England's foes – Danes, Muslims and Saxons – and also

> Picts, pagans and proven knights
> of Ireland and Argyll, and outlaws of the Highlands.

English archers confront them. Mordred flees to Wales. King Arthur has, in the hands of a few generations of poets, completely changed sides.

But he always belongs to the people, fed on romances and ballads. The anonymous poem *Gawain and the Green Knight* is the most earthy and local-feeling of any work written in English in medieval times. It was produced, probably in Lancashire or Cheshire, by an educated writer born around 1330; and it was only rediscovered in a manuscript during the nineteenth century. It is, like the previous poem, alliterative rather than rhymed, though there are short rhyming lines, and it brims with the mystery and chilliness of the old English north. Very early on the poet insists that it's the kind of story the common people knew:

> I'll tell it straight, as I in town heard it,
> with tongue;
> as it was said and spoken
> in story staunch and strong,
> with linked letters loaded,
> as in this land so long.*

He protests too much. What we are really going to get is an extremely complex, beautifully patterned work, full of symbolism, eroticism and a courtly ethic which has more to do with the French romances than anything else in English we know of. But the poet's assertion that Arthurian tales are part of popular culture – 'in town ... as it was said and spoken' – feels right. There must have been a huge, now lost oral culture of poems and stories in medieval England, as there was in the Gaelic lands of Ireland and Scotland and Wales.

The Gawain story is, on the surface, a simple one. Arthur and his knights are feasting at Christmas, looking for a seasonal game to play. Then the door blows open and a green giant arrives, not very jolly ...

---

* This translation is by A.S. Kline.

a dreadful man,
the most in the world's mould of measure high,
from the nape to the waist so swart and so thick,
and his loins and his limbs so long and so great
half giant on earth I think now that he was;
but the most of man anyway I mean him to be,
and that the finest in his greatness that might ride,
for of back and breast though his body was strong,
both his belly and waist were worthily small,
and his features all followed his form made
and clean.
Wonder at his hue men displayed,
set in his semblance seen;
he fared as a giant were made,
and over all deepest green.

He calmly rides, on his huge green horse, into the hall with a strange challenge: one of the knights can have a free go at beheading him with an axe, and if the giant survives, the knight must take a blow in return, not flinching, a year from now. They are understandably nervous, but Sir Gawain takes up the challenge, and slices off the giant's head. He promptly gets to his feet, picks it up, pops it under his arm and walks out. As he leaves, the severed head calmly and mockingly repeats the deal. Fast forward a year, and Gawain has set out on his quest through freezing dark forests to find the giant and offer his neck to the axe. He is riding through a landscape full of monsters and challenges, but also a real Britain:

He had no friend but his steed by furze and down,
and no one but God to speak with on the way,
till that he neared full nigh to northern Wales.
All the Isle of Anglesey on the left hand he held,
and fared over the fords by the forelands,
over at Holyhead, till he reached the bank

in the wilderness of Wirral – few thereabouts
that either God or other with good heart loved.

On Christmas Eve, he finally finds a mysterious castle that seems
to float in a green landscape untouched by winter. He is welcomed
by its lord, Bertilak. Over the next three days Gawain will stay in
the castle and they will exchange gifts. But Bertilak's wife tries hard
to seduce our hero while her husband is away hunting. He doesn't
give way, except for kisses and accepting a green garter from her.
Then he rides off to find the giant at his Green Chapel. The first
time he kneels for the axe he flinches away, and the giant mocks
him. The second time, the giant misses. The third time his blade
cuts Gawain, but only slightly. He reveals himself as Bertilak, who
has known all along about the attempted seduction – a test of
Gawain's nobility which he (almost) passed. Gawain returns to
Arthur's court to tell his story.

Laid out like that, the poem is a straightforward enough magical
romance – the monster, the wicked lady, the tempted hero, the test,
the happy outcome. It is structured around triplets – three jour-
neys, three scenes in court, three tests, and so on. It's a longer version
of the kind of story we can imagine being told around hundreds of
medieval hearths. But what my account misses is everything that is
really important here – the contrast between the warm, luxurious,
succulent world of the castles and the bare, icy, threatening land-
scape of cliffs and forests beyond; the psychological subtlety of
erotic temptation struggling with Christian morality; the genuine
menace of the green knight as he mocks Arthur's court. These aren't
idealisations or symbols but real people, caught up in a world of
magical threats and spiritual redemption that feels very much like
the world of the early 1400s. Here, for example, is Gawain snug in
bed in Bertilak's castle, as his wife tries to seduce him one morning
while her husband is out hunting the deer:

Thus larks the lord by linden-wood eaves,
while Gawain the good man gaily abed lies,
lurks till the daylight gleams on the walls,
under canopy full clear, curtained about.
And as in slumber he lay, softly he heard
a little sound at his door, and it slid open;
and he heaves up his head out of the clothes,
a corner of the curtain he caught up a little,
and watches warily to make out what it might be.
It was the lady, the loveliest to behold,
that drew the door after her full silent and still,
and bent her way to the bed; and the knight ashamed,
laid him down again lightly and feigned to sleep.
And she stepped silently and stole to his bed,
caught up the curtain and crept within,
and sat her full softly on the bedside
and lingered there long, to look when he wakened.
The lord lay low, lurked a full long while,
compassing in his conscience what this case might
mean or amount to, marvelling in thought.
But yet he said to himself: 'More seemly it were
to descry with speech, in a space, what she wishes.'
Then he wakened and wriggled and to her he turned,
and lifted his eyelids and let on he was startled,
and signed himself with his hand, as with prayer, to be
safer.
With chin and cheek full sweet,
both white and red together,
full graciously did she greet,
lips light with laughter.

'Good morning, Sir Gawain,' said that sweet lady,
'You are a sleeper unsafe, that one may slip hither.
Now are you taken in a trice, lest a truce we shape,
I shall bind you in your bed, that you may trust.'
All laughing the lady made her light jests.

This is as vividly imagined, and as sexy, as any modern novel. Chaucer himself couldn't have done it better, and it's a fit entrant, perhaps, for the Good Sex Awards. Here, by contrast, is a description of Bertilak's men slicing up the animals he's killed while out hunting. As you enjoy it, remember that we, like Gawain, are waiting for the moment, which cannot be far off, when he has to present his own neck to the green giant's blade ... This isn't really just about dead deer.

Some that were there searched them in assay,
and two fingers of fat they found on the feeblest.
Then they slit the slot, and seized the first stomach,
shaved it with sharp knives, and knotted the sheared.
Then lopped off the four limbs and rent off the hide,
next broke they the belly, the bowels out-taking,
deftly, lest they undid and destroyed the knot.
They gripped the gullet, and swiftly severed
the weasand from the windpipe and whipped out the guts.
Then sheared out the shoulders with their sharp knives,
hauled them through a little hole, left the sides whole.
Then they slit up the breast and broke it in twain.
And again at the gullet one then began
rending all readily right to the fork,
voiding the entrails, and verily thereafter
all the membranes by the ribs readily loosened ...

We are, all of us, only animals in the end, fragile bags of slithering flesh; if Gawain is tempted by the sins of the flesh, we have a horrible presentiment about where it will end for him. The symbolism of this poem is rich enough to keep whole departments of English academics hard at work for decades. The green giant is closely related to the 'green man' myths of Saxon England – in a way, he stands for authentic, menacing Britishness against the Frenchified civilisation of the beautiful castles. But the beheading test comes from ancient Welsh and Irish sources. The poem is partly about Christians trying to live in a world that remains unredeemed and pagan: there are complicated symbolic games based on the pentangle of Christian truth, and almost every aspect of Gawain's armour and clothing has a specific meaning. The whole story takes place at Christmas, the time of Christ's birth, and is therefore saturated with spiritual promise. In the end, our hero is redeemed. Yet beyond all that, this is a story about scared, horny human beings trying to enjoy themselves, do the right thing, and stay safe in a cold, dangerous world. There's nothing else like it in English.

That includes the other poems thought to be by the same poet – the moving Christian reflection on the death of his two-year-old daughter, 'Pearl', and two other religious poems, 'Patience' and 'Cleanness'. But for the great Christian poem of this period we have to travel due south from the Wirral, to the Malvern Hills of Worcestershire and Herefordshire. It's there that a shadowy figure, probably a cleric at Oxford, called William Langland, set his allegory of virtue and corruption, *Piers Plowman*. It has nothing to do with the world of Arthur or knightly virtues; it's an angry poem about the here-and-now of an England where corrupt clerics and greedy priests have far too much power. It's the first poem we've discussed which could be called in any real sense political. Like the work of the Gawain poet, in order to understand it most of us now need it translated – though only just. This is how it famously begins:*

In a summer season when soft was the sun,
I clothed myself in a cloak as I shepherd were,

---

* This modern translation is taken from the Harvard internet site.

Habit like a hermit's unholy in works,
And went wide in the world wonders to hear.
But on a May morning on Malvern hills,
A marvel befell me of fairy, methought.
I was weary with wandering and went me to rest
Under a broad bank by a brook's side,
And as I lay and leaned over and looked into the waters
I fell into a sleep for it sounded so merry.

Then began I to dream a marvellous dream,
That I was in a wilderness wist I not where.
As I looked to the east right into the sun,
I saw a tower on a toft worthily built;
A deep dale beneath a dungeon therein,
With deep ditches and dark and dreadful of sight
A fair field full of folk found I in between,
Of all manner of men the rich and the poor,
Working and wandering as the world asketh.
Some put them to plow and played little enough,
At setting and sowing they sweated right hard
And won that which wasters by gluttony destroy.

So here we are again in a recognisable English landscape – a gentler, more rolling landscape than that of the forested north-west, but like it a landscape being reshaped and restructured by belief. A hilltop becomes a tower, a symbol of Christian truth; a dale becomes a dark dungeon, standing for evil and the under-world. Between them, unheeding, are all the plain people of England, the kind of busy crowd a medieval writer would rarely come across, except at a fair. And we are away, in a country ravaged by unfairness, in which the poor sweat and the rich guzzle. Langland compares the poor to mice being torn by cruel cats. He's clearly a man who knows London and the ways of the wealthy, corrupt clerics and their allies. His vision, however, gives us a social portrait of the British of a kind we haven't had before. Here, for instance, he's having a go at lawyers – a favourite target of radical writers over the centuries.

> There hovered an hundred in caps of silk,
> Serjeants they seemed who practised at Bar,
> Pleading the law for pennies and pounds,
> And never for love of our Lord unloosing their lips.
> You might better measure the mist on the Malvern hills,
> Than get a sound out of their mouth unless money were
>   showed.
> Barons and burgesses and bondmen also
> I saw in this crowd as you shall hear later.
> Bakers and brewers and butchers a-many,
> Woollen-websters and weavers of linen,
> Tailors and tinkers, toll-takers in markets,
> Masons and miners and men of all crafts.
> Of all kinds of labourers there stood forth some;
> Ditchers and diggers that do their work ill
> And spend all the day singing ...
> Cooks and their knaves cried 'Pies, hot pies!
> Good pork and good goose!'

So, roadworkers standing around leaning on their shovels rather than getting on with it, and takeaway food ... The joy of *Piers Plowman* is often how extraordinarily modern it feels, behind the cloak of a medieval religious sermon. But it isn't modern; this is a view of the world in which everything has a religious meaning and significance. A poem like this one can remind us how different life must have felt when, for instance, events as banal as high winds and bad weather were thought to be a sign from God:

> He proved that these pestilences were purely for sin,
> And the south-west wind on Saturday at even
> Was plainly for pure pride and for no point else.
> Pear-trees and plum-trees were puffed to the earth

For example, ye men that ye should do better.
Beeches and broad oaks were blown to the ground,
Turned upwards their tails in token of dread
That deadly sin at doomsday shall undo them all.

This world is not our world, yet *Piers Plowman* keeps its wild vitality when Langland feels obliged to be explicit about the terrible behaviour he is condemning. It's not all the corruption of the rich, but also the swinish behaviour of the ordinary Briton. Here for instance is Gluttony hard at the beer in his local pub, drinking away with ratcatchers, roadsweepers, fiddlers, horse dealers and needle sellers:

There was laughing and lowering and 'Let go the cup!'
They sat so till evensong singing now and then,
Till Glutton had gulped down a gallon and a gill.
His guts 'gan to grumble like two greedy sows;
He pissed a pot-full in a paternoster-while;
And blew with the bugle at his backbone's end,
That all hearing that horn held their nose after
And wished it were stopped up with a wisp of furze.

It's perhaps only the fact that the amount of time taken to piss out so much beer is measured not in minutes but by how long it takes to say the Lord's Prayer that reminds us that this beery scene comes from a very different England.

I hope by now I've convinced you that medieval poetry in English is a bigger and more exciting field than just Chaucer's *Canterbury Tales*. Yet that portly, self-deprecating, white-bearded London civil servant is unavoidable, a mountain in our landscape – the man who transforms English poetry more than any other in the medieval period. His great contemporaries Gower and Lydgate have virtually disappeared from the common culture, but Chaucer is different, and always has been. He was published in Tudor times and appropriated, despite his Catholic world, by the new England of the Protestant reformers: Shakespeare certainly knew his work.

And indeed, we all know our Chaucer, don't we – jokes about farts and fat women, the long-winded knights, parsons and the other pilgrims as they jolt and bicker their way towards Canterbury, this Chaucer who is the essence of unabashed celebratory Englishness, and the father of English poetry. These days when we say 'Chaucerian' we seem to mean simply lecherous and drunk. But a prolonged swim in the ocean of English verse this extraordinary man produced reminds us that his world was much more European than simply English, and that he saw himself as the inheritor and passer-on of Latin, French and Italian culture. Indeed, everything in Chaucer looks not just south to Canterbury, but south to the Continent too. If the Gawain poet stands for the wintry north, and Langland with his crowd of folk sprawls across the Midlands, Chaucer is emphatically the poet of London. His victory is also the victory of London over the rest of Britain.

London in Chaucer's time, almost as much as London today, depended upon trade and intercourse with Europe. The courts of Chaucer's three kings – the Plantagenets Edward III and Richard II, and the Lancastrian Henry IV – were all deeply intertwined with French affairs. The to and froing of clerics, official embassies, artisans, merchants and bankers made London feel different from (and superior to) anywhere else in Britain. Chaucer himself came from a family of merchant wine-sellers, and spent his life on the fringes of the court. He served in the army in France, and was ransomed; he was connected to John of Gaunt through marriage; he received money as the king's valet and was sent abroad on royal commissions. He made repeated trips to France and Italy, where he may have met Petrarch and Boccaccio; he worked as a civil servant, responsible for maintaining the banks of the Thames, and received money from three different monarchs, neatly negotiating the complex and lethal politics of the medieval monarchy. Chaucer was, in short, what we would call a member of the London political establishment, as smoothly elite as Langland was rebelliously crude.

His early poetry owes a lot to the traditions of French courtly romance; later he would pick up the newly fashionable poetry of Florence and northern Italy; and only in later life, when he was well established, would he turn to the stories and idioms of the urban English. It's an unfair and ungenerous thought, but perhaps, along with his duller contemporary John Gower, he was simply too successful for the greater good of British poetry, helping push out the language and the alliterative techniques used further north.

Chaucer's earlier poetry, with strong French influences, isn't much about the contemporary world of medieval England. These early poems are fun, and make light work of the heavy learning they are based on; but they're not the Chaucer we know today. As he moves from French influence to Italian, with a longer, more flexible line, and steadily greater vocabulary, he comes more into focus. First in his almost novel-like poem of love betrayed, *Troilus and Criseyde*, and then in the *Tales* themselves, this small, sharp-eyed bureaucrat proves himself above all a brilliant observer – of everything from clothing to the twists and turns of how we fool ourselves.

But the more you read of Chaucer, the more you realise that his medieval characters are not much like us. They experience a complicated, religion-saturated existence. Saints are real, and Purgatory looms for sinners. Daily life is governed by the movement of the planets, and explained by a complex web of folklore. Living so close to animals, birdlife and flora, the Chaucerian English find allegory in everything. As Chaucer shows us in his 'Parliament of Fowls', every bird has its own stories and its own meaning:

The noble falcon, who with his feet will strain
At the king's glove; sparrow-hawk sharp-beaked,
The quail's foe; the merlin that will pain
Himself full oft the lark for to seek;
There was the dove with her eyes meek;
The jealous swan, that at his death does sing;
The owl too, that portent of death does bring;

The crane, the giant with his trumpet-sound;
The thief, the chough; the chattering magpie;
The mocking jay; the heron there is found;
The lapwing false, to foil the searching eye;
The starling that betrays secrets on high;
The tame robin; and the cowardly kite;
The rooster, clock to hamlets at first light;

The sparrow, Venus' son; the nightingale,
That calls forth all the fresh leaves new;
The swallow, murderer of the bees.*

And on and on ... But it isn't just birds that have special meanings in the medieval world. Almost everything carries a story, even – from the same poem – different kinds of wood:

The builder's oak, and then the sturdy ash;
The elm, for pillars and for coffins meant;
The piper's box-tree; holly for whip's lash;
Fir for masts; cypress, death to lament;
The ewe for bows; aspen for arrows sent;
Olive for peace; and too the drunken vine;
Victor's palm; laurel for those who divine.

However, as Chaucer's other poems make clear, this is a world in which numerous divine influences, including the gods of ancient Rome and Greece, are still felt and thought to be potent. At a social level there is a huge, complicated and expensive hierarchy of priests, nuns and their servants, always present. For the upper classes there is of course a chivalric honour code which matters more than life itself.

Yes, as every schoolchild knows – or used to know – Chaucer's characters have bawdy appetites, are corrupt or cruel, and regularly

---

* Translation from the poetryintranslation website.

fart. But as every student soon learns, this is a false familiarity. With its iron hierarchies of class and caste, its guilds, beggars, religious con-artists and its sense that allegory is ubiquitous, Chaucer's England is closer to the more remote parts of Hindu India than to anywhere in today's Britain. Far from being the rollicking essence of Englishness, his characters spent a great deal of their time over-seas – as did Chaucer himself. His knight, for instance, has fought in Alexandria in Egypt, in Prussia, Lithuania, Russia, Spain and North Africa, as well as modern-day Turkey and Syria. For Chaucer's religious characters, Rome is the real capital of the world. Or take that most famous and homely of the pilgrims on their way to Canterbury:

A good WIFE was there from next to BATH,
But pity was that she was somewhat deaf.
In cloth-making she was excellent,
Surpassing those of Ypres and of Ghent.
… Her kerchiefs were finely wove I found;
I dare to swear those weighed a good ten pounds,
That on a Sunday she wore on her head.
Her hose were of a fine scarlet red,
And tightly tied: her shoes full soft and new.
Bold was her face, and fair and red of hue.
Had been a worthy woman all her life;
Husbands at the church-door she had five,
Besides other company in her youth –
No need to speak of that just now, in truth.
And thrice had she been to Jerusalem;
She had crossed many a foreign stream.
At Boulogne she had been, and Rome,
St James of Compostella, and Cologne,
And she knew much of wandering by the way,
Gap toothed was she, truthfully to say.

We remember the five husbands, the jolly clothing, even the gap in her teeth – she starts to feel almost like a female Falstaff – but how often do we remind ourselves that the wife of Bath spent so much time gallivanting across Europe?

So why, some people will be wondering, is Chaucer still so vastly popular when so many medieval poets have faded from view? The great trick he pulls off in *The Canterbury Tales* is, as different characters tell different stories, discovering a multitude of voices. So the pious and learned Chaucer can mimic a foul-mouthed miller; and it's through this ventriloquism that we hear (we hope) the voices of the ruder, cruder medieval British. We also get that wonderful, concrete description Chaucer is so famous for. 'The Miller's Tale' starts with that oldest of stories – the foolish older man, in this case a carpenter, who has taken for his wife a much younger and sexier teenager called Alison. We know what's going to happen next. A lecherous student called Nicholas becomes Alison's lover, and persuades the carpenter that he has had a vision of the future. There is going to be a second flood, like Noah's; to escape drowning, the carpenter agrees to be suspended in a tub, usefully well out of the way of the two lovers. But it turns out there is a third man, Absalon, who works for the parish priest and is also in love with Alison:

Up rose this jolly lover, Absalon,
And gaily dressed to perfection is,
But first chews cardamom and liquorice,
To smell sweet, before he combs his hair.

Then he goes to Alison's window and begs for a kiss. She, the minx, has other ideas. What follows is filthy, but is also one of the most famous scenes in Chaucer:

Then Absalon first wiped his mouth full dry.
Dark was the night like to pitch or coal,
And at the window out she put her hole,
And Absalon, had better nor worse than this,

That with his mouth her naked arse he kissed
Before he was aware, had savoured it.
Back he started, something was amiss,
For well he knew a woman has no beard.
He felt something rough, and long-haired,
And said: 'Fie, alas, what have I done?'
'Tee-hee!' quoth she, and clapped the window shut,

No waxing, it seems, in medieval London. But now the story takes a darker hue. Absalon vows to take his revenge. He heats up a poker red-hot and returns to the window. He begs Alison for another kiss, in return for which he will give her a present:

First he coughed then he knocked withal
On the window, as loud as he dared
Then Alison answered: 'Who's there,
That knocks so? I warrant it's a thief!'
'Why no' quoth he, 'Not so, by my faith;
I am your Absalon, my sweet darling.
Of gold,' quoth he, 'I've brought you a ring.
My mother gave it me, so God me save.
Full fine it is, and carefully engraved;
This will I give you, if you will me kiss.'
Now Nicholas had risen for a piss,
And thought he would improve the jape:
He should kiss his arse ere he escape.
And he raised the window hastily,
And put his arse outside covertly,
Beyond the buttock, to the haunch-bone.
And then spoke up the clerk, Absalon:
'Speak, sweet bird; I know not where you art.'
Then Nicholas at once let fly a fart,
As great as if it were a thunder-clap,
The clerk was nearly blinded with the blast;
Yet he was ready with his iron hot,

41

And Nicholas right in the arse he smote.
Off went the skin a hand's breadth round and some;
The coulter had so burnt him on his bum,
That for the pain he thought he would die.

Could there be anything further from the bloodthirsty heroics of the alliterative poem about Arthur and his knights than this sordid tale of lower-class shenanigans? But there is an obvious connection which tells us another important truth about our forebears. It's really rather cruel. The miller, and presumably his listeners, took great delight in the branding of Nicholas, who suffered huge pain, albeit on the backside. Just as the reality of medieval warfare was extremely brutal, and there must have been many hideously deformed and maimed ex-soldiers wandering London, so too ordinary civilian life was cruel. Children tormented animals; old women were publicly burned to death as witches; the decomposing bodies of executed criminals were left hanging in the streets. Despite the intense religiosity, despite hundreds of thousands of priests and monks, despite the noble promises of the chivalric cult, despite assumptions about the afterlife and eternal punishment for sin, this was simply a less civilised country than it is today.

It may seem that I'm making far too much out of what was meant to be simply a coarse, funny poem, but there's so little in medieval poetry that directly describes life at the time. To the medieval mind, poetry had many purposes. It existed to educate and amuse on long winter nights; to pass on beliefs about religion and courtly, educated behaviour; to build a bridge back to the world of the ancients. But the assumption that poetry should directly reflect the dirty, often cruel and dangerous state of daily life is something that most poets would reject. Their world, apart from relative rarities such as 'The Miller's Tale', is an idealised and allegorical one: poets are forever falling into dreams in which they meet the Platonic representatives of honour, love, duty or whatever it might be.

This dream world would remain hugely popular long after Chaucer died. English poetry directly after Chaucer goes into a bit of a lull. The greatest group of his followers were writing at the end of the 1400s and the beginning of the 1500s in Scotland, and not surprisingly, the poetry of the so-called Scottish Chaucerians is full of dream and allegory, and translations from the classics. But Scotland, independent politically for almost two centuries, was becoming a distinctively different country: its court poets might ape and admire the culture of London, but the country itself was both rougher and more democratic. Scotland had its own chroniclers, and just like their English equivalents they tried to tie its history back to ancient days in the Mediterranean – we have already met Andrew of Wyntoun – but its epic poets emphasise something we don't hear much of from English poets at this time – freedom.

Since the wars of independence conducted by William Wallace and then Robert the Bruce against the English, culminating in the Battle of Bannockburn in 1314, Scotland had been free. It had adopted a different notion of kingship to England. In 1320 the Scots had sent a letter to the Pope expressing their view that independence from London meant a kind of freedom rare in medieval Europe. The so-called 'Declaration of Arbroath' asserted that 'for, as long as but a hundred of us remain alive, never will we on any conditions be brought under English rule. It is in truth not for glory, nor riches, nor honours that we are fighting, but for freedom – for that alone, which no honest man gives up but with life itself.' This is the spirit of the most famous Scottish medieval poem, written by John Barbour, an Aberdonian priest who studied in Oxford and Paris. His huge epic *The Brus* was completed at the Scottish court in the 1370s, on a commission from the great king's grandson, Robert II. In the tale of the independence wars, essentially an adventure story, the most famous lines are a reflection on the importance of political freedom:

A! Fredome is a noble thing
Fredome mays man to haiff lyking
Fredome all solace to man giffis,

He levys at es that freely levys.
A noble hart may haiff nane es
Na ellys nocht that may him ples
Gif fredome failyhe, for fre liking
Is yharnyt [desired] our all other thing.
Na he that ay has levyt fre
May nocht knaw weill the propyrte
The angyr na wrechyt dome [condition]
That is couplyt to foule thryldome,
But gif he had assayit it.

But if he did say, or try, it, he

Suld think fredome mar to prys
Than all the gold in warld that is.

This feels as if it was passionately written, and there are no equivalent passages in medieval poetry south of the border.

After the wars of independence, Scotland suffered a long period of terrible bad luck with its kings. That bad luck, however, gives us a rare example of poetry by a king which isn't half bad. In March 1406 the heir to the Scottish throne, the future King James I, set off by sea to avoid his enemies at home and escape to France. But when his vessel passed close to the English coast he was captured by pirates and handed over to Henry IV of England, beginning an eighteen-year captivity under different English kings. Clearly influenced by Chaucer, James wrote an autobiographical poem now known as *The King's Quair* (The King's Book). He falls asleep – as all poets do – and dreams of the philosopher Boethius – again, almost mandatory – before describing what actually happens to him. Here is his account of boarding ship and then being captured:

Purvait of all that was us necessarye,
With wynd at will, up airly by the morowe,
Streight unto schip, no longer wold we tarye,

The way we tuke, the tyme I tald to forowe.
With mony 'fare wele' and 'Sanct Johne to borowe'
Of falowe and frende, and thus with one assent
We pullit up saile and furth oure wayis went.

Upon the wawis weltering to and fro,
So infortunate was us that fremyt day
That maugré, playnly, quhethir we wold or no,
With strong hand, by forse, schortly to say,
Of inymyis takin and led away
We weren all, and broght in thair contree:
Fortune it schupe non othir wayis to be.

King James's story ends quite well. He hears a lady singing and is entranced by her. This will be his own bride in real life, Joan Beaufort, with whom he eventually returns to Scotland. There he wasn't a bad king, but became entangled in English wars, as Scottish kings mostly did, and was eventually murdered by his uncle, another occupational hazard of Scottish monarchy. But James shared one thing with the best of his subjects – his enthusiasm for Chaucer and the new developments in English verse. The Scottish renaissance was late and brief, but its flowering was extraordinary; and whatever the country's political freedom, for literary inspiration its writers looked south.

Gavin Douglas, a member of one of the most powerful Scottish families, and later an eminent churchman and diplomat, was the first person writing in any form of English to translate Virgil's *Aeneid*, producing a powerful and gripping version. Robert Henryson, a cleric from Fife, wrote a series of dream poems and witty animal fables, and also a coda to Chaucer, the *Testament of Cresseid*. His great virtue is down-to-earth directness. In his tale of the country mouse and the town mouse, taken from Aesop, Henryson really makes us feel the distinction between the life of a rural peasant, constantly threatened with starvation, and the snug, smug world of a well-to-do merchant in the town – indeed, his town mouse has been elected as a city burgess, freed from any obligation to pay taxes.

> This rurall mous into the wynter tyde
> Had hunger, cauld, and tholit grit distres.
> The tother mous that in the burgh couth byde,
> Was gild brother and made ane fre burges,
> Toll-fre alswa but custum mair or les
> And fredome had to ga quhairever scho list
> Amang the cheis and meill in ark and kist.

The town mouse goes to visit her sister in the country, but is deeply unimpressed with the poor food and humble abode, and persuades her to come to the town, where they feed richly:

> with vittell grit plentie,
> Baith cheis and butter upon skelfis hie,
> Flesche and fische aneuch, baith fresche and salt,
> And sekkis full of grotis, meile, and malt.

> Efter quhen thay disposit wer to dyne,
> Withowtin grace thay wesche and went to meit,
> With all coursis that cukis culd devyne,
> Muttoun and beif strikin in tailyeis greit.
> Ane lordis fair thus couth thay counterfeit
> Except ane thing, thay drank the watter cleir
> Insteid of wyne bot yit thay maid gude cheir.

All is going swimmingly, until first a steward and then a cat find them. The country mouse falls into a faint, and just escapes being eaten by the cat after being played with. The cat departs, and the town mouse reappears to find her sister:

> Out of hir hole scho come and cryit on hie,
> 'How, fair sister! Cry peip, quhairever ye be!'

This rurall mous lay flatlingis on the ground
And for the deith scho wes full sair dredand
For till hir hart straik mony wofull stound,
As in ane fever trimbillit fute and hand.
And quhan hir sister in sic ply hir fand,
For verray pietie scho began to greit,
Syne confort hir with wordis hunny sweit.

'Quhy ly ye thus? Ryse up, my sister deir,
Cum to your meit, this perrell is overpast.'
The uther answerit with a hevie cheir,
'I may not eit, sa sair I am agast.'

Here, as so often in Henryson, I think you can hear the very voices
of the Scottish people in the late 1400s. These and other fables tell
us about life as it's being lived. The town is full of luxuries like
cheese and cooked meats, but it's also a place of danger and rapacity.
Henryson looks life squarely in the face: elsewhere he writes about
leprosy and the plague. In the end, however, he has a very medieval
sensibility: everything has an allegorical meaning, and the purpose
of poetry is to point the moral. Here's part of the moral drawn to
the end of the story of the two mice, and it's a familiar Christian
one about the virtues of modesty and moderation. The best life is
one of 'sickerness' – security, or safety, with only modest
possessions:

Blissed be sempill lyfe withoutin dreid,
Blissed be sober feist in quietie.
Quha hes aneuch, of na mair hes he neid
Thocht it be littill into quantatie.
Grit aboundance and blind prosperitie
Oftymes makis ane evill conclusioun.
The sweitest lyfe thairfoir in this cuntrie
Is sickernes with small possessioun.

Aside from Chaucer himself, Robert Henryson seems the most lovable and humane of medieval poets. His slightly later and greater contemporary William Dunbar is a very different kettle of fish. More so than anyone before him, we feel we can get inside his mind, though it's not always attractive. Probably born south of Edinburgh around 1460, this courtier, priest and ambassador to England and Norway speaks in his own voice, in a way that feels new. He writes, for instance, about having a migraine headache:

My heid did yak yester nicht,
This day to mak that I na micht,
So sair the magryme dois me menyie
Persying my brow as ony ganyie
That scant I luik may on the licht.*

Dunbar wasn't a particularly nice man. He was always whingeing about money, enjoyed ferocious quarrels, and is the author of a spectacularly racist poem about a black African woman who arrives in Edinburgh by ship. But he has a directness that we rarely find before him. Here, for instance, is his furious address to the merchants of Edinburgh, whom he blames for leaving their city in an embarrassingly dilapidated state. May no one, he asks, go through the principal gates of the town without being assaulted by the stench of rotten fish – haddocks and skate – and the screams of old women and ferocious arguments, descending into mere abuse? Doesn't this dishonour the town before strangers?

May nane pas throw your principall gaittis
For stink of haddockis and of scattis,
For cryis of carlingis and debaittis,
For feusum flyttinis of defame.

---

* In Scots-English, 'yak' means ache; to 'mak' is to write poetry – still in Scotland today 'makar' means poet; and a 'ganyie' is an arrow.

Think ye not schame,
Befoir strangeris of all estaittis
That sic dishonour hurt your name?

The dirty, stinking lanes cut out the light from the parish church; the porches in front of the houses make them darker than anywhere else in the world – isn't it a shame that so few civic improvements have been made?

Your Stinkand Stull that standis dirk
Haldis the lycht fra your parroche kirk.
Your foirstairis makis your housis mirk
Lyk na cuntray bot heir at hame.
Think ye not schame,
Sa litill polesie to work,
In hurt and sclander of your name?

The high cross in the centre of the town should be a place of gold and silk; instead, it's all crud and milk. The public weighing beam stinks of shellfish, tripe and haggis:

At your Hie Croce quhar gold and silk
Sould be, thair is bot crudis and milk,
And at your Trone bot cokill and wilk,
Pansches, pudingis of Jok and Jame.
Think ye not schame,
Sen as the world sayis that ilk,
In hurt and sclander of your name? ...

Dunbar protests that tailors, cobblers and other low craftsmen crowd the streets, defiling them. A notorious passage leading to the main church, the so-called 'Stinking Style', means that the merchants are crammed together as in a honeycomb:

> Tailyouris, soutteris, and craftis vyll
> The fairest of your streitis dois fyll,
> And merchantis at the Stinkand Styll
> Ar hamperit in ane honycame.
> Think ye not schame
> That ye have nether witt nor wyll
> To win yourselff ane bettir name?

The entire town is a nest of beggars; scoundrels are everywhere, molesting decent people with their cries. Even worse, nothing has been properly provided for the honest poor:

> Your burgh of beggeris is ane nest,
> To schout thai swentyouris will not rest.
> All honest folk they do molest,
> Sa piteuslie thai cry and rame.
> Think ye not schame,
> That for the poore hes nothing drest,
> In hurt and sclander of your name?

As to the merchants themselves, who are supposed to be in charge of all this, their profits go up every day and their charitable works are less and less. You can't get through the streets for the cries of the crooked, the blind and the lame – shame on you.

> Your proffeit daylie dois incres,
> Your godlie workis, les and les.
> Through streittis nane may mak progres
> For cry of cruikit, blind, and lame.
> Think ye not schame,

That ye sic substance dois posses,
And will not win ane bettir name?

William Dunbar's great cry of anger against the corrupt and incompetent merchants running Edinburgh concludes with a plea for reform, proper pricing and better management. He was a junior member of the court of King James IV, and one likes to hope that his passionate protests had some effect; at any rate, it's the most vivid account of the reality of medieval streets in British poetry thus far – we could almost say English poetry, because Dunbar and his colleagues insisted that they wrote in 'Inglis', albeit strongly tinged with the special words and accents of contemporary Scotland.

James IV was one of the most impressive kings Scotland had had. He was multilingual, interested in everything from alchemy to shipbuilding, and he presided over a highly cultured court. Earlier, we noted the widespread influence of the old British languages – now broken up into Welsh, Scottish Gaelic, Irish and Cornish. The English wars against the Welsh had helped spread the idea that the old British were barbarians. We will see this in Shakespeare later on, and by late Tudor times the wars against the Irish kick-started a strain of intra-British racism which survives today. But even in Dunbar's Scotland, when King James was trying to pacify the Gaelic-speaking north (Dunbar used 'Erse' or Irish as the preferred term), there was a profound and mutually antagonistic cultural divide. In his 'Dance of the Seven Deadly Sins' Dunbar imagines Mahoun – the devil – celebrating with Highlanders, the foreign-tongued Irish or Gaels of the north. I could try to translate for you, but it's hardly worth it. The point is, they are barely human, and clog up even hell:

Than cryd Mahoun for a Heleand padyane.
Syne ran a feynd to feche Makfadyane
Far northwart in a nuke.
Be he the correnoch had done schout
Erschemen so gadderit him abowt,

In Hell grit rowme thay tuke.
Thae tarmegantis, with tag and tatter,
Full lowd in Ersche begowth to clatter
And rowp lyk revin and ruke.
The Devill sa devit wes with thair yell
That in the depest pot of Hell
He smorit thame with smuke.

Scotland, at least, was still deeply divided by language. In another famous poem, Dunbar engaged in what was called a 'flyting', a poetic competition of mutual abuse, with the poet Walter Kennedy. The two men would have stood opposite one another, probably at the court of King James, attacking each other and responding ingeniously to the insults; the competition would be judged on the complexity of the extemporised poetry as well as the invigorating level of abuse – almost identical to today's 'battle rap'. It's now thought that Dunbar probably wrote the whole thing himself, although if he did, he gave some very good lines of attack to his enemy, who portrays him as a dwarfish and treacherous fool, without any control over his bowels or bladder. Dunbar attacks Kennedy for writing in Irish; and what's interesting is that Kennedy came not from the Highlands, but from the Ayrshire coast in the Scottish south-west. The old British languages weren't yet in full retreat.

William Dunbar could write about almost everything – the terrible winter weather, the ups and downs of court life and its politics, dancing, eating, the corruption of friars and monks, the beauties of London and his desperate need for just a bit more money. But it would be a shame to leave this wonderful writer without his greatest poem, which returns us to the ubiquitous presence of death in late-medieval Britain. Plagues, hunger and disease, not to mention wars, raiding and executions, meant that corpses were a common sight and life expectancy was short. Bodies were generally buried close to the church or under its stones, which must have meant that the smell of decomposition was something everybody knew.

In 'Lament for the Makars', his elegy for dead poets, Dunbar gives full vent to his terror of death. We are told that he wrote the poem when he was sick himself, and there is nothing quite like it in British medieval poetry. *Timor mortis conturbat me* means, roughly speaking, 'The fear of death upends me.'

> I that in hail wes, and gladnes
> Am trublit now with gret seiknes,
> And feblit with infermite;
> *Timor mortis conturbat me.*
>
> Our pleasance heir is all vane glory,
> This fals warld is bot transitory,
> The flesche is brukle, the Fend is sle;
> *Timor mortis conturbat me.*
>
> The stait of man dois change and vary,
> Now sound, now seik, now blith, now sary,
> Now dansand mery, now like to dee;
> *Timor mortis conturbat me.*

The stanza that follows, in which Dunbar compares life to the wind rushing through reeds ('wicker'), seems to me a small miracle of poetic skill, in which the rhythm and the meaning are indistinguishable:

> No stait in erd heir standis sicker;
> As with the wynd wavis the wicker,
> Wavis this warldis vanite;
> *Timor mortis conturbat me.*

Death, says Dunbar, has taken the best from all the estates of life – heavily armed knights in the field, babies at the breast, champions, captains and beautiful ladies. Death has taken magicians and astrologers, rhetoricians, theologians, surgeons, physicians, and above all poets:

He hes done petuously devour,
The noble Chaucer, of makaris flour,
The Monk of Bery, and Gower, al thre,
Timor mortis conturbat me.

And he is taking Scotland's poets one by one, not forgetting Dunbar's old enemy:

In Dumfermelyne he has done roune
With Maister Robert Henrisoun ...
... Gud Maister Walter Kennedy
In poynt of dede lyis verily,
Gret reuth it were that so suld be;
Timor mortis conturbat me.

And so, eventually, that great clanging Latin bell can't be avoided by Dunbar himself, as he well knows:

Sen he hes all my brether tane,
He will nocht lat me lif alane,
On forse I man his nyxt me be;
Timor mortis conturbat me.

The poem has a special poignancy because, not so long after it was written, William Dunbar's whole world was destroyed on the battlefield. In 1513 his king and patron James IV honoured a treaty with the French and invaded Northumberland, where he was confronted by the Earl of Surrey and a large English army. What followed has been described as the last great medieval battle on British soil. Though both sides used artillery, not to great effect, most of the killing was done with billhooks and spears. James, who had lingered in chivalric manner before the battle, giving the English plenty of time to prepare, was slaughtered along with a dozen earls, almost all the senior clergy of Scotland and most of the chieftains – a shattering blow to a country just emerging from a long period

of feuding. The short Scottish renaissance that James had symbol-
ised, with its poets, architects, shipwrights and men of letters, came
to a juddering halt. *Timor mortis*, indeed.

3

Fanatics and Courtiers

In all the periods of poetry we've looked at so far, there is nothing quite as extraordinary as what happens in the 1500s – that great, bloody and turbulent century of Reformation. We begin it with the clearly medieval figures of the Chaucerians. Even if Dunbar feels different, it's still a recognisably medieval world, crammed with religious meaning and allegory, in which the old stories are still popular, whether Aesop or Arthur. We end the 1500s, however, with William Shakespeare nearing his zenith, and a fresh universe of new poets who feel almost modern in their directness. It's not that one world dies and a new one is born. Things aren't like that. But the great age of Catholic Christianity, the age of Latin learning, polychromatic cathedrals and a clear social hierarchy deriving from feudal times, was waning very quickly. Wars would carry on being fought, but mostly abroad. British culture, from Edinburgh to London, began to feel much more urban, less close to the sounds and smells of the countryside. Above all, a new religious sensibility, deriving from John Wycliffe and the early reformers, meant that people had a more direct relationship to the gospel; this seems to be connected to what we today would call individualism. Also, thanks to printing and the lack of domestic warfare, we suddenly have a much larger number of poets to choose from: simply, much more stuff survives.

Politically, the biggest change was the victory of the Tudor dynasty in England, those bringers of Protestantism and a more ruthless royal overlordship. It was the court of Henry VIII that would take poetry forward again, and so it is appropriate that the first major poet of England in this century was a highly political figure, and indeed the first Poet Laureate to be mentioned here. John Skelton probably came from Diss in Norfolk, and was an unruly, unpredictable but star figure at Oxford and Cambridge. Notorious for secretly marrying a wife while a vicar, and having a child – who he presented, naked, to his congregation – by her, he later became a great flayer of priestly corruption just as England was in revolt against the Roman Church. To start with he can sound old-fashioned and medieval, as in his jeering, triumphalist response to the death of Scotland's King James IV at Flodden:

> Kynge Jamy, Jomy your joye is all go.
> Ye summoned our kynge. Why dyde ye so?
>
> Ye have determyned to make a fraye,
> Our kynge than beynge out of the waye;
> But by the power and myght of God
> Ye were beten weth your owne rod.
> By your wanton wyll, syr, at a worde,
> Ye have loste spores, cote armure and sworde ...
>
> Of the out yles ye rough foted Scottes
> We have well eased you of the bottes.
> Ye rowe ranke Scottes and dronken Danes
> Of our Englysshe bowes ye have fette your banes.

It's not a lot more advanced than 'Na-na-na-na,' but Skelton was a much more sophisticated satirist than this, though known at the time and ever afterwards as a peculiarly sarcastic poet. And, often enough, nasty too. Alongside the conventions of chivalric love there was a bitterly misogynistic strain to English poetry. In the previous chapter I refrained from including the revoltingly racist poem by

Dunbar after he had seen a black woman in Edinburgh. But we shouldn't sanitise our own history, so here is Skelton ripping to pieces a woman whose main sin seems to be that she was elderly:

Her lothely lere
Is nothynge clere,
But ugly of chere,
Droupy and drowsy,
Scurvy and lowsy;
Her face all bowsy,
Comely crynkled,
Woundersly wrynkled,
Lyke a rost pygges eare,
Brystled wyth here.

Her lewde lyppes twayne,
They slaver, men sayne,
Lyke a ropy rayne,
A gummy glayre:
She is ugly fayre;
Her nose somdele hoked,
And camously croked,
Never stoppynge,
But ever droppynge;
Her skynne lose and slacke,
Grained lyke a sacke;
With a croked backe

Ugh. Skelton was tutor to the future Henry VIII, and became heavily embroiled in his fight with Cardinal Wolsey: the ferocious assaults on Church corruption, which deeply offended the cardinal and put Skelton in serious danger, were also however an expression of the growing anti-clerical mood of pre-Reformation England. Skelton's verse is always vigorous and exciting, and it's not hard to see why he was such a politically controversial figure. In his famous poem 'Speke, Parott' he uses the bird to deliver a tirade of abuse against Wolsey's Church. Like much of Skelton's writing, the poem is almost manic, and doesn't feel like a piece written to order, but rather the cry of an early reformer against the flabby, corrupt and greedy Church. Is it so different in tone to an angry blog post today directed at the political elite?

So many morall maters, and so lytell vsyd;
So myche newe makyng, and so madd tyme spente;
So myche translacion in to Englyshe confused;
So myche nobyll prechyng, and so lytell amendment;
So myche consultacion, almoste to none entente;
So myche provision, and so lytell wytte at nede;–
Syns Dewcalyons flodde* there can no clerkes rede.

So lytyll dyscressyon, and so myche reasonyng;
So myche hardy dardy, and so lytell manlynes;
So prodigall expence, and so shamfull reconyng;
So gorgyous garmentes, and so myche wrechydnese;
So myche portlye pride, with pursys penyles
So myche spente before, and so myche vnpayd behynde;–
Syns Dewcalyons flodde there can no clerkes fynde.

So myche forcastyng, and so farre an after dele;
So myche poletyke pratyng, and so lytell stondythe in
    stede;
So lytell secretnese, and so myche grete councell;
So manye bolde barons, there hertes as dull as lede;
So many nobyll bodyes vndyr on dawys hedd;
So royall a kyng as reynythe vppon vs all;–
Syns Dewcalyons flodde was nevyr sene nor shall.

---

* 'Deucalion's flood' refers to the Greek version of the Noah flood story, and therefore simply means 'since time immemorial'.

So many complayntes, and so smalle redresse;
So myche callyng on, and so smalle takyng hede;
So myche losse of merchaundyse, and so remedyles;
So lytell care for the comyn weall, and so myche nede;
So myche dowtfull daunger, and so lytell drede;
So myche pride of prelattes, so cruell and so kene;—
Syns Dewcalyons flodde, I trowe, was nevyr sene.

Skelton was a one-off, similar at times in tone to his contemporary William Dunbar. But he introduces us to the fact, unavoidable at this period, that poetry and the royal court intersected deeply. Particularly at Henry VIII's court, poetry became an essential part of daily life as perhaps it had never been before and has not been since. It was a world of incessant cod-Arthurian games, elaborate tournaments, masques and literary competitions; for an ambitious courtier, to be able to produce instant, fluent poems was a great advantage. These would not have been printed or publicly available – most would have been written on scraps of paper to be passed around the court from hand to hand. Thus a courtier might declare his love, or lament its passing. Because one such courtier, Sir Thomas Wyatt, was a minor genius, aspects of this artificial, highly-coloured world have survived.

A tall, handsome man who in a Holbein drawing looks like a heavily bearded modern hipster, Wyatt served both Henry VII and his son. He was suspected of having an affair with Anne Boleyn, and was imprisoned in the Tower by Henry VIII for adultery with her. There he witnessed other alleged adulterers being executed, and possibly Anne herself. Life at Henry VIII's court was dangerous, particularly for a glamorous and sexually driven man like Wyatt; and yet, despite flying close to the sun on numerous occasions, he survived to die of old age. From our point of view he is most important as the man who took Petrarch's new sonnet form and introduced it properly into English verse. In Wyatt's writing there is a specificity of description, and a humane directness, which make it sound as if it comes from a different century, almost a different planet, from Skelton's. The metaphor of timid deer for

women might seem offensive, but quickly collapses, in an almost
Shakespearean way:

> They flee from me that sometime did me seek
> With naked foot, stalking in my chamber.
> I have seen them gentle, tame, and meek,
> That now are wild and do not remember
> That sometime they put themself in danger
> To take bread at my hand; and now they range,
> Busily seeking with a continual change.
>
> Thanked be fortune it hath been otherwise
> Twenty times better; but once in special,
> In thin array after a pleasant guise,
> When her loose gown from her shoulders did fall,
> And she me caught in her arms long and small;
> Therewith all sweetly did me kiss
> And softly said, 'Dear heart, how like you this.'
>
> It was no dream: I lay broad waking.
> But all is turned thorough my gentleness
> Into a strange fashion of forsaking;
> And I have leave to go of her goodness,
> And she also, to use newfangleness.
> But since that I so kindly am served
> I would fain know what she hath deserved.

Well-travelled on the Continent and a multilingual Cambridge
scholar, Wyatt also introduced the Horatian ode into English, and
his address to his friend and fellow courtier John Poynz has all the
easy intimacy of Horace himself. The theme is the familiar one of
the poet retiring from court and explaining that he must do so
because he's had it with double dealing, oily hypocrisy and the other
necessities of life around the powerful. But in Wyatt's hands, what
could be a mere poetic exercise feels like a genuine plaint by a living

courtier in the cold climate of Henry's England: farewell to all the doublespeak of politics:

The friendly foe with his double face
Say he is gentle and courteous therewithal;
And say that Favel hath a goodly grace
In eloquence; and cruelty to name
Zeal of justice and change in time and place;
And he that suffer'th offence without blame
Call him pitiful; and him true and plain
That raileth reckless to every man's shame.
Say he is rude that cannot lie and feign;
The lecher a lover; and tyranny
To be the right of a prince's reign.
I cannot, I; no, no, it will not be!
This is the cause that I could never yet
Hang on their sleeves that way, as thou mayst see,
A chip of chance more than a pound of wit.
This maketh me at home to hunt and to hawk,
And in foul weather at my book to sit;
In frost and snow then with my bow to stalk;
No man doth mark whereso I ride or go:
In lusty leas at liberty I walk.
And of these news I feel nor weal nor woe,
Save that a clog doth hang yet at my heel.
No force for that, for it is ordered so,
That I may leap both hedge and dyke full well.
I am not now in France to judge the wine,
… Nor I am not where Christ is given in prey
For money, poison, and treason at Rome –
A common practice used night and day:
But here I am in Kent and Christendom
Among the Muses where I read and rhyme;
Where if thou list, my Poinz, for to come,
Thou shalt be judge how I do spend my time.

In its easy eloquence, its self-confidence, this is not so far removed, is it, from the great soliloquies we will soon be hearing on the Elizabethan stage? The Tudor court was a highly artificial human experience; but it produced an intensity of feeling, a closeness and a directness, which would soon be heard by the masses in makeshift theatres around the land. Grandees like Wyatt were confident enough to address their peers with a familiarity unknown in British poetry before. But it would spread.

So far, we've seen a misogynistic attack on women, and women presented as nervy, nibbling as the game for the courtly male hunter, but we haven't actually heard from any woman. Anne Askew was born in Lincolnshire in 1520, and became one of the best-known and most spectacular of Protestant martyrs. Her family was relatively wealthy, in land at least. Arranged marriages were common in Tudor England, largely for economic reasons. Girls were often married off as early as fourteen, and some of these unions would have been, by modern standards, forced marriages. Anne's father had planned to marry her older sister Martha to another local landowner, Thomas Kyne, but Martha died and Anne was substituted, aged fifteen. She bore Thomas two children, her first duty.

It wasn't a happy marriage; they disagreed about religion in particular. Although Henry VIII's long struggle with the papacy over his divorce from Catherine of Aragon was driving England towards the Protestant camp, there was still huge uncertainty and division over precisely what mix of traditional Catholic teaching and the new teaching of the reformers England would end up with. Relatively small doctrinal differences could become politically toxic. On this spectrum, Anne was a hard-core reformer; her husband was Catholic. While she was still little more than a teenager, Kyne kicked Anne out of the marital home. When she arrived in London she tried to divorce him on the grounds that he was an infidel, and that therefore the marriage could not be legal. Gutsy, but she failed.

A determined woman, Anne spoke out on the streets as a female preacher, and disseminated Protestant literature. Some of it came into the hands of courtiers, and probably also reached Katherine Parr, Henry VIII's sixth and final wife. Thomas Kyne pursued Anne, and had her arrested and brought back to Lincolnshire, but she escaped back to London and continued to preach. She was arrested and then brutally tortured, both at Newgate prison and the Tower of London, being almost split apart on the rack. Refusing to confess or to identify other Protestants she was burned alive at Smithfield, her body having first been sprinkled with gunpowder. She was so badly injured from her tortures that she had to be carried to her execution on a chair. Before she died, however, she composed poetry, of which the best-known example is her ballad from Newgate. If she hadn't been tortured by then, she was about to be. It's full, as we'd expect, of traditional Christian imagery:

Like as the armed knight
Appointed to the field,
With this world will I fight
And Faith shall be my shield.

Faith is that weapon strong
Which will not fail at need.
My foes, therefore, among
Therewith will I proceed.

As it is had in strength
And force of Christes way
It will prevail at length
Though all the devils say nay.

Behind the familiar Arthurian images we can feel the urgent drumbeat of a rebellious mind; and indeed it's a brave poem on many levels, including a direct attack on the royal authority:

More enmyes now I have
Than hairs upon my head.
Let them not me deprave
But fight thou in my stead.

On thee my care I cast.
For all their cruel spight
I set not by their haste
For thou art my delight.

I am not she that list
My anchor to let fall
For every drizzling mist
My ship substancial.

Not oft use I to wright
In prose nor yet in rime,
Yet will I shew one sight
That I saw in my time.

I saw a rial throne
Where Justice should have sit
But in her stead was one
Of moody cruel wit.

Anne Askew's horrific fate shouldn't blind us to the fact that she was, in her way, a fanatic. In the sermons and other writings by the reformers, and also by their enemies, no quarter is given. Another poem by her, in which she pictures herself as a poor, blind woman in a garden full of dangers and snares – the garden being her own body – provides a window for us into the Reformation mind in its full urgency. In today's world there is little, outside the more extreme edges of Islamism, that feels like this:

A garden I have which is unknown,
which God of his goodness gave to me,
I mean my body, wherein I should have sown
the seed of Christ's true verity.

My spirit within me is vexed sore,
my flesh striveth against the same:
My sorrows do increase more and more,
my conscience suffereth most bitter pain:

In Anne's world, the gardener working on her body is Satan, busy
trying to entrap her, with the older generation and the Catholics all
on his side:

Then this proud Gardener seeing me so blind,
he thought on me to work his will,
And flattered me with words so kind,
to have me continue in my blindness still.

He fed me then with lies and mocks,
for venial sins he bid me go
To give my money to stones and stocks,
which was stark lies and nothing so.

With stinking meat then was I fed,
for to keep me from my salvation,
I had trentals of mass, and bulls of lead,
not one word spoken of Christ's passion.

In me was sown all kind of feigned seeds,
with Popish ceremonies many a one,
Masses of requiem with other juggling deeds,
till God's spirit out of my garden was gone ...

…'Beware of a new learning,' quoth he, 'it lies,
which is the thing I most abhor,
Meddle not with it in any manner of wise,
but do as your fathers have done before.'

My trust I did put in the Devil's works,
thinking sufficient my soul to save,
Being worse than either Jews or Turks,
thus Christ of his merits I did deprave …

Towards the end of the poem Anne's imagery seems to prefigure her own violent ending. This is a world of savagery as well as of salvation:

Strengthen me good Lord in thy truth to stand,
for the bloody butchers have me at their will,
With their slaughter knives ready drawn in their hand
my simple carcass to devour and kill.

O Lord forgive me mine offense,
for I have offended thee very sore,
Take therefore my sinful body from hence,
Then shall I, vile creature, offend thee no more.

I would with all creatures and faithful friends
for to keep them from this Gardener's hands,
For he will bring them soon unto their ends,
with cruel torments of fierce firebrands.

The final lines, assuming they really are by Anne Askew and not a later Protestant propagandist, are genuinely horrific. She is going to leave her carcass on earth, she says:

Although to ashes it be now burned,
I know thou canst raise it again,
In the same likeness as thou it formed,
in heaven with thee evermore to remain.

Anne was one of sixty-three people listed in the famous *Foxe's Book of Martyrs* as being burned alive in the reign of Henry VIII alone. They include priests, courtiers, servants, musicians, professional actors or 'players', a tailor, Richard Mekins, 'a child that passed not the age of 15 years', Frenchmen and a Scot – a pretty good cross-section of Tudor society. There is also William Tracey, a squire from Worcestershire, the sixty-fourth victim – irritatingly for the authoriries he was already dead, so he was dug up and then burned. In the reign of Henry's daughter Mary nearly three hundred Protestants were burned alive, and it's an even fuller list, coming from every social class and almost every trade: upholsterers, shoe-makers, candlemakers, bricklayers, servants, carpenters, wheel-wrights, glovers, merchants, gentlemen and royal courtiers. Men and women, old and young, they came from every part of Britain. When the Protestants were in the saddle under the reigns of Edward VI and Elizabeth I, similar numbers of Catholics, many of them priests, were martyred in turn and beatified by the Vatican.

The punishment of death by burning alive was an ancient one, but was revived in Tudor times to cause the maximum fear – in a sense it was a terrorist punishment, worse than a public beheading. It was particularly popular for women like Anne Askew for a bizarre reason: male traitors had been traditionally hanged, drawn and quartered. For the crowd to see them being disembowelled alive, and often having their private parts cut off, they clearly needed to be naked. But while it was acceptable to torture and burn women alive, for them to be seen naked in public was indecent. William Blackstone, one of the fathers of English law, explained that 'For as the decency due to sex forbids the exposing and public mangling of their bodies, their sentence (which is to the full as terrible to sensation as the other) is to be drawn to the gallows and there be burned alive.'

It's a bleak view of Tudor London, and to balance it we could do worse than look at the writing of a very different woman. Isabella Whitney was Britain's first published professional writer of secular poetry. We don't know a lot about her, but she was from Cheshire and came down to London to work as a servant. Her verse — clear, punchy and very much from a woman's point of view — is a useful counterblast to the courtly sonnets and sexual innuendo of more famous male Tudor writers. Here she is, warning young gentle-women and maids in love about how men really behave. 'Mermaids' was a euphemism for prostitutes, in this case inverted and subverted to refer to wanton male lovers. Personally, I like to think it's also a reference here to the Mermaid Tavern, the favoured haunt in Cheapside of so many poets and playwrights, from John Donne to Fletcher and Beaumont. If so, Isabella was writing a direct response to the flamboyance of the Elizabethan wits.

Ye Virgins, ye from Cupid's tents
do bear away the foil
Whose hearts as yet with raging love
most painfully do boil ...

Beware of fair and painted talk,
beware of flattering tongues:
The Mermaids do pretend no good
for all their pleasant songs.

Some use the tears of crocodiles,
contrary to their heart:
And if they cannot always weep,
they wet their cheeks by art.

Ovid, within his Art of Love,
doth teach them this same knack
To wet their hand and touch their eyes,
so oft as tears they lack.

Here we have a woman's-eye view of the swooning swains and untrustworthy lovers described by so many sonneteers in codpieces.

Trust not a man at the first sight
but try him well before:
I wish all maids within their breasts
to keep this thing in store.

For trial shall declare his truth
and show what he doth think,
Whether he be a lover true,
or do intend to shrink.

And that's an image, I think, you would not find in John Donne or Shakespeare. In another, more famous poem, Isabella leaves her rather scanty worldly wealth to the city of London, a place which is less the doomy moral theatre of Anne Askew than a throbbing cockpit of trade and good things:

I, whole in body, and in minde,
but very weake in Purse:
Doo make, and write my Testament
for feare it wyll be wurse ...
... First for their foode, I Butchers leave,
that every day shall kyll:
By Thames you shal have Brewers store,
and Bakers at your wyll.
And such as orders doo obserue,
And pouring into London thrice a weeke:
I leave two Streets, full fraught therwith,
they neede not farre to seeke.
Watlyng Streete, and Canwyck streete,
I full of Wollen leave:
And Linnen store in Friday streete,
if they mee not deceave.

And those which are of callyng such,
that costlier they require:
I Mercers leave, with silke so rich,
as any would desyre.
In Cheape of them, they store shal finde
and likewise in that streete:
I Goldsmithes leave, with Iuels such,
as are for Ladies meete.
And Plate to furnysh Cubbards with,
full braue there shall you finde:
With Purle of Siluer and of Golde,
to satisfye your minde.
With Hoods, Bungraces, Hats or Caps,
such store are in that streete:
As if on t'one side you should misse
the t'other serues you feete.
For Nets of every kynd of sort,
I leave within the pawne:
French Ruffes, high Purles, Gorgets and Sleeves
of any kind of Lawne.
For Purse or Kniues, for Combe or Glasse,
or any needeful knacke
I by the Stoks have left a Boy,
wil aske you what you lack.
I Hose doo leave in Birchin Lane,
of any kynd of syse:
For Women stitchte, for men both Trunks
and those of Gascoyne gise.
Bootes, Shoes or Pantables good store,
Saint Martins hath for you:
… And for the men, few Streetes or Lanes,
but Bodymakers bee:
And such as make the sweeping Cloakes,
with Gardes beneth the Knee.
Artyllery at Temple Bar,

and Dagges at Tower hyll:
Swords and Bucklers of the best,
are nye the Fleete vntyll.
Now when thy Folke are fed and clad
with such as I have namde:
For daynty mouthes, and stomacks weake
some Iunckets must be framde.
Wherfore I Poticaries leave,
with Banquets in their Shop:
Phisicians also for the sicke,
Diseases for to stop.
Some Roysters styll, must bide in thee,
and such as cut it out:
That with the guiltlesse quarel wyl,
to let their blood about.
For them I cunning Surgions leave,
some Playsters to apply.
That Ruffians may not styll be hangde,
nor quiet persons dye.
For Salt, Otemeale, Candles, Sope,
or what you els doo want:
In many places, Shops are full,
I left you nothing scant ...

Here, in all its plenty, is the sprawling mercantile metropolis of modern times beginning to slide into view; here is a first version of the 'embarrassment of riches' described by Simon Schama in relation to the slightly later civilisation of the Dutch Republic. It is clear, however, that Isabella Whitney's London is also a harsh, challenging place where change is almost too fast-moving. As it still is.

Earlier, we saw how during Tudor times the world of the court began to intersect more closely with the ordinary urban imagination; like a dangerous magnet, the court attracted attention from everywhere. That's partly about the politics, increasingly aggressive, of religious reform. But nowhere is it clearer than in the develop-

ment of the period's most brilliant and long-lasting cultural inno-
vation – the English theatre. It can often seem as if William
Shakespeare and a select few contemporaries exploded upon the
world from nothing. But as the man said, nothing comes from
nothing. The truth is that the urban world of the sixteenth century
across England was brimming with spectacle and theatre long
before Shakespeare.

In trying to tell the story of the British through poetry there is a
particular problem which begins around now, and which I ought to
own up to. Just as in high medieval culture, so in early modern
culture, Britain was still a Latin-soaked society. If you wanted to get
on, if you wanted to be taken seriously, you had to be able to read
and speak Latin. In towns across Britain, grammar schools had
been established to birch and bully Latin conjugations into young
boys – and very occasionally girls too, though almost all the educa-
tion for them would have been accomplished in the home. Once
you had your Latin, the chance of a university education at Oxford,
Cambridge or St Andrews might be open to you. (The Scots were
well served: from 1451 Glasgow was an option, and from 1495
Aberdeen as well.) Without Latin, and preferably Greek, there was
no chance of a career in the Church, the law, or any literate profes-
sion connected to the court.

This double literacy had huge advantages for the educated
British. It meant that scholars from these islands could talk fluently
with their counterparts across the European Continent; and it
meant that they had access, directly, to the greatest of the classical
writers now becoming more and more freely available in Renaissance
Europe. But for poetry, it bred a problem. The educated poets were
doused, pickled and marinated in Latin and Greek authors. They
had been brought up to parse and translate Plautus, Livy, Ovid and
Cicero. Their poetic models came from Imperial Rome and ancient
Greece. Their minds were stocked, and over-stuffed, with stories
from classical mythology. So when they turned to write in English,
they naturally showed their proficiency by imitating the Greek and
Roman classics. Sometimes they did this so well you barely notice:

the early Shakespeare play *The Comedy of Errors* comes directly from Plautus. But often anthologies of British poetry from this time seem an endless procession of Roman nymphs and swains, busy copies of Ovid's *Metamorphoses* or, as we saw earlier, versions of Horace's odes. This is fine. It produces some highly enjoyable poetry. There is a lot of very, very clever writing, with bold and daring games, going on. But mostly it doesn't tell us much about the Britain of the period. For that we have to go to less clever, less fashionable verse by people further down the social scale, or who have turned their backs on the enticements of ancient Rome. Thus, in what follows there will be rather less than in most verse collections of Edmund Spenser's droll mimicries of medieval poets and Virgil – fewer Phoebes and Chloes, fewer Strephons – and more of the earthier, homespun verse of the ballads and the morality plays.

British theatrical traditions followed directly from medieval religious pageantry. Some, at least, of the great cycles of mystery plays, from York, Coventry, Wakefield and Chester, were still being performed in the first half of the 1500s, telling the stories of Noah, Cain and Abel, the New Testament and the saints in churches and marketplaces. Here was direct, simple, often funny drama which had to catch the attention of an illiterate peasant, or lose its audience. So long as the Catholic Church and the medieval guilds held on to their authority, these immensely popular and protracted (the York Cycle was composed of no fewer than forty-eight different tableaux) entertainments were an essential part of the religious education of millions of Britons, particularly in the north and Midlands of England.

But, like Christianity itself, religious theatre was changing fast, and by the 1540s there was a new kind of drama, equally didactic, in which vices and virtues appeared as characters in their own right. These morality plays, or 'interludes', went further in the representation of contemporary British people on the stage, albeit disguised as symbols. Vice, in particular, under many guises, represented the wickedness, lust, cruelty and arrogance that many in the audience would have recognised in the world around them. The young

William Shakespeare in Stratford-upon-Avon would have come across these plays – early in his life his father had the job of authorising performances in the town. The companies of players who took them around, travelling by cart and packhorse, enjoyed the protection of leading nobles, churchmen and sometimes the court itself; and the plays that have survived often have direct connections with the Tudor court, and were first performed there.

Henry Medwall, little known these days, was a crucial bridge between the medieval world and the Elizabethan stage. Often cited as the first known vernacular English dramatist, he was born in September 1461 in Southwark, then an anarchic and dangerous place, to a family of wool merchants and tailors. He had a relatively prosperous late-medieval upbringing, doused in Latin at a monastery before he went to Eton, and then to King's College, Cambridge, for more Latin. Alongside all the studying, he threw himself into musical and dramatic entertainments for banquets and other high days. He helped devise Christmas dramas and learned about the importance of mingling music and stories. Later he would serve as a notary public, a kind of lawyer, under Archbishop Morton, hanging on to the edges of the royal court (of Henry VII), rather as Chaucer had a century earlier. For much of his life Medwall was based at Lambeth Palace, where plays were performed in the Archbishop's Great Hall. It is suggested that Sir Thomas More himself may have acted in Medwall's first play, *Fulgens and Lucres*, in around 1497.

Medwall had learned his craft from the medieval morality plays, and he too makes symbols of his characters, but as extracts from his second play, *Nature*, show, he was learning to root them in the realities of contemporary life. Here, for example, is Pride, describing his exuberant long hairstyle:

I love it well to have side here
Half a foot beneath mine ear
For evermore I stand in fear
That mine neck should take cold!

I knit up all the night
And the daytime, comb it to down right
And then it crispeth and shyneth as bright
As any peryld gold ...

And as for his clothing, it's the latest London look:

My doublet is unlaced before,
A stomacher of satin and no more.
Rain it, snow it, never so sore,
Me thinketh I am too hot!
Then I have such a short gown
With wide sleeves that hang down –
They would make some lad in this town
A doublet and a coat.

Gluttony, meanwhile, lurches in with a lump of cheese and a bottle
of wine, announcing:

... Of all things earthly I hate to fast.
Four times a day I make repast,
Or thrice as I suppose,
And when I am well fed
Then get I me to a soft bed
My body to repose.

There take I a nap or twain
up I go straight and to it again!
Though nature be not ready,
Yet have I some meat of delight
For to provoke the appetite
and make the stomach greedy.

Envy tries to persuade Gluttony to arm himself for the wars – this was written just at the end of the Wars of the Roses – but Gluttony is having none of the weapons or armour. If he's going to the wars he's going to be a victualler, looking after the food and drink:

I was never wont to that gear.
But I may serve to be a Viteller,
and thereof shall he have store,
So that I may stand out of danger
of gunshot. But I will come no near(er)
– I warn you that before.

Now, no one is saying that this is great poetry, but it's perhaps not surprising that scholars have wondered whether Shakespeare's Falstaff is in some respects the child of Henry Medwall's Gluttony. We don't know if the great playwright saw this play when he was a boy, but it's exactly the kind of thing he would have seen, alongside exaggerated and ludicrous tragedies of the kind he mocked in *Hamlet*.

A slightly later contemporary of Medwall, John Heywood, born in Coventry in 1497, was one of the most celebrated wits and playwrights at the court of Henry VIII – as we have seen, a dangerous place to be. A Catholic who eventually fell foul of Henry's daughter Elizabeth, Heywood had six plays published. He was on the other side of the argument from poor Anne Askew, part of the circle around Sir Thomas More, and at one point he himself narrowly escaped hanging. He was less learned than Medwall – he had risen as a chorister, a musician and an actor – but again, his drama, though highly moralistic, is full of the smell and the street language of the age. These were plays which may have been created on the edges of the court, but then made their way outwards, being performed in private houses, the inns of court, and anywhere else where there was a hall big enough to accommodate the audience.

One of the most thoroughly enjoyable takes what is perhaps the classic British conversation to new levels. *The Play of the Weather* imagines that Jupiter, who bears an uncanny likeness in his grandiosity to Henry VIII, is considering reform of the chaotic British weather, which has been caused by disagreements between various other gods. His chief servant or courtier, 'Mery Report', is a rude, puckish creature, not a million miles away from Shakespeare's Ariel in *The Tempest*. Mery will be a good servant in this judgement, he tells Jupiter, because the weather means nothing to him personally:

> For all weathers I am so indifferent,
> without affection standing up so right –
> Sun light, moon light, star light, twilight, torch light,
> Cold, heat, moist, dry, hail, rain, frost, snow, lightning,
>   thunder,
> Cloudy, misty, windy, fair, foul, above head or under,
> Temperate or distemperate – Whatever it be
> I promise your lordship all is one to me.

So at least we know that the weather around 1533, when this play was probably written, wasn't so different from today's. The play is also about the antagonism and rivalry between different parts of the British economy, again a contemporary theme: among those asking for meteorological favours are a lordly huntsman, a woodsman, a merchant, the owner of a watermill and the owner of a windmill, a gentlewoman who wants to keep herself from being sunburnt, a laundress who needs good drying weather and a schoolboy who enjoys throwing snowballs. So it's clear that in moving from moral archetypes towards contemporary Britons, we have already come quite far.

Although Heywood was a serious man and a passionate Catholic, he was also typically Tudor in his enjoyment of bawdy and of raucous argument. And the play is surprisingly hard-edged in its economic assessment of England at the time. Remember the buzzing market of Isabella Whitney's London, its goods pouring in by merchant ships? Here is Heywood's merchant pleading with Jupiter for favourable winds, and a lack of mists and storms. He sounds at times like an early free-market economist:

> In the daily danger of our goods and life,
> First to consider the desert of our request,
> What wealth we bring the rest to our great care and strife –
> And then to reward us as ye shall think best.
>
> What were the surplusage of each commodity
> Which grows and increases in every land,
> Except exchange by such men as we be,
> By way of intercourse that lyeth on our hand?
>
> We brought from home things whereof there is plenty,
> And homeward we bring such things as they be scant.
> Who should afore us merchants accounted be?
> For were not we, the world should wish and want ...

What does this tell us? Certainly that there was a vigorous discussion going on about whether or not the merchant classes deserved their wealth and position. But the play takes on more sensitive questions as well. After a pompous gentleman demands good weather for his hunting, a forest ranger, in charge of hunting territory, eloquently protests his lot:

> Rangers and keepers of certain places
> As forests, parks, purlews and chases
> Where we be charged with all manner and game
> Small is our profit and great is our blame.
> Alas for our wages, what be we the near?
> What is forty shillings or five mark a year?

There is a distinct class edge to this. What would Henry VIII, that manically enthusiastic hunter, or indeed a local lord hosting such a play, make of this demand for higher wages? It would certainly have caused a hubbub of debate once the show was over. Similarly, after the libidinous gentlewoman has complained about her complexion being ruined by sun and rain, a working-class laundress gives her a terrific scolding. She too might have been as fair, except that she knew she had to work, partly because of the danger of idleness:

> It is not thy beauty that I disdain,
> But thine idle life that thou hast rehearsed,
> Which any good woman's heart would have pierced.
> For I perceive in dancing and singing,
> In eating and drinking and thine appareling,
> Is all the joy wherein thy heart is set.
> But naught of all this doth thine own Labour get.
> For how dost thou nothing but of thine own travail,
> Thou mightest go as naked as my nail.

The passages between the owners of the windmill and the water-mill fascinatingly compare the two ways of grinding meal, and their usefulness to ordinary farmers and peasants. But there's a lot of sly comedy to be had: the owner of the windmill, of course, wants maximum wind and little rain. But the watermiller explains that the blazing sun is a wonderful thing:

> And so for drought, if corn thereby increase
> The sun doth comfort and ripe all, doubtless
> And often the wind so leyth the corn, God wot,
> That never after can it right, but rot.

England's heavy rains are in fact essential: water is no mere commodity, but

> … thing of necessity,
> For washing, for scouring, all filth cleansing.
> Where water lacketh, what beastly being!

In brewing, in baking, in dressing of meat,
If ye lack water what could ye drink or eat?
Without water could live neither man nor beast,
For water preserveth both most and least.

The argument between the two millers quickly degenerates into a sexual competition about grinding; the pecking of their millstones becomes a fairly grotesque metaphor of the kind that Tudor audiences apparently liked. The puckish messenger, Mery, complains that his watermill is 'many times choked', to which the watermiller replies:

So will she be though you should burst your bones,
Except you be perfect in setting your stones ...

and advises him on good 'pecking'. Mery responds:

So saith my wife and that maketh all our checking.
She would have the mill pecked, pecked, pecked every day,
But by God, Millers must peck when they may.
So oft have we pecked that our stones wax right thin
and all our other gear not worth a pin ...

And on and on it goes. It's simple bawdy, not great poetry by any standards. But it tells us more about the life and talk of early modern England than all the lovelorn swains and surprised goddesses put together. There is a material directness about these Tudor 'interludes' from which Shakespeare and his contemporaries must certainly have learned. Here, for a final example, is the boy, explaining to Jupiter's servant why he needs ice and snow. He is clearly a classmate of Shakespeare's more famous schoolboy:

Forsooth Sir, my mind is this, at few words
All my pleasure is in catching of birds
And making of snowballs, and throwing the same.

For which purpose to have set in frame,
With my godfather God I would fain have spoken,
Desiring him to have sent me by some token
Where I might have had great frost for my pitfalls*
And plenty of snow to make my snowballs.
This once had, boys lives be such as no man leads
O, to see my snowballs light on my fellows heads
And to hear the birds, how they flicker their wings
in the pitfall, I say it passeth all things.

Perhaps, on reflection, he's more like an early English Dennis the Menace.

In the end Jupiter realises that everybody wants a different kind of weather, and that to help one would be to destroy somebody else:

All weathers in all places if men all times might hire,
Who could live by other?

Therefore he's going to leave the unpredictable and ever-changing British weather where it is; which at least gives people something to talk about for the next few hundred years. Everybody is pleased – the schoolboy offers to make some snowballs for Jupiter the next time he's back.

By the middle of the century, it's to drama that we look for the spirit of the times. That's the case with the religious fanaticism already discussed: another leading playwright of the pre-Shakespearean theatre was John Bale, whose morality plays were basically anti-Catholic tirades, slashing in every direction at enemies of the true Protestant faith. In his *Three Laws*, for instance, Sodomy appears on stage boasting about how successful he is, particularly with the Catholic clergy:

---

* A pitfall is a kind of bird trap.

In the first age I began,
And so persevered with man
And still will if I can
So long as he endure.
If monkish sects renew,
And popish priests continue
Which are of my retinue
To live I shall be sure.

Clean marriage they forbid,
Yet cannot their ways be hid ...

... In Rome with to me they fall,
Both Bishop and Cardinal
Monk, Friar, priest and all,
More rank than they are ants.
Example in Pope Julye,
Which sought to have in his fury
Two lads, and to use them beastly,
From the Cardinal of Nantes.

The accusation that priestly celibacy led straightforwardly to interfering with boys, particularly choirboys, seems to go back a long way; this is the uncensored language of the Protestant Reformation in full flood, many miles away from the aureate stanzas of the poets in the anthologies. Again, the boys who grew up to become the great playwrights of Elizabethan and Jacobean Britain were brought up on this kind of thing. In the same John Bale play, when Sodomy and Idolatry cackle together, surely we can hear the echo of the witches in *Macbeth*:

Let her tell forth her matter
With holy oil and watter,
I can so cloyne and clatter
That I can at the latter

More subtleties contrive
I can work wiles in battle,
if I do once but spattle
I can make corn and cattle
That they shall never thrive ...

John Bale in his 1539 play *Kynge Johan* is also the author of the first history play we know of in English; sadly, he makes that too into little more than a diatribe against the wickedness of the Catholic Church.

Much more genial plays are two versions of comedies by Terence, *Ralph Roister-Doister* from 1566, by the Eton and Westminster teacher Nicholas Udall; and *Gammer Gurton's Needle*, first acted a year later at Christ's College, Cambridge, and probably written by John Still, who later became the Bishop of Bath and Wells. These were two sober fellows – Udall was known for the severity of his thrashings of schoolboys, and Still was an eminent professor of divinity. But in each case they caught the tone of contemporary language in ways that none of the earlier morality plays had quite achieved. *Roister-Doister* is the story of the attempted wooing, then unsuccessful abduction, of a rich widow. Here is the villain's boy or servant, protesting at the effect on him of Ralph's frantic pursuit of his woman. The satirical asides on his work with the lute and gittern (a small stringed instrument of the time) are particularly wonderful.

... now that my maister is new set on wooing,
I trust there shall none of us finde lacke of doing:
Two pair of shoes a day will now be too little
To serve me, I must trot to and fro so mickle.
– Go bear me this token, carry me this letter,
Now this is the best way, now that way is better.
Up before day sirs, I charge you, an hour or twain,
Trudge, do me this message, and bring word quick again,
If one miss but a minute, then his armes and wounds,
I would not have slacked for ten thousand pounds.

Nay see I beseeche you, if my most trusty page,
Go not now about to hinder my marriage,
So fervent hot wooing, and so far from wiving,
I trow never was any creature living,
With every woman is he in some loves pang,
Then up to our lute at midnight, twangle-dome twang,
Then twang with our sonnets, and twang with our dumps,
And hey-hough from our heart, as heavy as lead lumps:
Then to our recorder with toodleloodle poope
As the howlet out of an ivy bushe should hoope.
Anon to our gitterne, thrumpledum, thrumpledum thrum,
Thrumpledum, thrumpledum, thrumpledum,
    thrumpledum thrum.

This is a play known mainly to scholars these days, but I hope I'm not alone in feeling that some of these lines are worthy of Shakespeare: it's the kind of thing we might have had from Malvolio at his most ridiculous.

In *Gammer Gurton's Needle* we have an even thinner plot – old lady loses her precious and valuable sewing needle in the leather trousers of her servant Hodge while mending them. Predictably it eventually turns up in his bottom. But again, the play is full of the authentic-sounding dialect of Cambridgeshire in Tudor times. Here is the opening speech, delivered by a servant who stumbles across the house in the immediate chaos of the needle's loss:

Many a mile have I walked, divers and sundry ways,
And many a good man's house have I been at in my days;
Many a gossip's cup in my time have I tasted,
And many a broach and spit have I both turned and
    basted,
Many a piece of bacon have I had out of their balks,
In running over the country, with long and weary walks;
Yet came my foot never within those door cheeks,
To seek flesh or fish, garlick, onions, or leeks,

That ever I saw a sort in such a plight
As here within this house appeareth to my sight.
There is howling and scowling, all cast in a dump,
With whewling and puling, as though they had lost a
    trump.

It's like eavesdropping on a culture that has vanished – genial, tough, robust people leading rawly physical lives. This play, as it happens, also contains the earliest English drinking song to have survived:

I cannot eat but little meat;
My stomach is not good;
But sure I think that I could drink
With him that weareth a hood. More
Drink is my life; although my wife
Some time do chide and scold,
Yet spare I not to ply the pot
Of jolly good ale and old.
Back and side go bare, go bare;
Both hand and foot go cold;
But, belly, God send thee good ale enough,
Whether it be new or old.

I love no roast but a brown toast,
Or a crab in the fire;
A little bread shall do me stead,
Much bread I never desire.
Nor frost, nor snow, nor wind, I trow,
Can hurt me if it would;
I am so wrapped within, and lapped
With jolly good ale and old …

The drinker goes on to curse sellers of thin ale, and like many pub-haunters today insists that he is all the better for a skinful the following morning. But as to his wife, happily it turns out that he isn't quite as misogynistic as it first appears. Indeed, she's a bit of a toper too:

> And Kytte, my wife, that as her life
> Loveth well good ale to seek,
> Full oft drinketh she that ye may see
> The tears run down her cheek.
> Then doth she troll to me the bowl
> As a good malt-worm should,
> And say, 'Sweetheart, I have taken my part
> Of jolly good ale and old.'

And so the pictures painted of Tudor society by the courtiers, the women who have been pushed out of their houses, the religious fanatics and the burgeoning playwrights all point towards a country that is recognisably ours. It's an unfair country, full of hypocrisy and special pleading, whose common people by and large ignore their rulers. Despite its fanaticism and brutality, and its terrible weather, it feels surprisingly warm.

4

England's
Miracle

An act of magic, we are told, requires bizarrely varied ingredients. In Shakespeare's time, apparently clever men were still trying to combine base minerals and rare chemicals to produce gold. His witches throw 'eye of newt and toe of frog, wool of bat and tongue of dog, adder's fork and blind-worm's sting, lizard's leg and owlet's wing' into their sinister cauldron. No gold was ever produced, and today we regard the witch-fever of Jacobean Britain as a horrible excuse for the torture and burning of old women. And yet, at the end of the sixteenth century something magical, almost miraculous, did happen in these islands. It reads and sounds like nothing less than a revolution in human consciousness. It was certainly a revolution in how humans understood one another, acted out on wet and greasy wooden platforms in front of a confused but captivated mob. The miracle is sometimes described by the two words 'William Shakespeare', but it went a bit wider than that. Although Shakespeare was the leader and prime genius of this revolution, there were others who deserve the name of genius – Kit Marlowe, Thomas Middleton, John Webster and Ben Jonson among them.

The revolution on the stage and in words can reasonably be compared to the collision that created the English language in the first place. As we have seen, it was the collision of Germanic, Latin, French and some British tongues that produced the endlessly flexible stew of English. By the late 1500s another collision was taking place. This time it wasn't simply about the 'word hoard', important though that was. At first sight, English culture wasn't unusual: across Continental Europe there was a peasantry, trading and farming peoples speaking diverse local languages and, as in England, an elite speaking Latin and looking back to classical authors for their inspiration. In London above all – that same London Isabella Whitney described so vividly in the previous chapter – many who had been classically educated were forced to sell their skills to those who had no such education.

When Shakespeare arrived in London he soon found his way to the anarchic, wild group of Cambridge- and Oxford-educated writers now known as the 'university wits' – Robert Greene, Thomas Nashe, George Peele and Christopher Marlowe himself, the acknowledged star of the early Elizabethan stage. As a non-university man Shakespeare would have been something of an outsider, though he was quick to collaborate and 'patch' plays with them. Later, starving and on his deathbed, Greene launched a famous attack on Shakespeare as a mere 'upstart crowe' – nothing but an actor, *sans* proper education, with ideas above his station. Ben Jonson, classically educated though never able to get to Cambridge because he was apprenticed to his bricklayer father-in-law, accused his friend Shakespeare of having 'little Latin and less Greek'.

What quickly became obvious was that this provincial man, crammed with the folklore, smells, sounds and words of the English Midlands, was well able to absorb translated stories from the classical and humanist writers, as well as having a basic grammar-school understanding of the Latinists. Thus he took his part amongst a highly literate and competitive elite who found that, thanks to a new market for entertainment, if they wanted to eat and dress well, if they dreamed of owning their own homes, they had to tell stories in English that would captivate the man in the street. Some at least found that if they took their Plautus and their Terence, stories from Latin Renaissance writers in Italy, and their understanding of the Latin chroniclers of older Britain, and then reshaped the stories and adapted their training in rhetoric and argument, and salted it all with the biting, vivid language of town and country people, they could make gold. They became alchemists of language.

The gold came slowly, penny by penny. The population of London when Shakespeare arrived in the 1580s was around 200,000, many of them recent migrants from the countryside or abroad, crammed into a small space still bounded by Roman walls. The theatres opening up as he began his career could accommodate around two thousand observers, and the big innovation was that, rather than a hat being passed around at the end of a performance, as had been the case when the companies toured England, audiences had to pay to get in. A penny bought you standing room, tuppence a basic seat, and three pennies a comfy chair out of the rain. So long as just a few per cent of the population came regularly, that provided a good income stream. Although there were plenty of rival ways of spending time for the overwhelmingly youthful, plague-threatened and competitive Londoners – brutal animal-baiting, bloodthirsty public punishments, taverns and the whore-houses of Southwark – these public theatres were simply more interesting. They were attacked relentlessly by puritan moralists who thought they gave the mob dangerous ideas, encouraging lawlessness and lechery, and who believed the audiences were engaged in sexual misbehaviour with one another. In fact, compared to the entertainments of cruelty, they were a clear advance in civilisation. At any rate, the denunciations, the warnings and the occasional eruptions of state censorship did little to diminish the popularity of this new, cutting-edge entertainment.

This wasn't the invention of William Shakespeare or any of his immediate contemporaries: as we have already seen, there were Tudor writers, from both the Catholic and the Protestant sides, who led the way from morality plays to the modern drama, and who were highly classically trained as well. Yet when the full colour of the theatrical revolution arrives, it does feel like magic. It happens remarkably fast. *The Spanish Tragedy* by Thomas Kyd arrives in the mid-1580s; so do the first plays by Christopher Marlowe, *Dido, Queen of Carthage* and the two parts of *Tamburlaine*, whose amoral plot provoked Shakespeare and whose thundering blank verse thrilled him. And we are off, though it will take Shakespeare himself some years before he puts on his first play, almost certainly *Henry VI Part One*. The first successful commercial theatre, called rather prosaically the Theatre, was opened by James Burbage in Shoreditch in 1576. The following year it was rivalled by the Curtain, and then came the Rose, the Swan and eventually, in 1599, the Globe.

It may not have felt like a revolution at the time. There had been plenty of plays put on in private theatres and in the relative privacy of the inns of court, as well as in the houses of grandees. And in towns around England plays had been performed out of doors too. The first English play in blank verse, the famously abominable *Gorboduc*, about a disputed succession to the throne, was performed at the Inner Temple before Queen Elizabeth as early as 1561. Far from being rarities, actors and acting companies were known throughout the country – they even travelled abroad, touring Germany and Denmark. And yet in little more than two decades what feels like a new art form was established, spread and produced a flood of astonishing work, much of which is still performed and enjoyed today.

It's hard to avoid the thought that this is one of the great triumphs of early capitalism. One of Shakespeare's best recent biographers, Stephen Greenblatt, explains why. A population of London's size, tempted by big new theatres, produced intense competition: 'To survive economically it was not enough to mount one or two successful plays a season and keep them up for reasonable runs. The companies had to induce people, large numbers of people, to get in the habit of coming to the theatre again and again, and this meant a constantly changing repertoire, as many as five or six plays per week. The sheer magnitude of the enterprise is astonishing: for each company, approximately twenty new plays per year in addition to some twenty plays carried over from previous seasons.' If you want to know why Shakespeare wrote so many plays, and had a hand in so many others, there is the reason. Money, advance, security, competition: to that extent, he lived in our world.

Before the Elizabethan theatres opened, there were relatively few openings for clever writers who weren't already rich, or had very rich patrons. Like the law and the Church, most of the roads to material advancement were blocked off by medieval regulations, by the 'squatter's rights' of well-established families, and by the rigidly hierarchical nature of early modern society itself. The old stories have it that Shakespeare fled to London after being caught poaching deer. Certainly his father's business was struggling, and even leaving aside his probable Catholic sympathies there wasn't much for him in Stratford. In London, however, coins could come tumbling into the hands of those who were ambitious, talented and hard-working enough to give the people what they wanted. You didn't need, necessarily, a grand patron – though almost all the companies had them, as a form of insurance and protection. What you needed was a buzz, curiosity and persistence. Very quickly a new market was formed. It was a highly competitive one. Write a bad play, or still worse, a boring play, and you were punished by empty places. Write a hit, and then another hit, and your name alone would draw the crowds.

Like modern television drama and cinema, this was entertainment which spanned the entire class structure, delighting Queen Elizabeth as well as illiterate boy apprentices. The theatre in Shakespeare's day still had plenty of formidable enemies. They certainly included servants of the state, paranoid about threats to the monarchy and the established order, as well as the puritans, who abominated all secular entertainments. And then there was the worst enemy of all, bubonic plague, whose regular visitations shut theatres, like other centres of mingling humanity, almost immediately. But above all there was a market, there was opportunity. And there had, therefore, to be product.

Shakespeare's England was still a land of martyrdom, spies and relentless, dangerous conflict between Protestants and Catholics. As early Protestant martyrs such as Anne Askew had been dealt with by Catholic authorities, so now in Elizabethan England, Catholics were treated. A lot of painstaking and learned research has been expended on the question of whether William Shakespeare himself was a Catholic, as if even today rival teams are desperate to recruit him posthumously onto their side. All that seems certain is that he and his family were deeply riven. His father, as one of the key civic officials in Stratford-upon-Avon, was directly involved in the Reformation programme of smashing Catholic statues, white-washing churches and sacking Catholic officials. On the other hand, he was almost certainly married to a Catholic woman, and a Catholic 'Confession of Faith' was found hidden in the roof of his house long after his death. He helped recruit Catholic teachers to his son's school, and got into trouble for failing to turn up regularly to Protestant worship, though that may have been more about embarrassment over his debts than religious belief. At any rate, he was a conflicted figure.

If, as seems likely, Shakespeare himself went to work as a teacher in northern Catholic houses before he came to London, then we must assume he had dangerously un-Protestant views of his own as a young man. Schoolfellows a little older than him fled to the Continent and returned as Catholic agents, and were duly hunted down, tortured and torn apart on the scaffold. Relatives were accused and publicly executed as well – Shakespeare may have seen their heads still rattling on poles when he first entered London across its famous bridge. The recent rediscovery of one of his First Folio collections of plays in France, where it had been in a Jesuit library, has highlighted his links with underground, Catholic England.

There are little hints and glints of Catholic teaching in Shakespeare's plays – most famously in *Hamlet* – but there is little real echo of the heart-racingly urgent and dangerous politics of contemporary religion. That should surprise nobody: Shakespeare was working under the watchful eyes of government censors and in front of a largely Protestant audience. His likely first company, the Queen's Players, had partly been formed to spread Protestant propaganda. All England was alive with special agents, or 'search-ers', and the government's fears were not unjustified – in 1580 Pope Gregory XIII had declared that the assassination of Queen

Elizabeth would not be a mortal sin, inciting English Catholics to a coup.

However, just as in the reign of Henry VIII, the religious war did produce some seriously good poetry, this time mainly from the point of view of the harried and desperate Catholic losers. It's perfectly possible that Shakespeare met the charismatic Jesuit agent and scholar Edmund Campion, who bravely debated with Protestant divines after he'd been tortured and imprisoned. He was confronted by Elizabeth herself, and later died the usual agonising death. Robert Southwell of Norfolk was one of the Jesuits in another mission, shortly after Campion, and came to a similar end, imprisoned, tortured and then hanged, drawn and quartered in 1595. A textual comparison by some scholars suggests that Southwell, connected to Shakespeare's famous patron the (Campion-befriending) Earl of Southampton, was an author who Shakespeare read closely. In the following extraordinary poem, penned in that year, while Shakespeare was writing *A Midsummer Night's Dream* and *Romeo and Juliet*, Southwell compares himself to a pounded nutmeg, and defiantly proclaims his martyrdom:

> The pounded spise both tast and scent doth please;
> In fadinge smoke the force doth incense showe;
> The perisht kernell springeth with increase;
> The lopped tree doth best and soonest growe.
> Gods spice I was, and poundinge was my due;
> In fadinge breath my incense favoured best;
> Death was my meane my kernell to renewe;
> By loppinge shott I upp to heavenly rest.
> Some thinges more perfit are in their decaye,
> Like sparke that going out geeves clerest light:
> Such was my happe, whose dolefull dying daye
> Begane my joye and termed fortunes spight.
> Alive a Queene, now dead I am a Saint;
> Once Mary cald, my name now Martyr is;
> From earthly raigne debarred by restrainte,

In liew wherof I raigne in heavenly blis.
My life, my griefe, my death, hath wrought my joye;
My freendes, my foyle, my foes, my weale procurd,
My speedie death hath scorned longe annoye,
And losse of life an endles life assurd.
My scaffolde was the bedd where ease I fownde;
The blocke a pillowe of eternall rest.
My headman cast mee in a blesfull sownde;
His axe cutt of my cares from combred brest.
Rue not my death, rejoyce at my repose;
It was no death to mee but to my woe,
The budd was opened to let owt the rose,
The cheynes unloosed to let the captive goe.
A Prince by birth, a prisoner by mishappe,
From crowne to crosse, from throne to thrall I fell.

Whether or not he was reading Southwell, the up-and-coming playwright and successful London actor William Shakespeare was also leaning with some political skill in the other direction. About this time he wrote the history play *King John*. It's not one of his greater efforts, and it follows the ferociously anti-Catholic play of the same name by John Bale. Like Bale, Shakespeare uses the opportunity to get in a bit of patriotic anti-papal baiting:

Thou canst not, Cardinal, devise a name
So slight, unworthy, and ridiculous
To charge me to an answer, as the Pope.
Tell him this tale, and from the mouth of England
And thus much more: that no Italian priest
Shall tithe or toll in our dominions;
But as we, under God, our supreme head,
So, under him, that great supremacy
Where we do reign we will alone uphold
Without th'assistance of a mortal hand.

Queen Elizabeth could hardly have put it better herself. We shouldn't look to Shakespeare for reportage on the most dangerous politics of his day. However, he does give us something even more useful – the ultimate window into a world in which faith, and in particular the fate of the soul after death, occupied almost everybody. In *Measure for Measure*, a play which to my ear is unforgiving of the smug certainties of any religious believers, the hero, Claudio, believes that in order to protect his sister Isabella's virtue he must reconcile himself to execution. A duke, Vincentio, urges him not to be frightened of death – as it were, the official line. Be 'absolute for death', he tells Claudio – death or life

> Shall thereby be the sweeter. Reason thus with life:
> If I do lose thee, I do lose a thing
> That none but fools would keep: a breath thou art,
> Servile to all the skyey influences,
> That dost this habitation, where thou keep'st,
> Hourly afflict: merely, thou art death's fool;

So far, so predictable. From pulpits up and down the country, preachers constantly urged their congregations to reconcile themselves to death. On scaffolds, and alongside the pyres prepared for religious martyrs, much the same conversation was going on. We know this from the endless sermons and tracts that have survived from the period; but how did ordinary English men and women feel in response? For that, we have to go to the greatest poet. Claudio, a living, breathing and terrified contemporary, is far from convinced, but to die, he tells himself, and go we know not where,

> To lie in cold obstruction and to rot;
> This sensible warm motion to become
> A kneaded clod; and the delighted spirit
> To bathe in fiery floods, or to reside
> In thrilling region of thick-ribbed ice;
> To be imprison'd in the viewless winds,

And blown with restless violence round about
The pendent world; or to be worse than worst
Of those that lawless and incertain thought
Imagine howling: 'tis too horrible!
The weariest and most loathed worldly life
That age, ache, penury and imprisonment
Can lay on nature is a paradise
To what we fear of death.

Paradise, purgatory or hell – the possibilities are simply too awesome and too terrifying for anyone but living saints or fanatics to face. And in the single most famous speech in the Shakespearean canon, Hamlet agrees with Claudio – the impossibility of knowing what comes after life terrifies all men. For Catholics, and indeed for many Protestants, the terrors of hell are so vivid, even after the paintings of damnation in the churches have been whitewashed over by the reformers, that they literally freeze action, in this case the possibilities of revenge or suicide. Daily life in early modern Britain could be, by our standards, almost intolerably harsh. Hunger, cold, danger, terrible illness and the constant threat of being expelled from the community were all regular ripples in the sea of troubles that was daily life. Just getting out, escaping, finally resting – what a wonderful prospect. Except, in a God-haunted world, it wasn't.

To be, or not to be: that is the question:
Whether 'tis nobler in the mind to suffer
The slings and arrows of outrageous fortune,
Or to take arms against a sea of troubles,
And by opposing end them? To die: to sleep;
No more; and by a sleep to say we end
The heart-ache and the thousand natural shocks
That flesh is heir to, 'tis a consummation
Devoutly to be wish'd. To die, to sleep;
To sleep: perchance to dream: ay, there's the rub;

For in that sleep of death what dreams may come
When we have shuffled off this mortal coil,
Must give us pause: there's the respect
That makes calamity of so long life;
For who would bear the whips and scorns of time,
The oppressor's wrong, the proud man's contumely,
The pangs of despised love, the law's delay,
The insolence of office and the spurns
That patient merit of the unworthy takes,
When he himself might his quietus make
With a bare bodkin? Who would fardels bear,
To grunt and sweat under a weary life,
But that the dread of something after death,
The undiscover'd country from whose bourn
No traveller returns, puzzles the will
And makes us rather bear those ills we have
Than fly to others that we know not of?
Thus conscience does make cowards of us all;
And thus the native hue of resolution
Is sicklied o'er with the pale cast of thought.

What is central to Shakespeare's tragic imagination is the understanding that, even without the fear of damnation, there is no way out – merely a universe of grey meaninglessness, which hems in the human life from either side. This is what the sinner and murderer Macbeth finally comes to believe in another of the tragedies:

To-morrow, and to-morrow, and to-morrow,
Creeps in this petty pace from day to day,
To the last syllable of recorded time;
And all our yesterdays have lighted fools
The way to dusty death. Out, out, brief candle!
Life's but a walking shadow, a poor player,
That struts and frets his hour upon the stage,
And then is heard no more. It is a tale

Told by an idiot, full of sound and fury,
Signifying nothing.

The arguments about whether Shakespeare was a secret Roman Catholic, struggling to disguise himself all his life, will go on. Most of the time, at least, he seems like a Christian who believes – unlike Christopher Marlowe – that divine judgement awaits a world of sinners. In that he's a man of his time; what makes him a poet for all time is his inability to reconcile himself to the rites and consolations of any particular religious form. Here, human experience remains scarier and more thrilling than even the Bible admits.

For Shakespeare, the great escape from Thanatos was, inevitably, Eros. Again and again he presents love as the only answer to the great challenge of death and oblivion. The love of the other can quieten, if it cannot quite cancel, the remorseless and deadly passage of time, as his sublime thirtieth sonnet sings:

When to the sessions of sweet silent thought
I summon up remembrance of things past,
I sigh the lack of many a thing I sought,
And with old woes new wail my dear time's waste:
Then can I drown an eye, unused to flow,
For precious friends hid in death's dateless night,
And weep afresh love's long since cancelled woe,
And moan the expense of many a vanished sight:
Then can I grieve at grievances foregone,
And heavily from woe to woe tell o'er
The sad account of fore-bemoaned moan,
Which I new pay as if not paid before.
But if the while I think on thee, dear friend,
All losses are restor'd and sorrows end.

In his thirty-third sonnet, Shakespeare goes further. Love is one with nature. It has the power of creation itself:

Full many a glorious morning have I seen
Flatter the mountain tops with sovereign eye,
Kissing with golden face the meadows green,
Gilding pale streams with heavenly alchemy;
Anon permit the basest clouds to ride
With ugly rack on his celestial face,
And from the forlorn world his visage hide,
Stealing unseen to west with this disgrace:
Even so my sun one early morn did shine,
With all triumphant splendour on my brow;
But out, alack, he was but one hour mine,
The region cloud hath mask'd him from me now.
Yet him for this my love no whit disdaineth;
Suns of the world may stain when heaven's sun staineth.

But what of Shakespeare's own experience of love? It is often pointed out that while his plays brim with hopeful, ardent suitors and erotic teasing, they are mostly silent when it comes to the experience of lifelong, marital love. This is surely related to Shakespeare's own early marriage to a woman eight or nine years older than he, who was pregnant by him. Anne Hathaway was a rare catch, a twenty-six-year-old orphan with some property of her own, able, unlike most women of her age, to make her own decisions about love and sex. But Shakespeare was only eighteen when they married, and most of what we know about him – granted, not very much – suggests that it wasn't an entirely happy union. It produced two adult daughters as well as a son, Hamnet, who died at the age of eleven. But Shakespeare spent most of his working life away from Anne, in London. He returned to her at Stratford-upon-Avon at the end of his career, but if his last will and testament is anything to go by, it was hardly an ardent reunion. His main will leaves her absolutely nothing – it all went to Susanna, the older daughter, and her husband – except, famously for a late codicil, leaving Anne 'my second-best bed with the furniture'. However you play it, it's not a compliment.

More significant, perhaps, than all of that is the fact that there are so few images of happy married life in Shakespeare's plays. Here is a man who can describe everything – war, lust, the pleasures of drunken debauchery, the agonies of young love, the furies and dementia of the old, the pleasures of male friendship – but who hardly ever gives us the state that is supposed to be at the centre of Tudor (and modern) social existence: marriage. Again and again, ill-matched lovers are briskly yoked together at the end of the play, and we are not encouraged to look ahead at what follows. The rare displays of marriage in action are hardly reassuring – think of the black, bleak compact of Lady and Lord Macbeth, or of the guilt-stricken lust of Hamlet's mother and uncle. We know that Shakespeare was perfectly capable of imagining a strong, sustaining, lifelong love, because he does as much in one of his greatest sonnets:

Let me not to the marriage of true minds
Admit impediments. Love is not love
Which alters when it alteration finds,
Or bends with the remover to remove:
O, no! it is an ever-fixed mark,
That looks on tempests and is never shaken;
It is the star to every wandering bark,
Whose worth's unknown, although his height be taken.
Love's not Time's fool, though rosy lips and cheeks
Within his bending sickle's compass come;
Love alters not with his brief hours and weeks,
But bears it out even to the edge of doom.
If this be error and upon me proved,
I never writ, nor no man ever loved.

Yet it seems that in his own experience, Love was Time's fool, and did indeed alter over months and years, if not weeks. Indeed, there is a disturbing loathing when it comes to describing love and sex between older people. The circumstances are hardly normal, of course, but remember Hamlet turning on his lustful mother:

O shame! where is thy blush? Rebellious hell,
If thou canst mutine in a matron's bones,
To flaming youth let virtue be as wax,
And melt in her own fire: proclaim no shame
When the compulsive ardour gives the charge,
Since frost itself as actively doth burn
And reason panders will ...
Nay, but to live
In the rank sweat of an enseamed bed,
Stew'd in corruption, honeying and making love
Over the nasty sty ...

In spirit, this is very close to one of the most ferocious poems Shakespeare ever produced, the notorious sonnet about the devastating effects of lust, a kind of madness that can destroy human happiness:

The expense of spirit in a waste of shame
Is lust in action: and till action, lust
Is perjured, murderous, bloody, full of blame,
Savage, extreme, rude, cruel, not to trust;
Enjoyed no sooner but despised straight;
Past reason hunted; and no sooner had,
Past reason hated, as a swallowed bait,
On purpose laid to make the taker mad.
Mad in pursuit and in possession so;
Had, having, and in quest to have extreme;
A bliss in proof, and proved, a very woe;
Before, a joy proposed; behind, a dream.
All this the world well knows; yet none knows well
To shun the heaven that leads men to this hell.

The sexual self-hatred that seems to underlie this sonnet can easily tip over into disgust for the object of love; and the following seems to me to be a poem that is not playful or clever, but essentially hating. It's apparently about 'false compare', or poetic overstatement, but the images we take from it are the black wires and the reeking breath:

> My mistress' eyes are nothing like the sun;
> Coral is far more red, than her lips red:
> If snow be white, why then her breasts are dun;
> If hairs be wires, black wires grow on her head.
> I have seen roses damasked, red and white,
> But no such roses see I in her cheeks;
> And in some perfumes is there more delight
> Than in the breath that from my mistress reeks.
> I love to hear her speak, yet well I know
> That music hath a far more pleasing sound:
> I grant I never saw a goddess go,
> My mistress, when she walks, treads on the ground:
> And yet by heaven, I think my love as rare,
> As any she belied with false compare.

I think it's important to include these poems, because it's too easy just to see Shakespeare as the champion of young, romantic love, the origin of the modern updates of *Romeo and Juliet*, and the hero of the brilliant but unhistorical hit movie *Shakespeare in Love*. The real author's views of love and sex are, in truth, a million miles away from the elevation of sexual love as the ultimate good in itself that characterises modern culture. Catholic or not, there is plenty of guilt, self-hatred and personal disappointment wired into Shakespearean attitudes towards love and sex. It's 'the answer'. But only sometimes, and for some lucky people. And even then, it's a subversive, dangerous, society-shaking force.

For the next big lesson Shakespeare teaches us about the differences between his world and that of the twenty-first century is the importance of hierarchy and order, up to – and including – monarchy. Hierarchy governed every aspect of daily life: wives and children were supposed to show respect to fathers and husbands;

apprentices were tightly bound to their employers, and faced severe punishments if they broke a host of complex rules; smaller gentry owed loyalty and obedience to the great magnates; and the entire country owed absolute obedience to the monarchy. Alongside this, of course, there was the parallel hierarchy, with its many gradations and pomposities, of the Church. But it's the monarchy, and the whole business of rulers and ruled, that is central to Shakespeare's notion of society.

In many ways Shakespeare invented the British monarchy as such a central component of the national identity. Right from the beginning of his career, with *Henry VI Part One*, through to its end and *The Tempest*, Shakespeare believes in order, and that order, properly understood, derives from a wise monarch. The weak, deluded or self-pitying ruler spreads discord and misery throughout the kingdom. The good ruler is not simply a morally attractive figure, but a political blessing on all under his authority.

There were very good reasons for this. Murder rates in early modern Britain were higher than we can begin to comprehend today. There was a good chance of being robbed and killed if you travelled; domestic violence was very high and tolerated; this was an armed and pressurised society in which the most significant social division was between those legally allowed to carry swords or pistols, and those forbidden to. Violence was everywhere. Shakespeare may have had his first chance at becoming an actor because a row between two more senior players resulted in a fatal stabbing; and Marlowe famously met his end in a Deptford brawl or assassination, with a dagger through his eye.

So it's hardly surprising that Shakespeare believes in order; and that a highly literate, impoverished young man trying to make his way in the seething chaos of one of the world's largest cities shows a certain nervousness about the mob. In the second part of *Henry VI* he portrays the medieval rebel Jack Cade as a deluded, violent and extremely dangerous mob orator, an enemy of grammar schools and learning, prepared to burn down London Bridge and behead his enemies, and whose dream of class victory amounts to slashing the price of bread and beer and declaring that the 'pissing conduit run nothing but claret wine this the first year of our reign'. Cade's followers dream of a massacre of lawyers – and indeed, like Maoist revolutionaries, of everyone who can read and write. These are the caricatures of a writer who fears disorder more than anything else, even the brutal punishments of the Tudor state.

Fear of disorder can be found almost everywhere in the Elizabethan theatre, even if the theatre itself was regarded as disorderly and threatening. In the play *Sir Thomas More*, partly written by Shakespeare, the great statesman confronts a London mob furious about immigration and determined to 'send them back' – nothing changes. More says:

> Grant them removed, and grant that this your noise
> Hath chid down all the majesty of England.
> Imagine that you see the wretched strangers,
> The babies at their backs, with their poor luggage
> Plodding to th'ports and coasts for transportation,
> And that you use it as Kings in your desires,
> Authority quite silenced by your brawl,
> And you in ruff of your opinions clothed:
> What had you got? I will tell you: you had taught
> How insolence and strong hand should prevail,
> How order should be quelled, and by this pattern
> Not one of you should live an aged man,
> For other ruffians, as their fancies wrought,
> With selfsame hand, self-reasons, and self-right,
> Would shark on you, and men like ravenous fishes
> Would feed on one another.

Underpinning it all is a tough-minded and very unmodern belief in the virtues of hierarchy, class and obedience. Much of the time, these days, we almost pretend in our worship of Shakespeare that it's not there. But it absolutely is: our greatest playwright was no kind of democrat. In *Sir Thomas More*, Shakespeare, or one of his collaborators, goes further still, telling the London rebels that to rise against the king is to rise against God. And if they succeed in rebellion, by undoing authority, they undo all order and will succeed only in making the world a still more dangerous place:

> ... Why, even your hurly
> Cannot proceed but by obedience.
> Tell me but this: what rebel captain,
> As mutinies are incident, by his name
> Can still the rout? Who will obey a traitor?
> Or how can well that proclamation sound
> When there is no addition but a rebel
> To qualify a rebel? You'll put down strangers,
> Kill them, cut their throats, possess their houses ...

All of which is to say no more than, in Shakespearean English, 'the revolution devours her children'. Shakespeare shows again and again his vivid understanding of the utter misery of being outcast from the state. In *King Lear*, the very greatest of his plays, unsocial man, torn by the storm and by madness, excluded from a functioning society, is merely a 'poor, bare forked animal'. In the world of the theatre, clothing was very important as a sign of social standing, belonging, authority. Now King Lear rips off his own clothes entirely, to make the point.

In writing about whipped beggars with nowhere to hide, and vividly describing the hunger of people at the bottom of the heap, Shakespeare shows that his sympathies naturally spread to the poor. But nothing, or almost nothing, is as terrifying as anarchy. And it's simply not true that Shakespeare did not know about democracy. As a widely read man he was well aware of the history of popular revolts in England, as well as the democratic experiments of republican Rome. It's just that as a man of his time, he doesn't believe democracy could ever work. In his Roman play *Coriolanus* he puts into the mouths of the common citizens themselves his explanation of why they can't successfully rule without an aristocratic leader: one explains that they are called 'the many-headed multitude', and another parses the thought:

We have been called so of many; not that our heads
are some brown, some black, some auburn, some bald,
but that our wits are so diversely coloured: and
truly I think if all our wits were to issue out of
one skull, they would fly east, west, north, south,
and their consent of one direct way should be at
once to all the points o' the compass.

And we can't be having that. In Shakespeare's world, whether it's Jack Cade's rebellion in London or the common people of Rome, who sound and dress like Londoners, the crowd is always wrong, ridiculous and often menacing. Coriolanus himself, admittedly a study in overweening and arrogant ambition, simply can't stick the idea of grovelling to the mob:

Most sweet voices!
Better it is to die, better to starve,
Than crave the hire which first we do deserve.
Why in this woolvish toge should I stand here,
To beg of Hob and Dick, that do appear,
Their needless vouches? Custom calls me to't:
What custom wills, in all things should we do't,
The dust on antique time would lie unswept,
And mountainous error be too highly heapt
For truth to o'er-peer. Rather than fool it so,
Let the high office and the honour go
To one that would do thus.

In the ancient conflict between the Roman mob and military dictatorship, Shakespeare uses an oily aristocrat, Menenius, to describe the traditional proper relationship between the different classes. In his fable, the other parts of the body rebel against the belly for gorging all the food – just as the rich take more than their fair share of social wealth. The belly replies:

> Your most grave belly was deliberate,
> Not rash like his accusers, and thus answer'd:
> 'True is it, my incorporate friends,' quoth he,
> 'That I receive the general food at first,
> Which you do live upon; and fit it is,
> Because I am the store-house and the shop
> Of the whole body: but, if you do remember,
> I send it through the rivers of your blood,
> Even to the court, the heart, to the seat o' the brain;
> And, through the cranks and offices of man,
> The strongest nerves and small inferior veins
> From me receive that natural competency
> Whereby they live: and though that all at once,
> You, my good friends,' – this says the belly, mark me, –
> *First Citizen.* Ay, sir; well, well.
> *Menenius Agrippa.* 'Though all at once cannot
> See what I do deliver out to each,
> Yet I can make my audit up, that all
> From me do back receive the flour of all,
> And leave me but the bran.'

Now of course, these are only the words of another Roman aristo-crat, and Shakespeare is the master of laying off one viewpoint against another. Nevertheless, the metaphor of the state as body would have been familiar and well understood to his audience. To us it may seem hilariously self-serving, but in the context of the original play it may well have felt like simple common sense.

The flipside to Shakespeare's distaste for anything resembling democracy is, of course, his insistence that rulers must be wise and virtuous – or rather, that any of their flaws and failings spread rapidly through the whole of society, causing distress to all. Good kings, bad kings, tyrants, the self-deluded, the saintly and the merely weak – Shakespeare is utterly obsessed by the problems of holding power. This explains, surely, the most distressing reversal in the entire canon, when lively, up-for-it Prince Hal turns on Falstaff, that great, incontinent, fleshly representation of all our baser appetites – the old slob we laugh at and we love – and coldly denies him:

I know thee not, old man: fall to thy prayers;
How ill white hairs become a fool and jester!
I have long dream'd of such a kind of man,
So surfeit-swell'd, so old and so profane;
But, being awaked, I do despise my dream.
Make less thy body hence, and more thy grace;
Leave gormandizing; know the grave doth gape
For thee thrice wider than for other men.
Reply not to me with a fool-born jest:
Presume not that I am the thing I was;
For God doth know, so shall the world perceive,
That I have turn'd away my former self;
So will I those that kept me company.
When thou dost hear I am as I have been,
Approach me, and thou shalt be as thou wast,
The tutor and the feeder of my riots:
Till then, I banish thee, on pain of death,
As I have done the rest of my misleaders,
Not to come near our person by ten mile ...

It is heartbreaking. Falstaff can't believe it. By some reports Queen Elizabeth herself could not believe it, and wanted Falstaff back in another play. But for Shakespeare good kingship is the ultimate social good, which justifies even this biblical denial.

In his careful obsession with the dynasties of England, Shakespeare does more than anyone else to identify the country itself with those who have ruled it. When we speak of Victorian Britain, or the Edwardian period, we are playing unacknowledged, anti-chronological tribute to Shakespeare. To identify the entire nation through the behaviour of its ruler seems an odd thing, but for Shakespeare the character of the monarch is the character of the country itself. Nowhere is this more explicit than when the elderly John of Gaunt confronts the disastrous-seeming reign of King Richard II, vain, impetuous and hugely in debt.

Methinks I am a prophet new inspired
And thus expiring do foretell of him:
His rash fierce blaze of riot cannot last,
For violent fires soon burn out themselves;
Small showers last long, but sudden storms are short;
He tires betimes that spurs too fast betimes;
With eager feeding food doth choke the feeder:
Light vanity, insatiate cormorant,
Consuming means, soon preys upon itself.
This royal throne of kings, this scepter'd isle,
This earth of majesty, this seat of Mars,
This other Eden, demi-paradise,
This fortress built by Nature for herself
Against infection and the hand of war,
This happy breed of men, this little world,
This precious stone set in the silver sea,
Which serves it in the office of a wall,
Or as a moat defensive to a house,
Against the envy of less happier lands,
This blessed plot, this earth, this realm, this England,
This nurse, this teeming womb of royal kings,
Fear'd by their breed and famous by their birth,
Renowned for their deeds as far from home,
For Christian service and true chivalry,
As is the sepulchre in stubborn Jewry,
Of the world's ransom, blessed Mary's Son,
This land of such dear souls, this dear dear land,
Dear for her reputation through the world,
Is now leased out, I die pronouncing it,

Like to a tenement or pelting farm:
England, bound in with the triumphant sea
Whose rocky shore beats back the envious siege
Of watery Neptune, is now bound in with shame,
With inky blots and rotten parchment bonds:
That England, that was wont to conquer others,
Hath made a shameful conquest of itself.

Shakespeare's England, the defiant survivor over the long, bloody wars against the Catholic monarchies of the Continent, still the unreconciled enemy of Scots and Irish, was, however, about to come to some kind of end. The death of Elizabeth and the succession of King James VI of Scotland, son of the same Queen Mary she had had beheaded, provided a 'Union of the Crowns' whose consequences and perplexities still surround us to this day. Shakespeare, ever the temporiser, was quickly at work on dramas calculated to appeal to the new king, an intellectual fascinated by exploration and overseas trade, and haunted by the (to him) vivid threat of witchcraft. What didn't Shakespeare foresee? The most obvious answer is religious civil war. Little more than thirty years after he died in retirement at Stratford in 1616, English Protestant revolutionaries would cut off the head of Charles I. Shakespeare knew very well the threat of puritan fanaticism. He saw friends, near family and fellow writers meet horrible ends on the scaffold for their determination to stick with the old religion. The world of the theatre in which, unlike so many of his contemporaries, he made his fortune and survived, rising to gentility, was always threatened by the chalky fingers and hysterical harangues of puritanical preachers. Occasionally, he turns directly back at them – the odious Angelo in *Measure for Measure* is the most obvious example. But even he could not have imagined what riot, disturbance and upending of the very principles of monarchy were brewing as he died.

5

Beyond the Nymphs and Swains: Renaissance Realities

William Shakespeare led a famously opaque life, leaving only scattered clues to his own existence. If he was a soldier, we've never heard about it. He wasn't a magistrate, or a public preacher, or an active courtier. He lived privately, and he wrote and acted and amassed some money – and that's about it. The same wasn't true of many of the other great Elizabethan and Jacobean poets. Though some poets had always lived around the frills of power – Chaucer is an obvious example, and so are Dunbar and Wyatt – it's really in this period that we see the most public poets of all, poets of action and engagement in public life. Sir Walter Raleigh, sea dog, explorer, courtier and finally the victim of royal politics, was also heavily engaged in the brutal and bloody English suppression of southwest Ireland. An even greater poet, Edmund Spenser, fought with Raleigh against the invading Spanish and Italian troops in Ireland, and tried to settle there. Both men were involved in a notorious massacre of papal soldiers who had surrendered at Smerwick; both believed that Catholic Ireland had to be suppressed by extreme force in order to secure Protestant England. In both cases the very notion of what it is to be British becomes hopelessly entangled with Tudor politics.

Edmund Spenser was regarded in his day as the most gloriously talented of British poets, Shakespeare excepted; and although he was London born, no English poet has been more closely associated with Ireland during one of its bloodiest periods. The so-called 'Munster Plantation' involved an attempt to settle Protestant gentry and farmers in what had been the domains of the powerful Desmond family, who led a spirited Catholic revolt against Tudor rule. Spenser was happy to take other people's land, and apparently disdained the Gaelic culture of the island; he was eventually burned out of his family home at Kilcolman during the long-lasting 1590s rebellion led by Hugh O'Neill of Tyrone and known as the Nine Years War. Spenser's verse tells us directly little or nothing of the events that shaped his life: *The Faerie Queene* is a lengthy and complex allegory championing the reign of Elizabeth and the Tudor dynasty, through cod-medieval language and courtly imagery. It does contain, however, passages which are moodily resonant and which seem to capture the tones of Munster in these murderous times:

That darkesome cave they enter, where they find
That cursed man, low sitting on the ground,
Musing full sadly in his sullein mind;
His grieisie locks, long growen and unbound,
Disordred hong about his shoulders round,
And hid his face; through which his hollow eyne
Lookt deadly dull, and stared as astound;
His raw-bone cheekes through penurie and pine,
Were shronke into his jawes, as he did never dine.

His garment naught but many ragged clouts,
With thornes together pind and patched was,
The which his naked sides he wrapt abouts;
And him beside there lay upon the gras
A drearie corse, whose life away did pas,
All wallowd in his owne yet luke-warm blood,
That from his wound yet welled fresh alas;
In which a rustie knife fast fixed stood,
And made an open passage for the gushing flood.

This feels, I think it's safe to say, as if it were written by a man who may have taken part in the Massacre of Smerwick. Much more typical of Spenser's golden eloquence is his famous marriage hymn, written for himself, which shows why his influence on English poetry has lasted so long. It begins like this:

Calme was the day, and through the trembling ayre,
Sweete breathing Zephyrus did softly play
A gentle spirit, that lightly did delay
Hot Titan's beames, which then did glyster fayre:
When whom I sullein care,
Through discontent of my long fruitlesse stay
In Princes Court, and expectation vayne
Of idle hopes, which still doe fly away
Like empty shaddowes, did afflict my brayne,
Walkt forth to ease my payne
Along the shore of silver streaming Themmes,
Whose rutty Banke, the which his River hemmes,
Was paynted all with variable flowers,
And all the meades adorned with daintie gemmes,
Fit to decke maydens bowres
And crowne their Paramours,
Against the Brydale day, which is not long:
Sweete Themmes runne softly, till I end my Song.

The mastery of rhythm, the self-consciously archaic language and the repopulation of British landscapes with classical figures proved addictive for later generations of English poets. For better or for worse, that's what 'Spenserian' means.

The Devonian freebooter, founder of the colony of Virginia and ruthless soldier Sir Walter Raleigh was a less considerable poet than Spenser, though his story of vaulting ambition, pride and vertiginous descent is even more dramatic. For his peers he was clearly charismatic, and if poetry can be charismatic then so too is Raleigh's. He is famous above all for his poems of regret, having lost the favour of Queen Elizabeth. He would eventually be executed by her successor James I at the age of sixty-four after many years languishing in the Tower of London. His poem 'The Lie' is, for my money, the most splendidly sod-you-all verse ever written, from a dangerous man who sees through all that's worst in his society:

Go, soul, the body's guest,
Upon a thankless errand;
Fear not to touch the best;
The truth shall be thy warrant:
Go, since I needs must die,
And give the world the lie.

Say to the court, it glows
And shines like rotten wood;
Say to the church, it shows
What's good, and doth no good:
If church and court reply,
Then give them both the lie.

Tell potentates, they live
Acting by others' action;
Not loved unless they give,
Not strong but by a faction.
If potentates reply,
Give potentates the lie.

Tell men of high condition,
That manage the estate,
Their purpose is ambition,
Their practice only hate:
And if they once reply,
Then give them all the lie.

Tell them that brave it most,
They beg for more by spending,
Who, in their greatest cost,
Seek nothing but commending.
And if they make reply,
Then give them all the lie.

Tell zeal it wants devotion;
Tell love it is but lust;
Tell time it is but motion;
Tell flesh it is but dust:
And wish them not reply,
For thou must give the lie.

Tell age it daily wasteth;
Tell honour how it alters;
Tell beauty how she blasteth;
Tell favour how it falters:
And as they shall reply,
Give every one the lie.

Tell wit how much it wrangles
In tickle points of niceness;
Tell wisdom she entangles
Herself in overwiseness:
And when they do reply,
Straight give them both the lie.

Tell physic of her boldness;
Tell skill it is pretension;
Tell charity of coldness;
Tell law it is contention:
And as they do reply,
So give them still the lie.

Tell fortune of her blindness;
Tell nature of decay;
Tell friendship of unkindness;
Tell justice of delay:
And if they will reply,
Then give them all the lie.

Tell arts they have no soundness,
But vary by esteeming;
Tell schools they want profoundness,
And stand too much on seeming:
If arts and schools reply,
Give arts and schools the lie.

Tell faith it's fled the city;
Tell how the country erreth;
Tell manhood shakes off pity
And virtue least preferreth:
And if they do reply,
Spare not to give the lie.

So when thou hast, as I
Commanded thee, done blabbing –
Although to give the lie
Deserves no less than stabbing –
Stab at thee he that will,
No stab the soul can kill.

It's the kind of poem one can imagine being roared in a tavern by a group of Renaissance wits. And indeed, there is a legend that it was Sir Walter Raleigh himself who founded the famous drinking club at the Mermaid Tavern in London's Cheapside, where most of the key dramatists of the Jacobean period gathered – though perhaps not Shakespeare himself. There is a roughness to the Raleigh poem, a crudeness which these days we associate more with the Restoration, but which was certainly part of the late Elizabethan and Jacobean world of poetry. You can find it in many of the dramatists, but also in the verses of the first working-class London poet we remember. John Taylor was a 'waterman' who ferried all classes up and down the River Thames, and across it to see plays at Southwark. He was the nearest thing Renaissance London had to a cabbie. His verses aren't exactly sophisticated, but if you want to know what London sounded like in the early 1600s, they are essential. He knew all too well the seedier side of life, and was scathing about his fares:

> Look how yon lecher's legs are worn away
> With haunting of the whore house every day:
> He knows more greasy panders, bawds, and drabs,
> And eats more lobsters, artichokes, and crabs,
> Blue roasted eggs, potatoes muscadine,
> Oysters, and pith that grows i'th' ox's chine,
> With many drugs, compounds, and simples store;
> Which makes him have a stomach to a whore.
> But one day he'll give o'er when 'tis too late,
> When he stands begging through an iron grate.

Similarly, some of the serving wenches we glimpse in the background of Shakespeare's tavern scenes are well known to the water poet:

> A lusty wench as nimble as an eel
> Would give a gallant leave to kiss and feel;
> His itching humour straightway was in hope
> To toy, to wanton, tally, buss and grope.
> 'Hold sir,' quoth she, 'My word I will not fail,
> For you shall feel my hand and kiss my tail.'

Bad behaviour in Jacobean times led not only to begging but to hanging, and the monthly executions at Tyburn provided Taylor with another subject:

I have heard sundry men oft times dispute
Of trees, that in one year will twice bear fruit.
But if a man note Tyburn, 'twill appear,
That that's a tree that bears twelve times a year.
I muse it should so fruitful be, for why
I understand the root of it is dry,
It bears no leaf, no bloom, or no bud,
The rain that makes it fructify is blood.
I further note, the fruit which it produces,
Doth seldom serve for profitable uses:
Except the skillful Surgeons industry
Do make Dissection of Anatomy.
It blooms, buds, and bears, all three together,
And in one hour, doth live, and die, and wither.
Like Sodom Apples, they are in conceit,
For touched, they turn to dust and ashes straight.
Besides I find this tree hath never been
Like other fruit trees, walled or hedged in,
But in the highway standing many a year,
It never yet was robbed, as I could hear.
The reason is apparent to our eyes,
That what it bears, are dead commodities:
And yet sometimes (such grace to it is given)
The dying fruit is well prepared for heaven,
And many times a man may gather thence
Remorse, devotion, and true penitence.
And from that tree, I think more fools ascend
To that Celestial joy, which shall never end.

Among the Mermaid drinkers, and Taylor's clients, were Ben
Jonson and John Donne, both of them very different men from
Raleigh, and poets who – unlike the loquacious cabbie – were
important public figures.

Jonson was no more nobly born than Shakespeare. He was a
native Londoner, whose father-in-law had been a brickmaker, and

while formidably intelligent and well educated, he seems to have had a thick brick chip on his shoulder all his life. But he was politically astute, and rose to be a key figure in the court of James I. His great comedies, *Volpone* and *Bartholomew Fair*, give us the sound and stench of Jacobean London with a specificity that goes beyond even Shakespeare. By common consent he's a much less great playwright, whose characters can seem merely gorgeously decorated cardboard cut-outs, representative of vices and virtues, the too-obvious children of medieval drama. Still, he was a wonderful poet.

Because we all like our history neat, it's easy to forget that so-called periods or chapters or ages overlap and bleed into one another. Thus, in what we now call the 'Renaissance' or early modern period, there is plenty of medievalism still lively and present. A great example of this is the rollicking Ben Jonson poem from one of his less well-known plays, in which the devil is invited to dinner and feeds upon a well-seasoned banquet of Jonson's contemporaries:

His stomach was queasy (he came hither coached)
The jogging had caused some crudities rise;
To help it he called for a puritan poached,
That used to turn up the eggs of his eyes.

And so recovered unto his wish,
He sat him down, and he fell to eat;
Promoter in plum broth was the first dish –
His own privy kitchen had no such meat.

Yet though with this he much were taken,
Upon a sudden he shifted his trencher,
As soon as he spied the bawd and the bacon,
By which you may note the devil's a wencher.

Six pickled tailors sliced and cut,
Sempsters and tirewomen, fit for his palate;
With feathermen and perfumers put
Some twelve in a charger to make a great sallet.

A rich fat usurer stewed in his marrow,
And by him a lawyer's head and green sauce:
Both which his belly took up like a harrow,
As if till then he had never seen sauce.

Then carbonadoed and cooked with pains,
Was brought up a cloven sergeant's face:
The sauce was made of his yeoman's brains,
That had been beaten out with his own mace.

Two roasted sherriffs came whole to the board;
(The feast had been nothing without 'em)
Both living and dead they were foxed and furred,
Their chains like sausages hung about 'em.

The very next dish was the mayor of a town,
With a pudding of maintenance thrust in his belly,
Like a goose in the feathers, dressed in his gown,
And his couple of hinch-boys boiled to a jelly.

A London cuckold hot from the spit,
And when the carver up had broken him,
The devil chopped up his head at a bit,
But the horns were very near like to choke him.

The chine of a lecher too there was roasted,
With a plump harlot's haunch and garlic,
A pandar's pettitoes, that had boasted
Himself for a captain, yet never was warlike.

A large fat pasty of a midwife hot;
And for a cold baked meat into the story,
A reverend painted lady was brought,
And coffined in crust till now she was hoary.

To these, an over-grown justice of peace,
With a clerk like a gizzard trussed under each arm;
And warrants for sippits, laid in his own grease,
Set over a chafing dish to be kept warm.

The jowl of a gaoler served for fish,
A constable soused with vinegar by;
Two aldermen lobsters asleep in a dish.
A deputy tart, a churchwarden pie.

All which devoured, he then for a close
Did for a full draught of Derby call;
He heaved the huge vessel up to his nose,
And left not till he had drunk up all.

Then from the table he gave a start,
Where banquet and wine were nothing scarce,
All which he flirted away with a fart,
From whence it was called the Devil's Arse.

This is recognisably a satire on the England of the 1620s, and yet its brutal, rollicking spirit is Chaucerian. Jonson was a man of very many voices. He took his classical heritage far more seriously than did Shakespeare; at his best he can be shockingly direct, as in his heartbreaking poem about the loss of a young son. We know that the death of children was a common, almost routine, part of early modern life. Shakespeare's son Hamnet died at the age of eleven, probably of the plague. Memories of him may dance through some of the great plays, but Shakespeare, characteristically, never addressed his loss directly. Jonson did.

Farewell, thou child of my right hand, and joy;
My sin was too much hope of thee, lov'd boy.
Seven years thou wert lent to me, and I thee pay,
Exacted by thy fate, on the just day.
O, could I lose all father now! For why
Will man lament the state he should envy?
To have so soon 'scap'd world's and flesh's rage,
And, if no other misery, yet age?
Rest in soft peace, and, ask'd, say here doth lie
Ben Jonson his best piece of poetry.
For whose sake, henceforth, all his vows be such,
As what he loves may never like too much.

Earlier on, we heard Shakespeare's ferocity about sexuality in one of his extraordinary sonnets. Jonson, also the author of some of the sweetest love poems in English, can be just as direct: 'doing' means exactly what you suspect it does.

Doing, a filthy pleasure is, and short;
And done, we straight repent us of the sport:
Let us not then rush blindly on unto it,
Like lustful beasts, that only know to do it:
For lust will languish, and that heat decay.
But thus, thus, keeping endless holiday,
Let us together closely lie and kiss,
There is no labour, nor no shame in this;
This hath pleased, doth please, and long will please; never
Can this decay, but is beginning ever.

Although Jonson was a poet of the city, his work on dramatic masques and his huge fame brought him many courtly and noble connections; and he is the master of a kind of poetry, and indeed a sensibility, which runs through English life in particular from the Tudor period to our own day. The so-called 'country house poem' was a very particular and artificial confection: the poet oils up to the landowner by suggesting that his land willingly and desperately gives itself to him. The oaks wish to be cut down to provide, the deer are all too keen to be sliced up into venison steaks, and so on. It's a conceit at once charming and completely ridiculous. Jonson's pioneering poem 'To Penshurst' was written to compliment Sir Robert Sidney, the Earl of Leicester, on his estate in Kent. Jonson paints a picture of a harmonious countryside, of plentiful order and moderation, which has the lush vividness of a Rubens landscape, and whose sensibility uncurls all the way down to Downton Abbey. It's ridiculous, idealised, and yet it bites into something in the English psyche too:

The lower land, that to the river bends,
Thy sheep, thy bullocks, kine, and calves do feed;
The middle grounds thy mares and horses breed.
Each bank doth yield thee conies; and the tops,
Fertile of wood, Ashore and Sidney's copse,
To crown thy open table, doth provide
The purpled pheasant with the speckled side;
The painted partridge lies in every field,
And for thy mess is willing to be killed.
And if the high-swollen Medway fail thy dish,
Thou hast thy ponds, that pay thee tribute fish,
Fat aged carps that run into thy net,
And pikes, now weary their own kind to eat,
As loath the second draught or cast to stay,
Officiously at first themselves betray;
Bright eels that emulate them, and leap on land
Before the fisher, or into his hand.
Then hath thy orchard fruit, thy garden flowers,
Fresh as the air, and new as are the hours.
The early cherry, with the later plum,
Fig, grape, and quince, each in his time doth come;
The blushing apricot and woolly peach
Hang on thy walls, that every child may reach.

And though thy walls be of the country stone,
They're reared with no man's ruin, no man's groan;
There's none that dwell about them wish them down;
But all come in, the farmer and the clown,
And no one empty-handed, to salute
Thy lord and lady, though they have no suit.
Some bring a capon, some a rural cake,
Some nuts, some apples; some that think they make
The better cheeses bring them ...

Jonson's enormous and capacious talent fathered an entire school of poets – the so-called 'tribe of Ben'. His rival and friend John Donne influenced only a few others. His was an odder, knottier and more intense genius, though today, perhaps because of that, he is far better known. Donne can perplex modern readers because he is both a great poet of love and eroticism, and a great religious poet. At times the two seem to mingle, apparently without curdling. But an urgent, vivid belief in God and redemption coexisted in an argumentatively religious society with equally urgent, vivid and profane urges. Donne wrote about sex and love in his youth, and then about Christ and the Church as he aged, but he wasn't two men. All through his life he was able to deploy a kind of intellectual avidity, a nervy restlessness that tore at whatever he was doing and thinking. This famous example may be the greatest poem about love-making ever written. He's urging his mistress to rip her clothes off:

Off with that girdle, like heaven's zone glistering,
But a far fairer world encompassing.
Unpin that spangled breastplate which you wear,
That th' eyes of busy fools may be stopped there.
Unlace yourself, for that harmonious chime
Tells me from you that now it is bed time.
Off with that happy busk, which I envy,
That still can be, and still can stand so nigh.
Your gown, going off, such beauteous state reveals,

As when from flowry meads th' hill's shadow steals.
Off with that wiry coronet and show
The hairy diadem which on you doth grow:
Now off with those shoes, and then safely tread
In this love's hallowed temple, this soft bed.
In such white robes, heaven's angels used to be
Received by men; thou, Angel, bring'st with thee
A heaven like Mahomet's Paradise; and though
Ill spirits walk in white, we easily know
By this these angels from an evil sprite:
Those set our hairs, but these our flesh upright.

License my roving hands, and let them go
Before, behind, between, above, below.
O my America! my new-found-land,
My kingdom, safeliest when with one man manned,
My mine of precious stones, my empery,
How blest am I in this discovering of thee!
To enter in these bonds is to be free;
Then where my hand is set, my seal shall be.

Full nakedness! All joys are due to thee,
As souls unbodied, bodies unclothed must be
To taste whole joys ...

Donne is so direct, his imagination so unflinching, that he can still shock in a way very few Renaissance poets can – as in his famous poem about a flea, which apart from anything else reminds us that the Renaissance, with unwashed clothes and hair, and the press of humanity into small timber buildings, was a formidably lousy period:

Mark but this flea, and mark in this,
How little that which thou deny'st me is;
It sucked me first, and now sucks thee,

And in this flea, our two bloods mingled be;
Thou knowest that this cannot be said
A sin, nor shame, nor loss of maidenhead.
Yet this enjoys before it woo,
And pampered, swells with one blood made of two,
And this, alas, is more than we would do.

Oh stay, three lives in one flea spare,
Where we almost, yea, more than married are.
This flea is you and I, and this
Our marriage bed, and marriage temple is;
Though parents grudge, and you, we are met
And cloistered in these living walls of jet.
Though use make you apt to kill me,
Let not to that self murder added be,
And sacrilege, three sins in killing three.

Cruel and sudden, hast thou since
Purpled thy nail in blood of innocence?
Wherein could this flea guilty be
Except in that drop which it sucked from thee?
Yet thou triumph'st, and sayest that thou
Find'st not thyself, nor me, the weaker now.
'Tis true, then learn how false fears be;
Just so much honour, when thou yieldst to me,
Will waste, as this flea's death took life from thee.

It's horrible, but it's clever and it's funny too; the same trick that Donne pulls off with overtly religious subjects, as when he compares being overmastered by God – overcome by religious ecstasy – to the seizure of a fortified city, or rape:

Batter my heart, three-personed God; for you
As yet but knock, breathe, shine, and seek to mend;
That I may rise and stand, o'erthrow me, and bend

Your force to break, blow, burn, and make me new.
I, like an usurped town, to another due,
Labour to admit you, but O, to no end;
Reason, your viceroy in me, me should defend,
But is captived, and proves weak or untrue.
Yet dearly I love you, and would be loved fain,
But am betrothed unto your enemy.
Divorce me, untie or break that knot again;
Take me to you, imprison me, for I,
Except you enthrall me, never shall be free,
Nor even chaste, except you ravish me.

What makes John Donne perennially interesting is not just the ingenuity of his extraordinary images, or his journey from libertine to devotional poet and preacher. Rather, he seems a man caught between the new learning which will produce, shortly after his lifetime, a revolution in science – the very close watching of material effects, the search for physical laws – and, on the other hand, hope that there is a divine plan and an overarching religious meaning to life. Again and again his poetry twists, turns and shudders between two rival ways of explaining life; again and again we are caught by his novelistic instinct of simply looking harder at what's around him. Here's an example from a complex poem about the soul, where Donne leaves off to contemplate the little twitches, spasms and writhings of a decapitated corpse – a bizarre and unlikely image in our terms, but almost humdrum in Jacobean London:*

Or as sometimes in a beheaded man,
Though at those two red Seas, which freely ran,
One from the trunk, another from the head,
His soul he sailed, to her eternal bed,
His eyes will twinkle, and his tongue will roll,
As though he beckoned, and called back his soul,

---

* I am grateful to my daughter Emily for this example.

He grasps his hands, and he pulls up his feet,
And seems to reach, and to step forth to meet
His Soul; when all these motions which we saw,
Are but as ice, which crackles at a thaw:
Or as a lute, which in moist weather, rings
Her knell alone, by cracking of her strings ...

Donne was writing at a time when old beliefs about the world were tumbling. Very soon the hitherto almost unchallenged ideas of authority and monarchy, so important in Shakespeare, would tumble as well. Puritan preachers were warning that the end of the world and the final judgement were at hand, and in the years after Elizabeth's death there does seem to have been a widespread belief not just that the good times were over, but that all times might be over before long. We see this most vividly in the darker Jacobean playwrights, such as Webster and Middleton. Christopher Marlowe had thrilled audiences a few decades earlier by expressing their fantasies about the overturning of power and the natural order. From the homosexual relationship of Edward II and Piers Gaveston to the impious fantasies of Dr Faustus, the gory, over-reaching ambition of Tamburlaine and the demonic plotting of the Jew of Malta, Marlowe again and again tears up on stage the ordered world around him. And yet, at the back of everything, we still feel that judgement of one kind or another is waiting. His world is anarchic and violent, blasphemous and constantly surprising; but it's not meaningless. The same however isn't true of, for instance, the pitch-dark dramas of John Webster.

Call for the robin-redbreast and the wren,
Since o'er shady groves they hover,
And with leaves and flowers do cover
The friendless bodies of unburied men.
Call unto his funeral dole
The ant, the field-mouse, and the mole,
To rear him hillocks that shall keep him warm,

And (when gay tombs are robb'd) sustain no harm;
But keep the wolf far thence, that's foe to men,
For with his nails he'll dig them up again.

That, Cornelia's dirge from *The White Devil*, is a vision of the world so bleak that we won't find it again until the twentieth-century poets, writing in the shadow of the Holocaust and Stalinism. T.S. Eliot mined Webster. Shakespeare comes close in *King Lear*, but flinches away from seeing life as meaningless. Webster, the lesser poet, doesn't flinch. Here is the shrouding of his tragic heroine the Duchess of Malfi:

Hark, now everything is still,
The screech-owl and the whistler shrill,
Call upon our dame aloud,
And bid her quickly don her shroud!
Much you had of land and rent;
Your length in clay's now competent:
A long war disturbed your mind;
Here your perfect peace is signed.
Of what is't fools make such vain keeping?
Sin their conception, their birth weeping,
Their life a general mist of error,
Their death a hideous storm of terror.
Strew your hair with powders sweet,
Don clean linen, bathe your feet,
And (the foul fiend more to check)
A crucifix let bless your neck:
'Tis now full tide 'tween night and day;
End your groan, and come away.

Webster wasn't alone: Thomas Middleton, one of the greatest dramatic poets of the age, can be as comfortless. At the end of his greatest play, *The Changeling*, the villainous De Flores is taunting his enemies:

130

Yes, and the while I coupled with your mate at Barley-
   break: now we are left in hell.
Vermandero: We are all there, it circumscribes us here.

Another character, Alsemero, agrees, blaming what's happened on
a strangeness in the moon:

... Here's beauty changed
To ugly whoredom; here, servant obedience
To a master-sin, imperious murder ...

What had gone wrong in the early years of the seventeenth century?
Was it simply the horror of contemplating the collapse of religious
certainties that had been more or less in people's heads for centuries?
The Reformation, kick-started in England by Henry VIII's erotic
fixation on Anne Boleyn, was a profoundly traumatic event: for many
traditional Catholic believers it involved not simply the destruction
of their monasteries, chapels and images, but also of the rituals by
which they had connected themselves to the dead, and hoped them-
selves to be remembered. It was a tearing-up not simply of authority
but of meaning, and it would lead to the religious wars of the 1600s.
These would rip apart all the kingdoms of Great Britain, and plunge
once quiet country towns into violence and near-anarchy. Other
factors included years of crop failure and the regular reappearance of
the Black Death: one of the original university wits, Thomas Nashe,
has left us, alongside some prodigious pornography and wonderful
prose works, perhaps the ultimate plague-infested lament of all:

Adieu, farewell earth's bliss!
This world uncertain is:
Fond are life's lustful joys,
Death proves them all but toys.
None from his darts can fly;
I am sick, I must die –
Lord, have mercy on us!

Rich men, trust not in wealth,
Gold cannot buy you health;
Physic himself must fade;
All things to end are made;
The plague full swift goes by;
I am sick, I must die –
Lord, have mercy on us!

Beauty is but a flower
Which wrinkles will devour;
Brightness falls from the air;
Queens have died young and fair;
Dust hath closed Helen's eye;
I am sick, I must die –
Lord, have mercy on us!

Strength stoops unto the grave,
Worms feed on Hector brave;
Swords may not fight with fate;
Earth still holds ope her gate;
Come, come! the bells do cry;
I am sick, I must die –
Lord, have mercy on us!

Wit with his wantonness
Tasteth death's bitterness;
Hell's executioner
Hath no ears for to hear
What vain art can reply;
I am sick, I must die –
Lord, have mercy on us!

Haste therefore each degree
To welcome destiny;
Heaven is our heritage,

Earth but a player's stage.
Mount we unto the sky;
I am sick, I must die –
Lord, have mercy on us!

As with Ben Jonson's earlier poem about the devil's dinner, this has
the starkness of much medieval verse. It reminds me of the French
poet Villon, and of Dunbar's 'Lament for the Makars', quoted earlier.
The next generation produced glorious religious verse which is
entirely different in tone – intimate, passionate and direct, as writers
responded to a revolution in feeling much more generous than the
darkness of the Jacobeans. In the next section we will turn to the
civil wars, and their effects upon the British. It's all too easy, however,
for us to describe the violence caused by religious disagreement and
completely miss the human essence of fervent religious belief.
People would kill one another because their arguments about the
nature of God went right to the heart of who they thought they
were. This period produces some of the bloodiest and most shameful
events in British history, but it also produces the finest religious and
spiritual verse written in English; and that's no contradiction.

George Herbert is, for my money, the greatest poet in the English
language after Shakespeare. He was a clergyman, born in Wales,
educated in London and Cambridge, who spent most of his life in
a tiny parish outside Salisbury. His formidable and intellectual
mother Magdalen was a close friend and patron of John Donne.
After failing to achieve worldly success despite his talents, Herbert
settled for the life of a country parson, ministering to his flock,
preaching and writing his devotional poetry for friends rather than
the public. He was closely associated with the Church of England
religious community at Little Gidding in Cambridgeshire. There's
not much more to be said, really. The mystery of his poetry lies in
its exquisite rhythms and perfect command of tone. Here is a man
who really does feel a personal relationship with God. In the famous
'Love (III)' he imagines himself as the shameful and reluctant guest
at God's banquet:

Love bade me welcome: yet my soul drew back,
Guilty of dust and sin.
But quick-ey'd Love, observing me grow slack,
From my first entrance in,
Drew nearer to me, sweetly questioning,
If I lack'd anything.

A guest, I answer'd, worthy to be here:
Love said, You shall be he.
I the unkind, ungrateful? Ah my dear,
I cannot look on thee.
Love took my hand, and smiling did reply,
Who made the eyes but I?

Truth Lord, but I have marr'd them: let my shame
Go where it doth deserve.
And know you not, says Love, who bore the blame?
My dear, then I will serve.
You must sit down, says Love, and tast me meat:
So I did sit and eat.

And here, in 'The Collar', he dramatises his own impatience with a quiet country life devoted to the always-listening, half-amused and patient God:

I struck the board, and cried, 'No more!
I will abroad.
What! shall I ever sigh and pine?
My lines and life are free; free as the road,
Loose as the wind, as large as store.
Shall I be still in suit?
Have I no harvest but a thorn
To let me blood, and not restore
What I have lost with cordial fruit?
Sure there was wine

Before my sighs did dry it; there was corn
Before my tears did drown it.
Is the year only lost to me?
Have I no bays to crown it?
No flowers, no garlands gay? all blasted?
All wasted?
Not so, my heart; but there is fruit,
And thou hast hands.
Recover all thy sigh-blown age
On double pleasures; leave thy cold dispute
Of what is fit and not; forsake thy cage,
Thy rope of sands,
Which petty thoughts have made, and made to thee
Good cable, to enforce and draw,
And be thy law,
While thou didst wink and wouldst not see.
Away! take heed;
I will abroad.
Call in thy death's-head there; tie up thy fears;
He that forbears
To suit and serve his need
Deserves his load.'
But as I rav'd, and grew more fierce and wild
At every word,
Me thoughts I heard one calling, 'Child';
And I replied, 'My Lord.'

Although Herbert's life was in many respects mercifully quiet, he suffered disappointment, bereavement, bad health and the other ordinary problems of human life. In his poem 'Affliction' he looks back on it all and wrestles with God. He pities himself, yet without a shred of self-pity:

When thou didst entice to thee my heart,
I thought the service brave:
So many joys I writ down for my part,
Besides what I might have
Out of my stock of natural delights,
Augmented with thy gracious benefits.

I looked on thy furniture so fine,
And made it fine to me:
Thy glorious household-stuff did me entwine,
And 'tice me unto thee.
Such stars I counted mine: both heav'n and earth
Paid me my wages in a world of mirth.

What pleasures could I want, whose King I served?
Where joys my fellows were?
Thus argu'd into hopes, my thoughts reserved
No place for grief or fear.
Therefore my sudden soul caught at the place,
And made her youth and fierceness seek thy face.

At first thou gav'st me milk and sweetnesses;
I had my wish and way:
My days were straw'd with flow'rs and happiness;
There was no month but May.
But with my years sorrow did twist and grow,
And made a party unawares for woe.

My flesh began unto my soul in pain,
'Sicknesses cleave my bones;
Consuming agues dwell in ev'ry vein,
And tune my breath to groans.'
Sorrow was all my soul; I scarce believed,
Till grief did tell me roundly, that I lived.

When I got health, thou took'st away my life,
And more; for my friends die:
My mirth and edge was lost; a blunted knife
Was of more use than I.
Thus thin and lean without a fence or friend,
I was blown through with ev'ry storm and wind.

Whereas my birth and spirit rather took
The way that takes the town;
Thou didst betray me to a lingering book,
And wrap me in a gown.
I was entangled in the world of strife,
Before I had the power to change my life.

Yet, for I threatened oft the siege to raise,
Not simpring all mine age,
Thou often didst with Academic praise
Melt and dissolve my rage.
I took thy sweetened pill, till I came where
I could not go away, nor persevere.

Yet lest perchance I should too happy be
In my unhappiness,
Turning my purge to food, thou throwest me
Into more sicknesses.
Thus doth thy power cross-bias me; not making
Thine own gift good, yet me from my ways taking.

Now I am here, what thou wilt do with me
None of my books will show:
I read, and sigh, and wish I were a tree;
For sure I then should grow
To fruit or shade: at least some bird would trust
Her household to me, and I should be just.

Yet though thou troublest me, I must be meek;
In weakness must be stout.
Well, I will change the service, and go seek
Some other master out.
Ah my dear God! though I am clean forgot,
Let me not love thee, if I love thee not.

George Herbert died in 1633, well before the political crisis which led to the civil wars, but he was an eloquent defender of the Anglican Communion, which can so easily be seen as a milky, compromising middle way between Catholicism and Puritan Protestantism. His defence of 'the British church' is also a rare and rather sweet defence of the middle way, and compromise generally.

I joy, dear mother, when I view
Thy perfect lineaments, and hue
Both sweet and bright.
Beauty in thee takes up her place,
And dates her letters from thy face,
When she doth write.

A fine aspect in fit array,
Neither too mean nor yet too gay,
Shows who is best.
Outlandish looks may not compare,
For all they either painted are,
Or else undress'd.

She on the hills which wantonly
Allureth all, in hope to be
By her preferr'd,
Hath kiss'd so long her painted shrines,
That ev'n her face by kissing shines,
For her reward.

She in the valley is so shy
Of dressing, that her hair doth lie
About her ears;
While she avoids her neighbour's pride,
She wholly goes on th' other side,
And nothing wears.

But, dearest mother, what those miss,
The mean, thy praise and glory is
And long may be.
Blessed be God, whose love it was
To double-moat thee with his grace,
And none but thee.

Like George Herbert, Henry Vaughan was a Church of England clergyman who spent much of his life ministering to a remote rural flock – in his case in the Welsh Brecon Beacons. Distantly related to Herbert, Vaughan experienced a religious rebirth, which he attributed in part to the older poet; and his religious poetry was deeply indebted to Herbert as well. Unlike Herbert, Vaughan was also a soldier. He fought in the Battle of Rowton Heath in 1645, for Charles I, and was present with the Royalists during the siege of Beeston Castle in Cheshire. He was never reconciled to the Cromwellian Commonwealth, and wrote semi-public poetry about the war. It doesn't, however, come near the greatest of his spiritual poetry in quality. After the defeat of the Royalists, and the banning of the Anglican Church that Herbert had so celebrated – including its essential *Book of Common Prayer* – Vaughan launched himself on what was effectively a one-person crusade to preserve the spirit of Anglicanism in the new age. His poetry becomes infused with spiritual longing, alongside a sense of loss; it's a reminder that history isn't simply battles and struggles, but also their long aftermaths:

My Soul, there is a country
Afar beyond the stars,

Where stands a winged sentry
All skillful in the wars;
There, above noise and danger
Sweet Peace sits, crown'd with smiles,
And One born in a manger
Commands the beauteous files.
He is thy gracious friend
And (O my Soul awake!)
Did in pure love descend,
To die here for thy sake.
If thou canst get but thither,
There grows the flow'r of peace,
The rose that cannot wither,
Thy fortress, and thy ease.
Leave then thy foolish ranges,
For none can thee secure,
But One, who never changes,
Thy God, thy life, thy cure.

Vaughan felt abandoned not just by the political world but by Britain itself – the country had taken a puritan path which he neither understood nor felt any sympathy for. The truer Christians of his original Anglican faith had departed the world itself:

They are all gone into the world of light!
And I alone sit ling'ring here;
Their very memory is fair and bright,
And my sad thoughts doth clear.

It glows and glitters in my cloudy breast,
Like stars upon some gloomy grove,
Or those faint beams in which this hill is drest,
After the sun's remove.

I see them walking in an air of glory,
Whose light doth trample on my days:
My days, which are at best but dull and hoary,
Mere glimmering and decays.

Perhaps it's because Vaughan had been forcibly separated from the rites and rituals of the Anglican Church that he reaches out to find spiritual images that can speak directly to us today. No poem of the seventeenth – or eighteenth, or nineteenth – century seems to me to include so eerily modern an understanding of the nature of time and space as Vaughan's glorious 'The World'. It's a spiritual vision, but Vaughan's experience of contemporary politics allows him to include in it one of the most convincing and unpleasant portraits of a politician in English verse:

I saw Eternity the other night,
Like a great ring of pure and endless light,
All calm, as it was bright;
And round beneath it, Time in hours, days, years,
Driv'n by the spheres
Like a vast shadow mov'd; in which the world
And all her train were hurl'd.
The doting lover in his quaintest strain
Did there complain;
Near him, his lute, his fancy, and his flights,
Wit's sour delights,
With gloves, and knots, the silly snares of pleasure,
Yet his dear treasure
All scatter'd lay, while he his eyes did pour
Upon a flow'r.

The darksome statesman hung with weights and woe,
Like a thick midnight-fog mov'd there so slow,
He did not stay, nor go;
Condemning thoughts (like sad eclipses) scowl

Upon his soul,
And clouds of crying witnesses without
Pursued him with one shout.
Yet digg'd the mole, and lest his ways be found,
Work'd under ground,
Where he did clutch his prey; but one did see
That policy;
Churches and altars fed him; perjuries
Were gnats and flies;
It rain'd about him blood and tears, but he
Drank them as free.

Had William Shakespeare sat down one afternoon in a tavern and written these lines, he'd have been proud of them; and they would have been amongst the most anthologised verses in the language.

6

Nothing Left But Laughter? Britain's Mullahs Confront the Problem of Pleasure

Across Britain, from Aberdeen in the throes of the Scottish reformation to the turmoil experienced in rural English parishes of Devon and Cornwall, along the south coast, from the Plantations of Ulster to the Cromwellian heartlands of East Anglia, the seventeenth century was an age of religious extremism, even of mania. There was a lot of politics in it too, of course, as the medieval doctrine of the divine right of kings collided with the rising self-confidence and rationalism of the middle classes; but for half a century or so we went collectively mad with each other. As we have seen, some of Britain's greatest poets saw through the mania, or simply ignored it, to produce the most luminous spiritual expressions ever achieved in English. Others, swaggeringly, turned their backs on piety and seriousness, producing deathless love lyrics and bawdy.

Fitting into both those categories, indeed a category all by himself, was the amazing Andrew Marvell, Puritan propagandist, apologist for Oliver Cromwell, country house poet and sexual hunter. Here is his famous 'To his Coy Mistress'. Perhaps a poem has never been created with such apparently single-minded determination to get a reluctant woman into bed. And it's very funny:

Had we but world enough, and time,
This coyness, Lady, were no crime.
We would sit down and think which way
To walk and pass our long love's day.
Thou by the Indian Ganges' side
Shouldst rubies find: I by the tide
Of Humber would complain. I would
Love you ten years before the Flood,
And you should, if you please, refuse
Till the conversion of the Jews.
My vegetable love should grow
Vaster than empires, and more slow;
A hundred years should go to praise
Thine eyes and on thy forehead gaze;
Two hundred to adore each breast,
But thirty thousand to the rest;
An age at least to every part,
And the last age should show your heart.
For, Lady, you deserve this state,
Nor would I love at lower rate.

But at my back I always hear
Time's wingèd chariot hurrying near;
And yonder all before us lie
Deserts of vast eternity.
Thy beauty shall no more be found,
Nor, in thy marble vault, shall sound
My echoing song; then worms shall try
That long preserved virginity,
And your quaint honour turn to dust,
And into ashes all my lust:
The grave's a fine and private place,
But none, I think, do there embrace.

Now therefore, while the youthful hue
Sits on thy skin like morning dew,
And while thy willing soul transpires
At every pore with instant fires,
Now let us sport us while we may,
And now, like amorous birds of prey,
Rather at once our time devour
Than languish in his slow-chapped power.
Let us roll all our strength and all
Our sweetness up into one ball,
And tear our pleasures with rough strife
Through the iron gates of life:
Thus, though we cannot make our sun
Stand still, yet we will make him run.

Both the theme – time is short, we won't be young forever, let's get on with it – and the wit are the essence of what is often called 'Cavalier poetry', after the mainly Royalist writers who specialised in it. There are so many casually brilliant erotic poems by Stuart lyricists that it's impossible to give more than a few examples. Overall, I think they need to be seen as the necessary reaction to the grimness described in the previous chapter, and that over-doomy, almost adolescent sense that the world is a dark place, about to end. To which the Cavaliers respond, in effect, 'Get 'em off.' Here is Sir John Suckling:

Why so pale and wan, fond lover?
Prithee, why so pale? –
Will, when looking well can't move her,
Looking ill prevail?
Prithee, why so pale?

Why so dull and mute, young sinner?
Prithee, why so mute? –
Will, when speaking well can't win her,

Saying nothing do't?
Prithee, why so mute?

Quit, quit, for shame! this will not move,
This cannot take her —
If of herself she will not love,
Nothing can make her:
The Devil take her!

And here's Richard Lovelace, another Royalist soldier, this time addressing a prostitute who becomes the patron saint of all women larger than size 10:

I cannot tell who loves the skeleton
Of a poor marmoset, naught but bone, bone.
Give me a nakedness with her clothes on.

Such whose white-satin upper coat of skin,
Cut upon a velvet rich incarnadin,
Has yet body (and of flesh) within.

Sure it is meant good husbandry in men,
Who so incorporate with aery lean,
To repair their sides, and get their rib again.

Hard hap unto that huntsman that decrees
Fat joys for all his sweat, whenas he sees,
After his 'say, naught but his keeper's fees.

Then Love, I beg, when next thou takest thy bow,
Thy angry shafts, and does heart-chasing go,
Pass rascal deer, strike me the largest doe.

These are poems which look back, in a rougher age, to the poems of Ben Jonson, composed for courtly masques but often with a cynical, even misogynistic undertone:

Still to be neat, still to be dressed
As you were going to a feast;
Still to be powdered, still perfumed –
Lady, it is to be presumed
Though art's hid causes are not found,
All is not sweet, all is not sound.

Give me a look, give me a face,
That makes simplicity grace;
Robes loosely flowing, her as free:
Such sweet neglect more taketh me
Than all the adulteries of art;
They strike mine eyes, but not my heart.

One of the central images in that short poem, about the lover being taken, or hooked like a fish on a line, reappears in my own favourite Cavalier poem, by the Devonshire clergyman Robert Herrick. Called simply 'Upon Julia's Clothes', its six lines are as near-perfect as English lyricism gets:

Whenas in silks my Julia goes,
Then, then, methinks, how sweetly flows
That liquefaction of her clothes.

Next, when I cast mine eyes and see
That brave vibration each way free;
O how that glittering taketh me!

When Jonson celebrates simplicity in the middle of the highly artificial and game-playing court of James I, it's as suspect as a modern Hollywood actress telling us she never diets; but in the hands of the clergyman Herrick, stuck off in his Devon village, it's more believable. Certainly he writes as if he means it:

A sweet disorder in the dress
Kindles in clothes a wantonness;
A lawn about the shoulders thrown
Into a fine distraction;
An erring lace, which here and there
Enthrals the crimson stomacher;
A cuff neglectful, and thereby
Ribbons to flow confusedly;
A winning wave, deserving note,
In the tempestuous petticoat;
A careless shoe-string, in whose tie
I see a wild civility; –
Do more bewitch me, than when art
Is too precise in every part.

Herrick himself was dryly eloquent on the paradox of a would-be fashionable city poet obliged to earn his crust in a countryside parsonage, yet still scribbling away for a literate audience that is, by the 1640s, growing at a huge pace:

More discontents I never had
Since I was born, than here;
Where I have been, and still am, sad,
In this dull Devonshire.
Yet justly too I must confess,
I ne'er invented such
Ennobled numbers for the press,
Than where I loath'd so much.

That reference to the press is significant: as the British Isles tore themselves apart, the appetite for news, explanation and commentary exploded. This is really when journalism begins. Some of the greatest poets of the age, including Donne, Herbert and Marvell, disdained print: their most important poetry circulated in hand-written copies to patrons and friends, and was only published after their deaths. This, however, is the first great age of the pamphlet, and the number of literate Britons was growing very fast. Both Marvell and his great friend John Milton were ardent pamphlet-eers, spreading their views through prose even more widely than through their poetry. But in this great age of religious argument, and of love poetry, the voice of women is very rarely heard. The misogyny of early modern Britain was bolstered during the Puritan revolution by a widespread identification of original sin with Eve.

It's interesting, therefore, that one of the very few published female poets concentrated her most successful rhetoric on defend-ing Eve, and therefore the position of women generally. Aemilia Lanier was part of the artistic elite congregated around the court: her father, Baptiste Bassano, was a Venetian musician hired by Elizabeth I. She had a long and apparently happy affair with a much older aristocrat, then unhappily married her cousin and lived to a ripe old age. Some scholars believe the family was Jewish, and that Aemilia was Shakespeare's 'dark Lady' from the sonnets, but the evidence is scanty. Much more important, for our purposes, is her own poetry. In 'Salve Deus Rex Judæorum' she argues that Adam is far more to blame for the betrayal of God and the arrival of original sin than Eve.

> Our mother Eve, who tasted of the tree,
> Giving to Adam what she held most dear,
> Was simply good, and had no power to see;
> The aftercoming harm did not appear.
> The subtle Serpent that our sex betrayed
> Before our fall so sure a plot had laid
>
> That under certain ignorance perceived
> No guile or craft that was by him intended;
> For had she known of what we were bereaved,

To his request she had not condescended.
But she, poor soul, by Cunning was deceived:
No hurt therein her harmless heart intended;
For she alleged God's word, which he denies,
That they should die, but even as gods be wise.

But surely Adam cannot be excused:
Her fault though great, yet he was most to blame;
What weakness offered, strength might have refused.
Being the Lord of all, the greater was his shame:
Although the serpent's craft had her abused,
God's holy Word or all his actions frame;
But he was lord and King of all the earth
Before poor Eve had either life or breath …

… And then to lay the fault on patience' back,
That we, poor women, must endure it all!
We know right well he did discretion lack,
Being not persuaded thereunto at all.
If Eve did err, it was for knowledge' sake;
The fruit being fair persuaded him to fall:
No subtle Serpent's falsehood did betray him;
If he would eat it, who had power to stay him?

This isn't the easiest verse, or the most smoothly flowing, but it is
an extremely forthright challenge to the downgrading of women as
vessels of sin which was the almost unchallenged male ideology of
Elizabethan England. Lanier doesn't shrink from drawing her own
conclusions:

Then let us have our liberty again,
And challenge to yourselves no sovereignty:
You came not in the world without our pain;
Make that a bar against your cruelty.
Your fault being greater, why should you disdain

Our being your equals, free from tyranny?
If one weak woman simply did offend,
This sin of yours hath no excuse nor end.

Had Lanier written no more than this, she would have been one of the most interesting voices of the period – certainly one that undercuts much of what we think we know about the Elizabethans and Jacobeans. But in an earlier part of the same collection of poetry, addressing her patron the Countess of Dorset, she takes on as well the whole assumption of aristocracy and noble birth ('greatness' here means simply birth, or breeding):

Greatness is no sure frame to build upon,
No worldly treasure can assure that place;
God makes both even, the cottage with the Throne:
All worldly honours there are counted base ...

Titles of honour which the world bestows
To none but the virtuous doth belong;
As beauteous bowers where true worth should repose,
And where his dwelling should be built most strong.
But when they are bestowed upon her foes,
Poor Virtue's friends endure the greatest wrong;
For they must suffer all indignity,
Until in heaven they better graced be.

What difference was there when the world began;
Was it not virtue that distinguished all?
All sprang but from one woman and one man;
Then how doth gentry come to rise and fall?

Lanier goes on to argue that the nobly born can never quite know their own origins. If they behave cruelly, or greedily, they lose whatever rights noble breeding apparently gave them:

Nor is he fit for honour or command
If base affections overrules his mind,
Or that self-will doth carry such a hand
As worldly pleasures have the power to blind,
So as he cannot see or understand
How to discharge that place to him assigned:
God's stewards must for all the poor provide,
If in God's house they purpose to abide.

An interesting and turbulent woman, Aemilia Lanier. She may have loyally addressed her verses to Queen Elizabeth and various aristocratic female patrons, but surely we can hear the early premonitions of that revolutionary spirit which will eventually bring down the Stuarts? Lanier may be the most unusual female voice of the period, but she certainly isn't the only one. Lady Mary Wroth came from a much more elevated family than Lanier, that tangled thicket of poets and statesmen the Sidneys; and for most of her life she was part of the Elizabethan and Jacobean court, a dancer in masques by Ben Jonson, well known to leading poets. Her husband, Sir Robert Wroth, was a favourite of King James, but also by most accounts a disloyal drunkard. Later, Mary had a long relationship with her cousin William Herbert, the third Earl of Pembroke, another patron of Shakespeare's. He, however, much richer, never married her.

Mary Wroth wrote a series of stunning sonnets and one of the first prose works by a woman to be published, and in both of them she confronts, through the thin disguise of classical allusion, the problem of being a woman in a swaggeringly male world. The sonnets, which seem at first glance so similar to those written by so many male poets in this age of sonnet-mania, convey a very different view of love and freedom. In the first one, Mary compares herself to a ship caught on the notorious Goodwin Sands off the English coast:

My paine still smother'd in my grieved brest,
Seekes for some ease, yet cannot passage finde,
To be discharg'd of this unwellcome guest,
When most I strive, more fast his burthens binde.
Like to a Ship on Goodwins cast by winde,
The more she strives, more deepe in Sand is prest,
Till she be lost: so am I in this kind
Sunck, and devour'd, and swallow'ed by unrest.
Lost, shipwrackt, spoyl'd, debar'd of smallest hope,
Nothing of pleasure left, save thoughts have scope,
Which wander may; goe then my thoughts and cry:
Hope's perish'd, Love tempest-beaten, Joy lost,
Killing Despaire hath all these blessings crost;
Yet Faith still cries, Love will not falsifie.

In another fine example, Wroth portrays the dilemma of being
pursued by jealous and prickly courtiers – a strange labyrinth:

Except my heart, which you bestow'd before,
And for a signe of Conquest gave away
As worthlesse to be kept in your choice store;
Yet one more spotlesse with you doth not stay.
The tribute which my heart doth truely pay,
Is faith untouch'd, pure thoughts discharge the score
Of debts for me, where Constancy beares sway,
And rules as Lord, unharm'd by Envies sore,
Yet other mischiefes faile not to attend,
As enimies to you, my foes must be,
Curst Jealousie doth all her forces bend
To my undoing, thus my harmes I see.
So though in Love I fervently doe burne,
In this strange Labyrinth how shall I turne?

She was clearly a passionate woman, and was reviled in her own
time for daring to break the conventions of courtly privacy. But for

Wroth, as for Lanier, the constant tension was between eroticism and freedom. To be conquered in love was not a simple thing, but a real defeat:

Am I thus conquer'd? have I lost the powers,
That to withstand, which joyes to ruine me?
Must I bee still, while it my strength devoures,
And captive leads me prisoner bound, unfree?
Love first shall leave mens phant'sies to them free,
Desire shall quench loves flames, Spring, hate sweet
    showres;
Love shall loose all his Darts, have sight, and see
His shame and wishings, hinder happy houres.
Why should we not loves purblinde charmes resist?
Must we be servile, doing what he list?
No, seeke some hoste to harbour thee: I flye
Thy babish tricks, and freedome doe professe;
But O my hurt makes my lost heart confesse:
I love, and must; so farewell liberty.

By the time Lady Mary Wroth died in 1652 the fashion for sonnets was long over, and liberty was being fought over with steel and gunpowder, rather than ink. This woman, who as a young girl had danced before Queen Elizabeth at Penshurst, lived long enough to see the British Isles being torn apart by the religious and political conflicts we tend today to remember as simply 'the Civil War'. When these wars finally arrived, they were so distressing and bloody that many poets pulled away, and shrank from directly describing what happened. Perhaps the truth is simply that war poetry, unless it is protest poetry, is generally rather dull. Abraham Cowley was a Royalist secret agent and soldier, and wrote directly about the war. This extract from his unfinished epic *The Civil War* describes the Battle of Newbury in 1643, a famous defeat for the royal forces. It isn't great poetry, but it does, I think, give a feel for a real battle by one who was actually there.

The cannon next their message 'gan to say —
On came the dreadful business of the day.
Here with sharp neighs the spriteful horses sound
And with proud tramplings beat the putrid ground.
The drums' grave voice and sullen noise of guns
With the shrill trumpets' brighter accent runs
(A dismal consort!) through the trembling air
Whilst groans of wounded men the burden bear.
Through dust and smoke (that day's untimely night)
The powder's nimble flames and restless light
Of glittering swords amaze and fright the eyes,
So through black storms the winged lightning flies!
Death in all shapes and in all habits dressed
(Such was his sportful rage) the field processed ...
... No place but saw some unexpected wound,
No part of man but some wild bullet found,
Uncertain fate o'er all the field did range —
Here strange deaths seen, and vary scapes as
    strange.

At this point in the battle the Cavaliers appeared to be winning, and pushed Essex, the Parliamentary leader, off the hill he had commanded:

At last bright victory over Charles his head
Thrust forth some beams — the clouds before it fled.
We forced the enclosures and the hill we won;
Ah, how much sweat and blood did down it run!

But now the struggle changes direction, and one by one the Cavalier commanders are killed. Lucius Cary, Viscount Falkland, is hit, and the poet is devastated — if nothing else this reminds us how important individual commanders were, and often still are, in the middle of a fight:

155

An eastern wind from Newbury rushing came:
It sighed, methought, it sighed out Falkland's name;
Falkland, methought, the hills all echoed round,
Falkland, methought, each bird did sadly sound.
A muse stood by me and just then I writ
My King's great acts in verses not unfit.
The troubled muse fell shapeless into air –
Instead of ink dropped from my pen a tear.
Oh, 'tis a deadly truth: Falkland is slain!
His noble blood all dyes the accursed plain.

The most vivid descriptions of war and regicide were kept for the new pamphlets, in angry prose. Some poetry, however, did take up its position, musket levelled, dagger drawn. Andrew Marvell, who in that earlier extract sounded exactly like a Cavalier being, well, cavalier, became a dedicated supporter of the Cromwellian movement. He served as an MP, castigated Cromwell's enemies abroad – at that time the Dutch – in hilariously intemperate terms – and wrote a 'Horation ode' to the man who had already moved from being the anti-royalist liberator to a military dictator in the making. This poem, a crucial document of the Civil War era, was written shortly after Cromwell's return from Ireland. There he had shattered the Royalist and Catholic forces, including Irish, English and Scottish mercenaries ranged against the Commonwealth. Cromwell's armies had been responsible for atrocities that remain vivid in the Irish imagination today, from the use of starvation to cow the population, to the notorious slaughters of civilians and priests, as well as surrendered soldiers, that followed the main sieges, of Drogheda above all. These war crimes are barely touched upon in Marvell's poem, which unlike his prose propaganda works wasn't even published at the time. The mood, to start with, is uncomplicated in its triumphalism:

The forward youth that would appear
Must now forsake his Muses dear,

Nor in the shadows sing
His numbers languishing.
'Tis time to leave the books in dust,
And oil th' unused armour's rust,
Removing from the wall
The corslet of the hall.
So restless Cromwell could not cease
In the inglorious arts of peace,
But through advent'rous war
Urged his active star:
And, like the three-forked lightning, first
Breaking the clouds where it was nursed,
Did thorough his own side
His fiery way divide.
For 'tis all one to courage high,
The emulous or enemy;
And with such, to enclose
Is more than to oppose.
Then burning through the air he went,
And palaces and temples rent;
And Caesar's head at last
Did through his laurels blast.
'Tis madness to resist or blame
The force of angry Heaven's flame;
And, if we would speak true,
Much to the man is due,
Who, from his private gardens, where
He lived reserved and austere,
As if his highest plot
To plant the bergamot,
Could by industrious valour climb
To ruin the great work of time,
And cast the Kingdom old
Into another mould.

This smashing action of the lightning on temples and palaces, and the fact that he burned through his own side as well, suggests an ambiguity about the great dictator. Marvell, thank God, proves himself far too good a poet to succumb to oily propaganda, and indeed gives more than gracious acknowledgement to Charles I's courage when he mounts the scaffold to be executed – not at all what one might expect from an ardent republican:

> ... thence the royal actor borne
> The tragic scaffold might adorn,
> While round the armed bands
> Did clap their bloody hands.
> He nothing common did or mean
> Upon that memorable scene,
> But with his keener eye
> The axe's edge did try;
> Nor call'd the gods with vulgar spite
> To vindicate his helpless right,
> But bowed his comely head
> Down as upon a bed.

It was this graciousness, and a certain political slipperiness, which allowed Marvell, when Cromwell's Commonwealth finally collapsed and Charles II was restored, to avoid the fate of so many. He was pardoned, became an MP in the Restoration Parliament – and satirised it – and was even able to obtain a pardon for the better-known and less temperate republican John Milton.

Certainly Marvell sounds temperate compared to the famous 'Diggers' Song' thought to have been composed by Gerrard Winstanley. Originally a weaver from Wigan, Winstanley was the nearest thing the times produced to a genuine revolutionary leader. The 1640s were years of hunger and distress. In the context of the war between Parliament and King, the diggers represent the most purely communist strain of thought – exactly the kind of mob Shakespeare was afraid of. They simply took over land owned by the gentry and farmed it themselves, in a provocative act against things as they were. In this song, Winstanley urges them to go much further:

You noble Diggers all, stand up now, stand up now,
You noble Diggers all, stand up now,
The waste land to maintain, seeing Cavaliers by name
Your digging does maintain, and persons all defame
Stand up now, stand up now.

Your houses they pull down, stand up now, stand up now,
Your houses they pull down, stand up now.
Your houses they pull down to fright your men in town
But the gentry must come down, and the poor shall wear
    the crown.
Stand up now, Diggers all.

With spades and hoes and plowes, stand up now, stand up
    now,
With spades and hoes and plowes stand up now,
Your freedom to uphold, seeing Cavaliers are bold
To kill you if they could, and rights from you to hold.
Stand up now, Diggers all.

Theire self-will is theire law, stand up now, stand up now,
Theire self-will is theire law, stand up now.
Since tyranny came in they count it now no sin
To make a gaol a gin, to starve poor men therein.
Stand up now, Diggers all.

The gentrye are all round, stand up now, stand up now,
The gentrye are all round, stand up now.
The gentrye are all round, on each side they are found,
Theire wisdom's so profound, to cheat us of our ground
Stand up now, stand up now.

The lawyers they conjoyne, stand up now, stand up now,
The lawyers they conjoyne, stand up now.
To arrest you they advise, such fury they devise,
The devill in them lies, and hath blinded both their eyes.
Stand up now, stand up now.

The clergy they come in, stand up now, stand up now,
The clergy they come in, stand up now.
The clergy they come in, and say it is a sin
That we should now begin, our freedom for to win.
Stand up now, Diggers all.

The tithes they yet will have, stand up now, stand up now,
The tithes they yet will have, stand up now.
The tithes they yet will have, and lawyers their fees crave,
And this they say is brave, to make the poor their slave.
Stand up now, Diggers all.

'Gainst lawyers and 'gainst Priests, stand up now, stand up
    now,
'Gainst lawyers and 'gainst Priests stand up now.
For tyrants they are both even flatt against their oath,
To grant us they are loath free meat and drink and cloth.
Stand up now, Diggers all.

The club is all their law, stand up now, stand up now,
The club is all their law, stand up now.
The club is all their law to keep men in awe,
But they no vision saw to maintain such a law.
Stand up now, Diggers all.

The Cavaleers are foes, stand up now, stand up now,
The Cavaleers are foes, stand up now;
The Cavaleers are foes, themselves they do disclose

By verses not in prose to please the singing boyes.
Stand up now, Diggers all.

To conquer them by love, come in now, come in now
To conquer them by love, come in now;
To conquer them by love, as itt does you behove,
For hee is King above, noe power is like to love,
Glory heere, Diggers all.

As a rousing call to revolution, it's impressive stuff; as poetry it's
pretty feeble. The diggers themselves, and the whole revolutionary
movement, soon fell out with Oliver Cromwell and the military
dictatorship he imposed – and yet the nearest thing Cromwell had
to a poet laureate is also among England's greatest poets. John
Milton's astonishing work *Paradise Lost*, the defining epic of the
English Protestant imagination, is far too long to be extracted here;
and in any case, extracts do it a terrible disservice. It is knotty and
at times forbidding, over-crammed with classical and erudite bibli-
cal references, mesmerising in the same way that Wagner's operas
are mesmerising – in short, it's worth it. In *Paradise Lost*, God is a
relatively unappealing figure, later described by William Blake as a
'schoolmaster of souls', while famously Milton seems half in love
with the devil. Certainly he was no kind of orthodox Christian.

The paradox of the Puritan revolution is encapsulated in Milton's
work: on the one hand he represents a courageous and flinty oppo-
sition to political and religious tyranny. He became a genuine revo-
lutionary, who believed established authority weighed down upon
and crushed man's spirit. His defence of freedom of the press
remains as potent today as it was in the middle of the seventeenth
century. And yet, on the other hand, this hostility to political
tyranny was based on a firm belief in what we might call, without
hyperbole, domestic tyranny. The Puritan wife was a quiet, utterly
obedient creature, the servant of her husband. Feminist critics have
long assaulted Milton for the way he turned wives and daughters
into literary drudges – though after he became blind, it's hard to see

how else his poetry could have been produced. What we shouldn't do, however, is to confuse our own beliefs about equality in marriage with the reality of Puritan Britain, where it was perfectly possible to combine paternal rule with genuine love. Milton's elegy for his second wife, who died a few months after giving birth, is a racking dream-sonnet, in which almost uncontrollable emotion is held in check, just, by its rigorous form.

> Methought I saw my late espoused saint
> Brought to me, like Alcestis, from the grave,*
> Whom Jove's great son to her glad husband gave,
> Rescu'd from death by force, though pale and faint.
> Mine, as whom wash'd from spot of child-bed taint
> Purification in the old Law did save,
> And such as yet once more I trust to have
> Full sight of her in Heaven without restraint,
> Came vested all in white, pure as her mind;
> Her face was veil'd, yet to my fancied sight
> Love, sweetness, goodness, in her person shin'd
> So clear as in no face with more delight.
> But Oh! as to embrace me she inclin'd,
> I wak'd, she fled, and day brought back my night.

Milton was a master of the elegy. A much earlier poem, 'Lycidas', was on the surface an elegy for Milton's Cambridge University friend Edward King, drowned at sea in 1637. But if you're expecting any direct reference to Mr King you will be disappointed. It's a self-consciously classical poem, rooted in the pastoral works of Virgil and his followers – Spenser included. Like Spenser, Milton, even at this early stage in his life, is able to combine references to the classical Mediterranean with a certain brisk northern Britishness. There is a dryness, a deliberately unseasonal starkness

---

* Alcestis was, in the story of Hercules, rescued at the last minute from Hades and returned to her husband.

here which is all Reformation, and nothing Augustan:

> Yet once more, O ye laurels, and once more
> Ye myrtles brown, with ivy never sere,
> I come to pluck your berries harsh and crude,
> And with forc'd fingers rude
> Shatter your leaves before the mellowing year.
> Bitter constraint and sad occasion dear
> Compels me to disturb your season due;
> For Lycidas is dead, dead ere his prime,
> Young Lycidas, and hath not left his peer.

Later in the poem, the young Puritan turns to attack the laxity and corruption of the English Church, at this point still under the influence of Archbishop Laud, before the tide has turned against King Charles I and the court:

> And when they list their lean and flashy songs
> Grate on their scrannel pipes of wretched straw,
> The hungry sheep look up, and are not fed,
> But, swoll'n with wind and the rank mist they draw,
> Rot inwardly, and foul contagion spread;
> Besides what the grim wolf with privy paw
> Daily devours apace, and nothing said,
> But that two-handed engine at the door
> Stands ready to smite once, and smite no more.

This is the outraged, addictive, rhetorical style which would cause Milton's pamphlets and poems to be publicly burned after the Restoration. He remained all his life a dedicated supporter of the republican revolution, a defender of freedom of the press, and a bitter critic of Romanising tendencies in the British Church. We can't leave Milton, however, without his greatest sonnet of all, that on his blindness, which is also the first well-known poem in English about disability from the point of view of the victim:

When I consider how my light is spent
E're half my days, in this dark world and wide,
And that one Talent which is death to hide,
Lodg'd with me useless, though my Soul more bent
To serve therewith my Maker, and present
My true account, lest he returning chide,
Doth God exact day-labour, light deny'd,
I fondly ask; But patience to prevent
That murmur, soon replies, God doth not need
Either man's work or his own gifts, who best
Bear his milde yoak, they serve him best, his State
Is Kingly. Thousands at his bidding speed
And post o're Land and Ocean without rest:
They also serve who only stand and waite.

Speaking of those who stand and wait, we also have to wonder how the Puritan revolution felt to the wives, childbearers and domestic servants who helped it happen. Here, as with contemporary Islamism, it would be very easy to portray it as an oppressive male plot, without realising that women were devout and determined Puritans too. Anne Bradstreet spent most of her working life in America, as one of the original Massachusetts colonists. She was born in Northampton in 1612 to a relatively affluent middle-class family. She married at eighteen, and in 1630 she, her husband Simon Bradstreet and her father set sail for Massachusetts. Life there would prove extremely hard, but Anne was a determined and in some ways unorthodox writer, holding her own in a society which strongly disapproved of female authors. Yet her poetry is most notable for its conjugal devotion – the world as seen by a devout Protestant wife and mother.

If ever two were one, then surely we.
If ever man were lov'd by wife, then thee.
If ever wife was happy in a man,
Compare with me, ye women, if you can.

I prize thy love more than whole Mines of gold
Or all the riches that the East doth hold.
My love is such that Rivers cannot quench,
Nor ought but love from thee give recompense.
Thy love is such I can no way repay.
The heavens reward thee manifold, I pray.
Then while we live, in love let's so persever
That when we live no more, we may live ever.

The Anne Bradstreet story is also a fine example of the dangers of looking too closely at contemporary portraiture. She is painted, literally, as a stern-faced, white-wimpled domestic saint. And yet, as the imagery in another poem written to her husband while he was away on public business makes clear, this marriage was as sensual as that of John Donne himself:

My head, my heart, mine eyes, my life, nay more,
My joy, my magazine, of earthly store,
If two be one, as surely thou and I,
How stayest thou there, whilst I at Ipswich lie?
So many steps, head from the heart to sever,
If but a neck, soon should we be together.
I, like the Earth this season, mourn in black,
My Sun is gone so far in's zodiac,
Whom whilst I 'joyed, nor storms, nor frost I felt,
His warmth such fridged colds did cause to melt.
My chilled limbs now numbed lie forlorn;
Return; return, sweet Sol, from Capricorn;
In this dead time, alas, what can I more
Than view those fruits which through thy heart I bore?
Which sweet contentment yield me for a space,
True living pictures of their father's face.
O strange effect! now thou art southward gone,
I weary grow the tedious day so long;

But when thou northward to me shalt return,
I wish my Sun may never set, but burn
Within the Cancer of my glowing breast,
The welcome house of him my dearest guest.

The days when historians spoke of the English Civil War are now long past, and rightly so. This was a conflict that engulfed the entire British Isles, and whose reverberations were felt in the new British colonies in America. Anne Bradstreet imagines a dialogue between New England and her bleeding, suffering mother, Old England, who explains that there has recently grown

'Twixt King and Peers a question of state:
Which is the chief – the law or else the King?
One said, 'It's He'; the other, 'No such thing!'
'Tis said, my better part in Parliament
To ease my groaning land, showed their intent
To crush the proud and right to each man deal,
To help the Church, and stay of the commonweal ...

But, Bradstreet explains, between the arguments, and despite the best intentions, contention grows between the people and the king. Once war begins, it isn't easy to stop, until the very existence of the British state is threatened. From the vantage point of Massachusetts, this is beginning to look like the end of Britain herself.

They worded it so long they fell to blows,
That thousands lay on heaps – here bleeds my woes:
I that no wars so many years have known
Am now destroyed and slaughtered by mine own;
But could the field alone this strife decide,
One battle, two, or three I might abide;
But these may be beginnings of more woe –
Who knows, but this may be my overthrow!
Oh, pity me in this sad perturbation,

My plundered towns, my houses' devastation,
My weeping virgins and my young men slain,
My wealthy trading fallen, my dearth of grain,
The seed times come, but ploughman hath no hope
Because he knows not who shall in his crop;
The poor they want their pay, their children bread,
Their woeful mothers' tears unpitied ...

It's interesting, isn't it, that after all the partisan pleading of
England's finest poets, it takes a Puritan woman from across the
Atlantic to show the genuinely devastating effects of what has
happened. But let's not be too hasty: for in Bradstreet's poem New
England replies to her mother in furiously partisan and anti-Cath-
olic rhetoric. She wants to see an end, a burning, of all the mitres,
surplices and other popish rubbish:

Copes, rochets, croziers, and such empty trash,
And let their names consume, but let the flash
Light Christendom, and all the world to see
We hate Rome's whore, with all her trumpery!

Not for the last time, we look in vain to America for religious
moderation. But although this was a period of religious hysteria
and war, away from the smoke and the denunciations there was
creativity and genuine devotion, as there always is. I began this
chapter with Andrew Marvell, and I'd like to end it with one of his
famous gardening poems. It's a luscious meditation on the fecund
English countryside, the Britain unchanged by war, which reaches
depths of meditative serenity that can be seen as a stinging rebuke
to the temper of the times. 'The Garden' is a defence of the mind –
its autonomy and inner power – against all the temptations and
entanglements of cluttered and disappointing daily life; and thus it's
a defence of poetry itself. Like many people, I prefer it to anything
by John Milton:

How vainly men themselves amaze
To win the Palm, the Oke, or Bayes;
And their uncessant Labours see
Crown'd from some single Herb or Tree,
Whose short and narrow verged Shade
Does prudently their Toyles upbraid;
While all Flow'rs and all Trees do close
To weave the Garlands of repose.

Fair quiet, have I found thee here,
And Innocence thy Sister dear!
Mistaken long, I sought you then
In busie Companies of Men.
Your sacred Plants, if here below,
Only among the Plants will grow.
Society is all but rude,
To this delicious Solitude.

No white nor red was ever seen
So am'rous as this lovely green.
Fond Lovers, cruel as their Flame,
Cut in these Trees their Mistress' name.
Little, Alas, they know, or heed,
How far these Beauties Hers exceed!
Fair Trees! where s'eer your barkes I wound,
No Name shall but your own be found.

When we have run our Passions heat,
Love hither makes his best retreat.
The Gods, that mortal Beauty chase,
Still in a tree did end their race:
Apollo hunted Daphne so,
Only that She might Laurel grow.
And Pan did after Syrinx speed,
Not as a Nymph, but for a Reed.

What wond'rous Life in this I lead!
Ripe Apples drop about my head;
The Luscious Clusters of the Vine
Upon my Mouth do crush their Wine;
The Nectaren, and curious Peach,
Into my hands themselves do reach;
Stumbling on Melons, as I pass,
Insnar'd with Flow'rs, I fall on Grass.

Mean while the Mind, from pleasure less,
Withdraws into its happiness:
The Mind, that Ocean where each kind
Does streight its own resemblance find;
Yet it creates, transcending these,
Far other Worlds, and other Seas;
Annihilating all that's made
To a green Thought in a green Shade.

7

The Restoration of What?
Satire, Science and Cynicism,
as Political Britain is Born

If there is a single glaringly obvious political fact taught by the contemporary world, it is this: civil wars (from the Balkans to Iraq to Northern Africa) don't end neatly. Raw stumps bleed on. After the turmoil must come the reckoning. And so it was in Britain with the restoration of King Charles II in 1660. Under the Commonwealth, Puritan values had been imposed. Holidays such as Christmas and Easter had been banned by Parliament, and a series of increasingly restrictive bans on the theatres and most public performances of music and poetry were imposed from September 1642 onwards. With the Restoration there was a reaction against all of this, a bouncing-back of libertine, celebratory and scandalous culture. It didn't mean, quite, that the cultural war between godly puritanism and worldly aristocracy was over; for war itself went on.

For the remainder of the Stuart dynasty, and into the reigns of William and Mary and the early Hanoverians, the British remained deeply divided over religion and legitimacy. In parts of the British Isles the civil wars were followed by further major bloodshed. There were rebellions against Catholic kings by Protestants, and against Protestant kings by Catholics. There was the family revolt of the Duke of Monmouth against James II, culminating in the Battle of Sedgemoor in 1685; then the ousted James's defeat by William at the Boyne in 1690; and finally the Jacobite rebellions of 1715 and

1745. But for most Britons, for most of the time, it's in this period that party politics and intrigue replace cavalry charges and public burnings. Although in theory the return of King Charles marked the final defeat of the republican revolution and its Commonwealth, in the longer view it was the values of the Puritan and parliamentary rebels which triumphed. Royal Catholicism and divine right were replaced by Protestant kings mostly subservient to Parliament.

At the same time, following Cromwell's creation of an effective national navy, the British begin to spread out across the oceans, forming the beginnings of the Empire. Charles II was the last British ruler to be humiliated at sea by foreigners – the triumphant navy of the Dutch Republic. His Protestant successors would accumulate victories over the major Catholic power of the age, the French, and acquire footholds in India, the Mediterranean and America.

We might expect, therefore, a coarser, more cynical poetry to reflect the triumph of party politics and the end of Puritan censorship. And, by and large, that's exactly what we get. It starts with the unabashedly filthy poetry of John Wilmot, Earl of Rochester, and of Aphra Behn, the almost ridiculously exotic Royalist woman playwright and poet. John Dryden and then Alexander Pope raised political satire to levels not achieved before or afterwards in English verse. Soon, classicism and 'good taste' appear to be pushing back the crudities and passions of the seventeenth century. That, at least, is the conventional story. In fact, as new anthologies make clear, the poetry of the British after Cromwell's Republic but before the loss of the American colonies is far more varied. There's nothing to compare to the ecstatic religious achievements of Herbert and Vaughan, and the cynical Cavalier lyricists were more impressive in their first flowering under Charles I than under his son. It's not until the end of the period and the extraordinary figure of William Blake that we get poetry which is genuinely radical. But on the way there are some remarkable poems which tell us a lot about class, sex, money and politics in this increasingly modern-seeming Britain.

In all English poetry, there is no more glamorous, absurd and unlikely figure than John Wilmot. His father, the first Earl of Rochester, was a Cavalier hero, who engineered the escape of Charles II to the Continent after the Battle of Worcester. The son was sent to Oxford and apparently 'debauched' by the age of thirteen. He became a courtier to the new king; was sent to the Tower of London after eloping with an heiress; then proved himself a war hero in two bloody sea battles with the Dutch; fell out again with the monarch; wrote bitter, highly intellectual and very rude satires; disguised himself as a female healer of sexual and fertility ailments; and died of venereal disease at the ripe old age of thirty-three. He may have repented on his deathbed. Or he may not have done. The insouciant Rochester style is perfectly expressed by this beautifully made, nihilistic lyric, which is, so far as I know, the first poem by a major British poet to celebrate sodomy:

Love a Woman! y'are an Ass,
'Tis a most insipid Passion,
To Chuse out for Happiness
The idlest part of God's Creation.

Let the Porter and the Groom,
Things design'd for Dirty Slaves,
Drudg in Fair *Aurelia*'s Womb,
To get Supplies for Age and Graves.

Farewel Woman, I intend
Henceforth ev'ry Night to sit
With my Lewd Well-natur'd Friend,
Drinking, to engender Wit.

Then give me Health, Wealth, Mirth, and Wine,
And if busie Love intrenches,
There's a sweet soft Page of mine,
Do's the Trick worth Forty Wenches.

Were that all Rochester could achieve, he'd barely be worth including here. But there's a darkness and a focused seriousness to his apparent loathing of the world which raises him as an artist. Nobody was more aware of his own debauches and squandered reputation than John Wilmot himself. His suicidal bravery in the sea battles suggests either a streak of existential rejection of the world more associated with the twentieth century, or that, after it, he was suffering from what we call today post-conflict trauma. In the following poem, 'To the Postboy', he ruthlessly assesses his own career:

Son of a whore, God damn you, can you tell
A peerless peer the readiest way to hell?
I've out-swilled Bacchus, sworn of my own make
Oaths would fright Furies, and make Pluto quake;
I've swived more whores more ways than Sodom's walls
E'er knew, or the College of Rome's Cardinals:
Witness heroic scars, Look here, ne'er go,
Cerecloths and ulcers from the top to toe;
Frighted at my own mischiefs I have fled,
And bravely left my life's defender dead;
Broke houses to break chastity, and dyed
That floor with murder which my lust denied:
Pox on it – why do I speak of these poor things;
I have blasphemed my God and libelled kings:
The readiest way to hell – come, quick, ne'er stir –
Boy: The readiest way, my Lord, 's by Rochester.

In what is perhaps his single most famous poem, 'Ane Satyre against Mankind', Rochester flays humanity itself: his sense of disgust at the so-called reasoning animal is gripping and convincing. It feels more like a tirade by a twenty-first-century animal-rights campaigner or philosopher than a seventeenth-century aristocrat:

Were I – who to my cost already am
One of those strange, prodigious creatures, man –
A spirit free to choose for my own share
What sort of flesh and blood I pleased to wear,
I'd be a dog, a monkey, or a bear,
Or anything but that vain animal,
Who is so proud of being rational.

His senses are too gross; and he'll contrive
A sixth, to contradict the other five;
And before certain instinct will prefer
Reason, which fifty times for one does err.
Reason, an ignis fatuus of the mind,
Which leaving light of nature, sense, behind,
Pathless and dangerous wand'ring ways it takes,
Through Error's fenny bogs and thorny brakes;
Whilst the misguided follower climbs with pain
Mountains of whimseys, heaped in his own brain;
Stumbling from thought to thought, falls headlong down,
Into Doubt's boundless sea where, like to drown,
Books bear him up awhile, and make him try
To swim with bladders of Philosophy;
In hopes still to o'ertake the escaping light;
The vapour dances, in his dancing sight,
Till spent, it leaves him to eternal night.
Then old age and experience, hand in hand,
Lead him to death, make him to understand,
After a search so painful, and so long,
That all his life he has been in the wrong:

Huddled in dirt the reasoning engine lies,
Who was so proud, so witty, and so wise ...

Civil war had produced, for some thinking people, a complete collapse in their belief in any coherent moral order at all. Rochester, in person a beneficiary of the new regime, never stopped flaying it. He once, by his own account, got into terrible trouble with Charles II by giving him the wrong poem – not one the monarch had asked him for, but the manuscript of a much ruder satire on the king himself. It wasn't this short and famous squib – which apparently Charles rather liked: he said it was true, because his words were his own but his actions were forced upon him by his political ministers:

Here lies a great and mighty King,
Whose promise none relied on;
He never said a foolish thing,
Nor ever did a wise one.

No, the satire Rochester handed to Charles was far worse. Banishment from the court seems a fairly modest response. Nervous readers might skip it.

I' th' isle of Britain, long since famous grown
For breeding the best cunts in Christendom,
There reigns, and oh! long may he reign and thrive,
The easiest King and best-bred man alive.
Him no ambition moves to get renown
Like the French fool, that wanders up and down
Starving his people, hazarding his crown.
Peace is his aim, his gentleness is such,
And love he loves, for he loves fucking much.
– Nor are his high desires above his strength:
His scepter and his prick are of a length;
And she may sway the one who plays with th' other,
And make him little wiser than his brother.
Poor prince! thy prick, like thy buffoons at Court,
Will govern thee because it makes thee sport.
'Tis sure the sauciest prick that e'er did swive,
The proudest, peremptoriest prick alive.

Though safety, law, religion, life lay on 't,
'Twould break through all to make its way to cunt.
Restless he rolls about from whore to whore,
A merry monarch, scandalous and poor.

Compared to that, today's rulers get away very lightly with *Have I Got News for You* and *Private Eye*.

With the Restoration and the reopening of the theatres we get a clutch of vigorous dramatists, only a few of them poets of real talent. The life of Aphra Behn is clouded in mystery and deliberate misinformation. But she seems to have been born the daughter of a barber, perhaps near Canterbury, and to have associated herself with the powerful Sidney family. She probably visited the small and dangerous sugar colony of Surinam on the coast of South America, possibly as a Royalist spy on its planters. She then married, probably a Dutch slave trader who may have died in the London plague of 1666. She was certainly an agent for the king in Holland, where she went under the name of Astrea, or simply 'agent 160'. Struggling to make her living as a humbly born (though beautiful and extremely clever) widow, she produced a series of plays, and verse good enough to catch the attention of colleagues such as John Dryden and Rochester. Her verse plays with gender and sexuality in ways that still seem radical. A partisan Royalist, a raging snob and a wily survivor, Behn is like no other literary figure of the age. She may be the first truly professional female writer – the first to live entirely off the earnings of her pen. In 'The Disappointment', Behn uses the conventions of pastoral courtship – Lysander loves Chloe – but spectacularly upends them to create a poem, very much from the female point of view, about male impotence.

In a lone Thicket, made for Love,
Silent as yielding Maids Consent,
She with a charming Languishment
Permits his force, yet gently strove?
Her Hands his Bosom softly meet,

But not to put him back design'd,
Rather to draw him on inclin'd,
Whilst he lay trembling at her feet;
Resistance 'tis to late to shew,
She wants the pow'r to say – Ah! what do you do?

Her bright Eyes sweat, and yet Severe,
Where Love and Shame confus'dly strive,
Fresh Vigor to Lisander give:
And whispring softly in his Ear,
She Cry'd – Cease – cease – your vain desire,
Or I'll call out – What wou'd you do?
My dearer Honour, ev'n to you,
I cannot – must not give – retire,
Or take that Life whose chiefest part
I gave you with the Conquest of my Heart.

But he as much unus'd to fear,
As he was capable of Love,
The blessed Minutes to improve,
Kisses her Lips, her Neck, her Hair!
Each touch her new Desires alarms!
His burning trembling Hand he prest
Upon her melting Snowy Breast,
While she lay panting in his Arms!
All her unguarded Beauties lie
The Spoils and Trophies of the Enemy.

And now, without Respect or Fear,
He seeks the Objects of his Vows;
His Love no Modesty allows:
By swift degrees advancing where
His daring Hand that Altar seiz'd,
Where Gods of Love do Sacrifice;
That awful Throne, that Paradise,

Where Rage is tam'd, and Anger pleas'd;
That Living Fountain, from whose Trills
The melted Soul in liquid Drops distils.

Her balmy Lips encountring his,
Their Bodies as their Souls are joyn'd,
Where both in Transports were confin'd,
Extend themselves upon the Moss.
Cloris half dead and breathless lay,
Her Eyes appear'd like humid Light,
Such as divides the Day and Night;
Or falling Stars, whose Fires decay;
And now no signs of Life she shows,
But what in short-breath-sighs returns and goes.

He saw how at her length she lay,
He saw her rising Bosom bare,
Her loose thin Robes, through which appear
A Shape design'd for Love and Play;
Abandon'd by her Pride and Shame,
She do's her softest Sweets dispence,
Offring her Virgin-Innocence
A Victim to Love's Sacred Flame;
Whilst th' or'e ravish'd Shepherd lies,
Unable to perform the Sacrifice.

Aphra Behn is one of the more glamorous and provocative female writers of the Restoration age, but she's not the most interesting: that is another Royalist, Margaret Cavendish, Duchess of Newcastle. The sister of one of the most successful Cavalier commanders of cavalry, executed for treason after the war, Margaret was Maid of Honour to Queen Henrietta Maria at Charles I's court, but as a writer what marks her out is her interest in the new philosophy of the early Enlightenment. In 'Of Many Worlds in This World' she shows how new instruments such as the microscope completely changed how people saw the universe. It may not be the most elegantly expressed poem in this collection, but it eerily looks forward to the twenty-first century and our belief in multiple dimensions and universes:

Just like as in a nest of boxes round,
Degrees of sizes in each box are found.
So, in this world, may many others be
Thinner and less, and less still by degree:
Although they are not subject to our sense,
A world may be no bigger than two-pence.
Nature is curious, and such works may shape,
Which our dull senses easily escape:
For creatures, small as atoms, may be there,
If every one a creature's figure bear.
If atoms four, a world can make, then see
What several worlds might in an ear-ring be:
For millions of those atoms may be in
The head of one small, little, single pin.
And if thus small, then ladies may well wear
A world of worlds, as pendants in each ear.

Margaret Cavendish produced huge numbers of semi-scientific treatises and poems; she is in her range of interests much more impressive than the male poets of the time. Reading her, we get a vivid idea of how the early-modern human mind was beginning to grapple with the disconcerting early revelations of science:

Small Atomes of themselves a World may make,
As being subtle, and of every shape:
And as they dance about, fit places finde,
Such Formes as best agree, make every kinde.
For when we build a house of Bricke, and Stone,
We lay them even, every one by one:

And when we finde a gap that's big, or small,
We seeke out Stones, to fit that place withall.
For when not fit, too big, or little be,
They fall away, and cannot stay we see.
So Atomes, as they dance, finde places fit,
They there remaine, lye close, and fast will sticke.
Those that unfit, the rest that rove about,
Do never leave, untill they thrust them out.
Thus by their severall Motions, and their Formes,
As severall work-men serve each other's turnes.
And thus, by chance, may a New World create:
Or else predestined to worke my Fate.

Today's scientists would describe things differently, but here we have the other side of the seventeenth-century mind – not the religious ecstasy and fanaticism we have met already, but the early years of the Royal Society and the Britain of Harvey, Boyle and Newton. Great poetry? Perhaps not; but there is a restlessness and energy about Margaret Cavendish's mind which I find refreshing. It doesn't just apply to science. 'The Hunting of the Hare' is a fascinating poem on many levels. First, it's a countryside poem by someone with an acute understanding of natural science, a close observer of animal behaviour. Second, although Margaret comes from an aristocratic and Cavalier background, it's a poem from the point of view not of the galloping huntsman but of the quarry. Is there a political undercurrent? Third, Margaret Cavendish's empathy for the hare, Wat (it makes me think of Robert Burns), makes this an unusual early 'animal rights' verse. Her scientific poems could have been composed by an unusually open-minded male aristocrat. This poem, which in full is longer than this version, surely could not have been:

Betwixt two ridges of ploughed land lay Wat
Pressing his body close to earth lay squat.
His nose upon his two forefeet close lies

Glaring obliquely with his great grey eyes
His head he always sets against the wind;
If turn his tail, his hairs blow up behind,
Which he too cold will grow; but he is wise,
And keeps his coat still down, so warm he lies.
Thus resting all the day, till sun doth set,
Then riseth up, his relief for to get,
Walking about until the sun doth rise;
Then back returns, down in his form he lies.
At last poor Wat was found as he there lay,
By huntsmen with their dogs which came that way.
Seeing, gets up and fast begins to run,
Hoping some way the cruel dogs to shun.
But they by nature have so quick a scent
That by their nose they trace what way he went ...

... Into a great thick wood he straightway gets,
Where underneath a broken bough he sits.
At every leaf what with the wind did shake
Did bring such terror, made his heart to ache.
That place he left; to champian plains he went,
Winding about for to deceive their scent,
And while they snuffling were to find his track
Poor Wat, being weary, his swift pace did slack ...

... The great slow hounds, their throats did set a base
The fleet swift hounds as tenors next in place;
The little beagles, they a treble sing,
And through the air their voice a round did ring,
Which made a consort as they ran along;
If they but words could speak, might sing a song,
The horns kept time, the hunters shout for joy,
And valiant seem, poor Wat for to destroy.
Spurring their horses to a full career,
Swim rivers deep, leap ditches without fear;

Endanger life and limbs, so fast will ride,
Only to see how patiently Wat died.
For why, the dogs so near his heels it did to get
That they their sharp teeth in his breach did set.
Then tumbling down, did fall with weeping eyes,
Gives up his ghost, and thus poor Wat he dies.
Men hooping loud, such acclamations make,
As if the devil they did prisoner take.
When they do but a shiftless creature kill,
To hunt, there needs no valiant soldier's skill.

There speaks the sister of a cavalry commander. This is, however, above all a poem of the countryside, written at a period in British poetry when the town appears to dominate – the political satires, the sex poems and the moralising of court poets. Yet the vast majority of British people were still countryside dwellers, rarely moving far from home.

Another poet who treats the realities of British country life at this time is Charles Cotton, an exiled Royalist gentleman and obsessive fisherman. In his 'quatrains' dealing with different times of the day, amid the classical references we can hear and see the authentic sounds and sights of seventeenth-century country life. This is an extract from 'Morning Quatrains':

Now doors and windows are unbarr'd,
Each-where are cheerful voices heard,
And round about 'Good-morrows' fly,
As if Day taught Humanity.
The chimnies now to smoke begin,
And the old wife sits down to spin,
Whilst Kate, taking her pail, does trip
Mull's swoll'n and straddl'ing paps to strip.
Vulcan now makes his anvil ring,
Dick whistles loud, and Maud doth sing,
And Silvio with his bugle horn

Winds an Imprime unto the Morn.
Now through the morning doors behold
Phoebus array'd in burning gold,
Lashing his fiery steeds, displays
His warm and all-enlight'ning rays.
Now each one to his work prepares,
All that have hands are labourers,
And manufactures of each trade
By op'ning shops are open laid.
Hob yokes his oxen to the team,
The angler goes unto the stream,
The woodman to the purlews hies,
And lab'ring bees to load their thighs.
Fair Amarillis drives her flocks,
All night safe-folded from the fox,
To flow'ry downs, where Colin stays,
To court her with his roundelays.
The traveller now leaves his inn
A new day's journey to begin,
As he would post it with the day,
And early rising makes good way.
The slick-fac'd school-boy satchel takes,
And with slow pace small riddance makes ...

And here is an extract from the evening version:

The shadows now so long do grow,
That brambles like tall cedars show,
Mole-hills seem mountains, and the ant
Appears a monstrous elephant.
A very little little flock
Shades thrice the ground that it would stock;
Whilst the small stripling following them
Appears a mighty Polypheme.
These being brought into the fold,

And by the thrifty master told
He thinks his wages are well paid,
Since none are either lost or stray'd.
Now lowing herds are each-where heard,
Chains rattle in the villain's yard,
The cart's on tail set down to rest,
Bearing on high the cuckold's crest.
The hedge is stripp'd, the clothes brought in,
Naught's left without should be within,
The bees are hiv'd, and hum their charm,
Whilst every house does seem a swarm.

Good narrative verse, which this is, is like good journalism: it depends upon attentiveness – sharp listening, close watching. Here, Cotton reminds me of the much-better-known William Cowper, who we'll meet later, and also of the more famous Andrew Marvell. At Oliver Cromwell's funeral, Marvell was one of three poets in attendance (Cotton would not have approved). The others were the courageous John Milton and the much younger son of a Puritan farming family, John Dryden. Milton was a man of unbending principle. Marvell was a trimmer. Dryden was a turncoat. As soon as Charles II was restored as king, Dryden symbolically scrunched up and threw away the fairly terrible adulatory verses he'd composed for the late Lord Protector and wrote a new poem, only a little better, to celebrate the returned monarch. 'Astrea Redux' views the republican rebellion against absolute monarchy as an absolute disaster:

The vulgar, gulled into rebellion, armed,
Their blood to action by the prize was warmed.
The sacred purple, then, and scarlet gown,
Like sanguine dye to elephants, was shewn.
Thus, when the bold Typhœus scaled the sky,
And forced great Jove from his own heaven to fly,
(What king, what crown, from treason's reach is free,

184

If Jove and Heaven can violated be?)
The lesser gods, that shared his prosperous state,
All suffered in the exiled Thunderer's fate.
The rabble now such freedom did enjoy,
As winds at sea, that use it to destroy:
Blind as the Cyclops, and as wild as he,
They owned a lawless savage liberty,
Like that our painted ancestors so prized,
Ere empire's arts their breast had civilised.
How great were then our Charles his woes, who thus
Was forced to suffer for himself and us!
He, tossed by fate, and hurried up and down,
Heir to his father's sorrows, with his crown,
Could taste no sweets of youth's desired age,
But found his life too true a pilgrimage.

Dryden is most famous for his political and cultural satires, ripping into leading politicians of the time, and his poetic rivals. For the modern reader, the problem is exactly what made him exciting in his day – the contemporary references. He can seem as faded as an out-of-date newspaper front page. We no longer care much about the foibles of minor poets like Shadwell, or the failures of the Duke of Monmouth. So Dryden can seem dry. That's a pity: his satires may not be as shocking as those of Rochester, but they are razor-sharp and well worth enjoying today, as we continue to despair of ambitious politicians, and to laugh at self-deluded celebrities. Here, in perhaps his most famous poem, *Absalom and Achitophel*, he reflects on Charles II's notorious enthusiasm for mistresses, and on his illegitimate son ('Absalom') the Duke of Monmouth, who led a doomed rebellion against his uncle, Charles's brother and successor James II:

In pious times, e'er Priest-craft did begin,
Before Polygamy was made a sin;
When man, on many, multiply'd his kind,

E'r one to one was, cursedly, confin'd:
When Nature prompted, and no law deny'd
Promiscuous use of Concubine and Bride;
Then, Israel's monarch, after Heaven's own heart,
His vigorous warmth did, variously, impart
To Wives and Slaves; And, wide as his Command,
Scatter'd his Maker's Image through the Land.
Michal, of Royal blood, the Crown did wear,
A Soyl ungratefull to the Tiller's care;
Not so the rest; for several Mothers bore
To Godlike David, several Sons before.
But since like slaves his bed they did ascend,
No True Succession could their seed attend.
Of all this Numerous Progeny was none
So Beautifull, so brave as Absalon:
Whether, inspir'd by some diviner Lust,
His father got him with a greater Gust;
Or that his Conscious destiny made way
By manly beauty to Imperiall sway.
Early in Foreign fields he won Renown,
With Kings and States ally'd to Israel's Crown.
In Peace the thoughts of War he could remove,
And seem'd as he were only born for love.
What e'er he did was done with so much ease,
In him alone, 'twas Natural to please.
His motions all accompanied with grace;
And Paradise was open'd in his face.
With secret Joy, indulgent David view'd
His Youthfull Image in his Son renew'd:
To all his wishes Nothing he deny'd,
And made the Charming Annabel his Bride.
What faults he had (for who from faults is free?)
His Father could not, or he would not see.
Some warm excesses, which the Law forbore,
Were constru'd Youth that purg'd by boyling o'r:

And Amnon's Murther, by a specious Name,
Was call'd a Just Revenge for injur'd Fame.
Thus Prais'd, and Lov'd, the Noble Youth remain'd,
While David, undisturb'd, in Sion raign'd.
But Life can never be sincerely blest:
Heaven punishes the bad, and proves the best.

And here Dryden turns his waspish gaze on the Earl of Shaftesbury
(Achitophel), a notorious meddler who Dryden makes sound
rather like Milton's Satan. The man himself, Anthony Ashley
Cooper, may now be remembered only by historians. But he is a
type not unknown to Westminster in the twenty-first century.
Sadly.

Of these the false Achitophel was first:
A Name to all succeeding Ages Curst.
For close Designs, and crooked Counsels fit;
Sagacious, Bold, and Turbulent of wit:
Restless, unfixt in Principles and Place;
In Power unpleas'd, impatient of Disgrace.
A fiery Soul, which working out its way,
Fretted the Pigmy Body to decay:
And o'r inform'd the Tenement of Clay.
A daring Pilot in extremity;
Pleas'd with the Danger, when the Waves went high
He sought the Storms; but for a Calm unfit
Would Steer too nigh the Sands, to boast his Wit.
Great Wits are sure to Madness near ally'd;
And thin Partitions do their Bounds divide;
Else, why should he, with Wealth and Honour blest,
Refuse his Age the needful hours of Rest?
Punish a Body which he could not please;
Bankrupt of Life, yet Prodigal of Ease?
And all to leave, what with his Toyl he won,
To that unfeather'd, two Leg'd thing, a Son;

Got, while his Soul did hudled Notions try;
And born a shapeless Lump, like Anarchy.
In Friendship False, Implacable in Hate:
Resolv'd to Ruine or to Rule the State.
To Compass this the Triple Bond he broke;
The Pillars of the publick Safety shok;
And fitted Israel for a foreign Yoke.
Then, seiz'd with Fear, yet still affecting Fame,
Usurp'd a Patriott's All-attoning Name.
So easie still it proves in Factious Times,
With publick Zeal to cancel private Crimes.
How safe is Treason, and how sacred ill,
Where none can sin against the People's Will:
Where Crouds can wink; and no offence be known,
Since in another's guilt they find their own.

To his own generation, Dryden seemed able to do everything – heroic dramas and tragedies, comedies, lyrics, satires and his superb translations of Virgil. He wrote at a time when poetry really mattered. One poetic feud led to him being beaten almost to death by thugs, who had been hired by none other than Rochester. He was also Britain's first official Poet Laureate, an ambiguous post which he got by outrageous oiling-up to Charles II. His poem about the Dutch wars and disasters of 1666, *Annus Mirabilis*, is cleverly done, and in its comparison of Britain with the Roman Empire it looks forward to one of the favourite tropes of the Victorians. It reminds me a bit of the hired poets who gushed to Stalin in the Soviet Union. This was the period when the British and Dutch were in deadly competition over the lucrative trade in spices such as nutmeg, more valuable by weight than gold. British jealousy of the successful Republic oozes from Dryden's account of war, which in truth didn't go well for the British.

In thriving arts long time had Holland grown,
Crouching at home and cruel when abroad:
Scarce leaving us the means to claim our own;
Our King they courted, and our merchants awed.

Trade, which, like blood, should circularly flow,
Stopp'd in their channels, found its freedom lost:
Thither the wealth of all the world did go,
And seem'd but shipwreck'd on so base a coast.

For them alone the heavens had kindly heat;
In eastern quarries ripening precious dew:
For them the Idumaean balm did sweat,
And in hot Ceylon spicy forests grew.

The sun but seem'd the labourer of the year;
Each waxing moon supplied her watery store,
To swell those tides, which from the line did bear
Their brimful vessels to the Belgian shore.

Thus mighty in her ships, stood Carthage long,
And swept the riches of the world from far;
Yet stoop'd to Rome, less wealthy, but more strong:
And this may prove our second Punic war.

What peace can be, where both to one pretend?
(But they more diligent, and we more strong)
Or if a peace, it soon must have an end;
For they would grow too powerful, were it long.

Behold two nations, then, engaged so far
That each seven years the fit must shake each land:
Where France will side to weaken us by war,
Who only can his vast designs withstand.

But Dryden paints the king as cautious, and the opposite of belli-
cose: in war after war, British leaders have claimed to clamour for
peace and to have been pushed to the brink by treacherous
foreigners:

> The loss and gain each fatally were great;
> And still his subjects call'd aloud for war;
> But peaceful kings, o'er martial people set,
> Each, other's poise and counterbalance are.
>
> He first survey'd the charge with careful eyes,
> Which none but mighty monarchs could maintain;
> Yet judged, like vapours that from limbecks rise,
> It would in richer showers descend again.
>
> At length resolved to assert the watery ball,
> He in himself did whole Armadoes bring:
> Him aged seamen might their master call,
> And choose for general, were he not their king.
>
> It seems as every ship their sovereign knows,
> His awful summons they so soon obey;
> So hear the scaly herd when Proteus blows,
> And so to pasture follow through the sea.
>
> To see this fleet upon the ocean move,
> Angels drew wide the curtains of the skies;
> And heaven, as if there wanted lights above,
> For tapers made two glaring comets rise.
>
> Whether they unctuous exhalations are,
> Fired by the sun, or seeming so alone:
> Or each some more remote and slippery star,
> Which loses footing when to mortals shown.

Or one, that bright companion of the sun,
Whose glorious aspect seal'd our new-born king;
And now a round of greater years begun,
New influence from his walks of light did bring.

Victorious York did first with famed success,
To his known valour make the Dutch give place:
Thus Heaven our monarch's fortune did confess,
Beginning conquest from his royal race.

With the divine support of the comets, an interminable sea battle
begins: the British win. The detail of Dryden's poetry suggests that
he was using first-hand contemporary accounts of the battle. His
entire intention is to rally the nation around Charles II. But this
was a year of disasters as well as battles – 1666 saw the plague, and
above all the great Fire of London. Unsurprisingly, the king takes a
heroic role in this as well. Dryden, who wrote the poem while he
was out of London fleeing from the plague, gives a wonderful and
vivid description of the effect of the conflagration on the crammed
city – even if he has to blame the 'Belgian' wind for fanning it in the
first place.

Here cries soon waken all the dwellers near;
Now murmuring noises rise in every street:
The more remote run stumbling with their fear,
And in the dark men jostle as they meet.

So weary bees in little cells repose;
But if night-robbers lift the well-stored hive,
An humming through their waxen city grows,
And out upon each other's wings they drive.

Now streets grow throng'd and busy as by day:
Some run for buckets to the hallow'd quire:
Some cut the pipes, and some the engines play;
And some more bold mount ladders to the fire.

In vain: for from the east a Belgian wind
His hostile breath through the dry rafters sent;
The flames impell'd soon left their foes behind,
And forward with a wanton fury went.

A quay of fire ran all along the shore,
And lighten'd all the river with a blaze:
The waken'd tides began again to roar,
And wondering fish in shining waters gaze ...

... The fire, meantime, walks in a broader gross;
To either hand his wings he opens wide:
He wades the streets, and straight he reaches cross,
And plays his longing flames on the other side.

At first they warm, then scorch, and then they take;
Now with long necks from side to side they feed:
At length, grown strong, their mother-fire forsake,
And a new colony of flames succeed.

To every nobler portion of the town
The curling billows roll their restless tide:
In parties now they straggle up and down,
As armies, unopposed, for prey divide.

One mighty squadron with a side-wind sped,
Through narrow lanes his cumber'd fire does haste,
By powerful charms of gold and silver led,
The Lombard bankers and the 'Change to waste.

Another backward to the Tower would go,
And slowly eats his way against the wind:
But the main body of the marching foe
Against the imperial palace is design'd.

Now day appears, and with the day the King,
Whose early care had robb'd him of his rest:
Far off the cracks of falling houses ring,
And shrieks of subjects pierce his tender breast.

The King directs operations. If things don't go well, then at least they don't go as disastrously as they might have done. Dryden finally paints a haunting picture of the London of ashes and tottering stone that the great fire left behind:

Night came, but without darkness or repose, —
A dismal picture of the general doom,
Where souls, distracted when the trumpet blows,
And half unready, with their bodies come.

Those who have homes, when home they do repair,
To a last lodging call their wandering friends:
Their short uneasy sleeps are broke with care,
To look how near their own destruction tends.

Those who have none, sit round where once it was,
And with full eyes each wonted room require;
Haunting the yet warm ashes of the place,
As murder'd men walk where they did expire.

Some stir up coals, and watch the vestal fire,
Others in vain from sight of ruin run;
And, while through burning labyrinths they retire,
With loathing eyes repeat what they would shun.

The most in fields like herded beasts lie down,
To dews obnoxious on the grassy floor;
And while their babes in sleep their sorrows drown,
Sad parents watch the remnants of their store.

Once again, loyalty to their hyperactive king will save the huddled masses; London will rise again. Dryden wins his royal pension by turning natural calamity into patriotic triumph. Interestingly, already, at this relatively early stage, he foresees the rise of London as a global mercantile and imperial capital which will overawe Britain's Continental rivals:

Now, like a maiden queen, she will behold,
From her high turrets, hourly suitors come;
The East with incense, and the West with gold,
Will stand, like suppliants, to receive her doom!

The silver Thames, her own domestic flood,
Shall bear her vessels like a sweeping train;
And often wind, as of his mistress proud,
With longing eyes to meet her face again.

The wealthy Tagus, and the wealthier Rhine,
The glory of their towns no more shall boast;
And Seine, that would with Belgian rivers join,
Shall find her lustre stain'd, and traffic lost.

The venturous merchant who design'd more far,
And touches on our hospitable shore,
Charm'd with the splendour of this northern star,
Shall here unlade him, and depart no more.

Our powerful navy shall no longer meet,
The wealth of France or Holland to invade;
The beauty of this town without a fleet,
From all the world shall vindicate her trade.

The country which in Dryden's early years had been a divided,
Puritan republic has become, at least in embryo, the monarchist
empire that it will remain for the next quarter of a millennium.

8

The Age of Reason. And Slavery, and Filth, and So On

The first half of the eighteenth century attracted labels that mostly now seem absurd. In the wake of the French and Scottish enthusiasm for Deist and scientific philosophies, it's been called 'the Enlightenment' or even 'the age of reason'. Referring back to the long period of Roman imperial peace, and a poem by Pope about George II, it's also been called 'the Augustan age'. Referring to the enthusiasm for politer, more regulated social behaviour, it's been called 'the age of politeness'. These labels all imply that the British reacted to both the religious extremism of the Commonwealth and to the pleasure-principle libertinism of the Restoration by dreaming of a new middle way. There is a certain amount of truth in that. But these ladies also suggest an age of mincing decorum, a gentle, genteel period. And there's almost no truth in that.

From the late 1600s to the 1750s we have the first age of empire and the rise of the Royal Navy as the nation's senior service, its worm-eaten monsters kept going, in Winston Churchill's immortal phrase, by 'rum, sodomy and the lash'. Empire brought with it new wealth and new moral dilemmas, including the slave trade and endless mercantile wars against the French. At home it was a period of outrageous corruption, and while government was nothing like as tyrannical as it had been under the Tudors or the Stuarts, early-eighteenth-century governments relied heavily on mass hangings, whippings and brandings, as well as the odd burning and decapitation. The Jacobite uprisings reminded people across Britain, not just in Scotland, that there was still an open wound between Catholic legitimists and Protestant Hanoverian loyalists. Scotland and England had been soldered together by the 1707 Act of Union, bitterly resented by minorities in both countries. This is also the first period of rapid industrialisation, in its crudest, smokiest and most dangerous phase. Alongside that, it's a time of rapid urbanisation. Over the course of the century London's population almost doubled to just under a million; Bristol, Edinburgh and Dublin were also expanding very quickly. Slum housing and filthy, ill-maintained sewers were nothing new in Britain, and would remain a problem in the centuries ahead; but Georgian London was a filthy, stinking and dangerous place.

In literature, the most important background development was technological democratisation: a mass press was now churning out newspapers throughout Britain. Even if most people were illiterate, reading aloud in taverns and coffee houses meant that news and the latest opinions were more widely spread than ever before. It wasn't just newspapers. Sermons, essays and poems were printed in magazine and book form and avidly consumed. This is the period when the novel as we know it was invented. So it would be surprising if the poetry of the age was purely an 'Augustan' rehash of classical authors, concentrating on the importance of refined sensibility and good manners.

And despite the generations brought up on Alexander Pope, the insufferably tedious James Thomson and Thomas Gray's 'Elegy', it turns out that there was a lot more going on. The truth is that anyone compiling a book such as this is, in turn, indebted to good anthologists. *The New Oxford Book of Eighteenth-Century Verse*, edited by Professor Roger Lonsdale, is a genuine breakthrough collection which has greatly expanded the ordinary reader's understanding of the period: what follows depends in part upon Lonsdale's pioneering work. Culture does move dialectically. There is a proposition, which invites its challenge or alternative. These struggle, and out of their conflict emerges a new proposition, and so on. This was Hegel's great insight, and Karl Marx's, and it still has force. The trouble is that, in trying to portray a fast-moving and complex society like Britain's, it's not nearly messy enough. We will move to the messiness later, but let's see if it's possible to paint with broad strokes first.

In very crude terms, the religious extremism of Puritan England provoked Restoration libertinism – repression led to licence; the next generation found both extremes too much and therefore championed order, politeness, poise – piety but not too much piety; love poetry but not pornography. Alexander Pope was also literature's Pope in this period, recasting British verse for the age after Milton, dominating everything around him. The trouble, from our point of view just now, is that he was a genius, and genius is specific, unusual, special. To understand the underlying choices the age thought it was making we are better off with a much less well-known poet, John Pomfret, a Bedfordshire vicar admired by Samuel Johnson. Pomfret's theme in 'The Choice' is that the right way to live is in moderation, avoiding all extremes. In a way it's the lifestyle version of George Herbert's defence of the Anglican Church described in an earlier chapter:

If heaven the grateful liberty would give
That I might choose my method how to live,
And all those hours propitious fate should lend,
In blissful ease and satisfaction spend:
Near some fair town I'd have a private seat,
Built uniform, not little, nor too great:
Better if on a rising ground it stood;
Fields on this side, on that a neighbouring wood;
It should within no other things contain
But what were useful, necessary, plain:
Methinks 'tis nauseous, and I'd ne'er endure
The needless pomp of gaudy furniture.
A little garden, grateful to the eye,
And a cool rivulet run murmuring by,

On whose delicious banks a stately row
Of shady limes or sycamores should grow;
At the end of which a silent study plac'd
Should be with all the noblest authors grac'd:
Horace and Virgil, in whose mighty lines
Immortal wit and solid learning shines;
Sharp Juvenal, and amorous Ovid too,
Who all the turns of love's soft passion knew;
He that with judgment reads his charming lines,
In which strong art with stronger nature joins,
Must grant his fancy does the best excel,
His thoughts so tender and express'd so well;
With all those moderns, men of steady sense,
Esteem'd for learning and for eloquence.
In some of these, as fancy should advise,
I'd always take my morning exercise:
For sure no minutes bring us more content
Than those in pleasing, useful studies spent.
I'd have a clear and competent estate,
That I might live genteelly, but not great;
As much as I could moderately spend,
A little more, sometimes t'oblige a friend.
Nor should the sons of poverty repine
Too much at fortune, they should taste of mine;
And all that objects of true pity were
Should be reliev'd with what my wants could spare.
For that our Maker has too largely given
Should be return'd, in gratitude to heaven.
A frugal plenty should my table spread,
With healthy, not luxurious dishes fed:
Enough to satisfy, and something more
To feed the stranger and the neighbouring poor.
Strong meat indulges vice, and pampering food
Creates diseases and inflames the blood.
But what's sufficient to make nature strong

And the bright lamp of life continue long
I'd freely take, and as I did possess,
The bounteous Author of my plenty bless.
I'd have a little vault, but always stor'd
With the best wines each vintage could afford.
Wine whets the wit, improves its native force,
And gives a pleasant flavour to discourse:
By making all our spirits debonair
Throws off the lees, the sediment of care.
But as the greatest blessing heaven lends
May be debauch'd and serve ignoble ends,
So, but too oft, the grape's refreshing juice
Does many mischievous effects produce.
My house should no such rude disorders know
As from high drinking consequently flow.

It's very sensible, and also slightly dull. Pomfret's moderation, however, was also meant to be an act of will, a determined effort to cope with life's terrors and disappointments by fixing them in a kind of grid – a frame of philosophical self-knowledge. The importance of poise is that it keeps you upright even in the most awful situations. A far greater example of what this can achieve is Jonathan Swift's famous poem about his own approaching death. These days Swift is much better known for his prose satires, such as *Gulliver's Travels* and *The Tale of a Tub*, but he's also one of the great Irish poets of all time. 'Verses on the Death of Dr Swift' begin with reflections on what we now call *Schadenfreude* – the way we enjoy the misfortunes even of our friends – before rising to this extraordinary stare into the mirror of mortality:

The time is not remote, when I
Must by the course of nature die;
When I foresee my special friends
Will try to find their private ends:
Tho' it is hardly understood

Which way my death can do them good,
Yet thus, methinks, I hear 'em speak:
'See, how the Dean begins to break!
Poor gentleman, he droops apace!
You plainly find it in his face.
That old vertigo in his head
Will never leave him till he's dead.
Besides, his memory decays:
He recollects not what he says;
He cannot call his friends to mind:
Forgets the place where last he din'd;
Plies you with stories o'er and o'er;
He told them fifty times before.
How does he fancy we can sit
To hear his out-of-fashion'd wit?
But he takes up with younger folks,
Who for his wine will bear his jokes.
Faith, he must make his stories shorter,
Or change his comrades once a quarter:
In half the time he talks them round,
There must another set be found.
For poetry he's past his prime:
He takes an hour to find a rhyme;
His fire is out, his wit decay'd,
His fancy sunk, his Muse a jade.
I'd have him throw away his pen;—
But there's no talking to some men!'
And then their tenderness appears,
By adding largely to my years:
'He's older than he would be reckon'd
And well remembers Charles the Second.
He hardly drinks a pint of wine;
And that, I doubt, is no good sign.
His stomach too begins to fail:
Last year we thought him strong and hale;

But now he's quite another thing:
I wish he may hold out till spring.'
Then hug themselves, and reason thus:
'It is not yet so bad with us.'

In its bald directness about death, its humour and its humanity, this seems to me a triumphant answer to John Donne's horror of death, and therefore a triumph of the Augustan belief in poise. Are poems ever really useful? I think this one is: a living and permanent remonstrance to self-pity. Swift can be shocking in less useful ways – his poem about an elderly prostitute going to bed is too disgusting to reprint here, and he's the only poet I know of who has written verses from the point of view of a pair of buttocks. But he's a great rebuke to the still-common idea that eighteenth-century poets wrote about idealised subjects and not about what was all around them. Swift is a great noticer – he notices how people behave in a sudden shower of rain, and the humbug they talk when a general dies. And in his tender but characteristically direct birthday verses to the great love of his life, Esther Johnson, or 'Stella', he deals with love and ageing:

All travellers at first incline
Where'er they see the fairest sign
And if they find the chambers neat,
And like the liquor and the meat,
Will call again, and recommend
The Angel Inn to every friend.
And though the painting grows decay'd,
The house will never lose its trade:
Nay, though the treach'rous tapster, Thomas,
Hangs a new Angel two doors from us,
As fine as daubers' hands can make it,
In hopes that strangers may mistake it,
We think it both a shame and sin
To quit the true old Angel Inn.

Now this is Stella's case in fact,
An angel's face a little crack'd.
(Could poets or could painters fix
How angels look at thirty-six)
This drew us in at first to find
In such a form an angel's mind;
And every virtue now supplies
The fainting rays of Stella's eyes.
See, at her levee crowding swains,
Whom Stella freely entertains
With breeding, humour, wit, and sense,
And puts them to so small expense;
Their minds so plentifully fills,
And makes such reasonable bills,
So little gets for what she gives,
We really wonder how she lives!
And had her stock been less, no doubt
She must have long ago run out.
Then, who can think we'll quit the place,
When Doll hangs out a newer face?
Nail'd to her window full in sight
All Christian people to invite.
Or stop and light at Chloe's head,
With scraps and leavings to be fed?
Then, Chloe, still go on to prate
Of thirty-six and thirty-eight;
Pursue your trade of scandal-picking,
Your hints that Stella is no chicken;
Your innuendoes, when you tell us,
That Stella loves to talk with fellows:
But let me warn you to believe
A truth, for which your soul should grieve;
That should you live to see the day,
When Stella's locks must all be gray,
When age must print a furrow'd trace

On every feature of her face;
Though you, and all your senseless tribe,
Could Art, or Time, or Nature bribe,
To make you look like Beauty's Queen,
And hold for ever at fifteen;
No bloom of youth can ever blind
The cracks and wrinkles of your mind:
All men of sense will pass your door,
And crowd to Stella's at four-score.

It's a poem, like the one on his own death, which is really about decency and mental strength: 'breeding, humour, wit, and sense' defy time itself. Here, again, is the boldest claim of the Augustan age. As every educated person knows, Swift was often much angrier and less forgiving, particularly about the atrocious state of Ireland under English rule. His prose 'Modest Proposal' advocates the selling of Irish children as delicacies for the rich to eat, thus dealing with overpopulation and failing agriculture at one blow. It's probably the most brilliant and savage political satire ever written in the British Isles, and there's nothing quite like it in Swift's poetry. Not quite: but his 'Satirical Elegy' on the death of the famous general John Churchill, Duke of Marlborough, is almost as angry, and so far as I know the greatest British anti-war poem written up to this date (1765). Marlborough was one of England's greatest generals, victor of a series of titanic battles against the French across Europe – Blenheim, Ramillies, Oudenarde – friend of the monarch and recipient of the enormously grand palace of Blenheim outside Oxford, gifted him by a grateful people. None of which impressed Swift at all: to him, Marlborough was a warmonger and slaughterer, and nothing more grand than that:

His Grace! impossible! what, dead!
Of old age too, and in his bed!
And could that mighty warrior fall,
And so inglorious, after all?

Well, since he's gone, no matter how,
The last loud trump must wake him now;
And, trust me, as the noise grows stronger,
He'd wish to sleep a little longer.
And could he be indeed so old
As by the newspapers we're told?
Threescore, I think, is pretty high;
'Twas time in conscience he should die!
This world he cumber'd long enough;
He burnt his candle to the snuff;
And that's the reason, some folks think,
He left behind so great a stink.
Behold his funeral appears,
Nor widows' sighs, nor orphans' tears,
Wont at such times each heart to pierce,
Attend the progress of his hearse.
But what of that? his friends may say,
He had those honours in his day.
True to his profit and his pride,
He made them weep before he died.

In terms of raw anger and disgust it might seem that you can't go
further than that. Swift does:

Come hither, all ye empty things!
Ye bubbles rais'd by breath of kings!
Who float upon the tide of state;
Come hither, and behold your fate!
Let pride be taught by this rebuke,
How very mean a thing's a duke;
From all his ill-got honours flung,
Turn'd to that dirt from whence he sprung.

Among Swift's circle of opposition Tory friends in London was the
Roman Catholic, diseased and almost dwarfish genius Alexander

Pope. The great exponent of heroic couplets – 'da-DUM, da-DUM, da-DUM, da-DUM, da-DUM' in paired rhymes – Pope found ways of making poetry that followed Milton without slavishly imitating him. In his *Essay on Man* of 1734 he attempts to justify the ways of God to man, in a sunnier, more optimistic way than Milton would have dreamt of – a rationalistic 'whatever it is, is right' worldview later rejected and satirised by the great French philosopher Voltaire. It's a higher, more philosophical version of the middle way that we found in Pomfret, though Pope's Catholicism leads him to be sceptical of scientific rationalism:

The proper study of Mankind is Man.
Placed on this isthmus of a middle state,
A Being darkly wise, and rudely great:
With too much knowledge for the Sceptic side,
With too much weakness for the Stoic's pride,
He hangs between; in doubt to act, or rest;
In doubt to deem himself a God, or Beast;
In doubt his mind or body to prefer;
Born but to die, and reas'ning but to err;
Alike in ignorance, his reason such,
Whether he thinks too little, or too much;
Chaos of Thought and Passion, all confus'd;
Still by himself, abus'd or disabus'd;
Created half to rise and half to fall;
Great Lord of all things, yet a prey to all,
Sole judge of truth, in endless error hurl'd;
The glory, jest and riddle of the world.
Go, wondrous creature! mount where science guides,
Go, measure earth, weigh air, and state the tides;
Instruct the planets in what orbs to run,
Correct old time, and regulate the sun;
Go, soar with Plato to th' empyreal sphere,
To the first good, first perfect, and first fair;
Or tread the mazy round his followers trod,

And quitting sense call imitating God;
As Eastern priests in giddy circles run,
And turn their heads to imitate the sun.
Go, teach Eternal Wisdom how to rule –
Then drop into thyself, and be a fool!

Pope was always a serious Christian believer, but as different a kind
of Catholic as one can imagine from the stern and passionate
Catholicism of the Counter-Reformation; his answer to Milton, as
it were, is that God's wisdom is to be trusted by humans with
limited understanding – essentially, lie back and enjoy it:

Hope humbly then; with trembling pinions soar;
Wait the great teacher Death; and God adore.
What future bliss, he gives not thee to know,
But gives that hope to be thy blessing now.
Hope springs eternal in the human breast:
Man never is, but always to be blest:
The soul, uneasy and confin'd from home,
Rests and expatiates in a life to come.

Alexander Pope's grappling with Milton, however, had a much
more popular and wittier result. 'The Rape of the Lock' is mock-
heroic, a burlesque answer to the magnificent but humourless
Paradise Lost. Published in 1712, it followed a real-life row between
Arabella Fermor and her would-be lover Lord Petre. Both of them
came from Catholic families and were therefore, like Pope himself,
living under the tight restrictions imposed by Anglican Britain. But
there is no shadow, no bitterness in the poem: Petre had snipped
off a lock of Arabella's hair without her permission, causing a furi-
ous row between the families. Pope turns this into a confrontation
involving a whole world of imps, sprites and spectral fairy creatures,
as airy as Milton's angelic horde, but smaller and far less frighten-
ing. Indeed, they are the nearest we get in later English poetry to
Shakespeare's *A Midsummer Night's Dream*. The dark-browed trag-

edy of Milton deliquesces into a frothy comedy, and Pope proves himself the nearest thing the unmusical English ever had to Mozart. Like some of the Master's operas, the poem is both bonkers and marvellously humane. The opening of the long poem gives a sense of how Pope plays with heroic conventions to comic effect. Belinda, his heroine, is lying late in bed and dreaming …

> Sol thro' white curtains shot a tim'rous ray,
> And op'd those eyes that must eclipse the day;
> Now lap-dogs give themselves the rousing shake,
> And sleepless lovers, just at twelve, awake:
> Thrice rung the bell, the slipper knock'd the ground,
> And the press'd watch return'd a silver sound.
> Belinda still her downy pillow press'd,
> Her guardian sylph prolong'd the balmy rest:
> 'Twas he had summon'd to her silent bed
> The morning dream that hover'd o'er her head;
> A youth more glitt'ring than a birthnight beau,
> (That ev'n in slumber caus'd her cheek to glow)
> Seem'd to her ear his winning lips to lay,
> And thus in whispers said, or seem'd to say.
> 'Fairest of mortals, thou distinguish'd care
> Of thousand bright inhabitants of air!
> If e'er one vision touch'd thy infant thought,
> Of all the nurse and all the priest have taught,
> Of airy elves by moonlight shadows seen,
> The silver token, and the circled green,
> Or virgins visited by angel pow'rs,
> With golden crowns and wreaths of heav'nly flow'rs,
> Hear and believe! thy own importance know,
> Nor bound thy narrow views to things below.
> Some secret truths from learned pride conceal'd,
> To maids alone and children are reveal'd:
> What tho' no credit doubting wits may give?
> The fair and innocent shall still believe.

Know then, unnumber'd spirits round thee fly,
The light militia of the lower sky;

The Shakespearean echoes are unmistakable. But later on, when the wicked peer is just about to take Belinda's scissors and cut off her lock, it starts to sound like a naughty version of Milton:

Just then, Clarissa drew with tempting grace
A two-edg'd weapon from her shining case;
So ladies in romance assist their knight
Present the spear, and arm him for the fight.
He takes the gift with rev'rence, and extends
The little engine on his fingers' ends;
This just behind Belinda's neck he spread,
As o'er the fragrant steams she bends her head.
Swift to the lock a thousand sprites repair,
A thousand wings, by turns, blow back the hair,
And thrice they twitch'd the diamond in her ear,
Thrice she look'd back, and thrice the foe drew near.

The peer now spreads the glitt'ring forfex wide,
T' inclose the lock; now joins it, to divide.
Ev'n then, before the fatal engine clos'd,
A wretched Sylph too fondly interpos'd;
Fate urg'd the shears, and cut the Sylph in twain,
(But airy substance soon unites again).
The meeting points the sacred hair dissever
From the fair head, for ever, and for ever!

Then flash'd the living lightning from her eyes,
And screams of horror rend th' affrighted skies.
Not louder shrieks to pitying Heav'n are cast,
When husbands or when lap-dogs breathe their last,
Or when rich China vessels, fall'n from high,
In glitt'ring dust and painted fragments lie!

As with Mozart, and with Swift, there are more serious messages hidden under the comedy. Mozart, a critic of aristocratic Austrian elites, died in poverty; Swift died mad. Comedy and the poise it requires provides a way of holding back the darkness. Pope's life was a hard one. He built himself an elaborate grotto by the Thames at Twickenham, yet his feuds with political and literary enemies meant he could only go out protected by a large dog and a loaded pistol. An outsider all his life, wit protected him against meaninglessness: his war against dull poets was a war to protect his sanity. In his late 'Epistle to Dr Arbuthnot' he speaks for all celebrity authors plagued by third-rate admirers:

> Shut, shut the door, good John! fatigu'd, I said,
> Tie up the knocker, say I'm sick, I'm dead.
> The dog-star rages! nay 'tis past a doubt,
> All Bedlam, or Parnassus, is let out:
> Fire in each eye, and papers in each hand,
> They rave, recite, and madden round the land.
>
> What walls can guard me, or what shades can hide?
> They pierce my thickets, through my grot they glide;
> By land, by water, they renew the charge;
> They stop the chariot, and they board the barge.
> No place is sacred, not the church is free;
> Ev'n Sunday shines no Sabbath-day to me:
> Then from the Mint walks forth the man of rhyme,
> Happy! to catch me just at dinner-time.
>
> Is there a parson, much bemus'd in beer,
> A maudlin poetess, a rhyming peer,
> A clerk, foredoom'd his father's soul to cross,
> Who pens a stanza, when he should engross?
> Is there, who, lock'd from ink and paper, scrawls
> With desp'rate charcoal round his darken'd walls?
> All fly to Twit'nam, and in humble strain

Apply to me, to keep them mad or vain.
Arthur, whose giddy son neglects the laws,
Imputes to me and my damn'd works the cause:
Poor Cornus sees his frantic wife elope,
And curses wit, and poetry, and Pope.

Life is so serious, you have to laugh at it. But the threat to civilisa-
tion and to sanity that comes from what Pope calls dullness – and
it includes propaganda, exaggeration, lies, all the threats we face
today – is an existential one. Wit for him is a moral quality. Right
at the end of his huge poem 'The Dunciad', he makes clear, for once,
what lies behind the Joker's face:

Religion blushing veils her sacred fires,
And unawares Morality expires.
Nor public Flame, nor private, dares to shine;
Nor human Spark is left, nor Glimpse divine!
Lo! thy dread Empire, Chaos! is restor'd;
Light dies before thy uncreating word:
Thy hand, great Anarch! lets the curtain fall;
And universal Darkness buries All.

Like Dryden, Pope was a great translator – in his case, Homer
rather than Virgil – but the gift he gave to other poets was to show
how the mock-heroic, rather than the heroic, can be used to allow
a description of almost everything. Instead of limiting what one can
write about, it opens up the world. This was a lesson learned by
Pope's great admirer Thomas Gray. His 'Elegy in a Country
Churchyard' is probably the best-known and most emblematic
English poem of the eighteenth century; as with Pope, we still
spend a lot of time quoting Gray unawares. But around the time he
wrote that poem he wrote another which is much more in the spirit
of Pope, and which introduces another very important aspect of
Britishness, developing quickly during this century – the soppy love
of pets, and in particular cats. Here is another elegy, but this time

to a favourite cat, 'drowned in a tub of gold fishes'. Anyone who has cats will recognise its descriptive genius. It also reminds us that this was a great new age of trade and materialism, when porcelain from China was all the rage (remember the smashed 'rich China vessels' in 'The Rape of the Lock'?).

'Twas on a lofty vase's side,
Where China's gayest art had dyed
The azure flowers that blow,
Demurest of the tabby kind,
The pensive Selima, reclined,
Gazed on the lake below.

Her conscious tail her joy declared;
The fair round face, the snowy beard,
The velvet of her paws,
Her coat, that with the tortoise vies,
Her ears of jet, and emerald eyes,
She saw; and purred applause.

Still had she gazed; but 'midst the tide
Two angel forms were seen to glide,
The genii of the stream:
Their scaly armour's Tyrian hue
Through richest purple to the view
Betrayed a golden gleam.

The hapless nymph with wonder saw:
A whisker first, and then a claw,
With many an ardent wish,
She stretched, in vain, to reach the prize.
What female heart can gold despise?
What cat's averse to fish?

Presumptuous maid! with looks intent
Again she stretched, again she bent,
Nor knew the gulf between:
(Malignant Fate sat by, and smiled)
The slippery verge her feet beguiled,
She tumbled headlong in.

Eight times emerging from the flood
She mewed to ev'ry wat'ry god
Some speedy aid to send.
No dolphin came, no nereid stirred;
Nor cruel Tom, nor Susan heard.
A fav'rite has no friend!

Gray's more famous elegy was written in the 1740s, composed, at least in part, in the graveyard of St Giles parish church in Stoke Poges, Buckinghamshire. Although inspired by the death of a friend, it's a general meditation on extinction which gains its peculiar power from the intense impression of a sleepy, barely-known English village community, peopled by decent folk doomed to be forgotten by history. To that extent, it's a reply to Shakespeare's despairing hope of immortality through remembrance, as expressed in his sonnets.

The Curfew tolls the knell of parting day,
The lowing herd wind slowly o'er the lea,
The plowman homeward plods his weary way,
And leaves the world to darkness and to me.

Now fades the glimmering landscape on the sight,
And all the air a solemn stillness holds,
Save where the beetle wheels his droning flight,
And drowsy tinklings lull the distant folds;

Save that from yonder ivy-mantled tow'r
The moping owl does to the moon complain
Of such as, wand'ring near her secret bow'r,
Molest her ancient solitary reign.

Beneath those rugged elms, that yew-tree's shade,
Where heaves the turf in many a mould'ring heap,
Each in his narrow cell for ever laid,
The rude Forefathers of the hamlet sleep.

The breezy call of incense-breathing Morn,
The swallow twitt'ring from the straw-built shed,
The cock's shrill clarion, or the echoing horn,
No more shall rouse them from their lowly bed.

For them no more the blazing hearth shall burn,
Or busy housewife ply her evening care:
No children run to lisp their sire's return,
Or climb his knees the envied kiss to share.

Oft did the harvest to their sickle yield,
Their furrow oft the stubborn glebe has broke:
How jocund did they drive their team afield!
How bow'd the woods beneath their sturdy stroke!

Let not Ambition mock their useful toil,
Their homely joys, and destiny obscure;
Nor Grandeur hear with a disdainful smile
The short and simple annals of the poor.

The boast of heraldry, the pomp of pow'r,
And all that beauty, all that wealth e'er gave,
Awaits alike th' inevitable hour:
The paths of glory lead but to the grave.

A little earlier I suggested that Alexander Pope, usually seen as an elite and rarefied writer, had opened the door to new ways of describing the daily reality of life. Another friend of his, and of Jonathan Swift's, was John Gay, these days mostly remembered for his sublime *Beggar's Opera* of 1728. This was something entirely new in the British theatre. At the time, London was obsessed by the imported exuberance of Italian opera, with its castrated singers and its incomprehensible arias. Gay responded with a robustly British piece, based on folk tunes and entirely in English, telling the story of robbers and murderers but also caricaturing Britain's first, and notoriously corrupt, Prime Minister, Robert Walpole. It was re-imagined in the twentieth century by Bertolt Brecht. More immediate for our purposes, however, are Gay's poems about daily life, above all his 'Trivia, or the Art of Walking the Streets of London', which pretty much does what it says on the tin, giving the modern reader a realistic account of what the early-eighteenth-century city was actually like to live in. The best time of day to walk around, then as now, was first thing:

> For ease and for dispatch, the morning's best;
> No tides of passengers the street molest.
> You'll see a draggled damsel, here and there,
> From Billingsgate her fishy traffic bear;
> On doors the sallow milk-maid chalks her gains;
> Ah! how unlike the milk-maid of the plains!
> Before proud gates attending asses bray,
> Or arrogate with solemn pace the way;
> These grave physicians with their milky cheer,
> The love-sick maid and dwindling beau repair;
> Here rows of drummers stand in martial file,
> And with their vellum thunder shake the pile,
> To greet the new-made bride. Are sounds like these
> The proper prelude to a state of peace?
> Now industry awakes her busy sons,
> Full charg'd with news the breathless hawker runs:

Shops open, coaches roll, carts shake the ground,
And all the streets with passing cries resound.

As the streets become busier and more crammed, the dangers
increase as well, including of getting smuts on brightly coloured
clothes:

Ye walkers too that youthful colours wear,
Three sullying trades avoid with equal care;
The little chimney-sweeper skulks along,
And marks with sooty stains the heedless throng;
When small-coal murmurs in the hoarser throat,
From smutty dangers guard thy threaten'd coat:
The dust-man's cart offends thy clothes and eyes,
When through the street a cloud of ashes flies;
But whether black or lighter dyes are worn,
The chandler's basket, on his shoulder borne,
With tallow spots thy coat; resign the way,
To shun the surly butcher's greasy tray,
Butchers, whose hands are dy'd with blood's foul stain,
And always foremost in the hangman's train.
Let due civilities be strictly paid.
The wall surrender to the hooded maid;
Nor let thy sturdy elbow's hasty rage
Jostle the feeble steps of trembling age;
And when the porter bends beneath his load,
And pants for breath, clear thou the crowded road.
But, above all, the groping blind direct,
And from the pressing throng the lame protect.
You'll sometimes meet a fop, of nicest tread,
Whose mantling peruke veils his empty head;
At ev'ry step he dreads the wall to lose,
And risks, to save a coach, his red-heel'd shoes;
Him, like the miller, pass with caution by,
Lest from his shoulder clouds of powder fly.

So this is a satirical account of London society, not just a guide to walking the streets. It also becomes geographically interesting – the old distinction between the hard-working, smelly east and the posher, calmer West End was already there in 1716. Pell-mell is what we call Pall Mall:

> ... who that rugged street would traverse o'er,
> That stretches, O Fleet-ditch, from thy black shore
> To the tower's moated walls! here steams ascend,
> That, in mix'd fumes, the wrinkled nose offend.
> Where chandler's cauldrons boil; where fishy prey
> Hide the wet stall, long absent from the sea;
> And where the cleaver chops the heifer's spoil,
> And where huge hogsheads sweat with trainy oil,
> Thy breathing nostril hold, but how shall I
> Pass, where in piles Carnavian cheeses lie;
> Cheese, that the table's closing rites denies,
> And bids me with the unwilling chaplain rise.
> O bear me to the paths of fair Pell-mell,
> Safe are thy pavements, grateful is thy smell;
> At distance rolls along the gilded coach,
> Nor sturdy car-men on thy walks encroach:
> No lets would bar thy ways, were chairs denied,
> The soft supports of laziness and pride;
> Shops breathe perfumes, through sashes ribbons glow,
> The mutual arms of ladies and the beau.

John Gay is, I find, an addictive poet; and much of the London he describes is still just visible. But he also wrote a lot about the countryside, including country sports, from the now despised hare-coursing:

> Let thy fleet greyhound urge his dying foe.
> With what delight the rapid course I view!
> How does my eye the circling race pursue!

He snaps deceitful air with empty jaws,
The subtle hare darts swift beneath his paws;
She flies, he stretches, now with nimble bound.
Eager he presses on, but overshoots his ground;
She turns, he winds, and soon regains the way,
Then tears with goary mouth the screaming prey.
What various sport does rural life afford!
What unbought dainties heap the wholesome board!

To shooting, in this case woodcock:

Now to the copse thy lesser spaniel take,
Teach him to range the ditch and force the brake;
Now closest coverts can protect the game:
Hark! the dog opens; take thy certain aim;
The woodcock flutters; how he wavering flies!
The wood resounds: he wheels, he drops, he dies.

But away from *Country Life* country life, other sports were taking
their modern form. William Somervile was a Warwickshire coun-
try gentleman, convivial and relatively unknown as a poet. He
deserves to be remembered, however, for a very early description of
cricket. In 'The Bowling-Green' of 1734, he makes it clear that the
pitch was already very carefully prepared:

... The Swain
Whets his unrighteous scythe, and shaves the plain.
Beneath each stroke the peeping flow'rs decline,
And all the unripened crop is swept away.
The heavy roller next he tugs along,
Whiffs his short pipe ...

Then the keen cricketers turn up, a complete cross-section of
English rural life:

Attorneys spruce in their plate-buttoned frocks,
And rosy Parsons, fat and orthodox;
Of ev'ry sect, Whigs, Papists and High-Fliers,
Cornuted aldermen, and hen-pecked squires;
Fox-hunters, quacks, scribblers in verse and prose,
And half-pay captains, and half-witted beaux.
On the green cirque the ready racers stand,
Disposed in pairs, and tempt the bowler's hand ...

What follows is witty verse which shows that the poet was a proper cricketer himself, or at least someone who well understood the game's frustrations. There is a priest, whom Somervile calls Zadoc, after Solomon's high priest, but who isn't as good a bowler as he'd like to be. He bowls wide to the left, and then overcompensates:

As if he meant to regulate its course
By power attractive and magnetic force.
Now almost in despair, he raves, he storms,
Writhes his unwieldy trunk in various forms:
Unhappy Proteus! Still in vain he tries
A thousand shapes, the bowl erroneous flies,
Deaf to his prayers, regardless of his cries.
His puffing cheeks with rising rage inflame,
And all his sparkling rubies glow with shame.

Somervile's reference to 'half-pay captains' reminds us that eighteenth-century Britain was a society mostly at war, and therefore heavily militarised. We have seen Jonathan Swift's ferociously anti-war poem, and it's matched by one by the novelist Tobias Smollett which I'll come to shortly. But war gave employment and lustre to many young men who regretted the peace treaties when they came. Richardson Pack was a professional soldier who fought with distinction in the War of the Spanish Succession before retiring to London and Aberdeen. In 1713 this European dynastic conflict was brought to an end by the Treaty of Utrecht (under which

Gibraltar was ceded to Britain). There was widespread rejoicing –
but not, suggests Richardson Pack, from one 'half-pay officer in the
country', as he writes to his friend in London:

> Curse on the star, dear Harry, that betrayed
> My choice from law, divinity or trade,
> To turn a rambling brother o' the blade!
> Of all professions sure the worst is war.
> How whimsical our fortune! How bizarre!
> This week we shine in scarlet and in gold:
> The next, the cloak is pawned – the watch is sold.
> Today we're company for any lord:
> Tomorrow not a soul will take our word.
> Like meteors raised in a tempestuous sky,
> A while we glitter, then obscurely die.
> Must heroes suffer such disgrace as this?
> O cursed effects of honourable peace!

At war, he'd been able to indulge himself in romantic love affairs
and vast quantities of champagne. Now things are very different.
He

> Must now retire, and languish out my days
> Far from the roads of pleasure or of praise:
> Quit sweet Hyde Park for dull provincial air,
> And change the Playhouse for a country fair;
> With sneaking Parsons beastly bumpers quaff,
> At low conceits and vile conundrums laugh;
> Toast to the Church and talk of Right Divine,
> And herd with Squires – more noisy than their swine.

These days he no longer eats well, while soldiers aren't in fashion
among the women. It's an unusual sidelight on a world of war, but
it sounds heartfelt. It was easier, of course, to lament the passing of
a conflict fought out on foreign soil.

Three decades after that complaint came the Jacobite uprising of 1745, and the last full-scale battle fought on British soil, at Culloden, where the forces of Prince Charles Edward Stuart were defeated by the Duke of Cumberland. The repression of Highland society which followed was brutal, and opened a wound in Scotland that took a very long time to heal. Tobias Smollett was the hugely popular and scandalous novelist, who left his native Scotland to work mainly in London and for the navy. His novels rarely treat of politics directly, but his first published work was a passionate post-Culloden lament:

> Mourn, hapless Caledonia, mourn
> Thy banish'd peace – thy laurels torn!
> Thy sons, for valour long renown'd,
> Lie slaughter'd on their native ground;
> Thy hospitable roofs no more
> Invite the stranger to the door;
> In smoky ruins sunk they lie,
> The monuments of cruelty.
>
> The wretched owner sees afar
> His all become the prey of war;
> Bethinks him of his babes and wife,
> Then smites his breast, and curses life!
> Thy swains are famish'd on the rocks
> Where once they fed their wanton flocks:
> Thy ravish'd virgins shriek in vain;
> Thy infants perish on the plain.
>
> What boots it then, in every clime
> Through the wide-spreading waste of time,
> Thy martial glory, crown'd with praise,
> Still shone with undiminish'd blaze?
> Thy towering spirit now is broke,
> Thy neck is bended to the yoke.

What foreign arms could never quell,
By civil rage and rancour fell ...

... O baneful cause! oh fatal morn,
Accursed to ages yet unborn!
The sons against their fathers stood,
The parent shed his children's blood.
Yet, when the rage of battle ceased,
The victor's soul was not appeased;
The naked and forlorn must feel
Devouring flames, and murdering steel!

The pious mother, doom'd to death,
Forsaken, wanders o'er the heath;
The bleak wind whistles round her head,
Her helpless orphans cry for bread;
Bereft of shelter, food, and friend,
She views the shades of night descend,
And stretch'd beneath the inclement skies
Weeps o'er her tender babes and dies.

While the warm blood bedews my veins,
And unimpair'd remembrance reigns,
Resentment of my country's fate
Within my filial breast shall beat;
And, spite of her insulting foe,
My sympathizing verse shall flow: —
'Mourn, hapless Caledonia! mourn
Thy banish'd peace, thy laurels torn!'

Smollett knew the military life very well, and some of the greatest passages in his novels concern its seamy underside: he had served in the Royal Navy as a surgeon. But nothing Smollett wrote about what it was really like to serve King George II on a man-of-war comes close to the anonymous poem 'A Sea-Chaplain's Petition to the Lieutenants in the Ward-Room, for the Use of the Quarter-Gallery'. It's an obscure-sounding title for a very basic request: the chaplain on board the ship no longer wants to have to defecate at the 'heads' along with the common sailors, but wishes for the comparative privacy and comfort of the place reserved for the officers.

> You who can grant, or can refuse, the pow'r
> Low from the stern to drop the golden show'r,
> When nature prompts, oh! patient deign to hear,
> If not a parson's, yet a poet's prayer!

He now understands, the chaplain continues, that away from the shore he no longer has the right to eat with the lieutenants. However:

> An humbler boon, and of a different kind
> (Grant, heav'n, it may a different answer find!),
> Attends you now (excuse the rhyme to write):
> 'Tis though I eat not with you, let me sh—e!

It's not just about embarrassment or privacy; we now get an unadorned account of toilet life at the carved prow of the vessel, those

> More vulgar tubes, which downward peep
> Near where the lion awes the raging deep,
> The waggish youth (I tell what I am told)
> Oft smear the sides with excremental gold;
> Say then, when pease, within the belly pent,
> Roar at the port and struggle for a vent,
> Say, shall I squat on dung remissly down,
> And with unseemly ordure stain the gown?
> Or shall I – terrible to think! – displode
> Against th'unbuttoned plush the smoky load,

223

The laugh of swabbers? – Heavens avert the jest,
And from th'impending scorn preserve your priest!

So much for the eighteenth century being, in poetry, the age of politeness. The wretched chaplain expresses his envy of the ship's cobbler, who has his own place to go, before reflecting on how he's wasted his life becoming educated and ordained, only to be cast off to worse toilets than 'the man of leather':

Ah! What avails it that, in days of yore,
Th'instructive lashes of the birch I bore;
For four long years with logic stuffed my head,
And, feeding thought, went supperless to bed …
… Since you, with whom my lot afloat is thrown
(O sense! O elegance! to land unknown!),
Superior rev'rence to the man refuse
Who mends your morals, than who mends your shoes

Alexander Pope this isn't, nor even Dean Swift. But there is real anger in it, about dignity and class: this short poem tells us more, I would suggest, about life in the Royal Navy at the time than many a history book.

The poet's reference to being birched makes one wonder about that other fundamental part of male life in the eighteenth century – the grim world of schooling. Mostly, we get only passing references in the poetry of the time. But there is a disturbing poem by William Shenstone, a Shropshire poet once widely admired but much less known today. In 'The Schoolmistress' he paints a picture of the grubby dame schools that covered the country as Britain's tatty system of primary education. 'An imitation of Spenser', it's clever in its own way, but to the modern eye it is no longer humorous:

In ev'ry village mark'd with little spire,
Embow'r'd in trees, and hardly known to fame,
There dwells, in lowly shed, and mean attire,
A matron old, whom we school-mistress name;
Who boasts unruly brats with birch to tame;
They grieven sore, in piteous durance pent,
Aw'd by the pow'r of this relentless dame;
And oft-times, on vagaries idly bent,
For unkempt hair, or task unconn'd, are sorely shent.

And all in sight doth rise a birchen tree,
Which learning near her little dome did stowe;
Whilom a twig of small regard to see,
Tho' now so wide its waving branches flow;
And work the simple vassals mickle woe;
For not a wind might curl the leaves that blew,
But their limbs shudder'd, and their pulse beat low;
And, as they look'd, they found their horror grew,
And shap'd it into rods, and tingled at the view.

So have I seen (who has not, may conceive,)
A lifeless phantom near a garden plac'd;
So doth it wanton birds of peace bereave,
Of sport, of song, of pleasure, of repast;
They start, they stare, they wheel, they look aghast:
Sad servitude! such comfortless annoy
May no bold Briton's riper age e'er taste!
Ne superstition clog his dance of joy,
Ne vision empty, vain, his native bliss destroy.

Near to this dome is found a patch so green,
On which the tribe their gambols do display;
And at the door impris'ning board is seen,
Lest weakly wights of smaller size should stray;
Eager, perdie, to bask in sunny day!

The noises intermix'd, which thence resound,
Do learning's little tenement betray:
Where sits the dame, disguis'd in look profound,
And eyes her fairy throng, and turns her wheel around.

Her cap, far whiter than the driven snow,
Emblem right meet of decency does yield:
Her apron dy'd in grain, as blue, I trowe,
As is the hare-bell that adorns the field:
And in her hand, for scepter, she does wield
Tway birchen sprays; with anxious fear entwin'd,
With dark distrust, and sad repentance fill'd;
And stedfast hate, and sharp affliction join'd,
And fury uncontroul'd, and chastisement unkind.

So far we have heard little from eighteenth-century women poets, but the theme of childhood introduces Mary Barber, a Dublin-based poet admired by Swift. She had nine children of her own, and wrote many of her best poems about or to them. She wasn't keen on the British mania for flagellating children, as a poem for her son makes clear. It's an early plea for what I suppose we would think of as modern education:

Our master, in a fatal hour,
Brought in this Rod, to shew his pow'r.
O dreadful birch! O baleful tree!
Thou instrument of tyranny!
Thou deadly damp to youthful joys!
The sight of thee our peace destroys.
Not Damocles, with greater dread,
Beheld the weapon o'er his head.

That sage was surely more discerning,
Who taught to play us into learning,
By graving letters on the dice:
May heav'n reward the kind device,
And crown him with immortal fame,
Who taught at once to read and game!

Take my advice; pursue that rule;
You'll make a fortune by your school.
You'll soon have all the elder brothers,
And be the darling of the mothers.

O may I live to hail the day,
When boys shall go to school to play!
To grammar rules we'll bid defiance;
For play will then become a science.

Anyone familiar with eighteenth-century portraiture would have noticed that boys, up to a certain age, were still mostly kitted out in dresses rather than trousers. After five or so, they were strapped into tight breeches, collars and shoes. Mary Barber was clearly sympathetic. She apparently encouraged her son to recite this:

What is it our mammas bewitches,
To plague us little boys with breeches?
To tyrant Custom we must yield,
Whilst vanquish'd Reason flies the field.
Our legs must suffer by ligation,
To keep the blood from circulation;
And then our feet, tho' young and tender,
We to the shoemakers surrender;
Who often makes our shoes so strait,
Our growing feet they cramp and fret;
Whilst, with contrivance most profound,
Across our insteps we are bound;

Which is the cause, I make no doubt,
Why thousands suffer in the gout.
Our wiser ancestors wore brogues,
Before the surgeons brib'd these rogues,
With narrow toes, and heels like pegs,
To help to make us break our legs.
Then, ere we know to use our fists,
Our mothers closely bind our wrists;
And never think our cloaths are neat,
Till they're so tight we cannot eat.
And, to increase our other pains,
The hatband helps to cramp our brains.
The cravat finishes the work,
Like bowstring sent from the Grand Turk.
Thus dress, that should prolong our date,
Is made to hasten on our fate.
Fair privilege of nobler natures,
To be more plagu'd than other creatures!
The wild inhabitants of air
Are cloath'd by heav'n with wondrous care:
Their beauteous, well-compacted feathers
Are coats of mail against all weathers;
Enamell'd, to delight the eye;
Gay as the bow that decks the sky.
The beasts are cloath'd with beauteous skins:
The fishes arm'd with scales and fins;
Whose lustre lends the sailor light,
When all the stars are hid in night.
O were our dress contriv'd like these,
For use, for ornament, and ease!

Dublin, not just under Swift's influence, became a major centre of poetry and literature during the eighteenth century. Edinburgh, the city of philosophers, followed some way behind. Apart from Allan Ramsay, the father of the more famous painter, by far the most important contemporary poet before Burns was Robert Fergusson. There is a striking statue of him on Edinburgh's Royal Mile. He's young, he's thin, and even cast in metal he looks peakily malnourished. He died, ridiculously young, at twenty-four, but not before he had mocked the grandees of Edinburgh to their furious embarrassment, and perfected a rollicking verse form that Burns would appropriate with startling success. In 'The Daft Days' he shows that the wild New Year celebrations for which Scotland is famous around the world go back a long way. The poem is in Scots, but mostly easily comprehensible when spoken out loud.

Now mirk December's dowie face
Glours our the rigs wi' sour grimace,
While, thro' his minimum of space,
The bleer-ey'd sun
Wi' blinkin light and stealing pace,
His race doth run.

From naked groves nae birdie sings,
To shepherd's pipe nae hillock rings,
The breeze nae od'rous flavour brings
From Borean cave,
And dwyning nature droops her wings,
Wi' visage grave.

Mankind but scanty pleasure glean
Frae snawy hill or barren plain,
Whan Winter, 'midst his nipping train,
Wi' frozen spear,
Sends drift owr a' his bleak domain,
And guides the weir ...

Fiddlers, your pins in temper fix,
And roset weel your fiddle-sticks,
But banish vile Italian tricks
From out your quorum,
Nor fortes wi' pianos mix,
Gie's Tulloch Gorum.*

For naught can cheer the heart sae weil
As can a canty Highland reel,
It even vivifies the heel
To skip and dance:
Lifeless is he what canna feel
Its influence.

Let mirth abound, let social cheer
Invest the dawning of the year;
Let blithesome innocence appear
To crown our joy,
Nor envy wi' sarcastic sneer
Our bliss destroy.

And thou, great god of Aqua Vitæ!
Wha sways the empire of this city,
When fou we're sometimes capernoity,
Be thou prepar'd
To hedge us frae that black banditti,
The City-Guard.†

No part of the British Isles was as godly as Scotland; and this is a godly age, a time of religious revivalism which has given us many of the hymns still sung up and down the country. Isaac Watts – 'When

---

* A wild fiddle tune.

† The notoriously aggressive and violent Edinburgh civic police, with whom Fergusson was always falling out.

I Survey the Wondrous Cross' – and Charles Wesley – 'Jesu, Lover of My Soul' – are two of the most famous hymn-writers of all. I, however, prefer the extraordinary Christopher Smart. Plagued with madness and dying in a debtors' prison, Smart was a genius, and admired as such by the great Samuel Johnson. His Christmas Day hymn, particularly in its second half, is in my view the single finest religious work between George Herbert and the present day.

Where is this stupendous stranger,
Swains of Solyma, advise?
Lead me to my Master's manger,
Show me where my Saviour lies.

O Most Mighty! O Most Holy!
Far beyond the seraph's thought,
Art thou then so mean and lowly
As unheeded prophets taught?

O the magnitude of meekness!
Worth from worth immortal sprung;
O the strength of infant weakness,
If eternal is so young!

If so young and thus eternal,
Michael tune the shepherd's reed,
Where the scenes are ever vernal,
And the loves be Love indeed!

See the God blasphem'd and doubted
In the schools of Greece and Rome;
See the pow'rs of darkness routed,
Taken at their utmost gloom.

Nature's decorations glisten
Far above their usual trim;

Birds on box and laurels listen,
As so near the cherubs hymn.

Boreas now no longer winters
On the desolated coast;
Oaks no more are riv'n in splinters
By the whirlwind and his host.

Spinks and ouzels sing sublimely,
'We too have a Saviour born';
Whiter blossoms burst untimely
On the blest Mosaic thorn.

God all-bounteous, all-creative,
Whom no ills from good dissuade,
Is incarnate, and a native
Of the very world He made.

Smart is also the author of the most extraordinary animal poem of
the eighteenth century, deeply odd though it is. It's about his cat,
Jeoffry; and it's a religious poem which, as in the above hymn,
extends the divine deep into the animal world. There's no real
excuse for including it in an account of Britishness through poetry,
except that we are an animal-loving people – and it's irresistible.

For I will consider my Cat Jeoffry.
For he is the servant of the Living God duly and daily
    serving him.
For at the first glance of the glory of God in the East he
    worships in his way.
For this is done by wreathing his body seven times round
    with elegant quickness.
For then he leaps up to catch the musk, which is the
    blessing of God upon his prayer.

For he rolls upon prank to work it in.

For having done duty and received blessing he begins to consider himself.

For this he performs in ten degrees.

For first he looks upon his forepaws to see if they are clean.

For secondly he kicks up behind to clear away there.

For thirdly he works it upon stretch with the forepaws extended.

For fourthly he sharpens his paws by wood.

For fifthly he washes himself.

For sixthly he rolls upon wash.

For seventhly he fleas himself, that he may not be interrupted upon the beat.

For eighthly he rubs himself against a post.

For ninthly he looks up for his instructions.

For tenthly he goes in quest of food.

For having consider'd God and himself he will consider his neighbour.

For if he meets another cat he will kiss her in kindness.

For when he takes his prey he plays with it to give it a chance.

For one mouse in seven escapes by his dallying.

For when his day's work is done his business more properly begins.

For he keeps the Lord's watch in the night against the adversary.

For he counteracts the powers of darkness by his electrical skin and glaring eyes.

For he counteracts the Devil, who is death, by brisking about the life.

For in his morning orisons he loves the sun and the sun loves him.

For he is of the tribe of Tiger ...

This reminds one of William Blake, and not simply for the tiger reference. Smart has Blake's utter originality of vision. We will come to Blake in the next chapter, but before we do there is one other essential mid-eighteenth-century poet who, like Smart, suffered from mental illness and found succour in evangelical Christianity. Is there anyone who can pull together the different strains of mock-heroic, desperate desire for poise, beady-eyed description, deep religious sentiment and delight in rural life that have linked so many of the poems in this section? Is there anyone who stands for the spirit of the age in the two generations after Pope? Step forward the slight, nervous-looking yet quietly devastating personality that is William Cowper.

Cowper was a brilliant student and unrequited lover who suffered a breakdown, and three times attempted to kill himself, before finding salvation among friends in the small Buckinghamshire town of Olney. There he met John Newton, a former slaver who had been converted to Christianity and who wrote 'Amazing Grace'. The anti-slavery movement had provided a major theme in English poetry, from the writings of Daniel Defoe to Hannah More and the Nigerian freed slave Olaudah Equiano, but Cowper wrote more elegantly and angrily on the theme than anyone else. He was simply a more sympathetic soul than Pope, and perhaps even more tortured. He understood very well the importance of rhythm, fresh air and routine in trying to hold back the fear of insanity; and he did his very best. He was an attentive listener and good friend to female companions, a lover of animals, and a witty society poet. Yet below all this, a bubbling and too-harsh sense of his own imminent damnation kept him from happiness. It was, as we've seen, a nautical age, and Cowper found the sea a ubiquitous and threatening metaphor, as in his most famous hymn, one which has dug deep into the consciousness of the British:

God moves in a mysterious way
His wonders to perform;
He plants His footsteps in the sea,
And rides upon the storm.

Deep in unfathomable mines
Of never-failing skill
He treasures up His bright designs,
And works His sovereign will.

Ye fearful saints, fresh courage take,
The clouds ye so much dread
Are big with mercy, and shall break
In blessings on your head.

Judge not the Lord by feeble sense,
But trust Him for His grace;
Behind a frowning providence
He hides a smiling face.

His purposes will ripen fast,
Unfolding every hour;
The bud may have a bitter taste,
But sweet will be the flower.

Blind unbelief is sure to err,
And scan his work in vain;
God is His own interpreter,
And He will make it plain.

In an even greater poem, 'The Castaway', Cowper draws a devastating analogy between the story of a British seaman lost overboard during a recent voyage of Admiral Anson, and his own sense of being psychologically and religiously adrift. In it we feel the full force of Protestant individualism, that shift in religious sensibility so foreign to Alexander Pope:

Obscurest night involv'd the sky,
Th' Atlantic billows roar'd,
When such a destin'd wretch as I,
Wash'd headlong from on board,
Of friends, of hope, of all bereft,
His floating home for ever left.

No braver chief could Albion boast
Than he with whom he went,
Nor ever ship left Albion's coast,
With warmer wishes sent.
He lov'd them both, but both in vain,
Nor him beheld, nor her again.

Not long beneath the whelming brine,
Expert to swim, he lay;
Nor soon he felt his strength decline,
Or courage die away;
But wag'd with death a lasting strife,
Supported by despair of life.

He shouted: nor his friends had fail'd
To check the vessel's course,
But so the furious blast prevail'd,
That, pitiless perforce,
They left their outcast mate behind,
And scudded still before the wind.

Some succour yet they could afford;
And, such as storms allow,
The cask, the coop, the floated cord,

Delay'd not to bestow.
But he (they knew) nor ship, nor shore,
Whate'er they gave, should visit more.

No voice divine the storm allay'd,
No light propitious shone;
When, snatch'd from all effectual aid,
We perish'd, each alone:
But I beneath a rougher sea,
And whelm'd in deeper gulfs than he.

It's possible that Cowper was saved from madness by the writing of
poetry – he thought so – and his biggest poem, 'The Task', begins
in a mock-heroic way Pope would thoroughly have approved of:
one of his female patrons gave him the job of writing a poem about
that humblest of objects, a sofa. Cowper's response raced away in
all directions, from descriptions of winter walks in the snow, the
delight of reading newspapers, the joy of garden sheds, English
patriotism, the horror of city filth, the delight of being curled up in
front of the fire with a book, to his most passionate denunciations
of slavery. Has any major English poem started with such a bathetic
line as 'I sing the sofa'? But has any rambled to greater effect? Here
he is on slavery:

My ear is pained,
My soul is sick with every day's report
Of wrong and outrage with which earth is filled.
There is no flesh in man's obdurate heart,
It does not feel for man. The natural bond
Of brotherhood is severed as the flax
That falls asunder at the touch of fire.
He finds his fellow guilty of a skin
Not coloured like his own, and having power
To enforce the wrong, for such a worthy cause
Dooms and devotes him as his lawful prey.

Lands intersected by a narrow frith
Abhor each other. Mountains interposed,
Make enemies of nations who had else
Like kindred drops been mingled into one.
Thus man devotes his brother, and destroys;
And worse than all, and most to be deplored
As human nature's broadest, foulest blot,
Chains him, and tasks him, and exacts his sweat
With stripes, that mercy with a bleeding heart
Weeps when she sees inflicted on a beast.
Then what is man? And what man seeing this,
And having human feelings, does not blush
And hang his head, to think himself a man?
I would not have a slave to till my ground,
To carry me, to fan me while I sleep,
And tremble when I wake, for all the wealth
That sinews bought and sold have ever earned.
No: dear as freedom is, and in my heart's
Just estimation prized above all price,
I had much rather be myself the slave
And wear the bonds, than fasten them on him.
We have no slaves at home. – Then why abroad?

That's as great political writing as we see in any of the speeches of
Wilberforce. But 'The Task' is a narrative poem of many moods, and
a simple delight in being alive is one of them. The winter walk
sequence is as glittering as anything by Tolstoy:

'Tis morning; and the sun, with ruddy orb
Ascending, fires the horizon; while the clouds,
That crowd away before the driving wind,
More ardent as the disk emerges more,
Resemble most some city in a blaze,
Seen through the leafless wood. His slanting ray
Slides ineffectual down the snowy vale,

And, tingeing all with his own rosy hue,
From every herb and every spiry blade
Stretches a length of shadow o'er the field.
Mine, spindling into longitude immense,
In spite of gravity, and sage remark
That I myself am but a fleeting shade,
Provokes me to a smile. With eye askance
I view the muscular proportion'd limb
Transform'd to a lean shank. The shapeless pair
As they design'd to mock me, at my side
Take step for step; and as I near approach
The cottage, walk along the plaster'd wall,
Preposterous sight! the legs without the man.
The verdure of the plain lies buried deep
Beneath the dazzling deluge; and the bents
And coarser grass, upspearing o'er the rest,
Of late unsightly and unseen, now shine
Conspicuous, and in bright apparel clad,
And fledged with icy feathers, nod superb.
The cattle mourn in corners, where the fence
Screens them, and seem half petrified to sleep
In unrecumbent sadness. There they wait
Their wonted fodder; not like hungering man,
Fretful if unsupplied; but silent, meek,
And patient of the slow-paced swain's delay.
He from the stack carves out the accustom'd load,
Deep plunging, and again deep plunging oft,
His broad keen knife into the solid mass:
Smooth as a wall the upright remnant stands,
With such undeviating even force
He severs it away: no needless care,
Lest storms should overset the leaning pile
Deciduous, or its own unbalanced weight.
Forth goes the woodman, leaving unconcern'd
The cheerful haunts of man; to wield the axe

And drive the wedge in yonder forest drear,
From morn to eve his solitary task.
Shaggy, and lean, and shrewd, with pointed ears
And tail cropp'd short, half lurcher and half cur,
His dog attends him. Close behind his heel
Now creeps he slow; and now, with many a frisk
Wide scampering, snatches up the driften snow
With ivory teeth, or ploughs it with his snout;
Then shakes his powder'd coat, and barks for joy.

Great English poets tend to be animal lovers, from Chaucer to
Adrian Mitchell, and the same is true of William Cowper. Smart
had his cat in the lunatic asylum with him. Cowper had a pet hare,
Tiney:

Here lies, whom hound did ne'er pursue,
Nor swifter greyhound follow,
Whose foot ne'er tainted morning dew,
Nor ear heard huntsman's hallo',

Old Tiney, surliest of his kind,
Who, nurs'd with tender care,
And to domestic bounds confin'd,
Was still a wild Jack-hare.

Though duly from my hand he took
His pittance ev'ry night,
He did it with a jealous look,
And, when he could, would bite.

His diet was of wheaten bread,
And milk, and oats, and straw,
Thistles, or lettuces instead,
With sand to scour his maw.

On twigs of hawthorn he regal'd,
On pippins' russet peel;
And, when his juicy salads fail'd,
Slic'd carrot pleas'd him well.

A Turkey carpet was his lawn,
Whereon he lov'd to bound,
To skip and gambol like a fawn,
And swing his rump around.

His frisking was at evening hours,
For then he lost his fear;
But most before approaching show'rs,
Or when a storm drew near.

Eight years and five round rolling moons
He thus saw steal away,
Dozing out all his idle noons,
And ev'ry night at play.

I kept him for his humour's sake,
For he would oft beguile
My heart of thoughts that made it ache,
And force me to a smile.

But now, beneath this walnut-shade
He finds his long, last home,
And waits in snug concealment laid,
Till gentler puss shall come.

He, still more aged, feels the shocks
From which no care can save,
And, partner once of Tiney's box,
Must soon partake his grave.

241

Cowper is clearly still part of the world that valued poise, gentility and belief in a British mildness, reacting to both Puritan zeal and Restoration cynicism – retire to the country, pay women arch compliments, fear God. Equally obviously, with his rage against injustice, his empathy and his inner leaping demons, he's looking ahead to a different national atmosphere. The Romantics claimed him as one of their own; and he's a suitable entry point for the looming age of revolution.

9

The
Revolution

During the second half of the eighteenth century and into the nineteenth, the British experienced a series of vast economic and social shocks, which add up to a revolution from above. The look of these islands changed dramatically; the way the British people lived changed dramatically; so did where they lived, and their relationship with the rest of the world. Like a chemical ignition, this was the result of different elements and forces, which had been present for a long time, suddenly being brought together. The first, which affected poetry most, was the change in the countryside. Anciently, most of Britain had been farmed using open field systems and common grazing – a land without grids of fence or hedge, worked by traditional communities, sharing and sprawling. The enclosure of some land, making it private property, had begun in medieval times, and was a feature of Tudor England in particular. But it was during the later decades of the eighteenth century that the Enclosure Acts most radically transformed the countryside. They tamed and reduced ancient ecosystems, but allowed the Industrial Revolution full rein. The productivity of the land leapt ahead. Much more food was produced, by far fewer people.

More sophisticated crop rotation, using turnips and clover; better ploughs and drilling machines; higher-yielding grain types – who could be against such things? And indeed, between 1700 and 1800 the average yields of wheat, barley, oats and rye almost doubled. More food means more people: the population also almost doubled in these years. At the beginning of the century it was around 5.7 million. That was, historically, a relatively 'normal' population – not much different from that of the high Middle Ages (say, around 1350) or at the beginning of the civil wars. Then, however, with the cheap food brought about by the agricultural revolution, our population rose to just a little under nine million. In today's terms, of course, that is tiny, but at the time it must have felt a huge change.

Particularly so because the population moved as well. Britain is not only surrounded by windy, navigable waters, but is partly built on coal, iron and other useful mineral resources. The Industrial Revolution began relatively modestly, in relatively out-of-the-way places. It took London a long time to notice, but there was a water-powered silk-spinning operation in Derby from the 1720s; Thomas Newcomen's basic steam engine, invented in Cornwall in 1712, was first used in the Black Country shortly afterwards to keep coalmines free from water; coke-fuelled blast furnaces were being used in Coalbrookdale, Shropshire, from 1709; Northampton had a spinning factory from 1743. As one technical innovation provoked the next in a tumbling cascade of change, the necessary labour force was tramping from the enclosed and changing rural landscape seeking work in the new factories and the new cities – industrial London, Birmingham, Stoke-on-Trent, Manchester, Glasgow. By the middle of the century, industrialisation was staining the air over great swathes of Britain, and was still accelerating at frenetic speed.

More food; more machines; more stuff; more people. And at the same time British naval superiority meant that new things were being imported from China, India and the American and Caribbean colonies. The cheap, addictive calories provided by sugar cane were matched by new, exotic little luxuries – tea and coffee, and chinaware and tobacco. Unguided by any statesman or party, unprepared by any philosopher, the British found themselves in the cockpit of the global shift in human behaviour we call capitalism.

How did it feel? What did ordinary people think of it? All changes threaten, and this one threatened millions. In the countryside, ancient ways of life were ending. In the cities, swarming numbers of the new poor seethed. Technologies created new jobs, and then suddenly they disappeared again. Despite the new luxuries and the new wealth, revolution was in the air. 'The rights of man' was the slogan invented not by any American revolutionary nor any French Jacobin, but by England's Thomas Paine. To the elites of Westminster and the royal court, the fashionable belief in 'democracy' was a terrifying threat. Would it not lead to the tumbrils rolling up The Strand?

For many poets, including some of the most influential outsiders in British literary history, the gusts of change were entirely exhilarating. We think of the young Wordsworth, before he turned into a crusty Tory, and revolutionary Shelley, and impetuous young John Keats. In truth, though, the spread of incendiary and challenging writing was much wider than that, and began well before William Wordsworth discovered France. Indeed, the impatient and hotheaded demand for change can be traced to the evangelical anti-slavery Christians of decades before. In this chapter I want to open up the range of what might be called the revolutionary British.

We start with the most gentle and perplexing revolutionary of all. William Blake saw God when he was a toddler, and experienced visions of angels throughout his life, including as he was sitting naked in his garden with his wife. He was a friend of many other British radicals, and a lifelong opponent of industrialism and repression. A boy and man of unusual sensitivity and strong passions, he was preoccupied by this problem above all: how does the artist respond to a fast-changing world without merely describing it, and without the traditional poetic and religious tools which – for instance – George Herbert or John Milton could turn to? An etcher and artist lacking the elite education of the day, Blake responded by creating his own cosmology, starting almost from scratch. He rejected the science of Newton and the rationalism of Locke in favour of his own confusing, brightly-coloured personal vision. Blake speculated that there had been an original man, whom he called Albion, who had been divided into four warring fragments of moral personality. Using scraps of Milton, the Bible, and his ideas of ancient British and druidical beliefs, he created complex allegorical poems which have still not been fully disentangled or explained. Probably they cannot be.

Blake not only produced some of the most intense, loaded lyrics ever written in English, but also lusciously illustrated visionary poems which are unlikely to appeal to the general reader, but contain passages worth savouring. The best of them include his 1793 poem 'Visions of the Daughters of Albion', whose central female character Oothoon is raped. The poem looks to America as a possible source of freedom from the hypocrisy, cruelty and rapacity of British society, and may have been influenced by Mary Wollstonecraft, whose *Vindication of the Rights of Woman* had been published in the previous year. If nothing else, it makes explicit Blake's detestation of his own times, from the way children were educated to the growing commercialisation of life and the countryside revolution, enriching clergy and landowners at the expense of farmworkers:

Does not the great mouth laugh at a gift, and the narrow
    eyelids mock
At the labour that is above payment? And wilt thou take
    the ape
For thy counsellor, or the dog for a schoolmaster to thy
    children?
Does he who contemns poverty, and he who turns with
    abhorrence
From usury feel the same passion, or are they moved alike?
How can the giver of gifts experience the delights of the
    merchant?
How the industrious citizen the pains of the
    husbandman?
How different far the fat fed hireling with hollow drum,

Who buys whole corn-fields into wastes, and sings upon
    the heath!
How different their eye and ear! How different the world
    to them!
With what sense does the parson claim the labour of the
    farmer?
What are his nets and gins and traps; and how does he
    surround him
With cold floods of abstraction, and with forests of
    solitude,
To build him castle and high spires, where kings and
    priests may dwell ...

But this is also a poem about the effect of religious hypocrisy and repression on sexuality, particularly of women. Blake believed that relations between men and women in the Britain of his day encouraged prurience and lust at the expense of true, generous human love – and that this perversion passed into the children of modern British marriages:

Must chilling, murderous thoughts obscure
The clear heaven of her eternal spring; to bear the wintry
    rage
Of a harsh terror, driv'n to madness, bound to hold a rod
Over her shrinking shoulders all the day, and all the night
To turn the wheel of false desire, and longings that wake
    her womb
To the abhorrèd birth of cherubs in the human form,
That live a pestilence and die a meteor, and are no more;
Till the child dwell with one he hates, and do the deed he
    loathes,
And the impure scourge force his seed into its unripe
    birth,
Ere yet his eyelids can behold the arrows of the day?

The poem ends with a magnificent denunciation of 'things as they are', and an affirmation of the beauty and sanctity of human life, that underpins everything Blake wrote. It has the energy and passion of John Milton himself:

Does the sun walk, in glorious raiment, on the secret floor
Where the cold miser spreads his gold; or does the bright
    cloud drop
On his stone threshold? Does his eye behold the beam
    that brings
Expansion to the eye of pity; or will he bind himself
Beside the ox to thy hard furrow? Does not that mild
    beam blot
The bat, the owl, the glowing tiger, and the king of night?
The sea-fowl takes the wintry blast for a cov'ring to her
    limbs,
And the wild snake the pestilence to adorn him with gems
    and gold;
And trees, and birds, and men behold their eternal joy.
Arise, you little glancing wings, and sing your infant joy!
Arise, and drink your bliss, for everything that lives is
    holy!

William Blake is much better known for his short lyrics, but they emerge, like little glittering offcuts, from his more difficult narrative poems. They contain small but energetic moral universes, but as a kind of propaganda they are deliberately disturbing. This is called 'The Poison Tree':

I was angry with my friend:
I told my wrath, my wrath did end.
I was angry with my foe:
I told it not, my wrath did grow.

And I watered it in fears,
Night and morning with my tears;
And I sunned it with smiles,
And with soft deceitful wiles.

And it grew both day and night,
Till it bore an apple bright.
And my foe beheld it shine.
And he knew that it was mine,

And into my garden stole
When the night had veiled the pole;
In the morning glad I see
My foe outstretched beneath the tree.

There are many more examples, but two of Blake's poems have dug their way into the consciousness of the British in a most unusual way. The first is 'The Tyger', a poem brimming with awe about creation at a time just before ideas of natural selection began to brew, but also perplexed at the one creation producing both cruelty and glory – experience and innocence wrapped up together in the same fallen world.

Tyger Tyger, burning bright,
In the forests of the night;
What immortal hand or eye,
Could frame thy fearful symmetry?

In what distant deeps or skies
Burnt the fire of thine eyes?
On what wings dare he aspire?
What the hand, dare seize the fire?

And what shoulder, & what art,
Could twist the sinews of thy heart?

And when thy heart began to beat,
What dread hand? & what dread feet?

What the hammer? what the chain,
In what furnace was thy brain?
What the anvil? what dread grasp,
Dare its deadly terrors clasp!

When the stars threw down their spears
And water'd heaven with their tears:
Did he smile his work to see?
Did he who made the Lamb make thee?

Tyger Tyger, burning bright,
In the forests of the night:
What immortal hand or eye,
Dare frame thy fearful symmetry?

The second of Blake's 'special' poems is of course 'Jerusalem', his splendid denunciation of industrialism and moral corruption which has, hilariously, become the unofficial theme – via the Suffragettes – of Conservative England. Blake would have been amused and appalled. He meant it to sting. It was a war-song against the way things are, not a celebration of them:

And did those feet in ancient time
Walk upon England's mountains green?
And was the holy Lamb of God
On England's pleasant pastures seen?

And did the Countenance Divine
Shine forth upon our clouded hills?
And was Jerusalem builded here
Among these dark Satanic mills?

Bring me my bow of burning gold:
Bring me my arrows of desire:
Bring me my spear: O clouds unfold!
Bring me my chariot of fire.

I will not cease from mental fight,
Nor shall my sword sleep in my hand
Till we have built Jerusalem
In England's green and pleasant land.

William Blake was the great revolutionary artist who changed the course of poetry in the eighteenth century, but there were plenty of other poets just as angry and, if more conventional, just as direct. 'Peter Pindar' was the pseudonym of the pugnacious, lantern-jawed Devon satirist John Wolcot. In his 'The Royal Tour' he didn't shrink from caricaturing King George III, down to his stutter, when on the seafront at Weymouth the king and his wife are confronted by a legless beggar, a former Royal Naval sailor.

A Sailor pops upon the Royal Pair,
On crutches borne – an object of despair:
His squalid beard, pale cheek, and haggard eye,
Though silent, pour for help a piercing cry.

'Who, who are you? What, what? hae, what are you?'
'A man, my liege, whom kindness never knew.'

'A sailor! Sailor, hae? You've lost a leg.'
'I know it, sir – which forces me to beg.
I've nine poor children, sir, besides a wife –
God bless them! The sole comforts of my life.'

'Wife and nine children, hae? – All, all alive?
No, no, no wonder that you cannot thrive.
Shame, shame, to fill your heart with such a train!

251

Shame to get brats for others to maintain!
Get, get a wooden leg, or one of cork:
Wood's cheapest – yes, get wood, and go to work.
But mind, mind, Sailor – hae, hae, hae – hear, hear –
Don't go to Windsor, mind, and cut one there:
That's dangerous, dangerous – there I place my traps –
Fine things, fine things, for legs of thieving chaps:
Best traps, my traps – take care – they bite, they bite,
And sometimes catch a dozen legs a night.'

The sailor explains that he is penniless, can't afford a wooden leg, and points out that he lost his first one serving his king and country. King George is unimpressed:

'Must not encourage vagrants – no, no, no –
Must not make laws, my lad, and break 'em too.
Where, where's your parish, hae? And where's your pass?
Well, make haste home – I've got, I've got no brass.'

This is surely as ferocious as any anti-war political poetry of the twentieth century, and considerably bolder than most of what's appeared in our own day. Yet radicals like Wolcot were increasingly caught by not wanting to appear to approve of the horrors of the French Revolution over the water, as he shows in his 'Hymn to the Guillotine':

Daughter of Liberty! whose knife
So busy chops the threads of life,
And frees from cumbrous clay the spirit;
Ah! why alone shall Gallia feel
The beauties of thy pond'rous steel?
Why must not Britain mark thy merit?

Hark! 'tis the dungeon's groan I hear;
And lo, a squalid band appear,

With sallow cheek, and hollow eye!
Unwilling, lo, the neck they bend;
Yet, through thy pow'r, their terrors end,
And with their heads the sorrows fly.

O let us view thy lofty grace;
To Britons shew thy blushing face,
And bless Rebellion's life – tir'd train!
Joy to my soul! she's on her way,
Led by her dearest friends, Dismay,
Death, and the Devil, and Tom Paine!

Paine was a friend of William Blake, and much admired by radicals across Britain. He would provide a catalytic role in two revolutions – the American and the French – and succour for many desperate Britons. Joseph Mather was an industrial worker, a file-maker, born in Sheffield's eloquently named Cack Alley. Methodist and ballad-maker, Mather composed this revolutionary hymn to the great radical:

God save great Thomas Paine,
His 'Rights of Man' explain
To every soul.
He makes the blind to see
What dupes and slaves they be,
And points out liberty,
From pole to pole.

Thousands cry 'Church and King'
That well deserve to swing,
All must allow:
Birmingham blush for shame,
Manchester do the same,
Infamous is your name,
Patriots vow.

Pull proud oppressors down,
Knock off each tyrant's crown,
And break his sword;
Down aristocracy,
Set up democracy,
And from hyprocrisy
Save us good Lord.

Why should despotic pride
Usurp on every side?
Let us be free:
Grant Freedom's arms success,
And all her efforts bless,
Plant through the universe
Liberty's Tree.

Facts are seditious things
When they touch courts and kings,
Armies are raised,
Barracks and bastilles built,
Innocence charged with guilt,
Blood most unjustly spilt,
Gods stand amazed.

Despots may howl and yell,
Though they're in league with hell
They'll not reign long;
Satan may lead the van,
And do the worst he can,
Paine and his 'Rights of Man'
Shall be my song.

It is, of course, an angry mimicry of the National Anthem. But
Joseph Mather, experiencing at first hand the human cost of
Britain's early Industrial Revolution, had good reason to be angry.

In another poem, a kind of anti-nature verse, he describes his home town as 'Sheffield the black':

Where slowly down the vale a river runs,
Of dark complexion like its crooked sons;
In a fair country, stands a filthy town,
By bugs and butchers held in high renown;
Sheffield the Black – in ugliness supreme;
Yet ugly Sheffield is my dirty theme.

Ah, luckless he, who in unhappy hour
Is doomed to walk our streets beneath the shower,
No friendly spout from the projecting paves,
The copious tribute of the clouds receives,
But headlong from the roof, in sooty showers,
Prone on the hapless passenger it pours.
While on our moonless evenings, dark and damp,
Imprudent thrift denies the public lamp
And many a dunghill graces many a street.

Whole streams of rubbish and whole seas of mud;
With turnip tops, potato peelings join,
And to their cast garments, peas and beans combine,
Providing pigs and ducks with goodly cheer;
To pigs and ducks our streets are ever dear,
May no audacious scavenger presume to wield the rake,
    the shovel or the broom.

Although we tend to see the blackened and hellish world of the early British Industrial Revolution through the eyes of Dickens, Engels and other Victorian writers, it was all too apparent by the end of the eighteenth century. James Woodhouse was a shoemaker and teacher whose descriptions of Birmingham and Wolverhampton remain vivid:

In parts, through prospects scattered far and near,
Part-glowing gleams and flickering flames appear,
Like new volcanoes made deep darkness nursed,
From cooking coals in ruddy brilliance burst;
While smoky curls in thickening columns rise,
Obscure the landscape and involve the skies.

Such urban descriptions, verbal versions of the paintings of Joseph Wright of Derby, aren't unique. But Woodhouse goes on to describe the actual noise and sight of the steam engines at work:

Here clanking engines vomit scalding streams,
And belch vast volumes of attendant steams –
There thundering forges, with pulsations loud
Alternate striking, pierce the pendant cloud;
While to these distant hills, respiring slow,
Furnaces' iron lungs loud-breathing blow,
Breaking abrupt on Superstition's ear,
And shrink the shuddering frame with shivering fear:
Obtruding on the heart, each heaving breath,
Some vengeful fiend, grim delegate of death!

This may not be the finest poetry, but without such dispatches from the front line of industrialism, as it were, it's harder to fully appreciate what William Blake was up to. Not every inhabitant of the new industrial cities, of course, was horrified – many celebrated what was happening. James Bisset moved from Perth in Scotland to Birmingham when he was thirteen to pursue a trade as a painter of enamelled boxes. He did well enough to buy a big house in later life, and opened Birmingham's first art gallery. In a long poem celebrating the city's vigour and wealth he imagines the old gods rambling through Birmingham:

They visited our Wharfs, and wond'ring, found
Some thousand tons of coal piled on the ground,
And scores of boats, in length full sixty feet,
With loads of mineral fuel quite replete;
Whilst carts and country waggons filled each space,
And loaded teams stood ranged around the place.
The gods beheld the whole with great surprise,
and asked, 'from whence we gained such large supplies?'

The lucky deities are then taken on a tour of chemical works, pin-makers, button factories and gun works, buckle-makers and toymakers. Unlike the radicals, James Bisset finds the prospect of women and children hard at work in the factories appealing and elevating:

Inventions curious, various kinds of toys,
Then occupied the time of men and boys,
And blooming girls at work were often seen,
And twice their ages joined was scarce fifteen,
Sent by their parents out their bread to seek,
Who'd earn, perhaps, some shillings in a week;
And many women, too, you might then see,
With children on their lap, or round the knee,
An honest livelihood intent to gain,
And their sweet infant race help to maintain.
Charmed with the sight, the gods the whole reviewed,
And seemed with admiration quite subdued.

In a society so hostile to the very idea of child labour, it's a shock to find an apparently adept and observant poet so cheerful about it. Blake, of course, took a very different view, lamenting the fate of the boy chimney sweeps in one of his most famous poems. So too did Mary Alcock, from Northamptonshire:

A chimney-sweeper's boy am I:
Pity my wretched fate!
Ah, turn your eyes; 'twould draw a tear,
Knew you my helpless state.

Far from my home, no parents I
Am ever doomed to see;
My master, should I sue to him,
He'd flog the skin from me.

Ah, dearest madam, dearest sir,
Have pity on my youth;
Though black, and covered o'er with rags,
I tell you naught but truth.

My feeble limbs, benumbed with cold,
Totter beneath the sack,
Which ere the morning dawn appears
Is loaded on my back.

My legs you see are burnt and bruised,
My feet are galled by stones,
My flesh for lack of food is gone,
I'm little else but bones.

Yet still my master makes me work,
Not spares me day or night;
His 'prentice boy he says I am,
And he will have his right.

'Up to the highest top', he cries,
'There all out chimney-sweep!'
With panting heart and weeping eyes,
Trembling I upwards creep.

But stop! no more – I see him come;
Kind sir, remember me!
Oh, could I hide me underground,
How thankful should I be!

Of the major poets who grappled with issues of political liberty, and the dark side of fast-changing rural and urban life, it's interesting that the two we remember both started out as ploughmen. In Ayrshire, Robert Burns found new ways to satirise the times, and celebrate his robust erotic life; hundreds of miles to the south, John Clare, perhaps the purest countryside poet in English history, would eventually go mad – driven so, perhaps, by the speed of change all around him.

Robert Burns has been very badly served by the annual boozy cult which has grown up around him, emphasising some of his most sentimental songs and his addiction to 'the lasses'. The real Burns was a tough-minded and radical figure whose best work punctures the hypocrisies of Presbyterian Scotland after the Union, and champions 'the bottom dog' just as much as did Blake. He is a top-flight poet, as admirers such as Wordsworth and Keats understood; but he has been obscured for English readers by his determination to write in the Scots dialect of Ayrshire. This was because, as he said himself, he simply wrote better in Scots, using the rich and salty word-hoard of the common people rather than trying to mimic London writers. The decision saved him from becoming yet another limp pre-Romantic poet, but it makes things harder for those not brought up with Scots. The result is that we know his lyrics and his songs better than his longer poems, though some of these, such as 'The Cotter's Saturday Night' and 'Tam O'Shanter', are very great indeed. Here is the opening of the latter, which shows that boozy men have always huddled together in welcoming pubs, and their wives have always been furious waiting for them:

When chapman billies leave the street,
And drouthy* neibors, neibors, meet;
As market days are wearing late,
And folk begin to tak the gate,
While we sit bousing at the nappy,
An' getting fou† and unco‡ happy,
We think na on the lang Scots miles,
The mosses, waters, slaps and stiles,
That lie between us and our hame,
Where sits our sulky, sullen dame,
Gathering her brows like gathering storm,
Nursing her wrath to keep it warm.

This truth fand honest Tam o' Shanter,
As he frae Ayr ae night did canter:
(Auld Ayr, wham ne'er a town surpasses,
For honest men and bonnie lasses).

O Tam! had'st thou but been sae wise,
As taen thy ain wife Kate's advice!
She tauld thee weel thou was a skellum,
A blethering, blustering, drunken blellum;
That frae November till October,
Ae market-day thou was na sober ...

Like so many of his generation – he was in his prime when the French Revolution broke out – Burns found himself torn between patriotism and a yearning for liberty. In his case, however, there was the question of which *patria* the patriotism was about – the new Hanoverian Great Britain, or the lost, broken Jacobite Scotland which Tobias Smollett had mourned. At different times Burns

---

* Thirsty.

† Drunk.

‡ Very.

leaned in different directions. What was consistent was his feeling for the poor and his contempt for the comfortably well-off and self-satisfied. His greatest satire is 'Holy Willie's Prayer': a hypocritical Presbyterian, who follows the doctrine that the saved are chosen by God ahead of time, squirms and oils up to the Creator. There's nothing else quite like this in British poetry, so I make no apology for including it in full.

O Thou, that in the heavens does dwell,
Wha, as it pleases best Thysel',
Sends ane to heaven an' ten to hell,
A' for Thy glory;
And no for onie guid or ill
They've done afore Thee!

I bless and praise Thy matchless might,
When thousands Thou hast left in night,
That I am here afore Thy sight,
For gifts an' grace.
A burning and a shining light
To a' this place.

What was I, or my generation,
That I should get sic exaltation,
I wha deserv'd most just damnation
For broken laws,
Sax thousand years ere my creation,
Thro' Adam's cause.

When from my mither's womb I fell,
Thou might hae plung'd me deep in hell,
To gnash my gooms, and weep and wail,
In burnin lakes,
Where damned devils roar and yell,
Chain'd to their stakes.

Yet I am here a chosen sample,
To show Thy grace is great and ample;
I'm here a pillar o' Thy temple,
Strong as a rock,
A guide, a buckler, and example,
To a' Thy flock.

O Lord, Thou kens what zeal I bear,
When drinkers drink, an' swearers swear,
An' singing here, an' dancin there,
Wi' great and sma';
For I am keepit by Thy fear
Free frae them a'.

But yet, O Lord! confess I must,
At times I'm fash'd wi' fleshly lust:
An' sometimes, too, in warldly trust,
Vile self gets in;
But Thou remembers we are dust,
Defil'd wi' sin.

O Lord! yestreen, Thou kens, wi' Meg –
Thy pardon I sincerely beg;
O! may't ne'er be a livin plague
To my dishonour,
An' I'll ne'er lift a lawless leg
Again upon her.

Besides, I farther maun allow,
Wi' Leezie's lass, three times I trow –
But Lord, that Friday I was fou,
When I cam near her;
Or else, Thou kens, Thy servant true
Wad never steer her.

Maybe Thou lets this fleshly thorn
Buffet Thy servant e'en and morn,
Lest he owre proud and high shou'd turn,
That he's sae gifted:
If sae, Thy han' maun e'en be borne,
Until Thou lift it.

Lord, mind Gaw'n Hamilton's deserts;
He drinks, an' swears, an' plays at cartes,
Yet has sae mony takin arts,
Wi' great and sma',
Frae God's ain priest the people's hearts
He steals awa'.

An' when we chasten'd him therefor,
Thou kens how he bred sic a splore,
An' set the warld in a roar
O' laughing at us; —
Curse Thou his basket and his store,
Kail an' potatoes.

Lord, hear my earnest cry and pray'r,
Against that Presbyt'ry o' Ayr;
Thy strong right hand, Lord make it bare
Upo' their heads;
Lord visit them, an' dinna spare,
For their misdeeds.

O Lord, my God! that glib-tongu'd Aiken,
My vera heart and flesh are quakin,
To think how we stood sweatin, shakin,
An' p—'d wi' dread,
While he, wi' hingin lip an' snakin,
Held up his head.

Lord, in Thy day o' vengeance try him,
Lord, visit them wha did employ him,
And pass not in Thy mercy by them,
Nor hear their pray'r,
But for Thy people's sake destroy them,
An' dinna spare.

But, Lord, remember me an' mine
Wi' mercies temporal and divine,
That I for grace an' gear may shine,
Excell'd by nane,
And a' the glory shall be Thine,
Amen, Amen!

Burns was a man of many moods – bawdy, sentimental, revolution-
ary, patriotic, as raw as clay and as refined as white sugar – so it's
impossible to begin to do him justice in a collection like this. But if
the revolutionary age was about a change in sensibility, new ways of
thinking about the world, then there are a couple of obvious Burns
poems which mark such a change they could hardly have been writ-
ten earlier, or by anybody else. 'A Man's a Man' – Burns himself
wrote in January 1795, 'the piece is not really poetry' – is the world-
famous anthem for universal brotherhood. It was influenced by
Thomas Paine, whose *Rights of Man* Burns had been reading. The
poet had also been affected by the trial of Thomas Muir, the
Scottish radical and democrat who had been led in chains to
Edinburgh after being seized for sedition. It's therefore a lean and
angry poem. As one of his biographers has noted, it's a triumph of
simple words: of its 263 words, 240 are monosyllables. Sometimes,
the plainer the better.

Is there for honest Poverty
That hings his head, an' a' that;
The coward slave – we pass him by,
We dare be poor for a' that!

For a' that, an' a' that.
Our toils obscure an' a' that,
The rank is but the guinea's stamp,
The Man's the gowd for a' that.

What though on hamely fare we dine,
Wear hoddin grey, an' a that;
Gie fools their silks, and knaves their wine;
A Man's a Man for a' that:
For a' that, and a' that,
Their tinsel show, an' a' that;
The honest man, tho' e'er sae poor,
Is king o' men for a' that.

Ye see yon birkie, ca'd a lord,
Wha struts, an' stares, an' a' that;
Tho' hundreds worship at his word,
He's but a coof for a' that:
For a' that, an' a' that,
His ribband, star, an' a' that:
The man o' independent mind
He looks an' laughs at a' that.

A prince can mak a belted knight,
A marquis, duke, an' a' that;
But an honest man's abon his might,
Gude faith, he maunna fa' that!
For a' that, an' a' that,
Their dignities an' a' that;
The pith o' sense, an' pride o' worth,
Are higher rank than a' that.

Then let us pray that come it may,
(As come it will for a' that,)
That Sense and Worth, o'er a' the earth,

Shall bear the gree, an' a' that.
For a' that, an' a' that,
It's coming yet for a' that,
That Man to Man, the world o'er,
Shall brothers be for a' that.

Its glorious, but it's not quite representative of Robert Burns, such
a wry and attentive humorist. Many people prefer 'To a Mouse',
which widens the circle of empathy to all living creatures. It has the
sense of balance of the early eighteenth century, combined with the
more empathetic and egalitarian instincts of its second half. People
were looking around them and noticing more than their forebears
had.

Wee, sleekit, cow'rin, tim'rous beastie,
O, what a panic's in thy breastie!
Thou need na start awa sae hasty,
Wi' bickering brattle!
I wad be laith to rin an' chase thee,
Wi' murd'ring pattle!

I'm truly sorry man's dominion,
Has broken nature's social union,
An' justifies that ill opinion,
Which makes thee startle
At me, thy poor, earth-born companion,
An' fellow-mortal!

I doubt na, whiles, but thou may thieve;
What then? poor beastie, thou maun live!
A daimen icker in a thrave
'S a sma' request;
I'll get a blessin wi' the lave,
An' never miss't!

Thy wee bit housie, too, in ruin!
It's silly wa's the win's are strewin!
An' naething, now, to big a new ane,
O' foggage green!
An' bleak December's winds ensuin,
Baith snell an' keen!

Thou saw the fields laid bare an' waste,
An' weary winter comin fast,
An' cozie here, beneath the blast,
Thou thought to dwell –
Till crash! the cruel coulter past
Out thro' thy cell.

That wee bit heap o' leaves an' stibble,
Has cost thee mony a weary nibble!
Now thou's turn'd out, for a' thy trouble,
But house or hald,
To thole the winter's sleety dribble,
An' cranreuch cauld!

But, Mousie, thou art no thy lane,
In proving foresight may be vain;
The best-laid schemes o' mice an' men
Gang aft agley,
An' lea'e us naught but grief an' pain,
For promis'd joy!

Still thou art blest, compar'd wi' me
The present only toucheth thee:
But, Och! I backward cast my e'e
On prospects drear!
An' forward, tho' I canna see,
I guess an' fear!

Scottish patriots will say that there is, in all the writing of the British Isles, nobody quite like Burns, and they are right. But there was another poet at the other end of the islands, very reminiscent of Robert Burns, with the same close attentiveness to the realities of rural life, the same eye for detail and the same wide-spreading sympathy. John Clare was the son of a Northamptonshire peasant farmer, and was only three when Burns died. Unlike Burns's experience of farming in Ayrshire, however, Clare saw at first hand the full effects of the enclosure movement which transformed East Anglia from an ancient blur of woodland, copses and higgledy-piggledy strip farming to the regimented food factory it is now. Neither Burns (though he spent much of his life in the cultured, dirty old city of Edinburgh) nor Clare (though he died after a long spell in Northamptonshire General Lunatic Asylum) experienced either industrialisation or the new urbanism for himself. They were both, to that extent, observers from the sidelines. Clare did not share Burns's radicalism, but his laments for the effects of the agricultural revolution have made him a patron saint for modern environmentalists and ecologists. George Monbiot has proposed that 13 July should be remembered each year for the birth of the poet as 'Clare Day', partly on the strength of his poem about a nightingale's nest. It's long and detailed, but that's the point: you can't know the price of progress unless you know what you are losing; and you can't know what you are losing unless you watch carefully.

> Up this green woodland-ride let's softly rove,
> And list the nightingale — she dwells just here.
> Hush! let the wood-gate softly clap, for fear
> The noise might drive her from her home of love;
> For here I've heard her many a merry year —
> At morn, at eve, nay, all the live-long day,
> As though she lived on song. This very spot,
> Just where that old-man's-beard all wildly trails
> Rude arbours o'er the road, and stops the way —
> And where that child its blue-bell flowers hath got,

Laughing and creeping through the mossy rails –
There have I hunted like a very boy,
Creeping on hands and knees through matted thorn
To find her nest, and see her feed her young.
And vainly did I many hours employ:
All seemed as hidden as a thought unborn.
And where those crimping fern-leaves ramp among
The hazel's under boughs, I've nestled down,
And watched her while she sung; and her renown
Hath made me marvel that so famed a bird
Should have no better dress than russet brown.
Her wings would tremble in her ecstasy,
And feathers stand on end, as 'twere with joy,
And mouth wide open to release her heart
Of its out-sobbing songs. The happiest part
Of summer's fame she shared, for so to me
Did happy fancies shapen her employ;
But if I touched a bush, or scarcely stirred,
All in a moment stopt. I watched in vain:
The timid bird had left the hazel bush,
And at a distance hid to sing again.
Lost in a wilderness of listening leaves,
Rich Ecstasy would pour its luscious strain,
Till envy spurred the emulating thrush
To start less wild and scarce inferior songs;
For while of half the year Care him bereaves,
To damp the ardour of his speckled breast;
The nightingale to summer's life belongs,
And naked trees, and winter's nipping wrongs,
Are strangers to her music and her rest.
Her joys are evergreen, her world is wide –
Hark! there she is as usual – let's be hush –
For in this black-thorn clump, if rightly guest,
Her curious house is hidden. Part aside
These hazel branches in a gentle way,

And stoop right cautious 'neath the rustling boughs,
For we will have another search to day,
And hunt this fern-strewn thorn-clump round and round;
And where this reeded wood-grass idly bows,
We'll wade right through, it is a likely nook:
In such like spots, and often on the ground,
They'll build, where rude boys never think to look –
Aye, as I live! her secret nest is here,
Upon this white-thorn stump! I've searched about
For hours in vain. There! put that bramble by –
Nay, trample on its branches and get near.
How subtle is the bird! she started out,
And raised a plaintive note of danger nigh,
Ere we were past the brambles; and now, near
Her nest, she sudden stops – as choking fear,
That might betray her home. So even now
We'll leave it as we found it: safety's guard
Of pathless solitudes shall keep it still.
See there! she's sitting on the old oak bough,
Mute in her fears; our presence doth retard
Her joys, and doubt turns every rapture chill.
Sing on, sweet bird! may no worse hap befall
Thy visions, than the fear that now deceives.
We will not plunder music of its dower,
Nor turn this spot of happiness to thrall;
For melody seems hid in every flower,
That blossoms near thy home. These harebells all
Seem bowing with the beautiful in song;
And gaping cuckoo-flower, with spotted leaves,
Seems blushing of the singing it has heard.
How curious is the nest; no other bird
Uses such loose materials, or weaves
Its dwelling in such spots: dead oaken leaves
Are placed without, and velvet moss within,
And little scraps of grass, and, scant and spare,

What scarcely seem materials, down and hair;
For from men's haunts she nothing seems to win.
Yet Nature is the builder, and contrives
Homes for her children's comfort, even here;
Where Solitude's disciples spend their lives
Unseen, save when a wanderer passes near
That loves such pleasant places. Deep adown,
The nest is made a hermit's mossy cell.
Snug lie her curious eggs in number five,
Of deadened green, or rather olive brown;
And the old prickly thorn-bush guards them well.
So here we'll leave them, still unknown to wrong,
As the old woodland's legacy of song.

There's the world the enclosures destroyed. There's the price paid for an industrialised and more populous country; and John Clare, who lived a hard life made worse by his alcoholism and periods of madness, dares us to forget it.

The only other poet who can really compare to John Clare in the particularity and directness of his description of England at the time of the enclosures and industrialisation is another rural man, but different in every other way. George Crabbe was a doctor and then a clergyman from the East Anglian coast, who spent his life in livings around the south of England. His long career meant that he emerged in the London of Samuel Johnson and Edmund Burke, the Tory politician-philosopher who became a patron of Crabbe's, and lived long enough to be admired by Walter Scott and Byron. Yet he's essentially pre-Romantic. In long descriptive poems and tales written in heroic couplets, he's a poet far more interested in describing the world around him – largely a rather depressing rural and small-town world, though full of memorable characters – than describing or exploring his own character, still less his soul. He is often compared to a realistic novelist, and if we want to look in any detail at what English rural life was actually like as the eighteenth century moved into the nineteenth, Crabbe is essential. He's not as poignant as Clare, and he has a pious, essentially pessimistic world-view that puts some people off. But at his best he is gloriously vigorous and informative. He wasn't 'political' in the sense that many poets were, but he had a lively sympathy for the poor and excluded which mirrors that of Wordsworth. In the early poem 'The Village', Crabbe describes an elderly farmworker,

> Who, propp'd on that rude staff, looks up to see
> The bare arms broken from the withering tree,
> On which, a boy, he climb'd the loftiest bough,
> Then his first joy, but his sad emblem now.
>
> He once was chief in all the rustic trade;
> His steady hand the straightest furrow made;
> Full many a prize he won, and still is proud
> To find the triumphs of his youth allow'd;
> A transient pleasure sparkles in his eyes,
> He hears and smiles, then thinks again and sighs:
> For now he journeys to his grave in pain;
> The rich disdain him; nay, the poor disdain;
> Alternate masters now their slave command,
> Urge the weak efforts of his feeble hand,
> And, when his age attempts its task in vain,
> With ruthless taunts, of lazy poor complain.

Here, from the same poem, is Crabbe's description of the poor-house, at the time a ubiquitous institution where everyone who couldn't afford to keep themselves ended up in misery and squalor. That Crabbe's lines strongly impressed such leading Tories as Johnson and Burke reminds us how cautious we have to be about making assumptions based on crude political categories:

> Yon house that holds the parish-poor,
> Whose walls of mud scarce bear the broken door;
> There, where the putrid vapours, flagging, play,

And the dull wheel hums doleful through the day; —
There children dwell who know no parents' care;
Parents, who know no children's love, dwell there!
Heart-broken matrons on their joyless bed,
Forsaken wives, and mothers never wed;
Dejected widows with unheeded tears,
And crippled age with more than childhood fears;
The lame, the blind, and, far the happiest they!
The moping idiot and the madman gay.

Here too the sick their final doom receive,
Here brought, amid the scenes of grief, to grieve,
Where the loud groans from some sad chamber flow,
Mix'd with the clamours of the crowd below;
Here, sorrowing, they each kindred sorrow scan,
And the cold charities of man to man:
Whose laws indeed for ruin'd age provide,
And strong compulsion plucks the scrap from pride;
But still that scrap is bought with many a sigh,
And pride embitters what it can't deny.

Say ye, oppress'd by some fantastic woes,
Some jarring nerve that baffles your repose;
Who press the downy couch, while slaves advance
With timid eye, to read the distant glance;
Who with sad prayers the weary doctor tease,
To name the nameless ever-new disease;
Who with mock patience dire complaints endure,
Which real pain and that alone can cure;
How would ye bear in real pain to lie,
Despised, neglected, left alone to die?
How would ye bear to draw your latest breath,
Where all that's wretched paves the way for death?

Such is that room which one rude beam divides,
And naked rafters form the sloping sides;
Where the vile bands that bind the thatch are seen,
And lath and mud are all that lie between;
Save one dull pane, that, coarsely patch'd, gives way
To the rude tempest, yet excludes the day:
Here, on a matted flock, with dust o'erspread,
The drooping wretch reclines his languid head;
For him no hand the cordial cup applies.

When, later in his career, Crabbe turns to directly describing the political controversies raging across Britain at the time of the French Revolution, he gives us both the sense of living arguments, and the acrid atmosphere of the day. In the first of *The Tales of 1812*, he portrays Justice Bolt, a high Tory churchman. Bolt is a man who prides himself on his public speaking, who loves the sound of his own voice, and so when he's travelling in a distant city – perhaps Manchester or Birmingham – he innocently turns up to one of the hundreds of discussion clubs in England at the time. Big mistake:

Now, dinner past, no longer he supprest
His strong dislike to be a silent guest;
Subjects and words were now at his command –
When disappointment frown'd on all he plann'd;
For, hark! – he heard amazed, on every side,
His church insulted and her priests belied;
The laws reviled, the ruling power abused,
The land derided, and its foes excused: –
He heard and ponder'd – What, to men so vile,
Should be his language? – For his threat'ning style
They were too many; – if his speech were meek,
They would despise such poor attempts to speak:
At other times with every word at will,
He now sat lost, perplex'd, astonish'd, still.

Here were Socinians, Deists, and indeed
All who, as foes to England's Church, agreed;
But still with creeds unlike, and some without a creed:
Here, too, fierce friends of liberty he saw,
Who own'd no prince and who obey no law;
There were reformers of each different sort,
Foes to the laws, the priesthood, and the court;
Some on their favourite plans alone intent,
Some purely angry and malevolent:
The rash were proud to blame their country's laws;
The vain, to seem supporters of a cause;
One call'd for change, that he would dread to see;
Another sigh'd for Gallic liberty!
And numbers joining with the forward crew,
For no one reason – but that numbers do.
'How,' said the Justice, 'can this trouble rise,
This shame and pain, from creatures I despise?'
And Conscience answer'd – 'The prevailing cause
Is thy delight in listening to applause;
Here, thou art seated with a tribe, who spurn
Thy favourite themes, and into laughter turn
Thy fears and wishes: silent and obscure,
Thyself, shalt thou the long harangue endure;
And learn, by feeling, what it is to force
On thy unwilling friends the long discourse:
What though thy thoughts be just, and these, it seems,
Are traitors' projects, idiots' empty schemes;
Yet minds, like bodies, cramm'd, reject their food,
Nor will be forced and tortured for their good!'
At length, a sharp, shrewd, sallow man arose,
And begg'd he briefly might his mind disclose;
'It was his duty, in these worst of times,
T'inform the govern'd of their rulers' crimes.'

Bolt is too intimidated, too scared, to take on this republican, a lawyer called Hammond. Later on, he gets his chance to hit back: Crabbe is usually thought of as a slightly dreary describer of places and people, but he can be very funny indeed. Here is Justice Bolt working himself up into a fine old temper:

> Alarm'd by this, he lash'd his soul to rage,
> Burn'd with strong shame, and hurried to engage.
> As a male turkey straggling on the green,
> When by fierce harriers, terriers, mongrels seen,
> He feels the insult of the noisy train
> And skulks aside, though moved by much disdain;
> But when that turkey, at his own barn-door,
> Sees one poor straying puppy and no more,
> (A foolish puppy who had left the pack,
> Thoughtless what foe was threat'ning at his back)
> He moves about, as ship prepared to sail,
> He hoists his proud rotundity of tail,
> The half-seal'd eyes and changeful neck he shows,
> Where, in its quick'ning colours, vengeance glows;
> From red to blue the pendent wattles turn,
> Blue mix'd with red, as matches when they burn;
> And thus th' intruding snarler to oppose,
> Urged by enkindling wrath, he gobbling goes.
> So look'd our hero in his wrath, his cheeks
> Flush'd with fresh fires and glow'd in tingling streaks.

In a culture which still seems obsessed by Wordsworth and Keats, I recommend Crabbe and Clare as better observers of the real England. George Crabbe's nature descriptions are full of desolation – lonely beaches, rivers clogged by weeds, grim heathland. John Clare's England, geographically just up the road from Crabbe country, is sunnier and more swarming with life. It's well worth tramping through, and inhaling, for its descriptions of schoolboys, peasant workers, badgers, noble old trees and the rest. Yet it's Clare's reflec-

tively autobiographical poem, simply called 'I Am', that provides the
fitting final words for this chapter on the British revolutions. If you
want to understand the sense of disorientation and loss that change
at such a rate produced, here are the essential lines; here's one of
George Crabbe's unfortunate rural workers actually speaking in his
own words:

I am: yet what I am none cares or knows,
My friends forsake me like a memory lost;
I am the self-consumer of my woes,
They rise and vanish in oblivious host,
Like shades in love and death's oblivion lost;
And yet I am! and live with shadows tost

Into the nothingness of scorn and noise,
Into the living sea of waking dreams,
Where there is neither sense of life nor joys,
But the vast shipwreck of my life's esteems;
And e'en the dearest – that I loved the best –
Are strange – nay, rather stranger than the rest.

I long for scenes where man has never trod;
A place where woman never smil'd or wept;
There to abide with my creator, God,
And sleep as I in childhood sweetly slept:
Untroubling and untroubled where I lie;
The grass below – above the vaulted sky.

10
Romantic Agonies

That last poem, John Clare's 'I Am', was composed late in his life, in the lunatic asylum, probably around 1845. But it's an emblematic Romantic work because it introduces something troubling about English Romanticism. The movement, associated with William Wordsworth, John Keats, Samuel Taylor Coleridge, Percy Shelley and (I think rather bizarrely) Lord Byron, is one of the glories of English letters. After Shakespeare, Keats is probably the best-loved English poet of all. So what's the problem? If you think of the work of the great poets we've discussed so far, from Chaucer through to John Donne, George Herbert, Swift, Burns and right up to John Clare, in each case a powerful personality and temperament shine through; but in each case these are writers describing aspects of the world around them, and problems of the human condition first and foremost. Their prime subject is not themselves – not even with Blake or Smart, the most idiosyncratic of poets.

This changes when the Romantic revolution arrives. Wordsworth, in particular, writes obsessively about himself. Landscape, memory, the social world of eighteenth-century Britain, even the French Revolution, he finds significant mainly because of their effect on his own personal development. The poet now becomes central to the project of poetry. It was an addictive idea: although he disdained Wordsworth (and was very funny about him), Byron's poetry seemed more about Byron than about the rest of the world.

Coleridge's *Rime of the Ancient Mariner* and 'Kubla Khan' are strange enough to escape the charge of self-obsession, even though these days we are taught to read the second poem mainly as an account of Coleridge's opium addiction. Keats the story, 'Keats the motion picture', overwhelm Keats the highly sophisticated poet ... And all the way through the nineteenth and twentieth centuries, poet after poet looks inward or into the mirror, or at the best backwards to other poets, for his or her prime subjects. I've found it very noticeable, writing this, that as we leave the eighteenth century, vivid descriptions of life as it actually is in Britain become harder, not easier, to find; and that is the fault (if it is a fault) of the Romantic movement. Wordsworth, beloved as he is, is the prime culprit, and the origin of a period of self-obsession in British verse – when The Poet, with swirling cape and flowing locks, jutting jaw and one hand on his breast, begins to pose, a little irritatingly, in front of the mere poem.

And yes, this only happens because Wordsworth is a great poet, and therefore so many people mimic him; just as we get lots of bubbling 'music' in Victorian poetry as scores of lesser talents try to copy Keats. But even so. And it starts early with Wordsworth. Take one of his famous 'Lucy' poems. It's not really a poem about an obscure girl in the Lake District – look at the last line.

She dwelt among the untrodden ways
Beside the springs of Dove,
A Maid whom there were none to praise
And very few to love:

A violet by a mossy stone
Half hidden from the eye!
Fair as a star, when only one
Is shining in the sky.

She lived unknown, and few could know
When Lucy ceased to be;
But she is in her grave, and, oh,
The difference to me!

Or take the opening of his 'Tintern Abbey', which appeared in the first edition of the famous *Lyrical Ballads* in 1798. It seems an uncomplicated tribute to the landscape of the Wye Valley, albeit with much less detail and vivid sensuality than we would get from, say, John Clare:

Five years have passed; five summers, with the length
Of five long winters! and again I hear
These waters, rolling from their mountain-springs
With a soft inland murmur. – Once again
Do I behold these steep and lofty cliffs,
That on a wild secluded scene impress
Thoughts of more deep seclusion; and connect
The landscape with the quiet of the sky.
The day is come when I again repose
Here, under this dark sycamore, and view
These plots of cottage-ground, these orchard-tufts,
Which at this season, with their unripe fruits,
Are clad in one green hue, and lose themselves
'Mid groves and copses. Once again I see
These hedge-rows, hardly hedge-rows, little lines
Of sportive wood run wild: these pastoral farms,
Green to the very door; and wreaths of smoke
Sent up, in silence, from among the trees!
With some uncertain notice, as might seem
Of vagrant dwellers in the houseless woods,
Or of some Hermit's cave, where by his fire
The Hermit sits alone.

It's very beautiful, if oddly general, but the idea of the hermit now reveals the poem's real subject – not the landscape, but the landscape's effect on William Wordsworth's inner soul:

> These beauteous forms,
> Through a long absence, have not been to me
> As is a landscape to a blind man's eye:
> But oft, in lonely rooms, and 'mid the din
> Of towns and cities, I have owed to them,
> In hours of weariness, sensations sweet,
> Felt in the blood, and felt along the heart;
> And passing even into my purer mind
> With tranquil restoration:– feelings too
> Of unremembered pleasure: such, perhaps,
> As have no slight or trivial influence
> On that best portion of a good man's life,
> His little, nameless, unremembered, acts
> Of kindness and of love. Nor less, I trust,
> To them I may have owed another gift,
> Of aspect more sublime; that blessed mood,
> In which the burthen of the mystery,
> In which the heavy and the weary weight
> Of all this unintelligible world …

At which point – very sorry – he's lost me. In fact Wordsworth's best poems are those which grapple directly with what's changing inside himself. 'Intimations of Immortality' deals with something we find in many earlier poets, including Donne and Vaughan, as well as William Blake – the sense, or suspicion, that the human soul arrives on earth already imbued with a sense of delight and Paradise, a God-given inner joy which is slowly but remorselessly choked off by the business of being alive. Nobody, however, has said it as well as Wordsworth does here; and after this poem there's no point, frankly, in trying to say it again:

There was a time when meadow, grove, and stream,
The earth, and every common sight,
To me did seem
Apparelled in celestial light,
The glory and the freshness of a dream.
It is not now as it hath been of yore;—
Turn wheresoe'er I may,
By night or day.
The things which I have seen I now can see no more.

The Rainbow comes and goes,
And lovely is the Rose,
The Moon doth with delight
Look round her when the heavens are bare,
Waters on a starry night
Are beautiful and fair;
The sunshine is a glorious birth;
But yet I know, where'er I go,
That there hath passed away a glory from the earth.

Now, while the birds thus sing a joyous song,
And while the young lambs bound
As to the tabor's sound,
To me alone there came a thought of grief:
A timely utterance gave that thought relief,
And I again am strong:
The cataracts blow their trumpets from the steep;
No more shall grief of mine the season wrong;
I hear the Echoes through the mountains throng,
The Winds come to me from the fields of sleep,
And all the earth is gay;
Land and sea
Give themselves up to jollity,
And with the heart of May
Doth every Beast keep holiday;—

Thou Child of Joy,
Shout round me, let me hear thy shouts, thou happy
   Shepherd-boy.

Ye blessèd creatures, I have heard the call
Ye to each other make; I see
The heavens laugh with you in your jubilee;
My heart is at your festival,
My head hath its coronal,
The fulness of your bliss, I feel – I feel it all.
Oh evil day! if I were sullen
While Earth herself is adorning,
This sweet May-morning,
And the Children are culling
On every side,
In a thousand valleys far and wide,
Fresh flowers; while the sun shines warm,
And the Babe leaps up on his Mother's arm:–
I hear, I hear, with joy I hear!
But there's a Tree, of many, one,
A single field which I have looked upon,
Both of them speak of something that is gone;
The Pansy at my feet
Doth the same tale repeat:
Whither is fled the visionary gleam?
Where is it now, the glory and the dream?

Our birth is but a sleep and a forgetting:
The Soul that rises with us, our life's Star,
Hath had elsewhere its setting,
And cometh from afar:
Not in entire forgetfulness,
And not in utter nakedness,
But trailing clouds of glory do we come
From God, who is our home:

Heaven lies about us in our infancy!
Shades of the prison-house begin to close
Upon the growing Boy,
But he beholds the light, and whence it flows,
He sees it in his joy;
The Youth, who daily farther from the east
Must travel, still is Nature's Priest,
And by the vision splendid
Is on his way attended;
At length the Man perceives it die away,
And fade into the light of common day.

Wordsworth shows us that, amid all the political turmoil of the time, an ever more self-confident individualism was taking root in the British imagination. If one was going to be snippy about it, one might say that we were becoming a less social people, and a more introspective civilisation. That thought would presumably have horrified the young William Wordsworth, a vigorous enthusiast for the ideals of the French Revolution.

Indeed, one of the great advantages of Wordsworth in a project like this is that, charting his own mind, he charts a wider shift in the national mood, from a generous-spirited if perhaps naïve belief in brotherhood as the revolutionary ideas first spread, through to a much more nervous, patriotic distaste for the bloodshed of the Revolution as it developed. Wordsworth was in the vanguard of both the fervour and the embarrassed reaction against it. He was in France during the Revolution, and fell in love there. He wrote about this later on, but at the time he wrote his *Descriptive Sketches*, which were published in England in January 1793, just after the execution of King Louis XVI and just before Britain and France declared war. They were considered treasonable, and led to Wordsworth, with his sister Dorothy and his friend Coleridge, being spied upon by British government agents.

And oh, fair France! though now the traveller sees
Thy three-striped banner fluctuate on the breeze;
Though martial songs have banished songs of love,
And nightingales desert the village grove,
Scared by the fife and rumbling drum's alarms,
And the short thunder, and the flash of arms;
That cease not till night falls ...
– Yet, hast thou found that Freedom spreads her power
Beyond the cottage-hearth, the cottage-door:
All nature smiles, and owns beneath her eyes
Her fields peculiar, and peculiar skies ...
But foes are gathering – Liberty must raise
Red on the hills her beacon's far-seen blaze;
Must bid the tocsin ring from tower to tower! –
Nearer and nearer comes the trying hour!
Rejoice, brave Land, though pride's perverted ire
Rouse hell's own aid, and wrap thy fields in fire:
Lo, from the flames a great and glorious birth;
As if a new-made heaven were hailing a new earth!

Looking back on this period, Wordsworth gave perhaps the best ever description of the inflamed state of a young man captivated by the possibility of a revolutionary transformation in society:

Bliss was it in that dawn to be alive,
But to be young was very heaven! – Oh! times,
In which the meagre, stale, forbidding ways
Of custom, law, and statute, took at once
The attraction of a country in romance!
When Reason seemed the most to assert her rights,
When most intent on making of herself
A prime Enchantress – to assist the work
Which then was going forward in her name!
Not favoured spots alone, but the whole earth,
The beauty wore of promise, that which sets

(As at some moment might not be unfelt
Among the bowers of paradise itself)
The budding rose above the rose full blown.
What temper at the prospect did not wake
To happiness unthought of? The inert
Were roused ...

The Jacobin Revolution, with the widespread slaughter not only of aristocrats and the royal family but of priests, nuns, and many who simply fell out with the faction in power, quickly began to alter the atmosphere in Britain. Napoleon Bonaparte's dictatorship and general European war further hardened feelings, and Wordsworth was not alone in experiencing embarrassment about his former views and moving steadily towards support for the Conservative government. His friend Robert Southey did the same. Clare declared himself a simple 'king and country' man. Even Robert Burns signed up for the royal militia and wrote a patriotic anti-French song. But Wordsworth's apostasy was dramatic and full-hearted. He ended up writing ecclesiastical sonnets, supporting the death penalty and, in 'Ode to Duty', for instance, wholeheartedly renouncing his earlier self:

I, loving freedom, and untried;
No sport of every random gust,
Yet being to myself a guide,
Too blindly have reposed my trust:
And oft, when in my heart was heard
Thy timely mandate, I deferred
The task, in smoother walks to stray;
But thee I now would serve more strictly, if I may.

Through no disturbance of my soul,
Or strong compunction in me wrought,
I supplicate for thy control;
But in the quietness of thought:

Me this unchartered freedom tires;
I feel the weight of chance-desires:
My hopes no more must change their name,
I long for a repose that ever is the same.

Stern Lawgiver! yet thou dost wear
The Godhead's most benignant grace;
Nor know we anything so fair
As is the smile upon thy face:
Flowers laugh before thee on their beds
And fragrance in thy footing treads;
Thou dost preserve the stars from wrong;
And the most ancient heavens, through Thee, are fresh
    and strong.

To humbler functions, awful Power!
I call thee: I myself commend
Unto thy guidance from this hour;
Oh, let my weakness have an end!
Give unto me, made lowly wise,
The spirit of self-sacrifice;
The confidence of reason give;
And in the light of truth thy Bondman let
    me live!

Wordsworth had become a major national figure who would go on to be Poet Laureate. Long-lived and outspoken, his political views really mattered, particularly in the period after Waterloo, when Britain experienced widespread political unrest and repression. His change of views horrified and dismayed many of his friends, who had been passionate republicans and remained so throughout the Napoleonic period. Percy Bysshe Shelley expressed his sadness in a poem directed at Wordsworth:

Poet of Nature, thou hast wept to know
That things depart which never may return:
Childhood and youth, friendship and love's first glow,
Have fled like sweet dreams, leaving thee to mourn.
These common woes I feel. One loss is mine
Which thou too feel'st, yet I alone deplore.
Thou wert as a lone star, whose light did shine
On some frail bark in winter's midnight roar:
Thou hast like to a rock-built refuge stood
Above the blind and battling multitude:
In honoured poverty thy voice did weave
Songs consecrate to truth and liberty, –
Deserting these, thou leavest me to grieve,
Thus having been, that thou shouldst cease to be.

The understanding of Wordsworth's greatness that Shelley shows in that poem reminds us how ungenerous it would be to end on a sour note. In terms of what it was like to be alive towards the end of the eighteenth century, the best poetry that Wordsworth produced is his autobiographical account of his Lake District boyhood in the long and evergreen *Prelude*. His was, still, an unfettered childhood, which allowed him to ramble, row boats, and in this case, to ice-skate:

And in the frosty season, when the sun
Was set, and visible for many a mile
The cottage windows through the twilight blaz'd,
I heeded not the summons: – happy time
It was, indeed, for all of us; to me
It was a time of rapture: clear and loud
The village clock toll'd six; I wheel'd about,
Proud and exulting, like an untired horse,
That cares not for its home. – All shod with steel,
We hiss'd along the polish'd ice, in games
Confederate, imitative of the chase

And woodland pleasures, the resounding horn,
The Pack loud bellowing, and the hunted hare.
So through the darkness and the cold we flew,
And not a voice was idle; with the din,
Meanwhile, the precipices rang aloud,
The leafless trees, and every icy crag
Tinkled like iron, while the distant hills
Into the tumult sent an alien sound
Of melancholy, not unnoticed, while the stars,
Eastward, were sparkling clear, and in the west
The orange sky of evening died away.

Looking back as a historian, it's all too easy to focus on the inconveniences, unfairness and general unpleasantness of life in earlier times. Wordsworth provides an excellent antidote, reminding us what a great deal of fun and freedom was also to be had in an emptier, fresher land:

We were a noisy crew, the sun in heaven
Beheld not vales more beautiful than ours,
Nor saw a race in happiness and joy
More worthy of the ground where they were sown.
I would record with no reluctant voice
The woods of autumn and their hazel bowers
With milk-white clusters hung; the rod and line,
True symbol of the foolishness of hope,
Which with its strong enchantment led us on
By rocks and pools, shut out from every star
All the green summer, to forlorn cascades
Among the windings of the mountain brooks.
– Unfading recollections! at this hour
The heart is almost mine with which I felt
From some hill-top, on sunny afternoons
The Kite high up among the fleecy clouds
Pull at its rein, like an impatient Courser,

Or, from the meadows sent on gusty days,
Beheld her breast the wind, then suddenly
Dash'd headlong; and rejected by the storm.

Wordsworth's lifelong friend, rival and comrade was the Devonshire poet Samuel Taylor Coleridge. Like Wordsworth he was an early revolutionary, plotting to set up a commune in Pennsylvania, where he could escape the conventions and limitations of life in Britain. Unlike Wordsworth, Coleridge rarely touched upon politics in his poetry; but when he did, he was even more savage. In the late 1790s the government of William Pitt the Younger gave military support to a French royalist uprising in the Vendée region. It was bloody. Coleridge responded with 'Fire, Famine and Slaughter: A War Eclogue'. Here, Slaughter is explaining to Fire and Famine that Pitt has sent her:

He came by stealth, and unlocked my den,
And I have drunk the blood since then
Of thrice three hundred thousand men.
Both: Who bade you do it?
Slaughter: The same! the same!
Letters four do form his name.
He let me loose, and cried Halloo!
To him alone the praise is due.
Famine: Thanks, sister, thanks! the men have bled,
Their wives and their children faint for bread.
I stood in a swampy field of battle;
With bones and skulls I made a rattle,
To frighten the wolf and carrion-crow
And the homeless dog – but they would not go.
So off I flew: for how could I bear
To see them gorge their dainty fare?

Coleridge, who later apologised to the prime minister, was hardly pulling his punches. In the poem he expands the attack to include the brutal effects of British repression in Ireland following the uprising there in 1797. In this case, it is Fire who speaks:

Sisters! I from Ireland came!
Hedge and corn-fields all on flame,
I triumphed o'er the setting sun!
And all the while the work was done,
On as I strode with my huge strides,
I flung back my head and I held my sides,
It was so rare a piece of fun
To see the sweltered cattle run
With uncouth gallop through the night,
Scared by the red and noisy light!
By the light of his own blazing cot
Was many a naked rebel shot:
The house-stream met the flame and hissed,
While crash! fell in the roof, I wist,
On some of those old bed-rid nurses,
That deal in discontent and curses.

Inseparable from their revolutionary fervour, Coleridge shared a sense of dislocation with Wordworth, whom he hugely influenced. Self-exile to rural obscurity was a prudent act. England in their day must have seemed much larger, and its remoter spots much more remote. In 'Frost at Midnight' we crouch alongside Coleridge and his sleeping child, one dark night long ago in Devon:

The Frost performs its secret ministry,
Unhelped by any wind. The owlet's cry
Came loud – and hark, again! loud as before.
The inmates of my cottage, all at rest,
Have left me to that solitude, which suits
Abstruser musings: save that at my side

My cradled infant slumbers peacefully.
'Tis calm indeed! so calm, that it disturbs
And vexes meditation with its strange
And extreme silentness. Sea, hill, and wood,
This populous village! Sea, and hill, and wood,
With all the numberless goings-on of life,
Inaudible as dreams! the thin blue flame
Lies on my low-burnt fire, and quivers not;
Only that film, which fluttered on the grate,
Still flutters there, the sole unquiet thing.
Methinks, its motion in this hush of nature
Gives it dim sympathies with me who live,
Making it a companionable form,
Whose puny flaps and freaks the idling Spirit
By its own moods interprets, every where
Echo or mirror seeking of itself,
And makes a toy of Thought …

At least for a short period, so close was Coleridge's relationship
with Wordsworth that it's almost impossible to work out who most
influenced whom; but Coleridge's sense of alienation from the
world around him was at least as intense as that of the Lakeland
poet. For me, 'Dejection: an Ode' demonstrates that Coleridge does
it better. I said before that Coleridge was a less political poet, and
that's true, but the Romantic alienation which we find also in
Continental radicals such as Heine and Schubert is itself a political
perspective. The artist rejects things as they are.

A grief without a pang, void, dark, and drear,
A stifled, drowsy, unimpassioned grief,
Which finds no natural outlet, no relief,
In word, or sigh, or tear –
O Lady! in this wan and heartless mood,
To other thoughts by yonder throstle woo'd,
All this long eve, so balmy and serene,

Have I been gazing on the western sky,
And its peculiar tint of yellow green:
And still I gaze – and with how blank an eye!
And those thin clouds above, in flakes and bars,
That give away their motion to the stars;
Those stars, that glide behind them or between,
Now sparkling, now bedimmed, but always seen:
Yon crescent Moon, as fixed as if it grew
In its own cloudless, starless lake of blue;
I see them all so excellently fair,
I see, not feel, how beautiful they are!

My genial spirits fail;
And what can these avail
To lift the smothering weight from off my breast?
It were a vain endeavour,
Though I should gaze for ever
On that green light that lingers in the west:
I may not hope from outward forms to win
The passion and the life, whose fountains are within.

Again unlike Wordsworth, Coleridge responds by creating entirely new worlds of his own. *The Rime of the Ancient Mariner*, which first appeared in *Lyrical Ballads*, and the hallucinatory 'Kubla Khan' of 1797 are each connected to the real Britain of the turn of the century, in which stories of harsh sea voyages and tales of discovery in China were popular, but Coleridge's magical music turns each into something quite other, rich and strange. Here are the famous stanzas of the former when the albatross has been shot and the ship is becalmed. To the most highly intelligent and well-informed minds of the age, this world was still a much more mysterious and at times threatening place:

All in a hot and copper sky,
The bloody Sun, at noon,

Right up above the mast did stand,
No bigger than the Moon.

Day after day, day after day,
We stuck, nor breath nor motion;
As idle as a painted ship
Upon a painted ocean.

Water, water, every where,
And all the boards did shrink;
Water, water, every where,
Nor any drop to drink.

The very deep did rot: O Christ!
That ever this should be!
Yea, slimy things did crawl with legs
Upon the slimy sea.

About, about, in reel and rout
The death-fires danced at night;
The water, like a witch's oils,
Burnt green, and blue and white.

This poem, and 'Kubla Khan', are important not just because they
are two of the greatest imaginative achievements of English verse,
but because they would inspire generations of later poets to create
equally exotic imaginary worlds – refuges in language from the
urban, mercantile and apparently humdrum realities of nineteenth-
century life. But nobody did it as well as this:

In Xanadu did Kubla Khan
A stately pleasure-dome decree:
Where Alph, the sacred river, ran
Through caverns measureless to man
Down to a sunless sea.

So twice five miles of fertile ground
With walls and towers were girdled round:
And there were gardens bright with sinuous rills,
Where blossomed many an incense-bearing tree;
And here were forests ancient as the hills,
Enfolding sunny spots of greenery.

But oh! that deep romantic chasm which slanted
Down the green hill athwart a cedarn cover!
A savage place! as holy and enchanted
As e'er beneath a waning moon was haunted
By woman wailing for her demon-lover!
And from this chasm, with ceaseless turmoil seething,
As if this earth in fast thick pants were breathing,
A mighty fountain momently was forced:
Amid whose swift half-intermitted burst
Huge fragments vaulted like rebounding hail,
Or chaffy grain beneath the thresher's flail:
And 'mid these dancing rocks at once and ever
It flung up momently the sacred river.
Five miles meandering with a mazy motion
Through wood and dale the sacred river ran,
Then reached the caverns measureless to man,
And sank in tumult to a lifeless ocean:
And 'mid this tumult Kubla heard from far
Ancestral voices prophesying war!
The shadow of the dome of pleasure
Floated midway on the waves;
Where was heard the mingled measure
From the fountain and the caves.
It was a miracle of rare device,
A sunny pleasure-dome with caves of ice!

John Keats, the leading figure in the second generation of the
Romantic poets, self-consciously harked back to Wordsworth –
while despairing of his politics – and came to know Coleridge
personally when they lived on opposite sides of Hampstead Heath
in north London. Dying at just twenty-five, after only six years of
serious poetic composition, Keats was much mocked by reviewers
in his lifetime. It was only in Victorian Britain that he came to be
seen as the ultimate Romantic, a poet loved as none had been since
Shakespeare. Socially, the key to the Keats story is the single word
'insecurity'. Born the son of an ostler and later the manager of a
London tavern, he lost both his parents by the age of fourteen and
was plagued by money troubles all his life. His first career, which he
took seriously, was medicine: he trained as a doctor in London,
though he never properly practised, being determined above all to
be a poet. The gentlemanly reviewers who controlled the reputa-
tions of writers lampooned him for his low social origins, suggest-
ing he would be better off serving in a chemist's shop. They found
his sensual style offensive and 'low', describing his work as an exam-
ple of 'the Cockney School'. He probably also suffered for his politi-
cal views, which were radical and republican, though never
expressed as forcibly as those of his friend and rival Shelley.

This matters in the history of British poetry because of Keats's
reaction to it all. Essentially, following Coleridge, he created his
own poetic world, a soft-edged and languorous universe of sound
which captivated adolescents for generations to come. He had been
lucky in his schooling, going to a liberal institution which encour-
aged him to study earlier poets: for Keats, therefore, poetry became
a kind of alternative world of its own, in which Chaucer, Dante,
Milton, Spenser and Chapman were as real and present as any
nineteenth-century contemporaries. For him the actual London in
the early part of the nineteenth century was full of snubs and snob-
bery, material failure and illness. Poetry wasn't a way of describing
the world around him. It was another place entirely, with its own
higher values and sensibility. This was a further, and more extreme,
extension of Wordsworth's individualism and self-absorption. For

better or worse, it captivated poets of the rest of the century, and well into the next.

Keats was able to do this because he had technical skills – an ability to match sound, rhythm and sense – more perfect than anyone else's. He died young and he had a tragic love life, but that's not why he matters; it's the sheer craft of the writing that has kept him so alive for so long. The opening of 'Endymion', which gained him terrible reviews, asserts his 'poetry beyond life' creed:

A thing of beauty is a joy for ever:
Its loveliness increases; it will never
Pass into nothingness; but still will keep
A bower quiet for us, and a sleep
Full of sweet dreams, and health, and quiet breathing.
Therefore, on every morrow, are we wreathing
A flowery band to bind us to the earth,
Spite of despondence, of the inhuman dearth
Of noble natures, of the gloomy days,
Of all the unhealthy and o'er-darkn'd ways
Made for our searching: yes, in spite of all,
Some shape of beauty moves away the pall
From our dark spirits. Such the sun, the moon,
Trees old and young, sprouting a shady boon
For simple sheep; and such are daffodils
With the green world they live in; and clear rills
That for themselves a cooling covert make
'Gainst the hot season; the mid-forest brake,
Rich with a sprinkling of fair musk-rose blooms:
And such too is the grandeur of the dooms
We have imagined for the mighty dead;
An endless fountain of immortal drink,
Pouring unto us from Heaven's brink.

It's intoxicating, but there is a wooziness about it, a soft-edged qual-ity which suggests that Keats was not quite the countryman he would like to have been. His bucolic idylls aren't quite English; they often have a slightly suspicious whiff of the Mediterranean about them, as if Italian painters and Greek poets had been at work around the edges. John Clare, a real countryman, certainly thought so. Clare said that Keats 'often described nature as she appeared to his fancies and not as he would have described her had he witnessed the things he described'. That this is both right, and yet not the last word, is shown by the nightingale question. We've already seen Clare's vivid, detailed poem about real nightingales and their real nests. Here, by contrast, is the first half of Keats's 'Ode to a Nightingale', allegedly the result of listening to one in his friend Charles Brown's Hampstead garden.

> My heart aches, and a drowsy numbness pains
> My sense, as though of hemlock I had drunk,
> Or emptied some dull opiate to the drains
> One minute past, and Lethe-wards had sunk:
> 'Tis not through envy of thy happy lot,
> But being too happy in thy happiness, –
> That thou, light-winged Dryad of the trees,
> In some melodious plot
> Of beechen green, and shadows numberless,
> Singest of summer in full-throated ease.
>
> O for a draught of vintage, that hath been
> Cooled a long age in the deep-delved earth,
> Tasting of Flora and the country green,
> Dance, and Provencal song, and sun-burnt mirth!
> O for a beaker full of the warm South,
> Full of the true, the blushful Hippocrene,
> With beaded bubbles winking at the brim,
> And purple-stained mouth;
> That I might drink, and leave the world unseen,
> And with thee fade away into the forest dim:

Fade far away, dissolve, and quite forget
What thou among the leaves hast never known,
The weariness, the fever, and the fret
Here, where men sit and hear each other groan;
Where palsy shakes a few, sad, last grey hairs,
Where youth grows pale, and spectre-thin, and dies;
Where but to think is to be full of sorrow
And leaden-eyed despairs;
Where beauty cannot keep her lustrous eyes,
Or new love pine at them beyond tomorrow.

Away! away! for I will fly to thee,
Not charioted by Bacchus and his pards,
But on the viewless wings of Poesy,
Though the dull brain perplexes and retards:
Already with thee! tender is the night,
And haply the Queen-Moon is on her throne,
Clustered around by all her starry fays;
But here there is no light,
Save what from heaven is with the breezes blown
Through verdurous glooms and winding mossy ways.

I cannot see what flowers are at my feet,
Nor what soft incense hangs upon the boughs,
But, in embalmed darkness, guess each sweet
Wherewith the seasonable month endows
The grass, the thicket, and the fruit-tree wild;
White hawthorn, and the pastoral eglantine;
Fast-fading violets covered up in leaves;
And mid-May's eldest child,
The coming musk-rose, full of dewy wine,
The murmurous haunt of flies on summer eves.

Darkling I listen; and for many a time
I have been half in love with easeful Death,

Called him soft names in many a mused rhyme,
To take into the air my quiet breath;
Now more than ever seems it rich to die,
To cease upon the midnight with no pain,
While thou art pouring forth thy soul abroad
In such an ecstasy!
Still wouldst thou sing, and I have ears in vain –
To thy high requiem become a sod.

Thou wast not born for death, immortal Bird ...

It's not really England, is it? And yet it's a more beautiful poem than
anything John Clare ever managed to achieve. Here is Clare's 'To
Autumn', which I think is a small masterpiece, technically as well as
observationally:

The thistledown's flying, though the winds are all still,
On the green grass now lying, now mounting the hill,
The spring from the fountain now boils like a pot;
Through stones past the counting it bubbles red-hot.

The ground parched and cracked is like overbaked bread,
The greensward all wracked is, bents dried up and dead.
The fallow fields glitter like water indeed,
And gossamers twitter, flung from weed unto weed.

Hill-tops like hot iron glitter bright in the sun,
And the rivers we're eying burn to gold as they run;
Burning hot is the ground, liquid gold is the air;
Whoever looks round sees Eternity there.

All right, I know this is unfair – it's probably technically the most
perfect poem in the English language – but here by contrast is
Keats's 'Ode to Autumn':

Season of mists and mellow fruitfulness,
Close bosom-friend of the maturing sun;
Conspiring with him how to load and bless
With fruit the vines that round the thatch-eaves run;
To bend with apples the mossed cottage-trees,
And fill all fruit with ripeness to the core;
To swell the gourd, and plump the hazel shells
With a sweet kernel; to set budding more,
And still more, later flowers for the bees,
Until they think warm days will never cease,
For Summer has o'er-brimmed their clammy cell.

Who hath not seen thee oft amid thy store?
Sometimes whoever seeks abroad may find
Thee sitting careless on a granary floor,
Thy hair soft-lifted by the winnowing wind;
Or on a half-reaped furrow sound asleep,
Drowsed with the fume of poppies, while thy hook
Spares the next swath and all its twinèd flowers;
And sometimes like a gleaner thou dost keep
Steady thy laden head across a brook;
Or by a cider-press, with patient look,
Thou watchest the last oozings, hours by hours.

Where are the songs of Spring? Ay, where are they?
Think not of them, thou hast thy music too, –
While barrèd clouds bloom the soft-dying day,
And touch the stubble-plains with rosy hue;
Then in a wailful choir, the small gnats mourn
Among the river sallows, borne aloft
Or sinking as the light wind lives or dies;
And full-grown lambs loud bleat from hilly bourn;
Hedge-crickets sing; and now with treble soft
The redbreast whistles from a garden-croft,
And gathering swallows twitter in the skies.

Again, wherever this is, it's not East Anglia. But it's an entirely different kind of countryside – a state of mind, a shaft of insight into the condition of being alive, a place of imagination which has been created by Keats and now lives with us and inside us forever. It's not hard, is it, to understand why Keats transfixed his successors?

Though not all of them, of course: George Gordon, Lord Byron, despised Keats, whom he called 'that dirty little blackguard'. That both poets are generally bracketed together as Romantics only goes to show how loose and unsatisfactory the label really is. If Wordsworth and Coleridge had, in their different ways, changed what poetry was about by turning it into an account of their inner selves, Byron took things to a new extreme: he made himself, in his own daily life, a Romantic or 'poetic' hero. The life of the poet had become central to the poetry; now a poet stepped beyond the poetry, or at least used it as part of a wider project of self-projection. To complicate things further, Byron looked back to poets of almost a century earlier, Alexander Pope and John Dryden, as his heroes, and he seems more like the wicked Lord Rochester than anybody else in his own period. He's a strange mixture of eighteenth-century aristocracy, Restoration 'blood' and modern radical – but then again, so was much about the period of the Regency, as old King George III subsided into madness and allowed his indolent son to set the tone of the country.

Byron was born too late, in 1788, in either Dover or London, to experience the first fervour of the French Revolution. His father was a notoriously spendthrift and wild Scottish aristocratic sea captain; his mother was a fat, and according to her son, stupid heiress. He was born with a club foot, and this infirmity is generally thought to have driven him from a young age to sporting and sexual excesses to compensate. In the famous words of one of his mistresses, Lady Caroline Lamb, Byron was 'mad, bad, and dangerous to know'. His fellow second-generation Romantic poet, Percy Bysshe Shelley, described him as 'exceedingly interesting', but regretted that he was a slave to violent and vulgar prejudices, 'and as mad as a Hatter'.

There's a lot about Byron that seems very much of our own times – his cynical exploitation of what we would now call 'celebrity culture'; his deliberately shocking use of humour; his frank bi-sexuality; and on a more serious note, his crusades for freedom in far-off, exotic lands: all those poets who set off to help republican Spain in the 1930s were in some sense the heirs of Byron and his campaign to help free Greece from the Turkish Empire, which led to his early death in 1824. He wrote a series of romping verse romances which helped kick-start the Gothic craze across Europe, as well as meltingly beautiful lyrics, and very funny letters. But he is mostly remembered for two long, loose, mock-epic narrative poems, *Childe Harold's Pilgrimage* and *Don Juan*. Both are written in ottava rima, the usefully discursive and flexible stanza form which became popular in England with the Elizabethans, and which allows Byron to adopt the confidential, lordly, easy-going tone his admirers love so much.

Thus, in poetic terms, after Coleridge and Wordsworth, Byron can feel old-fashioned. He was a great literary fighter, and proclaimed his indifference to the first generation of Romantics, huddled up in the Lake District. In *Don Juan* Byron savages Southey for turning from radical to Tory, before turning his attention to others. Coleridge had recently started to write on German metaphysics:

> And Coleridge, too, has lately taken wing,
> But like a hawk encumber'd with his hood,
> Explaining Metaphysics to the nation –
> I wish he would explain his Explanation.

Ouch. As for Wordsworth himself, then hard at work on his huge narrative poem:

And Wordsworth, in a rather long 'Excursion'
(I think the quarto holds five hundred pages),
Has given a sample from the vasty version
Of his new system to perplex the sages;
'Tis poetry – at least by his assertion,
And may appear so when the dog-star rages –
And he who understands it would be able
To add a story to the Tower of Babel.

You – Gentlemen! by dint of long seclusion
From better company, have kept your own
At Keswick, and, through still continu'd fusion
Of one another's minds, at last have grown
To deem as a most logical conclusion,
That Poesy has wreaths for you alone:
There is a narrowness in such a notion,
Which makes me wish you'd change your lakes for Ocean.

Those extracts give a sense of Byron's world-weary tone. He had
grown up in a generation for which British wars against Napoleonic
France were the backdrop to everyday life. The wars had given Britain
a series of patriotic songs, and new heroes who had given their names
to streets and pubs, helping to instill a fresh sense of national warrior
pride in the wake of Trafalgar and Waterloo. Part of Byron's shock
tactics (a little like poets after the First World War) was to mock the
whole bloody business. Here he is, in *Don Juan* again:

I want a hero: an uncommon want,
When every year and month sends forth a new one,
Till, after cloying the gazettes with cant,
The age discovers he is not the true one;
Of such as these I should not care to vaunt,
I'll therefore take our ancient friend Don Juan,
We all have seen him, in the pantomime,
Sent to the Devil somewhat ere his time.

Vernon, the butcher Cumberland, Wolfe, Hawke,
Prince Ferdinand, Granby, Burgoyne, Keppel, Howe,
Evil and good, have had their tithe of talk,
And filled their sign-posts then, like Wellesley now;
Each in their turn like Banquo's monarchs stalk,
Followers of fame, 'nine farrow' of that sow:
France, too, had Buonaparte and Dumourier
Recorded in the Moniteur and Courier.

Barnave, Brissot, Condorcet, Mirabeau,
Pétion, Clootz, Danton, Marat, La Fayette
Were French, and famous people, as we know;
And there were others, scarce forgotten yet,
Joubert, Hoche, Marceau, Lannes, Desaix, Moreau,
With many of the military set,
Exceedingly remarkable at times,
But not at all adapted to my rhymes.

Nelson was once Britannia's god of War,
And still should be so, but the tide is turn'd;
There's no more to be said of Trafalgar,
'Tis with our hero quietly inurn'd;
Because the army's grown more popular,
At which the naval people are concern'd;
Besides, the Prince is all for the land-service,
Forgetting Duncan, Nelson, Howe, and Jervis.

Brave men were living before Agamemnon
And since, exceeding valorous and sage,
A good deal like him too, though quite the same none;
But then they shone not on the poet's page,
And so have been forgotten: I condemn none,
But can't find any in the present age
Fit for my poem (that is, for my new one);
So, as I said, I'll take my friend Don Juan.

This is intended to make the reader complicit, to wallow in feeling superior to the simple-minded patriotic mob of every class and two nations, at least. Byron appealed to the disaffected younger generation, who were sick to the back teeth of war stories and solemn patriotism. His poems were a weapon against their easily-offended elders, rather as children of the 1970s brandished Mick Jagger and David Bowie to offend a later wartime generation. Like them, Byron worked hard on his own image. Was he the haunted traveller Childe Harold? Was he the wicked corsair? Was he Don Juan? Byron, like his anti-hero, travelled widely in Europe and enjoyed many sexual affairs, including with boys and, it was alleged, his own half-sister. Brooding, unpredictable, dangerous and brilliant – the poet saturated his work with his own personality to the point where fact and fiction bled hopelessly into one another. He attracted myths and cloaked himself in them, right up to the moment of his death.

Here and now, he's useful above all because he tells us such a lot about the more cynical mood that flowed through parts of Britain after the endless and successful wars against Napoleon. These had brought income tax, great hardship for many of the labouring poor, and town centres where legless or otherwise mutilated former soldiers begged for money. From 1811 to 1820 the self-indulgent Prince Regent oversaw a London establishment which seemed to have lost its moral compass. The old king, who had led the country during the wars in America and France, was mad. The soon-to-be George IV was not mad, but he was bad, at least in the eyes of many of his subjects. Byron's worldly, insouciant poetry seems tailor-made for the age. Like some later celebrity-rebels, he wanted it every way. He was serious about his politics, savaging the government for instance for its treatment of rebel Ireland, and deadly serious when it came to the Greek rebellion. And yet the authentic 'Byron touch' is unable to grapple with seriousness itself:

I would to heaven that I were so much clay,
As I am blood, bone, marrow, passion, feeling –
Because at least the past were passed away –

And for the future – (but I write this reeling,
Having got drunk exceedingly today,
So that I seem to stand upon the ceiling)
I say – the future is a serious matter –
And so – for God's sake – hock and soda water!

Don Juan again – and yet how does this sit with the genuine fury expressed about the government's treatment of the Irish? Lord Castlereagh became the Foreign Secretary of the British government in the late Napoleonic period, but he had also, as Irish Secretary, been responsible for the suppression of the Irish rebellion of 1798. Byron summons the spirit of that old republican, John Milton:

Think'st thou, could he – the blind Old Man – arise
Like Samuel from the grave, to freeze once more
The blood of monarchs with his prophecies,
Or be alive again – again all hoar
With time and trials, and those helpless eyes,
And heartless daughters – worn – and pale – and poor;
Would he adore a sultan? he obey
The intellectual eunuch *Castlereagh*.

Cold-blooded, smooth-faced, placid miscreant!
Dabbling its sleek young hands in Erin's gore,
And thus for wider carnage taught to pant,
Transferr'd to gorge upon a sister shore,
The vulgarest tool that Tyranny could want,
With just enough of talent, and no more,
To lengthen fetters by another fix'd,
And offer poison long already mix'd.

An orator of such set trash of phrase
Ineffably – legitimately vile,
That even its grossest flatterers dare not praise,

307

Nor foes – all nations – condescend to smile, –
Not even a sprightly blunder's spark can blaze
From that Ixion grindstone's ceaseless toil,
That turns and turns to give the world a notion
Of endless torments and perpetual motion.

A bungler even in its disgusting trade,
And botching, patching, leaving still behind
Something of which its masters are afraid,
States to be curb'd and thoughts to be confined,
Conspiracy or Congress to be made –
Cobbling at manacles for all mankind –
A tinkering slave-maker, who mends old chains,
With God and man's abhorrence for its gains.

It's magnificent in its cold anger – or it would be, if we could take
Byron entirely seriously. People couldn't then, despite his Europe-
wide fame; and most readers can't now. The same goes, sadly, for his
beautiful love lyrics: because we know so much about the man,
including his enthusiasm for sodomising his lovers, how can we
really swoon over something as luscious and pure-seeming as this?

She walks in beauty, like the night
Of cloudless climes and starry skies;
And all that's best of dark and bright
Meet in her aspect and her eyes;
Thus mellowed to that tender light
Which heaven to gaudy day denies.

One shade the more, one ray the less,
Had half impaired the nameless grace
Which waves in every raven tress,
Or softly lightens o'er her face;
Where thoughts serenely sweet express,
How pure, how dear their dwelling-place.

And on that cheek, and o'er that brow,
So soft, so calm, yet eloquent,
The smiles that win, the tints that glow,
But tell of days in goodness spent,
A mind at peace with all below,
A heart whose love is innocent!

Innocent, I think, is a word Byron never quite understood. All of which said, he remains gloriously readable. This is not something we can say about Shelley, the last of the 'great' Romantics, the friend of both Byron and Keats, drowned off Italy in 1822. Like Byron, Shelley had to grapple with the solemnity and the reactionary politics of Europe after the defeat of Napoleon, and in particular the repressive and unimaginative British governments of the day. Like Byron, Shelley never gave up his youthful revolutionary fire (dying young, that great career move). But unlike Byron, Shelley's problem is not his cynicism, but his windy seriousness. Adored by the Victorians, even as they deplored his atheism, Shelley's longer and more visionary poems came to seem like so much over-coloured wind, great billows of enthusiastic nonsense. Opinion is moving back his way. Among the poems which express the full extremity of Romantic despair and longing by the 1820s is his famous lament for the dead John Keats:

I weep for Adonais – he is dead!
O, weep for Adonais! though our tears
Thaw not the frost which binds so dear a head!
And thou, sad Hour, selected from all years
To mourn our loss, rouse thy obscure compeers,
And teach them thine own sorrow, say: 'With me
Died Adonais; till the Future dares
Forget the Past, his fate and fame shall be
An echo and a light unto eternity!'

Shelley had an extraordinary lyric skill. A few poems have dug their way into the British imagination, and stay there. 'Ozymandias' is his wry commentary on the pomp of earthly power, and what inevitably comes to it. It should be engraved at the entrance to the House of Commons:

I met a traveller from an antique land
Who said: 'Two vast and trunkless legs of stone
Stand in the desert. Near them, on the sand,
Half sunk, a shattered visage lies, whose frown,
And wrinkled lip, and sneer of cold command,
Tell that its sculptor well those passions read
Which yet survive, stamped on these lifeless things,
The hand that mocked them and the heart that fed.
And on the pedestal these words appear –
"My name is Ozymandias, king of kings:
Look on my works, ye Mighty, and despair!"
Nothing beside remains. Round the decay
Of that colossal wreck, boundless and bare
The lone and level sands stretch far away.'

But in terms of the British experience in this period there is nothing to match 'The Mask of Anarchy', the finest protest poem ever written in English. The great victory of Waterloo in 1815 had disgorged huge numbers of demobilised servicemen into civilian life. The following year, the eruption of Mount Tambora in Indonesia created across much of Europe and North America 'the year without a summer', and caused the failure of the British harvest – the last time, before the opening up of global grain trade, that the English were faced with a natural disaster big enough to cause starvation. The new Corn Laws, introduced to protect the interests of British landowners by slapping tariffs on imported grain, made food more expensive and the situation worse. An unpopular government was struggling to hold the line against the reform of the political system, to allow the industrial cities a fair representation in Parliament. Thus, politically, a perfect storm was brewing.

In August 1819 Shelley was in exile in Italy. At St Peter's Fields in Manchester a huge crowd gathered to protest in favour of parliamentary reform, and was charged by cavalry. Fifteen people were killed, and hundreds wounded by the slashing sabres. Shelley responded in a poem which begins like this:

As I lay asleep in Italy
There came a voice from over the Sea,
And with great power it forth led me
To walk in the visions of Poesy.

I met Murder on the way –
He had a mask like Castlereagh –
Very smooth he looked, yet grim;
Seven blood-hounds followed him:

All were fat; and well they might
Be in admirable plight,
For one by one, and two by two,
He tossed them human hearts to chew
Which from his wide cloak he drew.

Next came Fraud, and he had on,
Like Eldon, an ermined gown;
His big tears, for he wept well,
Turned to mill-stones as they fell.

And the little children, who
Round his feet played to and fro,
Thinking every tear a gem,
Had their brains knocked out by them.

Clothed with the Bible, as with light,
And the shadows of the night,
Like Sidmouth, next, Hypocrisy
On a crocodile rode by.

And many more Destructions played
In this ghastly masquerade,
All disguised, even to the eyes,
Like Bishops, lawyers, peers, or spies.

Last came Anarchy: he rode
On a white horse, splashed with blood;
He was pale even to the lips,
Like Death in the Apocalypse.

And he wore a kingly crown;
And in his grasp a sceptre shone;
On his brow this mark I saw –
'I am God, and King, and Law!'

With a pace stately and fast,
Over English land he passed,
Trampling to a mire of blood
The adoring multitude.

And a mighty troop around,
With their trampling shook the ground,
Waving each a bloody sword,
For the service of their Lord.

And with glorious triumph, they
Rode through England proud and gay,
Drunk as with intoxication
Of the wine of desolation.

O'er fields and towns, from sea to sea,
Passed the Pageant swift and free,
Tearing up, and trampling down;
Till they came to London town.

And each dweller, panic-stricken,
Felt his heart with terror sicken
Hearing the tempestuous cry
Of the triumph of Anarchy.

For with pomp to meet him came,
Clothed in arms like blood and flame,
The hired murderers, who did sing
'Thou art God, and Law, and King.'

Part of the story of the British in the nineteenth century is the story of lack of revolution, of slow but sure parliamentary reform, and social reforms which hold back not the anger of the dispossessed, but any revolutionary force strong enough to topple 'God, and Law, and King'. Better times returned. A growing empire, able to export any surplus population to take other people's lands, and able to import luxuries from around the world, meshed gears with the world's first Industrial Revolution. For the British, in short, things would begin to get much better. Romantic poetry, which belonged to the period of crisis between the French Revolution and the Peterloo Massacre, ebbed away. A new seriousness entered British poetry. The Victorians were buttoning their waistcoats, fixing their bonnets, and preparing for their moment.

11
The British
Age

If any age can be said to have been 'the British age' it was the nine-
teenth century, or as it is normally referred to after the long-lived
queen, the Victorian era. Briefly, the British became the premier
world power, possessors of a vast empire, huge wealth based on the
world's first industrial revolution, and in the Royal Navy the most
formidable military operation on the planet. As one would expect,
it was therefore also an age of military and militaristic poetry, of
self-congratulation, and of the obsession with class that fast-chang-
ing material wealth brings. So much is obvious. But the Victorians
were also wrestling with new and unsettling ideas, from Darwinism
and evolution through natural selection, to spreading atheism and
the new doctrine of socialism. Far from being complacent, much of
the poetry of the period is introspective, challenging and self-
critical. There are passionate revivals of religious faith, celebrations
of domesticity, and a growing and urgent fascination with the rest
of the world.

Victorian poetry, like Victorian architecture, can seem a fairy city
of pastiche, from the medievalism of Tennyson's *Idylls of the King* to
the Venetian and Florentine settings of Browning or the Persian
effusions of Edward FitzGerald. This is also the age of exoticism
and Orientalism. None of which is much use in an attempt to tell
the epic story of what it was like being British, through poetry. But,
as with Victorian architecture, the sheer energy and variety is capti-

vating. As with the architecture, there are plain domestic buildings all around the polychromatic palaces. And as with buildings topped off with fourteenth-century spires, or windows borrowed from the Grand Canal, in Victorian poetry what seems outlandish may turn out on closer inspection to be both very British and very up-to-date.

Felicia Hemans came from a family that was in many ways the epitome of the new Britain. Her father was a Lancashire wine importer; one of her brothers became a highly distinguished Imperial soldier; another, Chief Commissioner of Police in Ireland; the third, a senior official in Canada. She herself married an Irish army officer, though the marriage didn't last very long. She dedicated her first poems to the Prince of Wales, despite which Shelley admired her; when she died, Wordsworth wrote an elegy. And indeed, her most famous poem, 'Casabianca', is exactly what we would expect from a young, patriotic woman of the Empire:

The boy stood on the burning deck
Whence all but he had fled;
The flame that lit the battle's wreck
Shone round him o'er the dead.
Yet beautiful and bright he stood,
As born to rule the storm;
A creature of heroic blood,
A proud, though childlike form.

The flames roll'd on ... he would not go
Without his father's word;
That father, faint in death below,
His voice no longer heard.

He call'd aloud ... 'Say, father, say
If yet my task is done!'
He knew not that the chieftain lay
Unconscious of his son.

'Speak, father!' once again he cried
'If I may yet be gone!'
And but the booming shots replied,
And fast the flames roll'd on.

Upon his brow he felt their breath,
And in his waving hair,
And looked from that lone post of death,
In still yet brave despair;

And shouted but once more aloud,
'My father, must I stay?'
While o'er him fast, through sail and shroud
The wreathing fires made way,

They wrapt the ship in splendour wild,
They caught the flag on high,
And stream'd above the gallant child,
Like banners in the sky.

There came a burst of thunder sound ...
The boy – oh! where was he?
Ask of the winds that far around
With fragments strewed the sea.

With mast, and helm, and pennon fair,
That well had borne their part;
But the noblest thing which perished there
Was that young faithful heart.

This quintessentially Victorian belief in pluck and patriotism led the unlucky Hemans to be ruthlessly parodied and mocked in the twentieth century. Her light poem of tribute to the English home has never recovered from what Noël Coward did to it in a famous song. Here's the opening of her poem:

The stately homes of England
How beautiful they stand!
Amidst their tall ancestral trees,
O'er all the pleasant land!
The deer across their green sward bound
Through shade and sunny gleam,
And the swan glides past them with the sound
Of some rejoicing stream.

The merry homes of England!
Around their hearths by night,
What gladsome looks of household love
Meet in the ruddy light!
There woman's voice flows forth in song,
Or childhood's tale is told;
Or lips move tunefully along
Some glorious page of old.

The cottage homes of England!
By thousands on her plains,
They are smiling o'er the silv'ry brook,
And round the hamlet-fanes;
Through glowing orchards forth they peep,
Each from its nook of leaves;
And fearless there the lowly sleep,
As the bird beneath their eaves.

Sentimental, no doubt. But rather moving, surely? And here is
Coward:

The stately homes of England
How beautiful they stand,
To prove the upper classes
Have still the upper hand.
Though the fact that they have to be rebuilt,

And frequently mortgaged to the hilt
Is inclined to take the gilt
Off the gingerbread,
And certainly damps the fun
Of the eldest son –
But still, we won't be beaten,
We'll scrimp and scrape and save.
The playing fields of Eton
Have made us frightfully brave.

Was there no more to Felicia Hemans than this? Fortunately there was much more, though it has only recently begun to be appreciated. She was in her way an early feminist poet, or at least a poet who returned again and again to the plight of women repressed and struggling for a voice, as in the opening of 'A Spirit Returns':

Thy voice prevails – dear friend, my gentle friend!
This long-shut heart for thee shall be unsealed,
And though thy soft eye mournfully will bend
Over the troubled stream, yet once revealed
Shall its freed waters flow; then rocks must close
For evermore, above their dark repose.

There is a suicidal undercurrent to her work, completely counter to the brisk moralism of the boy on the burning deck, as in her poem on the death of Sappho:

Sound on, thou dark, unslumbering sea!
Sound in thy scorn and pride!
I ask not, alien world, from thee,
What my own kindred earth hath still denied.

And yet I loved that earth so well,
With all its lovely things!
— Was it for this the death-wind fell
On my rich lyre, and quench'd its living strings?

— Let them lie silent at my feet!
Since broken even as they,
The heart whose music made them sweet,
Hath pour'd on desert-sands its wealth away.

Yet glory's light hath touch'd my name,
The laurel-wreath is mine —
— With a lone heart, a weary frame —
O restless deep! I come to make them thine!

Give to that crown, that burning crown,
Place in thy darkest hold!
Bury my anguish, my renown,
With hidden wrecks, lost gems, and wasted gold.

Thou sea-bird on the billow's crest,
Thou hast thy love, thy home;
They wait thee in the quiet nest,
And I, the unsought, unwatch'd-for — I too come!

I, with this winged nature fraught,
These visions wildly free,
This boundless love, this fiery thought —
Alone I come — oh! give me peace, dark sea!

The same ambivalence between accepting wholeheartedly the religious and imperial enthusiasms of the age, and private scepticism, is found in a much greater poet, also from Lancashire. A schoolboy at Thomas Arnold's famously Christian-muscular Rugby, and for a time a passionate High Church enthusiast, Arthur Hugh Clough was best known for his gung-ho call for soldiers to stick with it, a cleverly composed and more general injunction against defeatism. It has the compression and crispness of Kipling at his best.

Say not the struggle naught availeth,
The labour and the wounds are vain,
The enemy faints not, nor faileth,
And as things have been they remain.

If hopes were dupes, fears may be liars;
It may be, in yon smoke conceal'd,
Your comrades chase e'en now the fliers,
And, but for you, possess the field.

For while the tired waves, vainly breaking,
Seem here no painful inch to gain,
Far back, through creeks and inlets making,
Comes silent, flooding in, the main.

And not by eastern windows only,
When daylight comes, comes in the light;
In front the sun climbs slow, how slowly!
But westward, look, the land is bright!

Not everything that appeals to gym masters is preposterous. Clough is a fascinating study in Victorian enthusiasms, turning his back on the established Church and having his head turned by overseas travel, notably during the Italian revolution, when he was in Rome and Venice. As a thoroughly trained classicist he had a superb metrical skill, which he turned to contemporary subjects rather than to cod-classical ones. His 'Amours de Voyage', written in 1850 after he had witnessed the fight for the short-lived Roman Republic, defeated by the French coming to the aid of the Pope against Mazzini and his Italian patriots, is his masterpiece. He uses the long classical line, the hexameter, for chatty verse-letters from

Claude, a rather limp English traveller, to his friend Eustace back home. Claude is, like most Victorian Englishmen, an instinctive liberal constitutionalist; but he's deeply unimpressed by Abroad, and the political enthusiasms of foreigners. Clough conveys the living tone of contemporary English conversation, and has an eye for detail that is more than merely novelistic:

> I, who avoided it all, am fated, it seems, to describe it.
> I, who nor meddle nor make in politics, – I who sincerely
> Put not my trust in leagues nor any suffrage by ballot,
> Never predicted Parisian millenniums, never beheld a
> New Jerusalem coming down dressed like a bride out of
>   heaven
> Right on the Place de la Concorde, – I, nevertheless, let
>   me say it,
> Could in my soul of souls, this day, with the Gaul at the
>   gates shed
> One true tear for thee, thou poor little Roman Republic;
> What, with the German restored, with Sicily safe to the
>   Bourbon,
> Not leave one poor corner for native Italian exertion?
> France, it is foully done! and you, poor foolish England, –
> You, who a twelvemonth ago said nations must choose for
>   themselves, you
> Could not, of course, interfere, – you, now, when a nation
>   has chosen –
> Pardon this folly!

Claude is getting caught up with the passions of the Italian republicans. Like many British people in later conflicts, the more he sees of it, the more he feels his country ought to have intervened. But it's too late now. So how brave will he be, if he has to be? Not very.

Now supposing the French or the Neapolitan soldier
Should by some evil chance come exploring the Maison
    Serny
(Where the family English are all to assemble for safety),
Am I prepared to lay down my life for the British female?
Really, who knows? One has bowed and talked, till, little
    by little,
All the natural heat has escaped of the chivalrous spirit.
Oh, one conformed, of course; but one doesn't die for
    good manners,
Stab or shoot, or be shot, by way of graceful attention.

Now the fighting starts for real. But somehow daily life goes on, and
Claude, clutching his guidebook ('Murray'), gets the surreal mood
in a way that shows Clough was a naturally gifted reporter.

Yes, we are fighting at last, it appears. This morning as
    usual,
Murray, as usual, in hand, I enter the Caffè Nuovo;
Seating myself with a sense as it were of a change in the
    weather,
Not understanding, however, but thinking mostly of
    Murray,
And, for to-day is their day, of the Campidoglio Marbles;
Caffè-latte! I call to the waiter, – and Non c'è latte,
This is the answer he makes me, and this is the sign of a
    battle.
So I sit: and truly they seem to think any one else more
Worthy than me of attention. I wait for my milkless nero,
Free to observe undistracted all sorts and sizes of persons,
Blending civilian and soldier in strangest costume, coming
    in, and
Gulping in hottest haste, still standing, their coffee,
    – withdrawing
Eagerly, jangling a sword on the steps, or jogging a musket

Slung to the shoulder behind. They are fewer, moreover,
    than usual,
Much and silenter far; and so I begin to imagine
Something is really afloat. Ere I leave, the Caffè is empty,
Empty too the streets, in all its length the Corso
Empty, and empty I see to my right and left the
    Condotti …

It's a brilliant work, well worth reading in full. Clough himself was an agonised liberal, who later in life worked closely with Florence Nightingale. The Victorian age was one of great religious faith, clashing with sharp agnosticism and doubt, and Clough reflects it all. His 'The Latest Decalogue' is the definitive thumbnail guide to Victorian ambiguities:

Thou shalt have one God only; who
Would be at the expense of two?
No graven images may be
Worshipp'd, except the currency:
Swear not at all; for, for thy curse
Thine enemy is none the worse:
At church on Sunday to attend
Will serve to keep the world thy friend:
Honour thy parents; that is, all
From whom advancement may befall:
Thou shalt not kill; but need'st not strive
Officiously to keep alive:
Do not adultery commit;
Advantage rarely comes of it:
Thou shalt not steal; an empty feat,
When it's so lucrative to cheat:
Bear not false witness; let the lie
Have time on its own wings to fly:
Thou shalt not covet; but tradition
Approves all forms of competition.

This could easily be taken as a clever-Dick sneer against all religious belief, but it certainly wasn't that. The Victorians are interesting when they are unsure, not when they are sure. Clough, again:

'There is no God,' the wicked saith,
'And truly it's a blessing,
For what He might have done with us
It's better only guessing.'

'There is no God,' a youngster thinks,
'Or really, if there may be,
He surely did not mean a man
Always to be a baby.'

'There is no God, or if there is,'
The tradesman thinks, ''twere funny
If He should take it ill in me
To make a little money.'

'Whether there be,' the rich man says,
'It matters very little,
For I and mine, thank somebody,
Are not in want of victual.'

Some others, also, to themselves,
Who scarce so much as doubt it,
Think there is none, when they are well,
And do not think about it.

But country folks who live beneath
The shadow of the steeple;
The parson and the parson's wife,
And mostly married people;

Youths green and happy in first love,
So thankful for illusion;
And men caught out in what the world
Calls guilt, in first confusion;

And almost everyone when age,
Disease, or sorrows strike him,
Inclines to think there is a God,
Or something very like Him.

For all the previous centuries that this book has covered, the British seem to have been overwhelmingly a nation of Christian believers. Perhaps it was social control. Maybe there were always many doubters and agnostics, even atheists, but they kept their thoughts to themselves. But Christian faith was clearly absolutely central to the culture. Declared atheists were extremely rare – Christopher Marlowe and, for a time, Lord Rochester are the only atheist poets so far I can think of. But now new scientific discoveries in geology, and then biology, were upending ideas about the planet's antiquity, its origin, and the specialness of the human race – that is, ideas about God, and faith itself. This was a substantial trauma for millions of thinking people, best expressed in a poem by Matthew Arnold, the son of the founder of Rugby school, where Clough was educated. Arnold's poetry is very clever, lean and classical, and does absolutely nothing for me, with the exception of the deservedly famous 'Dover Beach', his lament on the disappearance of faith in an age of materialism:

The sea is calm to-night.
The tide is full, the moon lies fair
Upon the straits; – on the French coast the light
Gleams and is gone; the cliffs of England stand,
Glimmering and vast, out in the tranquil bay.
Come to the window, sweet is the night-air!
Only, from the long line of spray

Where the sea meets the moon-blanch'd land,
Listen! you hear the grating roar
Of pebbles which the waves draw back, and fling,
At their return, up the high strand,
Begin, and cease, and then again begin,
With tremulous cadence slow, and bring
The eternal note of sadness in.

Sophocles long ago
Heard it on the Aegean, and it brought
Into his mind the turbid ebb and flow
Of human misery; we
Find also in the sound a thought,
Hearing it by this distant northern sea.

The Sea of Faith
Was once, too, at the full, and round earth's shore
Lay like the folds of a bright girdle furl'd.
But now I only hear
Its melancholy, long, withdrawing roar,
Retreating, to the breath
Of the night-wind, down the vast edges drear
And naked shingles of the world.

Ah, love, let us be true
To one another! for the world, which seems
To lie before us like a land of dreams,
So various, so beautiful, so new,
Hath really neither joy, nor love, nor light,
Nor certitude, nor peace, nor help for pain;
And we are here as on a darkling plain
Swept with confused alarms of struggle and flight,
Where ignorant armies clash by night.

Of all the institutions that bound together the Victorian worldview – the monarchy, the Church of England, the Empire – none was more important than the institution of marriage. Marriage brought security and respectability; it was the universal dividing line between success in life, and an unfulfilled existence. The great bard of Victorian marriage was the Roman Catholic convert Coventry Patmore. Essex-born, Patmore was a painter and an amateur scientist before he turned to poetry; lack of family money meant that he spent many years as a relatively lowly assistant in the British Museum. But it was his marriage to Emily Andrews in 1847 that seems to have been the pivotal moment in his life. His poetry wasn't instantly successful, and he would eventually marry twice more, but his long narrative poem celebrating marriage, *The Angel in the House*, eventually became immensely popular. It is an easy-to-read verse novel, generally cheerful in tone, but its strongly anti-feminist message made it notorious to twentieth-century intellectuals. A short extract explains the moral behind it:

Man must be pleased; but him to please
Is woman's pleasure; down the gulf
Of his condoled necessities
She casts her best, she flings herself.
How often flings for naught! and yokes
Her heart to an icicle or whim,
Whose each impatient word provokes
Another, not from her, but him;
While she, too gentle even to force
His penitence by kind replies,
Waits by, expecting his remorse,
With pardon in her pitying eyes ...

Patmore's 'surrendered wife' would be intolerable to later generations, but provides an authentic glimpse into how many conventional Victorians saw ideal married relationships – at least, they bought the book in cartloads. Part of the reason for that, no doubt, is that Patmore conveys an urgent, authentic and almost naïve sense of married love. Alongside the demand – or hope – that the wife should be an angelic restraint on male barbarity, there is plenty of evidence of humble connubial bliss. This is about the pain of parting, on a completely ordinary day:

It was not like your great and gracious ways!
Do you, that have naught other to lament,
Never, my Love, repent
Of how, that July afternoon,
You went,
With sudden, unintelligible phrase,
And frighten'd eye,
Upon your journey of so many days
Without a single kiss, or a good-bye?
I knew, indeed, that you were parting soon;
And so we sate, within the low sun's rays,
You whispering to me, for your voice was weak,
Your harrowing praise.
Well, it was well
To hear you such things speak,
And I could tell
What made your eyes a growing gloom of love,
As a warm South-wind sombres a March grove.
And it was like your great and gracious ways
To turn your talk on daily things, my Dear,
Lifting the luminous, pathetic lash
To let the laughter flash,
Whilst I drew near,
Because you spoke so low that I could scarcely hear.
But all at once to leave me at the last,
More at the wonder than the loss aghast,
With huddled, unintelligible phrase,
And frighten'd eye,
And go your journey of all days
With not one kiss, or a good-bye,

And the only loveless look the look with which you pass'd:
'Twas all unlike your great and gracious ways.

Patmore was taken up by the religious painters of the Pre-Raphaelite
brotherhood – there is a full portrait of him by John Singer Sargent.
In later life his Roman Catholic faith was hugely important to him,
and his most famous short poem, 'Magna est Veritas' – the truth is
great – is light-hearted, smug and yet oddly moving, like so much
else he wrote:

Here, in this little Bay,
Full of tumultuous life and great repose,
Where, twice a day,
The purposeless, gay ocean comes and goes,
Under high cliffs, and far from the huge town,
I sit me down.
For want of me the world's course will not fail:
When all its work is done, the lie shall rot;
The truth is great, and shall prevail,
When none cares whether it prevail or not.

The obvious and essential antidote to Coventry Patmore is George
Meredith's terrifying fifty-sonnet sequence, *Modern Love*, about the
breakdown of a marriage, following double infidelity. The novelist's
own marriage collapsed after his wife, the daughter of his fellow
novelist Thomas Love Peacock, left him for another man. Meredith's
own dense novels are relatively little read these days, but as we
become more tuned in to the potential miseries of marriage, *Modern
Love* has become more and more popular. Where Patmore is opti-
mistic, Meredith is despairing; where Patmore paints with soppy
colours, Meredith tears his nails across the image. Here's how the
sequence begins, with two miserable people in bed together:

By this he knew she wept with waking eyes:
That, at his hand's light quiver by her head,

The strange low sobs that shook their common bed
Were called into her with a sharp surprise,
And strangely mute, like little gasping snakes,
Dreadfully venomous to him. She lay
Stone-still, and the long darkness flowed away
With muffled pulses. Then, as midnight makes
Her giant heart of Memory and Tears
Drink the pale drug of silence, and so beat
Sleep's heavy measure, they from head to feet
Were moveless, looking through their dead black years,
By vain regret scrawled over the blank wall.
Like sculptured effigies they might be seen
Upon their marriage-tomb, the sword between;
Each wishing for the sword that severs all.

And here, later in the story, is a horrifying dinner party, at which
the brittle conversation fails to disguise the death of love:

At dinner, she is hostess, I am host.
Went the feast ever cheerfuller? She keeps
The Topic over intellectual deeps
In buoyancy afloat. They see no ghost.
With sparkling surface-eyes we ply the ball:
It is in truth a most contagious game:
HIDING THE SKELETON, shall be its name.
Such play as this the devils might appall!
But here's the greater wonder; in that we,
Enamoured of an acting naught can tire,
Each other, like true hypocrites, admire;
Warm-lighted looks, love's ephemerae,
Shoot gaily o'er the dishes and the wine.
We waken envy of our happy lot.
Fast, sweet and golden shows the marriage-knot.
Dear guests, you now have seen love's corpse-light shine.

Coventry Patmore felt that he had been saved from misery by his Christian faith, and later in his life he formed a strong friendship with another Roman Catholic poet, who never married, and who has a good claim to be the most important religious poet in English between Henry Vaughan and T.S. Eliot. Gerard Manley Hopkins, like Patmore, came from a middle-class Essex family, and to start with wanted to be a painter. His father was a relatively well-known poet and journalist, and the family were intensely religious, albeit still inside the Anglican Church. At Oxford, Hopkins fell under the influence of the Anglo-Catholics and eventually converted, becoming a Jesuit priest. He was hardly alone in that – led by Cardinal Manning, many serious-minded Anglicans moved to Rome in the 1850s and 60s: the architect Augustus Pugin was among them.

Hopkins had always had extreme and ascetic tendencies. He was almost certainly a repressed homosexual, who embraced his vows of chastity and poverty with some relief. His verse is characterised by 'sprung rhythm': each line contains a strictly limited number of feet, but after a first stressed syllable there are an indeterminate number of unstressed syllables. This is supposed to mimic the rhythms of natural speech; in Hopkins's hands, or rather voice, it produces an ecstatic, tumbling effect. Earlier religious poets, such as John Donne and George Herbert, had been much concerned with the problem and fear of death; Hopkins more resembles Vaughan in his delighted enthusiasm for the natural world. He is a poet of celebration and gusto, rather than of lamentation, though at times as riddled by self-doubt and self-disgust as any metaphysical. This, no doubt, explains his huge current popularity. I find his most overtly Catholic poems, such as 'The Wreck of the *Deutschland*', the least compelling. But he writes like absolutely nobody else – a unique voice. Perhaps it isn't surprising that he found it hard to reach contemporary readers, and had to wait for more radical times in poetry to become truly popular:

As kingfishers catch fire, dragonflies draw flame;
As tumbled over rim in roundy wells

Stones ring; like each tucked string tells, each hung bell's
Bow swung finds tongue to fling out broad its name;
Each mortal thing does one thing and the same:
Deals out that being indoors each one dwells;
Selves – goes itself; myself it speaks and spells,
Crying What I do is me: for that I came.

I say more: the just man justices;
Keeps grace: that keeps all his goings graces;
Acts in God's eye what in God's eye he is –
Christ. For Christ plays in ten thousand places,
Lovely in limbs, and lovely in eyes not his
To the Father through the features of men's faces.

Hopkins's great achievement is to so interleave his ecstatic enjoyment of the world – and again and again you see the eye of a closely observant painter – with his religious faith that the two things become completely inextricable, and therefore the poem convinces even those (like this writer) who are faithless. Here are the two greatest examples, for my money as fine short poems as any written in the nineteenth century:

Glory be to God for dappled things –
For skies of couple-colour as a brinded cow;
For rose-moles all in stipple upon trout that swim;
Fresh-firecoal chestnut-falls; finches' wings;
Landscape plotted and pieced – fold, fallow, and plough;
And áll trádes, their gear and tackle and trim.

All things counter, original, spare, strange;
Whatever is fickle, freckled (who knows how?)
With swift, slow; sweet, sour; adazzle, dim;
He fathers-forth whose beauty is past change:
Praise him.

And:

> The world is charged with the grandeur of God.
> It will flame out, like shining from shook foil;
> It gathers to a greatness, like the ooze of oil
> Crushed. Why do men then now not reck his rod?
> Generations have trod, have trod, have trod;
> And all is seared with trade; bleared, smeared with toil;
> And wears man's smudge and shares man's smell: the soil
> Is bare now, nor can foot feel, being shod.
>
> And for all this, nature is never spent;
> There lives the dearest freshness deep down things;
> And though the last lights off the black West went
> Oh, morning, at the brown brink eastward, springs –
> Because the Holy Ghost over the bent
> World broods with warm breast and with ah! bright
>   wings.

And, yes, he pants a bit, doesn't he? Hopkins's Oxford was a hothouse, a place where over-intellectual, intense, argumentative young men pushed almost everything a little too far. However, below the self-importance there was a lot of fun to be had. Charles Dodgson, the son of a clergyman, overlapped with Hopkins at Oxford, and although he too took religious orders and never married, he was not tempted to become a Catholic. A brilliant mathematician and pioneering photographer, he is of course better known as Lewis Carroll, creator of *Alice in Wonderland* and lifelong admirer of rather small girls. Dodgson wrote serious verse as a young man, and wanted it to be taken seriously; but his real genius was for fantasy, and the subversive jokes of his alternative created world. Among the many 'nonsense' poems he is remembered for, 'Jabberwocky' is surely the greatest, rooted in Anglo-Saxon as securely as Tolkien's Middle Earth is rooted in early English:

'Twas brillig, and the slithy toves
Did gyre and gimble in the wabe:
All mimsy were the borogoves,
And the mome raths outgrabe.

'Beware the Jabberwock, my son!
The jaws that bite, the claws that catch!
Beware the Jubjub bird, and shun
The frumious Bandersnatch!'

He took his vorpal sword in hand:
Long time the manxome foe he sought –
So rested he by the Tumtum tree,
And stood a while in thought.

And, as in uffish thought he stood,
The Jabberwock, with eyes of flame,
Came whiffling through the tulgey wood,
And burbled as it came!

One two! One two! And through and through
The vorpal blade went snicker-snack!
He left it dead, and with its head
He went galumphing back.

'And hast thou slain the Jabberwock?
Come to my arms, my beamish boy!
Oh frabjous day! Callooh! Callay!'
He chortled in his joy.

'Twas brillig, and the slithy toves
Did gyre and gimble in the wabe:
All mimsy were the borogoves,
And the mome raths outgrabe.

Magnificent – but not perhaps brimming with laughter. More typical of the Lewis Carroll touch, which is relentlessly subversive of authority, is this perennial favourite:

'You are old, father William,' the young man said,
'And your hair has become very white;
And yet you incessantly stand on your head –
Do you think, at your age, it is right?'

'In my youth,' father William replied to his son,
'I feared it might injure the brain;
But, now that I'm perfectly sure I have none,
Why, I do it again and again.'

'You are old,' said the youth, 'as I mentioned before,
And you have grown most uncommonly fat;
Yet you turned a back-somersault in at the door –
Pray what is the reason for that?'

'In my youth,' said the sage, as he shook his grey locks,
'I kept all my limbs very supple
By the use of this ointment – one shilling a box –
Allow me to sell you a couple?'

'You are old,' said the youth, 'and your jaws are too weak
For anything tougher than suet;
Yet you finished the goose, with the bones and the beak –
Pray, how did you manage to do it?'

'In my youth,' said his father, 'I took to the law,
And argued each case with my wife;
And the muscular strength, which it gave to my jaw,
Has lasted the rest of my life.'

'You are old,' said the youth, 'one would hardly suppose
That your eye was as steady as ever;
Yet you balanced an eel on the end of your nose –
What made you so awfully clever?'

'I have answered three questions, and that is enough,'
Said his father. 'Don't give yourself airs!
Do you think I can listen all day to such stuff?
Be off, or I'll kick you down stairs!'

That's a poem, I suggest, which is as representative of the Victorian
spirit as is anything by Coventry Patmore, or indeed Tennyson. We
may no longer think of it as poetry, but the Victorian world was
awash with satirical verse – Edward Lear's limericks, nonsense
poems made up in families, light ballads sold in shops and on the
streets, and, above all, the hugely popular and often suggestive songs
of the music halls. The Victorians were tightly-laced, devout and
class-conscious, utterly confused about the new sciences and over-
confident about their nation's destiny. But they also laughed, a lot.

In terms of their impact on the Victorian reading public, the two
titans of the mid-nineteenth century were Alfred Lord Tennyson,
the Poet Laureate who succeeded Wordsworth, and Robert
Browning. Tennyson is first and foremost a creator of hugely popu-
lar verse fantasies, including his Arthurian series, 'Odysseus' and
'The Lady of Shalott', as well as official verses marking Britain's
imperial progress. It is characteristic of the age that the best of
these, 'The Charge of the Light Brigade', is in fact about a heroic but
idiotic military action: that strange, semi-suicidal British pluck
which culminated at Passchendaele was already well established in
the middle of the nineteenth century.

Half a league, half a league,
Half a league onward,
All in the valley of Death
Rode the six hundred.

'Forward, the Light Brigade!
Charge for the guns!' he said:
Into the valley of Death
Rode the six hundred.

'Forward, the Light Brigade!'
Was there a man dismay'd?
Not tho' the soldier knew
Some one had blunder'd:
Their's not to make reply,
Their's not to reason why,
Their's but to do and die:
Into the valley of Death
Rode the six hundred.

Cannon to right of them,
Cannon to left of them,
Cannon in front of them
Volley'd and thunder'd;
Storm'd at with shot and shell,
Boldly they rode and well,
Into the jaws of Death,
Into the mouth of Hell
Rode the six hundred.

Flash'd all their sabres bare,
Flash'd as they turn'd in air
Sabring the gunners there,
Charging an army, while
All the world wonder'd:
Plunged in the battery-smoke
Right thro' the line they broke;
Cossack and Russian
Reel'd from the sabre-stroke
Shatter'd and sunder'd.

Then they rode back, but not
Not the six hundred.

Or anything like as many: the action in October 1854 resulted in
nearly three hundred men killed or wounded, and more than three
hundred horses dying. The Crimean War would be important for
the Victorians mainly because it demonstrated considerable mili-
tary incompetence and disorganisation, a generation after
Wellington's armies had been disbanded. Mostly, however, Tennyson
preferred to dive back deep into British history for his conflict
poetry. Much of it is rousing and luscious but helps us in describing
the British mood in the nineteenth century, no better than the poly-
chromatic bricks of St Pancras station help us to understand the
development of Victorian science. For the modern reader, in general,
it is the long, much starker poem *In Memoriam* that shows Tennyson
at his best, and best nails the spirit of the times. Arthur Henry
Hallam was a close Cambridge University friend of Tennyson's who
died of a stroke in Vienna in 1833; it took seventeen years for
Tennyson to complete his reflections on life, love, fate and friend-
ship. Just as Milton responded to the death of his Cambridge friend
Henry King with 'Lycidas', a poem which goes beyond the individual
bereavement to make more general points, so too does Tennyson.
But, more than two hundred years later, Tennyson produces a far
balder, less classical poem of grief, which in its way has never been
bettered. Just listen to these comfortless strokes:

Dark house, by which once more I stand
Here in the long unlovely street,
Doors, where my heart was used to beat
So quickly, waiting for a hand,

A hand that can be clasp'd no more –
Behold me, for I cannot sleep,
And like a guilty thing I creep
At earliest morning to the door.

He is not here; but far away
The noise of life begins again,
And ghastly thro' the drizzling rain
On the bald street breaks the blank day.

The poem has many moods, however, and Tennyson argues himself into a knowing stoicism about loss which remains moving and even useful:

I envy not in any moods
The captive void of noble rage,
The linnet born within the cage,
That never knew the summer woods:

I envy not the beast that takes
His licence in the field of time,
Unfetter'd by the sense of crime,
To whom a conscience never wakes;

Nor, what may count itself as blest,
The heart that never plighted troth
But stagnates in the weeds of sloth;
Nor any want-begotten rest.

I hold it true, whate'er befall;
I feel it, when I sorrow most;
'Tis better to have loved and lost
Than never to have loved at all.

How, though, does the poet cope with the challenges to Christian faith all around him? *Vestiges of the Natural History of Creation* is not a book much remembered today. But when it was published, anonymously, in 1844 it created a sensation. Prince Albert read it to Queen Victoria. Its author, the Scottish journalist Robert Chambers, tried to show that all life, including human life, was the result of evolutionary changes which could be traced back to the origins of the solar system itself. The book was nothing like as coherent or as solidly based as Charles Darwin's *On the Origin of Species*, which would follow fourteen years later, but it got all Britain talking. Here is Tennyson's response. The speaker is Nature herself:

'So careful of the type?' but no.
From scarped cliff and quarried stone
She cries, 'A thousand types are gone:
I care for nothing, all shall go.

'Thou makest thine appeal to me:
I bring to life, I bring to death:
The spirit does but mean the breath:
I know no more.' And he, shall he,

Man, her last work, who seem'd so fair,
Such splendid purpose in his eyes,
Who roll'd the psalm to wintry skies,
Who built him fanes of fruitless prayer,

Who trusted God was love indeed
And love Creation's final law —
Tho' Nature, red in tooth and claw
With ravine, shriek'd against his creed —

Who loved, who suffer'd countless ills,
Who battled for the True, the Just,
Be blown about the desert dust,
Or seal'd within the iron hills?

No more? A monster then, a dream,
A discord. Dragons of the prime,
That tare each other in their slime,
Were mellow music match'd with him.

O life as futile, then, as frail!
O for thy voice to soothe and bless!
What hope of answer, or redress?
Behind the veil, behind the veil.

Tennyson's career was a very long one. He was famous for most of his life. In the Victorian age poets could be famous, the celebrities of a deep-thinking and fast-moving literary culture. Tennyson showed, if anyone needed to, that in the nineteenth century poetry still really mattered. He sold in vast numbers, and his new poems were eagerly devoured and discussed. Poets were expected to deal with everything that mattered, from politics and military strategy to religion and the domestic life. Poetry wasn't in any kind of intellectual ghetto, as it's been pressed back and pinioned today.

Robert Browning, Tennyson's great rival and sometimes his friend, was almost as much of a celebrity. He also was a poet of many moods. His great invention was the dramatic monologue, to be read on the page, creating the voices of historical (often Italian) figures as they reflect on their lives. He could also, however, produce hugely popular patriotic poetry, such as this, from his self-imposed exile in Italy:

Oh, to be in England
Now that April's there,
And whoever wakes in England
Sees, some morning, unaware,
That the lowest boughs and the brushwood sheaf
Round the elm-tree bole are in tiny leaf,
While the chaffinch sings on the orchard bough
In England – now!

And after April, when May follows,
And the whitethroat builds, and all the swallows!
Hark, where my blossomed pear-tree in the hedge
Leans to the field and scatters on the clover

Blossoms and dewdrops – at the bent spray's edge –
That's the wise thrush; he sings each song twice over,
Lest you should think he never could recapture
The first fine careless rapture!
And though the fields look rough with hoary dew,
All will be gay when noontide wakes anew
The buttercups, the little children's dower
– Far brighter than this gaudy melon-flower!

Browning's massive *The Ring and the Book*, retelling an Italian murder story from the late 1600s, is his single biggest achievement. Most readers today prefer the shorter monologues, for their lapel-grabbing immediacy. Here's the start of 'Bishop Bloughram's Apology':

No more wine? then we'll push back chairs and talk.
A final glass for me, though: cool, i' faith!
We ought to have our Abbey back, you see.
It's different, preaching in basilicas,
And doing duty in some masterpiece
Like this of brother Pugin's, bless his heart!
I doubt if they're half baked, those chalk rosettes,
Ciphers and stucco-twiddlings everywhere;
It's just like breathing in a lime-kiln: eh?
These hot long ceremonies of our church
Cost us a little – oh, they pay the price,
You take me – amply pay it! Now, we'll talk.

Following Browning, many later poets went in for the higher ventriloquism – Ezra Pound is a good example – but his great fame and influence came at a price, namely the outrageous overshadowing of his arguably more talented wife, Elizabeth Barrett. Born in County Durham in 1806, she came from a rich family which had made its wealth from farming land, and from Jamaican sugar plantations and mills. The tension between Elizabeth's strongly moral, dissenting religious views and the sources of her father's wealth affected her all her life: she became a leading slave-trade abolitionist, and a campaigner for humane restrictions on child labour in factories. Alongside this, and despite a lifelong and crippling illness, almost certainly tuberculosis, she produced a huge volume of poetry and was popular enough to be considered for the post of Poet Laureate when Tennyson got the job. Her secret marriage to Robert Browning infuriated her family, who disowned her and cut her off. The Brownings then decamped to Italy, and she died in Florence in 1861. Elizabeth Barrett was from youth a believer in women's rights and a reader of Mary Wollstonecraft; her remarkable poem 'Lord Walter's Wife' shows how far real Victorians were from naïvety about sex: never have the myth of female passivity, and the truth of male hypocrisy, been more expertly skewered:

'But why do you go?' said the lady, while both sat under
    the yew,
And her eyes were alive in their depth, as the kraken
    beneath the sea-blue.

'Because I fear you,' he answered; – 'because you are far
    too fair,
And able to strangle my soul in a mesh of your gold-
    coloured hair.'

'Oh that,' she said, 'is no reason! Such knots are quickly
    undone,
And too much beauty, I reckon, is nothing but too much
    sun.'

'Yet farewell so,' he answered; – 'the sunstroke's fatal at
    times.
I value your husband, Lord Walter, whose gallop rings still
    from the limes.'

'Oh that,' she said, 'is no reason. You smell a rose through a
   fence:
If two should smell it what matter? who grumbles, and
   where's the pretense?'

'But I,' he replied, 'have promised another, when love was
   free,
To love her alone, alone, who alone from afar loves me.'

'Why, that,' she said, 'is no reason. Love's always free I am
   told.
Will you vow to be safe from the headache on Tuesday,
   and think it will hold?'

'But you,' he replied, 'have a daughter, a young child, who
   was laid
In your lap to be pure; so I leave you: the angels would
   make me afraid.'

'Oh that,' she said, 'is no reason. The angels keep out of the
   way;
And Dora, the child, observes nothing, although you
   should please me and stay.'

At which he rose up in his anger – 'Why now, you no
   longer are fair!
Why, now, you no longer are fatal, but ugly and hateful, I
   swear.'

At which she laughed out in her scorn: 'These men! Oh
   these men overnice,
Who are shocked if a colour not virtuous is frankly put on
   by a vice.'

Her eyes blazed upon him – 'And you! You bring us your
   vices so near
That we smell them! You think in our presence a thought
   'twould defame us to hear!

'What reason had you, and what right, – I appeal to your
   soul from my life –
To find me so fair as a woman? Why, sir, I am pure, and a
   wife.

'Is the day-star too fair up above you? It burns you not.
   Dare you imply
I brushed you more close than the star does, when Walter
   had set me as high?

'If a man finds a woman too fair, he means simply adapted
   too much
To use unlawful and fatal. The praise! – shall I thank you
   for such?

'Too fair? – not unless you misuse us! and surely if, once
   in a while,
You attain to it, straightaway you call us no longer too fair,
   but too vile ...'

Although only an extract, that, I think, gives a fair sense of the
cutting edge of this remarkable woman, whose beady eyes glare out
from between her fashionable ringlets. As an anti-slavery
campaigner who had no illusions about the political problems at
home, she wrote her 'Curse for a Nation' against American slavery.
She's called to curse the Americans by an angel, but begins by argu-
ing with the angel: in effect, how can someone from a political
culture as corrupt as Britain's point the finger across the Atlantic?

I heard an angel speak last night,
And he said 'Write!
Write a Nation's curse for me,
And send it over the Western Sea.'

I faltered, taking up the word:
'Not so, my lord!
If curses must be, choose another
To send thy curse against my brother.

'For I am bound by gratitude,
By love and blood,
To brothers of mine across the sea,
Who stretch out kindly hands to me.'

'Therefore,' the voice said, 'shalt thou write
My curse to-night.
From the summits of love a curse is driven,
As lightning is from the tops of heaven.'

'Not so,' I answered. 'Evermore
My heart is sore
For my own land's sins: for little feet
Of children bleeding along the street:

'For parked-up honours that gainsay
The right of way:
For almsgiving through a door that is
Not open enough for two friends to kiss:

'For love of freedom which abates
Beyond the Straits:
For patriot virtue starved to vice on
Self-praise, self-interest, and suspicion:

'For an oligarchic parliament,
And bribes well-meant.
What curse to another land assign,
When heavy-souled for the sins of mine?'

'Therefore,' the voice said, 'shalt thou write
My curse to-night.
Because thou hast strength to see and hate
A foul thing done within thy gate.'

'Not so,' I answered once again.
'To curse, choose men.
For I, a woman, have only known
How the heart melts and the tears run down.'

'Therefore,' the voice said, 'shalt thou write
My curse to-night.
Some women weep and curse, I say
(And no one marvels), night and day.

'And thou shalt take their part to-night,
Weep and write.
A curse from the depths of womanhood
Is very salt, and bitter, and good.'

So thus I wrote, and mourned indeed,
What all may read.
And thus, as was enjoined on me,
I send it over the Western Sea.

So much for the apology – but when the American curse gets going,
it's quite a denunciation:

The Curse

Because ye have broken your own chain
With the strain
Of brave men climbing a Nation's height,
Yet thence bear down with brand and thong
On souls of others, – for this wrong
This is the curse. Write.

Because yourselves are standing straight
In the state
Of Freedom's foremost acolyte,
Yet keep calm footing all the time
On writhing bond-slaves, – for this crime
This is the curse. Write.

Because ye prosper in God's name,
With a claim
To honour in the old world's sight,
Yet do the fiend's work perfectly
In strangling martyrs, – for this lie
This is the curse. Write.

Ye shall watch while strong men draw
The nets of feudal law
To strangle the weak;
And, counting the sin for a sin,
Your soul shall be sadder within
Than the word ye shall speak.
This is the curse. Write.

When good men are praying erect
That Christ may avenge His elect
And deliver the earth,
The prayer in your ears, said low,

Shall sound like the tramp of a foe
That's driving you forth.
This is the curse. Write.

When wise men give you their praise,
They shall praise in the heat of the phrase,
As if carried too far.
When ye boast your own charters kept true,
Ye shall blush; for the thing which ye do
Derides what ye are.
This is the curse. Write.

When fools cast taunts at your gate,
Your scorn ye shall somewhat abate
As ye look o'er the wall;
For your conscience, tradition, and name
Explode with a deadlier blame
Than the worst of them all.
This is the curse. Write.

Go, wherever ill deeds shall be done,
Go, plant your flag in the sun
Beside the ill-doers!
And recoil from clenching the curse
Of God's witnessing Universe
With a curse of yours.
This is the curse. Write.

That is a genuinely frightening poem from the mind of a radical
dissenter, raging against the cruelties of smug, mid-century
Victorian life. Elizabeth Barrett Browning is known today more for
her hauntingly beautiful love lyrics and sonnets. This serves her
badly.

12

Plush, Mush and a Handful of Titans

Late-Victorian and Edwardian Britain presents a paradox to poetry lovers. On the one hand, with universal education and a press never more literate, widely read and diverse, it was a great age for reading. It was also the period of many new literary reviews. Yet most of the poetry of the period turns out to be disappointing – mushy, pallid, derivative. It was a turbulent period, with the zenith of Empire bringing huge wealth to the British middle classes, who were able to look out and know more about the rest of the world than ever before. Explorers, scientists and lecturers were bringing new knowledge to all parts of Britain. Politically, the rise of the trade unions and socialism brought open conflict onto the streets of the country ahead of the First World War. The mighty Liberal Party was threatened by the last stand of the aristocratic House of Lords, and by increasingly dangerous turbulence in Ireland. Yet very little of this is reflected in poetry, except the most vapid and forgettable occasional verse. The so-called Georgian poets, energetically promoted by Edward Marsh's magazine *Georgian Verse*, are little-read today. The most radical poetic movement, the Decadents led by Oscar Wilde, now seems merely wearisome; Wilde himself only finds real poetic form when he gets onto the subject of his own sexual martyrdom and imprisonment. In all of this, there are however some big figures.

One of them, Rudyard Kipling, remains controversial today because of his supposed hyper-patriotic enthusiasm for an imperial project that was causing misery in many parts of the world. A second, Thomas Hardy, was known to generations as one of England's greatest novelists before it became apparent that he was, first and foremost, the greatest poet since the Romantics, and perhaps greater than them too. It's a terrible thing to say, but one of the outcomes of 1914 was to save British poetry by giving it a subject beyond all others. Of the major figures who engaged freshly with the English countryside, one, Edward Thomas, died in the war. The other, A.E. Housman, was a brilliant Latin scholar who spent most of his life in cloistered academia, tortured by the need to repress his homosexuality.

Before we come to them, we need to look at the other poetry which was popular from the late 1900s until the First World War. One of the disadvantages poets faced in this Britain was the apparently mesmerising and deadening influence of the Pre-Raphaelites, who covered the country in swirls of prettified medieval claptrap, the worst of Victorianism. If that seems harsh, dear reader, read on. Here is Dante Gabriel Rossetti, founder of the original Pre-Raphaelite brotherhood, in characteristic form. He had a thing about damozels, and his paintings feature dark-tressed, huge-jawed women with mad eyes. Each, I suppose, to his own.

> The blessèd damozel lean'd out
> From the gold bar of Heaven;
> Her eyes were deeper than the depth
> Of waters still'd at even;
> She had three lilies in her hand,
> And the stars in her hair were seven.
>
> Her robe, ungirt from clasp to hem,
> No wrought flowers did adorn,
> But a white rose of Mary's gift,
> For service meetly worn;
> Her hair that lay along her back
> Was yellow like ripe corn.

Herseem'd she scarce had been a day
One of God's choristers;
The wonder was not yet quite gone
From that still look of hers;
Albeit, to them she left, her day
Had counted as ten years.

(To one, it is ten years of years.
… Yet now, and in this place,
Surely she lean'd o'er me – her hair
Fell all about my face …
Nothing: the autumn-fall of leaves.
The whole year sets apace.)

It was the rampart of God's house
That she was standing on;
By God built over the sheer depth
The which is Space begun;
So high, that looking downward thence
She scarce could see the sun.

It lies in Heaven, across the flood
Of ether, as a bridge.
Beneath, the tides of day and night
With flame and darkness ridge
The void, as low as where this earth
Spins like a fretful midge.

Fretful midge, indeed. Dante Gabriel's sister, Christina Rossetti, was a much better poet, and her vividly-coloured, rollicking 'Goblin Market' is a reliable guess for any collection of Victorian poetry. But she too suffers from flowery sentimentalism, and a whiff of an ill-remembered fourteenth century:

Twist me a crown of wind-flowers;
That I may fly away
To hear the singers at their song,
And players at their play.
Put on your crown of wind-flowers:
But whither would you go?
Beyond the surging of the sea
And the storms that blow.
Alas! your crown of wind-flowers
Can never make you fly:
I twist them in a crown to-day,
And to-night they die.

It's more than sentimentalism, though. There is a morbidity, a long-ing for death, which pervades the movement. Christina again:

When I am dead, my dearest,
Sing no sad songs for me;
Plant thou no roses at my head,
Nor shady cypress tree:
Be the green grass above me
With showers and dewdrops wet;
And if thou wilt, remember,
And if thou wilt, forget.

I shall not see the shadows,
I shall not feel the rain;
I shall not hear the nightingale
Sing on, as if in pain:
And dreaming through the twilight
That doth not rise nor set,
Haply I may remember,
And haply may forget.

By far the most socially engaged of these poets was the Christian socialist and brilliantly talented designer William Morris. But even he is deep in the medievalism he believed key to escaping the dislocations and unhappiness of modern market society. Mostly, this means that instead of writing directly through his poetry about the world around him, he's harking wistfully back:

Through thick Arcadian woods a hunter went,
Following the beasts upon a fresh spring day;
But since his horn-tipped bow but seldom bent,
Now at the noontide naught had happed to slay,
Within a vale he called his hounds away,
Hearkening the echoes of his lone voice cling
About the cliffs and through the beech-trees ring.

But when they ended, still awhile he stood,
And but the sweet familiar thrush could hear,
And all the day-long noises of the wood,
And o'er the dry leaves of the vanished year
His hounds' feet pattering as they drew anear,
And heavy breathing from their heads low hung,
To see the mighty corner bow unstrung.

Even when Morris turns directly to 'condition of England' questions, there is a medieval veil drawn across the subject. This poem insists that God is the God of the poor – *Deus est Deus pauperum* – but is it really a work from the industrial and socialist world at all?

There was a lord that hight Maltete,
Among great lords he was right great,
On poor folk trod he like the dirt,
None but God might do him hurt.
Deus est Deus pauperum.

354

With a grace of prayers sung loud and late
Many a widow's house he ate;
Many a poor knight at his hands
Lost his house and narrow lands.
Deus est Deus pauperum.

He burnt the harvests many a time,
He made fair houses heaps of lime;
Whatso man loved wife or maid
Of Evil-head was sore afraid.
Deus est Deus pauperum.

He slew good men and spared the bad;
Too long a day the foul dog had,
E'en as all dogs will have their day;
But God is as strong as man, I say.
Deus est Deus pauperum.

Member of no movement, and certainly not a socialist, Algernon
Charles Swinburne points the way to another, rather strange, prob-
lem with later Victorian poetry. Sensitive, highly classically-trained
writers, cut off in universities and then surrounded by coteries of
their own kind, produced verse that was almost too technically
good – mellifluous, post-Keatsian in its music, which lisps and
swoons and billows, rather like the music of Delius – and yet in the
end is not *about* anything very much. This is the opening of
Swinburne's tribute to Charles Baudelaire, the far greater French
Decadent:

Shall I strew on thee rose or rue or laurel,
Brother, on this that was the veil of thee?
Or quiet sea-flower moulded by the sea,
Or simplest growth of meadow-sweet or sorrel,
Such as the summer-sleepy Dryads weave,
Waked up by snow-soft sudden rains at eve?

355

Or wilt thou rather, as on earth before,
Half-faded fiery blossoms, pale with heat
And full of bitter summer, but more sweet
To thee than gleanings of a northern shore
Trod by no tropic feet?

For always thee the fervid languid glories
Allured of heavier suns in mightier skies;
Thine ears knew all the wandering watery sighs
Where the sea sobs round Lesbian promontories,
The barren kiss of piteous wave to wave
That knows not where is that Leucadian grave
Which hides too deep the supreme head of song.
Ah, salt and sterile as her kisses were,
The wild sea winds her and the green gulfs bear
Hither and thither, and vex and work her wrong,
Blind gods that cannot spare.

Poets brought up in the shadow of this kind of stuff must have asked themselves what poetry was any longer allowed to be about – what was its fit subject? The Decadent movement deployed the languorous death-wish as a weapon against optimistic bourgeois Christianity; aestheticism against athleticism. It must have seemed a good idea at the time, but it produced poetry which simply seems too limp, too yellow, too affected. The hearty, boorish mockers maybe had a point. One of the most characteristic of the Decadent poets, much read and influential in his time, was Arthur Symons. He is highly sensitive to colour, and tends to write about moments:

Mauve, black, and rose,
The veils of the jewel, and she, the jewel, a rose.

First, the pallor of mauve,
A soft flood flowing about the body I love.

Then, the flush of the rose,
A hedge of roses about the mystical rose.

Last, the black, and at last
The feet that I love, and the way that my love has passed.

The following poem is simply called 'Pastel: Masks and Faces':

The light of our cigarettes
Went and came in the gloom:
It was dark in the little room.

Dark, and then, in the dark,
Sudden, a flash, a glow,
And a hand and a ring I know.

And then, through the dark, a flush
Ruddy and vague, the grace
(A rose!) of her lyric face.

It's not medieval, or cod-medieval. It has a certain, quite compelling, compression, and it's about modern people – note the cigarettes. Even the colour mauve, used in clothing in the previous poem, was a relatively recent chemical invention. Symons and his colleagues had found a new way to write. But in the end this kind of thing works better in oil paint than syllables. Oscar Wilde himself proves it:

Against these turbid turquoise skies
The light and luminous balloons
Dip and drift like satin moons
Drift like silken butterflies;

Reel with every windy gust,
Rise and reel like dancing girls,

Float like strange transparent pearls,
Fall and float like silver dust.

Now to the low leaves they cling,
Each with coy fantastic pose,
Each a petal of a rose
Straining at a gossamer string.

Then to the tall trees they climb,
Like thin globes of amethyst,
Wandering opals keeping tryst
With the rubies of the lime.

These were hugely talented, ambitious men; and it's hard to resist
the suspicion that what they really lacked, living relatively comfort-
able lives, was a proper subject. Oscar Wilde found his in the worst
possible way, after his homosexuality led to his imprisonment in the
extremely harsh Reading Gaol. His famous ballad is full of wisdom,
and achieves the hypnotic power of Coleridge:

I walked, with other souls in pain,
Within another ring,
And was wondering if the man had done
A great or little thing,
When a voice behind me whispered low,
'That fellow's got to swing.'

Dear Christ! the very prison walls
Suddenly seemed to reel,
And the sky above my head became
Like a casque of scorching steel;
And, though I was a soul in pain,
My pain I could not feel.

I only knew what hunted thought
Quickened his step, and why
He looked upon the garish day
With such a wistful eye;
The man had killed the thing he loved
And so he had to die.

Yet each man kills the thing he loves
By each let this be heard,
Some do it with a bitter look,
Some with a flattering word,
The coward does it with a kiss,
The brave man with a sword!

Some kill their love when they are young,
And some when they are old;
Some strangle with the hands of Lust,
Some with the hands of Gold:
The kindest use a knife, because
The dead so soon grow cold.

Some love too little, some too long,
Some sell, and others buy;
Some do the deed with many tears,
And some without a sigh:
For each man kills the thing he loves,
Yet each man does not die.

He does not die a death of shame
On a day of dark disgrace,
Nor have a noose about his neck,
Nor a cloth upon his face,
Nor drop feet foremost through the floor
Into an empty place

There were other ways to escape the languorous fingers of Edwardian decadence. Some would escape it in the trenches of Flanders. Others, above all William Butler Yeats, escaped it by eventually growing up. In the twentieth century Yeats would become one of the greatest Irish poets of all time. But how well remembered would he be, were it only for his Edwardian verses of the 'Celtic Twilight'?

> We who are old, old and gay,
> O so old!
> Thousands of years, thousands of years,
> If all were told:
> Give to these children, new from the world,
> Silence and love;
> And the long dew-dropping hours of the night,
> And the stars above:
> Give to these children, new from the world,
> Rest far from men.
> Is anything better, anything better?
> Tell us it then:
> Us who are old, old and gay,
> O so old!
> Thousands of years, thousands of years,
> If all were told.

Yeats is a poet of the very first order, and even his relatively young poetry shows what could still be done within the confines of late-Victorian and Decadent traditions. We will come to him properly later on, but it is astonishing that 'The Lake Isle of Innisfree' was published as early as 1893. It has all the languor, though not the morbidity, of the Decadent movement, and its love of twilight and subtle colour effects. But it has a magic that Symons and even Wilde never got close to:

I will arise and go now, and go to Innisfree,
And a small cabin build there, of clay and wattles made:
Nine bean-rows will I have there, a hive for the
    honeybee,
And live alone in the bee-loud glade.
And I shall have some peace there, for peace comes
    dropping slow,
Dropping from the veils of the morning to where the
    cricket sings;
There midnight's all a glimmer, and noon a purple glow,
And evening full of the linnet's wings.
I will arise and go now, for always night and day
I hear lake water lapping with low sounds by the shore;
While I stand on the roadway, or on the pavements grey,
I hear it in the deep heart's core.

Yeats, who helps to bulk up so many anthologies of English poetry, is of course anything but English. But the same is true of Rudyard Kipling. Born in India, he spoke Hindi before he spoke English. As a small boy he was sent to the Home Counties first with a family who took in boarders, and then at boarding school, and loathed the experience, feeling unsettled in the country that was in theory 'home'. In adult life he settled briefly in London after roaming America, but he then went back to the United States, and might well have made his home there permanently had it not been for a bitter political row. He would put down roots in England, in a seventeenth-century stone house, but he was always heading off to South Africa, or to France. Much of his best poetry comes from the India of the Raj, and if the young Kipling appears to have any real home, it's the British Army.

Kipling was indeed the poet of Empire, but he was a questioning poet, impatient of anything easy. Of all the writers included in this collection, nobody was as purely male a poet as Kipling. He could be a wonderful mimic, but only of male voices. His virtues – pluck, determination, comradeship – are soaked in testosterone. His marriage wasn't notably happy. All his life, male friendships mattered very much.

Once, every second educated household in Britain would have had some Kipling on the shelf – generally small, red-leather-bound volumes with a neat gold swastika stamped on the spine (the Indian symbol of good luck, chosen by Kipling long before German anti-Semites appropriated it; in his old age, as Hitler was establishing himself in power, Kipling had the swastikas removed from new editions). He has hardly vanished from popular culture even today, thanks to the Disney takeover of his children's story *The Jungle Book* and to the poem 'If', recently voted the most popular British poem. T.S. Eliot admired him, but he fell dramatically in popularity from the 1960s onwards, being regarded as a hopeless white supremacist and imperialist. George Orwell, as so often, hit him fairly and squarely on the head when he said that Kipling 'dealt largely in platitudes, and since we live in a world of platitudes, much of what he said sticks. Even his worst follies seem less shallow and less irritating than the "enlightened" utterances of the same period.' Kipling can be sententious, but he certainly expanded the circle of things poetry could be about, embracing travel, engineering, history and ethnography alongside his military songs and his religious ones. Here is one of his relatively early poems, 'Christmas in India' – not, I think, very well known, but wonderfully vivid in its observation and riotous energy. If we want to know something about what it was like to live in the British Raj, then this kind of poetry certainly helps:

Dim dawn behind the tamarisks – the sky is saffron-
    yellow –
As the women in the village grind the corn,
And the parrots seek the riverside, each calling to his
    fellow
That the Day, the staring Easter Day is born.
Oh the white dust on the highway! Oh the stenches in the
    byway!

Oh the clammy fog that hovers
And at Home they're making merry 'neath the white and
    scarlet berry –
What part have India's exiles in their mirth?

Full day behind the tamarisks – the sky is blue and staring –
As the cattle crawl afield beneath the yoke,
And they bear One o'er the field-path, who is past all hope
    or caring,
To the ghat below the curling wreaths of smoke.
Call on Rama, going slowly, as ye bear a brother lowly –
Call on Rama – he may hear, perhaps, your voice!
With our hymn-books and our psalters we appeal to other
    altars,
And to-day we bid 'good Christian men rejoice!'

High noon behind the tamarisks – the sun is hot above us –
As at Home the Christmas Day is breaking wan.
They will drink our healths at dinner – those who tell us
    how they love us,
And forget us till another year be gone!
Oh the toil that knows no breaking! Oh the Heimweh,
    ceaseless, aching!
Oh the black dividing Sea and alien Plain!
Youth was cheap – wherefore we sold it,
Gold was good – we hoped to hold it,
And to-day we know the fulness of our gain.

Grey dusk behind the tamarisks – the parrots fly together –
As the sun is sinking slowly over Home;
And his last ray seems to mock us shackled in a lifelong
    tether
That drags us back how'er so far we roam.
Hard her service, poor her payment – she is ancient,
    tattered raiment –

India, she the grim Stepmother of our kind.
If a year of life be lent her, if her temple's shrine we enter,
The door is shut — we may not look behind.

Black night behind the tamarisks — the owls begin their
    chorus —
As the conches from the temple scream and bray.
With the fruitless years behind us, and the hopeless years
    before us,
Let us honour, O my brother, Christmas Day!
Call a truce, then, to our labours — let us feast with friends
    and neighbours,
And be merry as the custom of our caste;
For if 'faint and forced the laughter', and if sadness follow
    after,
We are richer by one mocking Christmas past.

It's not exactly an example of the puffed chest, is it? Kipling's sympa-
thies were with the makers of the Empire — soldiers and engineers
— and generally not with the comfortable middle classes back home.
The best of his verse catches the rhythms of ordinary conversation
far from the polite world of Edwardian Britain — none better than
the still-stinging 'Tommy':

I went into a public-'ouse to get a pint o' beer,
The publican 'e up an' sez, 'We serve no red-coats here.'
The girls be'ind the bar they laughed an' giggled fit to die,
I outs into the street again an' to myself sez I:
O it's Tommy this, an' Tommy that, an' 'Tommy, go away';
But it's 'Thank you, Mister Atkins', when the band begins
    to play,
The band begins to play, my boys, the band begins to play,
O it's 'Thank you, Mister Atkins', when the band begins to
    play.

I went into a theatre as sober as could be,
They gave a drunk civilian room, but 'adn't none for me;
They sent me to the gallery or round the music-'alls,
But when it comes to fightin', Lord! they'll shove me in the
    stalls!
For it's Tommy this, an' Tommy that, an' 'Tommy, wait
    outside';
But it's 'Special train for Atkins' when the trooper's on the
    tide,
The troopship's on the tide, my boys, the troopship's on
    the tide,
O it's 'Special train for Atkins' when the trooper's on the
    tide.

Yes, makin' mock o' uniforms that guard you while you
    sleep
Is cheaper than them uniforms, an' they're starvation
    cheap;
An' hustlin' drunken soldiers when they're goin' large a bit
Is five times better business than paradin' in full kit.
Then it's Tommy this, an' Tommy that, an' 'Tommy, 'ow's
    yer soul?'
But it's 'Thin red line of 'eroes' when the drums begin to
    roll,
The drums begin to roll, my boys, the drums begin to roll,
O it's 'Thin red line of 'eroes' when the drums begin to
    roll.

We aren't no thin red 'eroes, nor we aren't no blackguards
    too,
But single men in barricks, most remarkable like you;
An' if sometimes our conduck isn't all your fancy paints,
Why, single men in barricks don't grow into plaster saints;
While it's Tommy this, an' Tommy that, an' 'Tommy, fall
    be'ind',

But it's 'Please to walk in front, sir', when there's trouble in
  the wind,
There's trouble in the wind, my boys, there's trouble in the
  wind,
O it's 'Please to walk in front, sir', when there's trouble in
  the wind.

You talk o' better food for us, an' schools, an' fires, an' all:
We'll wait for extry rations if you treat us rational.
Don't mess about the cook-room slops, but prove it to our
  face
The Widow's Uniform is not the soldier-man's disgrace.
For it's Tommy this, an' Tommy that, an' 'Chuck him out,
  the brute!'
But it's 'Saviour of 'is country' when the guns begin to
  shoot;
An' it's Tommy this, an' Tommy that, an' anything you
  please;
An' Tommy ain't a bloomin' fool — you bet that Tommy
  sees!

That, like his poem about an army execution, 'Danny Deever', is
well known and much loved. But Kipling's imagination ranged
wide, deep back in history and in his own time, embracing nautical
engineers such as Mr McAndrew, a Scottish Calvinist reflecting in
a ship's boiler room. The poem continues with a great deal of tech-
nical detail, expertly dealt with in metrical form, but the following
extract gives a sense of it:

From coupler-flange to spindle-guide I see Thy Hand, O
  God —
Predestination in the stride o' yon connectin'-rod.
John Calvin might ha' forged the same — enorrmous,
  certain, slow —
Ay, wrought it in the furnace-flame — my 'Institutio'.

I cannot get my sleep to-night; old bones are hard to
  please;
I'll stand the middle watch up here – alone wi' God an'
  these
My engines, after ninety days o' race an' rack an' strain
Through all the seas of all Thy world, slam-bangin' home
  again.
Slam-bang too much – they knock a wee – the crosshead-
  gibs are loose;
But thirty thousand mile o' sea has gied them fair
  excuse …

During the nineteenth century, British naval superiority had
allowed the Empire to swell by some ten million square miles, and
four hundred million new subjects. Large swathes of the world
beyond the formal Empire, from Argentina to China, were also
under Britain's effective economic domination. Such an enormous
swelling, happening so fast, must come at a price. Part of the price
was a complacent widespread racialism: the British came to think
themselves simply better, more grown-up and more moral than
anybody else. Kipling's poem 'The White Man's Burden' – in fact
written in 1899 to jolly up the Americans as they effectively took
over the Philippines – seems to exemplify this sense of racial and
cultural superiority. Today, it does seem offensive – but read it care-
fully and you see that it is very far from celebratory:

Take up the White Man's burden –
Send forth the best ye breed –
Go bind your sons to exile
To serve your captives' need;
To wait in heavy harness
On fluttered folk and wild –
Your new-caught, sullen peoples,
Half devil and half child.

Take up the White Man's burden –
In patience to abide,
To veil the threat of terror
And check the show of pride;
By open speech and simple,
An hundred times made plain.
To seek another's profit,
And work another's gain.

Take up the White Man's burden –
The savage wars of peace –
Fill full the mouth of Famine
And bid the sickness cease;
And when your goal is nearest
The end for others sought,
Watch Sloth and heathen Folly
Bring all your hope to naught.

Take up the White Man's burden –
No tawdry rule of kings,
But toil of serf and sweeper –
The tale of common things.
The ports ye shall not enter,
The roads ye shall not tread,
Go make them with your living,
And mark them with your dead!

Take up the White Man's burden –
And reap his old reward:
The blame of those ye better,
The hate of those ye guard –
The cry of hosts ye humour
(Ah, slowly!) toward the light: –
'Why brought ye us from bondage,
Our loved Egyptian night?'

Take up the White Man's burden –
Ye dare not stoop to less –
Nor call too loud on freedom
To cloak your weariness;
By all ye cry or whisper,
By all ye leave or do,
The silent, sullen peoples
Shall weigh your Gods and you.

Take up the White Man's burden –
Have done with childish days –
The lightly proffered laurel,
The easy, ungrudged praise.
Comes now, to search your manhood
Through all the thankless years,
Cold-edged with dear-bought wisdom,
The judgment of your peers!

Kipling was saved from simple-minded jingoism by his religious pessimism. Nowhere is this clearer than in the poem 'Recessional', which he wrote for Queen Victoria's Diamond Jubilee of 1897. The moment called for something triumphalist, something not too complicated. Kipling failed to oblige:

God of our fathers, known of old –
Lord of our far-flung battle-line –
Beneath whose awful Hand we hold
Dominion over palm and pine –
Lord God of Hosts, be with us yet,
Lest we forget, lest we forget!

The tumult and the shouting dies –
The captains and the kings depart –
Still stands Thine ancient sacrifice,
An humble and a contrite heart.

Lord God of Hosts, be with us yet,
Lest we forget, lest we forget!

Far-call'd our navies melt away –
On dune and headland sinks the fire –
Lo, all our pomp of yesterday
Is one with Nineveh and Tyre!
Judge of the Nations, spare us yet,
Lest we forget, lest we forget!

If, drunk with sight of power, we loose
Wild tongues that have not Thee in awe –
Such boasting as the Gentiles use
Or lesser breeds without the Law –
Lord God of Hosts, be with us yet,
Lest we forget, lest we forget!

For heathen heart that puts her trust
In reeking tube and iron shard –
All valiant dust that builds on dust,
And guarding calls not Thee to guard –
For frantic boast and foolish word,
Thy Mercy on Thy People, Lord!

Had Kipling been a 'jingo', then for him the First World War, to which he was completely committed, offering himself as a propagandist to the British government, would have been a terrible punishment. His beloved son John, rejected by the army when he volunteered because of his poor eyesight, was helped into the Irish Guards by his father. He died, apparently horribly, with his face torn off, at the Battle of Loos in 1915, shortly after his eighteenth birthday. Kipling's poem 'My Boy Jack' may or may not have been written to express his grief and remorse at his son's fate (it's as likely to be about a generic lost sailor), but a poem he wrote at the end of the war, 'A Death-Bed', which deals with the consequences of all-mighty state power – represented for Kipling by the Kaiser's Germany – is devastating in its account of the realities of trench life. From this poem on, when we talk about Britain's great war poets we have to include Kipling, who envisages the Kaiser dying of throat cancer:

This is the State above the Law.
'The State exists for the State alone.'
[This is a gland at the back of the jaw,
And an answering lump by the collar-bone.]

Some die shouting in gas or fire;
Some die silent, by shell and shot.
Some die desperate, caught on the wire –
Some die suddenly. This will not.

'Regis suprema voluntas Lex'
[It will follow the regular course of – throats.]
Some die pinned by the broken decks,
Some die sobbing between the boats.

Some die eloquent, pressed to death
By the sliding trench as their friends can hear
Some die wholly in half a breath.
Some – give trouble for half a year.

'There is neither Evil nor Good in life
Except as the needs of the State ordain.'
[Since it is rather too late for the knife,
All we can do is to mask the pain.]

Some die saintly in faith and hope –
One died thus in a prison-yard –
Some die broken by rape or the rope;
Some die easily. This dies hard.

'I will dash to pieces who bar my way.
Woe to the traitor! Woe to the weak!'
[Let him write what he wishes to say.
It tires him out if he tries to speak.]

Some die quietly. Some abound
In loud self-pity. Others spread
Bad morale through the cots around.
This is a type that is better dead.

'The war was forced on me by my foes.
All that I sought was the right to live.'
[Don't be afraid of a triple dose;
The pain will neutralize all we give.

Here are the needles. See that he dies
While the effects of the drug endure ...
What is the question he asks with his eyes? –
Yes, All-Highest, to God, be sure.]

But we can't leave Kipling without mentioning his most famous poem, 'If'. In any account of Britishness, it's important for its Christian stoicism – the ideals, or perhaps rather the temperament, that built the Empire. It was originally written in 1910 about the actions of a blundering mercenary, Leander Starr Jameson, admired by Kipling but who helped provoke the Boer War. Yet it still speaks to millions of people, and has been claimed in India as the essence of the message of the *Bhagavad Gita*. Mock if you like; mock if you dare. Its form is advice, from a father to his son:

If you can keep your head when all about you
Are losing theirs and blaming it on you,
If you can trust yourself when all men doubt you,
But make allowance for their doubting too;
If you can wait and not be tired by waiting,

Or being lied about, don't deal in lies,
Or being hated, don't give way to hating,
And yet don't look too good, nor talk too wise:

If you can dream – and not make dreams your master;
If you can think – and not make thoughts your aim;
If you can meet with Triumph and Disaster
And treat those two impostors just the same;
If you can bear to hear the truth you've spoken
Twisted by knaves to make a trap for fools,
Or watch the things you gave your life to, broken,
And stoop and build 'em up with worn-out tools:

If you can make one heap of all your winnings
And risk it on one turn of pitch-and-toss,
And lose, and start again at your beginnings
And never breathe a word about your loss;
If you can force your heart and nerve and sinew
To serve your turn long after they are gone,
And so hold on when there is nothing in you
Except the Will which says to them: 'Hold on!'

If you can talk with crowds and keep your virtue,
Or walk with Kings – nor lose the common touch,
If neither foes nor loving friends can hurt you,
If all men count with you, but none too much;
If you can fill the unforgiving minute
With sixty seconds' worth of distance run,
Yours is the Earth and everything that's in it,
And – which is more – you'll be a Man, my son.

Kipling wasn't alone in turning to the voices of the street and an earthy colloquialism, so unlike the Georgian poets, and so refreshing. The Scottish poet John Davidson, the son of an evangelical minister, was educated in science at the Highlanders' Academy,

Greenock, and spent his early years as a schoolteacher in Scotland before moving to London. His politics seem to have been almost the opposite of Kipling's, and his interest in science gave him unusual insight – his poems about snow, and the weather, are unlike anybody else's – but what he shared with Kipling was an instinct for the ballad, and an ear for how people at the end of the nineteenth century actually spoke. Here are parts of his famous 'Thirty Bob a Week', the lament of a very ordinary London office clerk – the grandson, as it were, of many Dickens characters, and a figure you can find in the fiction of the time, but rarely in poetry. He begins by lamenting that he is not a man of genius and wealth. He's an early version of that familiar modern figure, the overworked commuter.

I couldn't touch a stop and turn a screw,
And set the blooming world a-work for me,
Like such as cut their teeth – I hope, like you –
On the handle of a skeleton gold key;
I cut mine on a leek, which I eat it every week:
I'm a clerk at thirty bob as you can see.

But I don't allow it's luck and all a toss;
There's no such thing as being starred and crossed;
It's just the power of some to be a boss,
And the bally power of others to be bossed:
I face the music, sir; you bet I ain't a cur;
Strike me lucky if I don't believe I'm lost!

For like a mole I journey in the dark,
A-travelling along the underground
From my Pillar'd Halls* and broad Suburbean Park,
To come the daily dull official round;
And home again at night with my pipe all alight,
A-scheming how to count ten bob a pound.

---

* The clerk's ironic description of his small suburban house.

And it's often very cold and very wet,
And my missus stitches towels for a hunks;
And the Pillar'd Halls is half of it to let –
Three rooms about the size of travelling trunks.
And we cough, my wife and I, to dislocate a sigh,
When the noisy little kids are in their bunks.

But you never hear her do a growl or whine,
For she's made of flint and roses, very odd;
And I've got to cut my meaning rather fine,
Or I'd blubber, for I'm made of greens and sod:
So p'rhaps we are in Hell for all that I can tell,
And lost and damn'd and served up hot to God.

I ain't blaspheming, Mr. Silver-tongue;
I'm saying things a bit beyond your art:
Of all the rummy starts you ever sprung,
Thirty bob a week's the rummiest start!
With your science and your books and your the'ries about
    spooks,
Did you ever hear of looking in your heart?

I didn't mean your pocket, Mr., no:
I mean that having children and a wife,
With thirty bob on which to come and go,
Isn't dancing to the tabor and the fife:
When it doesn't make you drink, by Heaven! it makes you
    think,
And notice curious items about life.

And it's this way that I make it out to be:
No fathers, mothers, countries, climates – none;
Not Adam was responsible for me,
Nor society, nor systems, nary one:

A little sleeping seed, I woke – I did, indeed –
A million years before the blooming sun.

I woke because I thought the time had come;
Beyond my will there was no other cause;
And everywhere I found myself at home,
Because I chose to be the thing I was;
And in whatever shape of mollusc or of ape
I always went according to the laws.

I was the love that chose my mother out;
I joined two lives and from the union burst;
My weakness and my strength without a doubt
Are mine alone for ever from the first:
It's just the very same with a difference in the name
As 'Thy will be done.' You say it if you durst!

They say it daily up and down the land
As easy as you take a drink, it's true;
But the difficultest go to understand,
And the difficultest job a man can do,
Is to come it brave and meek with thirty bob a week,
And feel that that's the proper thing for you.

It's a naked child against a hungry wolf;
It's playing bowls upon a splitting wreck;
It's walking on a string across a gulf
With millstones fore-and-aft about your neck;
But the thing is daily done by many and many a one;
And we fall, face forward, fighting, on the deck.

By the end of the poem we are back close to the territory of William
Blake, though without his supernatural system – Davidson's is a
rather comfortless, materialistic stoicism, and after a long immer-
sion in his poems one isn't surprised to find that he died of suicide,

by drowning. The twentieth-century Scottish poet Hugh MacDiarmid wrote one of his most moving lyrics about Davidson – and again, the older poet in his agnosticism, and his interest in science, was a precursor of much that came later. Like Kipling, he was a great noticer. This comes from his poem 'A Loafer':

I hang about the streets all day,
At night I hang about;
I sleep a little when I may,
But rise betimes the morning's scout;
For through the year I always hear
Afar, aloft, a ghostly shout.

My clothes are worn to threads and loops;
My skin shows here and there;
About my face like seaweed droops
My tangled beard, my tangled hair;
From cavernous and shaggy brows
My stony eyes untroubled stare.

I move from eastern wretchedness
Through Fleet Street and the Strand;
And as the pleasant people press
I touch them softly with my hand,
Perhaps I know that still I go
Alive about a living land.

Where Davidson differed from most of the poets of his own time was in his commitment to a scientific view of the world. And the Edwardian period is indeed the first great age of popular science. After the great breakthroughs of the Victorians, the basic laws of physics, evolution and chemistry were spreading through schools and colleges, and go-ahead people, such as the popular novelist H.G. Wells, felt that a grounding in science was essential to being properly educated. But how would science affect British poetry, still mostly wallowing in its gauzy bucolic medievalism? Davidson's poem 'Snow' isn't an unqualified success, but it's a damned good try at seeing the natural world anew.

'Who affirms that crystals are alive?'
I affirm it, let who will deny:
Crystals are engendered, wax and thrive,
Wane and wither; I have seen them die.

Trust me, masters, crystals have their day,
Eager to attain the perfect norm,
Lit with purpose, potent to display
Facet, angle, colour, beauty, form.

Water-crystals need for flower and root
Sixty clear degrees, no less, no more;
Snow, so fickle, still in this acute
Angle thinks, and learns no other lore:

Such its life, and such its pleasure is,
Such its art and traffic, such its gain,
Evermore in new conjunctions this
Admirable angle to maintain.

Crystalcraft in every flower and flake
Snow exhibits, of the welkin free:
Crystalline are crystals for the sake,
All and singular, of crystalry.

Yet does every crystal of the snow
Individualize, a seedling sown
Broadcast, but instinct with power to grow
Beautiful in beauty of its own.

Every flake with all its prongs and dints
Burns ecstatic as a new-lit star:
Men are not more diverse, finger prints
More dissimilar than snow-flakes are.

Worlds of men and snow endure, increase,
Woven of power and passion to defy
Time and travail: only races cease,
Individual men and crystals die.

Thomas Hardy was older than Davidson by seventeen years – he
was born in 1840 in Dorset – and he lived a lot longer. He was also
a much greater poet, indeed one of the greatest poets in British
literature; but he shared certain interesting traits with Davidson.
He too was a profoundly pessimistic man, with a great interest in
scientific and modern thought. Though he had an emotional attach-
ment to the Anglican Church, Hardy couldn't accept the traditional
religious view of the world, and famously once advised a clergyman
to study Darwin and followers such as Herbert Spencer. Davidson
and Hardy are both writers attempting to make sense of a world
which now has a God-shaped hole in it; and as such, they speak for
millions of less talented Britons at the time. Hardy's 'The
Convergence of the Twain' was written in response to the sinking
of the *Titanic* in 1912, but also expresses his dark view of fate, and
the follies of a culture that had come to think itself superior to
nature. For those of us today who suspect that our fast-growing
and greedy civilisation will one day get its comeuppance, this is an
almost essential text:

I
In a solitude of the sea
Deep from human vanity,
And the Pride of Life that planned her, stilly couches she.

II
Steel chambers, late the pyres
Of her salamandrine fires,
Cold currents thrid, and turn to rhythmic tidal lyres.

III
Over the mirrors meant
To glass the opulent
The sea-worm crawls – grotesque, slimed, dumb,
    indifferent.

IV
Jewels in joy designed
To ravish the sensuous mind
Lie lightless, all their sparkles bleared and black and blind.

V
Dim moon-eyed fishes near
Gaze at the gilded gear
And query: 'What does this vaingloriousness down here?'
    …

VI
Well: while was fashioning
This creature of cleaving wing,
The Immanent Will that stirs and urges everything

VII
Prepared a sinister mate
For her – so gaily great –
A Shape of Ice, for the time far and dissociate.

VIII
And as the smart ship grew
In stature, grace, and hue
In shadowy silent distance grew the Iceberg too.

IX
Alien they seemed to be;
No mortal eye could see
The intimate welding of their later history.

X
Or sign that they were bent
By paths coincident
On being anon twin halves of one August event,

XI
Till the Spinner of the Years
Said 'Now!' And each one hears,
And consummation comes, and jars two hemispheres.

The underlying pessimism of Hardy, and other Edwardian writers, is so noticeable that it's hard for the modern reader not to see it as an eerie premonition of the horrors of the First World War to come. Ezra Pound, the American poet working in London while Hardy was writing his best poetry, declared famously that poets were 'the antennae of the race'. Hardy proves it in his 'Channel Firing', which imagines the buried dead in a Dorset church reacting to British naval gunnery practice in the Channel. What's extraordinary – even spooky – is that it was written and published in 1914, well before the war had begun.

That night your great guns, unawares,
Shook all our coffins as we lay,
And broke the chancel window-squares,
We thought it was the judgement day

And sat upright. While drearisome
Arose the howl of wakened hounds:
The mouse let fall the altar-crumb,
The worms drew back into the mounds,

The glebe cow drooled. Till God called, 'No;
It's gunnery practice out at sea
Just as before you went below;
The world is as it used to be:

'All nations striving strong to make
Red war yet redder. Mad as hatters
They do more for Christés sake
Than you who are helpless in such matters.

'That this is not the judgment hour
For some of them's a blessed thing,
For if it were they'd have to scour
Hell's floor for so much threatening ...

'Ha, ha. It will be warmer when
I blow the trumpet (if indeed
I ever do; for you are men,
And rest eternal sorely need).'

So down we lay again. 'I wonder,
Will the world ever saner be,'
Said one, 'than when He sent us under
In our indifferent century!'

And many a skeleton shook his head.
'Instead of preaching forty year,'
My neighbour Parson Thirdly said,
'I wish I had stuck to pipes and beer.'

Again the guns disturbed the hour,
Roaring their readiness to avenge,
As far inland as Stourton Tower,
And Camelot, and starlit Stonehenge.

But I am in danger here of suggesting that Hardy is in some way a political poet. He is not. He is a poet of ideas, and of his time, certainly, but his best work is personal, above all in the *Poems of 1912 –13,* when he looks back with intense regret and shame on his failed marriage to his first wife Emma. He had been faithless. She had turned her back on him, scandalised by his anti-religious views. As Hardy goes back to try to recapture their early love in the places they knew best, he achieves an almost unbearable honesty about failure in human love. Here are two of my favourites from the sequence. The first is called 'The Voice':

Woman much missed, how you call to me, call to me,
Saying that now you are not as you were
When you had changed from the one who was all to me,
But as at first, when our day was fair.
Can it be you that I hear? Let me view you, then,
Standing as when I drew near to the town
Where you would wait for me: yes, as I knew you then,
Even to the original air-blue gown!
Or is it only the breeze, in its listlessness
Travelling across the wet mead to me here,
You being ever dissolved to wan wistlessness,
Heard no more again far or near?

Thus I; faltering forward,
Leaves around me falling,
Wind oozing thin through the thorn from norward,
And the woman calling.

The second, referring to one of their favourite walks, is called 'At Castle Boterel'. If, kind reader, you don't feel your eyes welling at the end of it, there's something wrong with you.

As I drive to the junction of lane and highway,
And the drizzle bedrenches the waggonette,
I look behind at the fading byway,
And see on its slope, now glistening wet,
Distinctly yet

Myself and a girlish form benighted
In dry March weather. We climb the road
Beside a chaise. We had just alighted
To ease the sturdy pony's load
When he sighed and slowed.

What we did as we climbed, and what we talked of
Matters not much, nor to what it led, –
Something that life will not be balked of
Without rude reason till hope is dead,
And feeling fled.

It filled but a minute. But was there ever
A time of such quality, since or before,
In that hill's story? To one mind never,
Though it has been climbed, foot-swift, foot-sore,
By thousands more.

Primaeval rocks form the road's steep border,
And much have they faced there, first and last,
Of the transitory in Earth's long order;
But what they record in colour and cast
Is – that we two passed.

And to me, though Time's unflinching rigour,
In mindless rote, has ruled from sight
The substance now, one phantom figure
Remains on the slope, as when that night
Saw us alight.

I look and see it there, shrinking, shrinking,
I look back at it amid the rain
For the very last time; for my sand is sinking,
And I shall traverse old love's domain
Never again.

Thinking of the British landscape, and feelings of pessimism ahead of the First World War, there's one other essential poet. A.E. Housman was considered to be the most brilliant classical scholar of his day – and his day was crammed with brilliant classical scholars. A gay man at a time when this was criminal and extremely dangerous, his best-known sequence of verses was called 'A Shropshire Lad' – a kind of long anthem to doomed youth, and an elegy to an English pastoral Eden which seemed, as the new century loomed, to be vanishing:

Into my heart an air that kills
From yon far country blows:
What are those blue remembered hills,
What spires, what farms are those?

That is the land of lost content,
I see it shining plain,
The happy highways where I went
And cannot come again.

And:

Far in a western brookland
That bred me long ago
The poplars stand and tremble
By pools I used to know.

There, in the windless night-time,
The wanderer, marvelling why,
Halts on the bridge to hearken
How soft the poplars sigh.

He hears: no more remembered
In fields where I was known,
Here I lie down in London
And turn to rest alone.

There, by the starlit fences,
The wanderer halts and hears
My soul that lingers sighing
About the glimmering weirs.

Housman's sense of the English countryside was as history-drenched as Thomas Hardy's – an endlessly lived-in, lived-on narrative. But in Housman's Shropshire the actual countrymen seem vaguer, sketched in, rather than the dialect-speaking, three-dimensional characters of Hardy's Dorset. This perhaps reflects the underlying story Housman tells – an England being emptied of bold young men, sent off to fight and die for the Empire abroad. But it means that, again and again, the most vivid characters in Housman's verses are ghosts.

On Wenlock Edge the wood's in trouble;
His forest fleece the Wrekin heaves;

The gale, it plies the saplings double,
And thick on Severn snow the leaves.

'Twould blow like this through holt and hanger
When Uricon* the city stood;
'Tis the old wind in the old anger,
But then it threshed another wood.

Then, 'twas before my time, the Roman
At yonder heaving hill would stare;
The blood that warms an English yeoman,
The thoughts that hurt him, they were there.

There, like the wind through woods in riot,
Through him the gale of life blew high;
The tree of man was never quiet:
Then 'twas the Roman, now 'tis I.

The gale, it plies the saplings double,
It blows so hard, 'twill soon be gone:
Today the Roman and his trouble
Are ashes under Uricon.

Housman seems to have been a mostly lonely man, and mostly repressed, famous for his savage treatment of less talented scholars. But he wrote one very powerful poem about the war against homosexuals, after the trial of Oscar Wilde. It is, I suppose, the first gay protest poem in English literature:

Oh who is that young sinner with the handcuffs on his
    wrists?
And what has he been after that they groan and shake
    their fists?

---

* Housman's name for a Roman settlement under what is now Wroxeter.

And wherefore is he wearing such a conscience-stricken
    air?
Oh they're taking him to prison for the colour of his hair.

'Tis a shame to human nature, such a head of hair as his;
In the good old time 'twas hanging for the colour that it is;
Though hanging isn't bad enough and flaying would be fair
For the nameless and abominable colour of his hair.

Oh a deal of pains he's taken and a pretty price he's paid
To hide his poll or dye it of a mentionable shade;
But they've pulled the beggar's hat off for the world to see
    and stare,
And they're taking him to justice for the colour of his hair.

Now 'tis oakum for his fingers and the treadmill for his
    feet,
And the quarry-gang on Portland in the cold and in the
    heat,
And between his spells of labour in the time he has to
    spare
He can curse the God that made him for the colour of his
    hair.

We are now on the very edge of the First World War, the first definitive shock to inherited notions of Britishness in modern times. But to get some sense of what the war would do to established ideas of patriotism and Britain's place in the world, we must end with Sir Henry Newbolt. Like Kipling a poet fashioned through the rhythms and language of hymns, popular verse and the music hall, Newbolt was educated at Clifton College, part of the new generation of public schools formed to provide the Empire with austere, stoical and reliable public servants. A comfortably-off barrister as well as a highly successful writer, Newbolt might seem to be the very epitome of the smug and conventional imperialist

Englishman of Edwardian times, just as Clifton College might seem the epitome of the kind of school that produced such men. But real life is messier, and more interesting. Sir Henry spent much of his life in a three-way affair involving his wife and their mutual, thus bisexual, lover. Clifton was in fact an unusually open-minded school, welcoming in boys from poorer backgrounds and reserving a special house for Jewish boys. Nevertheless, there isn't much room for doubt in Newbolt's most famous poem, 'Vita Lampeda', or 'the lamp of life'. Written in 1892, it was massively popular. When the war started, Sir Henry volunteered for the government's propaganda bureau; this poem was especially mocked and hated by a new generation shivering and dying in the trenches:

There's a breathless hush in the Close to-night —
Ten to make and the match to win —
A bumping pitch and a blinding light,
An hour to play and the last man in.
And it's not for the sake of a ribboned coat,
Or the selfish hope of a season's fame,
But his captain's hand on his shoulder smote
'Play up! play up! and play the game!'
The sand of the desert is sodden red, —
Red with the wreck of a square that broke; —
The Gatling's jammed and the Colonel dead,
And the regiment blind with dust and smoke.
The river of death has brimmed his banks,
And England's far, and Honour a name,
But the voice of a schoolboy rallies the ranks:
'Play up! play up! and play the game!'
This is the word that year by year,
While in her place the school is set,
Every one of her sons must hear,
And none that hears it dare forget.
This they all with a joyful mind
Bear through life like a torch in flame,

And falling fling to the host behind —
'Play up! play up! and play the game!'

Hardly anyone, presumably, sets out to be a war poet: it's a fate that happens to some unlucky people at some unlucky moments. Rupert Brooke, remembered as one of the most uncomplicatedly patriotic of the First World War poets, actually spent most of his life as a peacetime poet, before being killed by an infected mosquito bite off Greece in 1915. If, somewhere in our collective consciousness, we have a half-buried notion that poets 'ought' to be particularly good-looking, then Rupert Brooke is probably to blame. Yeats called him 'the best looking young man in England', and photographs display a floppy-haired, chisel-jawed youth with a curiously intense stare. Today's children are taught the war poets from the latter end of the conflict – the most disaffected, angry anti-war poets there have ever been. But Rupert Brooke was rather more of the Sir Henry Newbolt way of thinking. He had a fierce prejudice for England and the English. His poem 'The Old Vicarage, Grantchester', a romantic hymn to the small village outside Cambridge, is now mostly famous for its closing lines: 'Stands the Church clock at ten to three? And is there honey still for tea?' But it begins with Brooke in Berlin, where he was recuperating from an unhappy and complicated romantic tangle, and in a sourly homesick frame of mind:

Just now the lilac is in bloom,
All before my little room;
And in my flower-beds, I think,
Smile the carnation and the pink;
And down the borders, well I know,
The poppy and the pansy blow ...
Oh! there the chestnuts, summer through,
Beside the river make for you
A tunnel of green gloom, and sleep
Deeply above; and green and deep
The stream mysterious glides beneath,

Green as a dream and deep as death.
– Oh, damn! I know it! and I know
How the May fields all golden show,
And when the day is young and sweet,
Gild gloriously the bare feet
That run to bathe ...
'Du lieber Gott!'

Here am I, sweating, sick, and hot,
And there the shadowed waters fresh
Lean up to embrace the naked flesh.
Temperamentvoll German Jews
Drink beer around; – and THERE the dews
Are soft beneath a morn of gold.
Here tulips bloom as they are told;
Unkempt about those hedges blows
An English unofficial rose;
And there the unregulated sun
Slopes down to rest when day is done,
And wakes a vague unpunctual star,

Interesting, isn't it, that for the casual English anti-Semite of 1912,
German Jews are just part of the German furniture, drinking their
beer? Brooke stands up for the liberal English idyll, an unregulated
country where the state is not yet powerful; his xenophobia,
however, reeks. He throws himself into a historical reverie about
the glories of the English countryside, before radically changing
mood and energetically libelling, in a very funny passage, many of
his countrymen:

God! I will pack, and take a train,
And get me to England once again!
For England's the one land, I know,
Where men with Splendid Hearts may go;
And Cambridgeshire, of all England,

The shire for Men who Understand;
And of THAT district I prefer
The lovely hamlet Grantchester.
For Cambridge people rarely smile,
Being urban, squat, and packed with guile;
And Royston men in the far South
Are black and fierce and strange of mouth;
At Over they fling oaths at one,
And worse than oaths at Trumpington,
And Ditton girls are mean and dirty,
And there's none in Harston under thirty,
And folks in Shelford and those parts
Have twisted lips and twisted hearts,
And Barton men make Cockney rhymes,
And Coton's full of nameless crimes,
And things are done you'd not believe
At Madingley on Christmas Eve.
Strong men have run for miles and miles,
When one from Cherry Hinton smiles;
Strong men have blanched, and shot their wives,
Rather than send them to St. Ives;
Strong men have cried like babes, bydam,
To hear what happened at Babraham.

What does this tell us? Two things, I think. First, that it's by now possible to be both patriotic and satirical about the realities of English life, particularly if you're looking down on them. Edwardian culture was more relaxed than Victorian culture, especially amongst intellectuals – and Rupert Brooke was a friend of the so-called Bloomsbury group. Brooke really means it when he says that England is the only place to live; but he also means it when he describes a countryside full of misbehaving and unappetising peasants. England, more than Scotland or Wales, was still a highly hierarchical and class-conscious society; Rupert Brooke was a flamboyant representative of the snobs at the top.

Second, it reminds us that this was also still a country of intense local rivalries. Small towns and villages did indeed tell terrible stories about one another, and most people's sense of identity was closely bound up with the village, or the few urban streets, in which they happened to be born and to live. Edwardians, particularly from the poorer classes, did not travel very far, unless they were on military or imperial duties. Their strong sense of locality, a kind of civic patriotism almost, would lead to the 'Pals" battalions of Kitchener's conscript army – young men, all from the same small area, joining up, serving and often dying together. Only now, at the end of the poem, does Rupert Brooke change tone again, in his famous celebration:

But Grantchester! ah, Grantchester!
There's peace and holy quiet there,
Great clouds along pacific skies,
And men and women with straight eyes,
Lithe children lovelier than a dream,
A bosky wood, a slumbrous stream,
And little kindly winds that creep
Round twilight corners, half asleep.
In Grantchester their skins are white;
They bathe by day, they bathe by night;
The women there do all they ought;
The men observe the Rules of Thought.
They love the Good; they worship Truth;
They laugh uproariously in youth;
(And when they get to feeling old,
They up and shoot themselves, I'm told) …

Ah God! to see the branches stir
Across the moon at Grantchester!
To smell the thrilling-sweet and rotten
Unforgettable, unforgotten
River-smell, and hear the breeze

Sobbing in the little trees.
Say, do the elm-clumps greatly stand
Still guardians of that holy land?
The chestnuts shade, in reverend dream,
The yet unacademic stream?
Is dawn a secret shy and cold
Anadyomene, silver-gold?
And sunset still a golden sea
From Haslingfield to Madingley?
And after, ere the night is born,
Do hares come out about the corn?
Oh, is the water sweet and cool,
Gentle and brown, above the pool?
And laughs the immortal river still
Under the mill, under the mill?
Say, is there Beauty yet to find?
And Certainty? and Quiet kind?
Deep meadows yet, for to forget
The lies, and truths, and pain? … oh! yet
Stands the Church clock at ten to three?
And is there honey still for tea?

Brooke's patriotism goes a long way towards explaining why so
many young Englishmen volunteered so quickly to go to France and
die. It's a patriotism we have largely lost, partly because of the twen-
tieth-century wartime experiences, and partly because we know so
much more about the rest of the world. But we are allowed to regret
the loss: it gave those who felt it a sense of confidence and warm
belonging that gurgled away with the bloodied rainwater of
Flanders:

If I should die, think only this of me:
That there's some corner of a foreign field
That is for ever England. There shall be
In that rich earth a richer dust concealed;

A dust whom England bore, shaped, made aware,
Gave, once, her flowers to love, her ways to roam,
A body of England's, breathing English air,
Washed by the rivers, blest by suns of home.

And think, this heart, all evil shed away,
A pulse in the eternal mind, no less
Gives somewhere back the thoughts by England given;
Her sights and sounds; dreams happy as her day;
And laughter, learnt of friends; and gentleness,
In hearts at peace, under an English heaven.

13

The Poets of More
Than One War

During the first quarter of the twenty-first century, a time of solemn commemorations, when the last of those who fought in the First World War are now dead, many of us have learned to revise the harsh judgements made about that conflict from the 1960s onwards. It wasn't a pointless war. The Kaiser's Germany, though nothing like Hitler's Germany, was an extremely aggressive, militaristic and indeed anti-Semitic state which believed that its own security required the military defeat of France and Russia. Had it been victorious there would have been a new order on the European Continent which would have been devastating for British power. Nor was it a war entirely led by stupid generals, sacrificing hundreds of thousands of men for no point whatever. The generals, who had never come across the military effect of new technologies such as massed machine guns, barbed wire, poison gas and high-explosive shells, weren't stupid so much as lacking the necessary experience and information. British leaders such as Lord Haig may have learned too slowly and have been infuriatingly complacent, but they were hardly alone: the Russian, German and French commanders behaved very similarly. Finally, whatever the ghastly slaughters of 1915 to 1917 for a few hundred yards of bloodsoaked mud, in the final year of the war the British Army won hugely important and decisive victories, partly thanks to excellent leadership and coordination, which stand alongside those of the Dukes of Marlborough and Wellington.

Today we tend to emphasise more the unprecedented effect of the war on the organisation of British society. This was when the state made a massive if necessary power grab, which would change the lives of millions of us throughout the century ahead.

Given all this, what can the famous war poets teach us that isn't banal? The horrors of the trenches have become one of the great clichés of British culture. That doesn't detract in any way from what actually happened – but we know all that. The hammering of Siegfried Sassoon and Wilfred Owen into the heads of generations of children who, beyond them, had learned not to like poetry, has been a powerful weapon for pacifism – if such an oxymoron can hold. In fact, the war poetry of 1914 to 1918 can still tell us a great deal. By and large, and perhaps unexpectedly, its anger is not directed at German soldiers or leaders. Yet the message is rarely that the war is completely futile, either: even poets who came close to such a view mostly tried to return to the fighting sooner or later. Rather, it creates a new and more nuanced patriotism than the 'Go England' anti-Germanism of Rupert Brooke; British landscapes represent all that is good. But the behaviour of the people away from the front, whether they be pompous middle-ranking military officers or baying patriotic crowds, is mostly feeble, uncomprehending or disgusting. Poets like Newbolt and Brooke didn't cut much ice in Flanders for very long. To be fair to them, they had no more idea of what was coming than anybody else, and Brooke died too quickly to comprehend the nature of the war.

The question of what a war poet is remains hard to answer definitively. Most of them, of course, were young men with some poetic ambitions who found themselves in khaki and in France. But not all. We have seen, through Kipling, that it was perfectly possible to be a good – by which I mean accurate and biting – war poet without being there. Nor was it necessary to survive until the worst slaughters at the Somme and Passchendaele. The Scottish poet Charles Hamilton Sorley, killed by a sniper at the Battle of Loos in 1915, is an interesting study in how quickly attitudes changed. A patriotic, Protestant public schoolboy, his early military verse has a

Rupert Brooke-ish patriotic fervour: this is a good war, for God and King:

All the hills and vales along
Earth is bursting into song,
And the singers are the chaps
Who are going to die perhaps.
O sing, marching men,
Till the valleys ring again.
Give your gladness to earth's keeping,
So be glad, when you are sleeping.

Cast away regret and rue,
Think what you are marching to,
Little live, great pass.
Jesus Christ and Barabbas
Were found the same day.
This died, that, went his way.
So sing with joyful breath.
For why, you are going to death.
Teeming earth will surely store
All the gladness that you pour.

Earth that never doubts nor fears
Earth that knows of death, not tears,
Earth that bore with joyful ease
Hemlock for Socrates,
Earth that blossomed and was glad
'Neath the cross that Christ had,
Shall rejoice and blossom too
When the bullet reaches you.
Wherefore, men marching
On the road to death, sing!
Pour gladness on earth's head,
So be merry, so be dead.

From the hills and valleys earth
Shouts back the sound of mirth,
Tramp of feet and lilt of song
Ringing all the road along.
All the music of their going,
Ringing swinging glad song-throwing,
Earth will echo still, when foot
Lies numb and voice mute.
On marching men, on
To the gates of death with song.
Sow your gladness for earth's reaping,
So you may be glad though sleeping.
Strew your gladness on earth's bed,
So be merry, so be dead.

That's the war of so many memorial sculptures after it – jingling, confident men going willingly to their deaths for their beliefs. But Sorley thought deeply, and quite quickly produced a remarkable poem of potential reconciliation, entitled simply 'To Germany':

You are blind like us. Your hurt no man designed,
And no man claimed the conquest of your land.
But gropers both through fields of thought confined
We stumble and we do not understand.
You only saw your future bigly planned,
And we, the tapering paths of our own mind,
And in each other's dearest ways we stand,
And hiss and hate. And the blind fight the blind.

When it is peace, then we may view again
With new-won eyes each other's truer form
And wonder. Grown more loving-kind and warm
We'll grasp firm hands and laugh at the old pain,
When it is peace. But until peace, the storm
The darkness and the thunder and the rain.

In his final poem – and we know it's his final poem because it was recovered from his kit after his death – Sorley achieves a very different tone from his earlier work. It's a poem about death, but it embraces the harsh suspicion that there is no heaven, or hell, or divine reconciliation to come, that had so haunted the late Victorians and the pre-war Edwardian poets:

When you see millions of the mouthless dead
Across your dreams in pale battalions go,
Say not soft things as other men have said,
That you'll remember. For you need not so.
Give them not praise. For, deaf, how should they know
It is not curses heaped on each gashed head?
Nor tears. Their blind eyes see not your tears flow.
Nor honour. It is easy to be dead.
Say only this, 'They are dead.' Then add thereto,
'Yet many a better one has died before.'
Then, scanning all the o'ercrowded mass, should you
Perceive one face that you loved heretofore,
It is a spook. None wears the face you knew.
Great death has made all his for evermore.

Edward Thomas was an Anglo-Welsh poet who joined up more or less as Sorley was killed, and who died himself in 1917, in the third Battle of Arras. A journalist and critic, Thomas was much influenced by the great American poet Robert Frost. His own verse reminds one of John Clare: he had a real countryman's sense of the populated countryside, crammed with eccentric and wilful people. Like Sorley, he struggled hard to find a new kind of patriotism that paid full due to his love of British landscapes, while not falling into simpleminded jingoism. Perhaps his best-loved poem is his nostalgic tribute to an obscure railway station:

Yes, I remember Adlestrop –
The name, because one afternoon
Of heat the express-train drew up there
Unwontedly. It was late June.

The steam hissed. Someone cleared his throat.
No one left and no one came
On the bare platform. What I saw
Was Adlestrop – only the name.

And willows, willow-herb, and grass,
And meadowsweet, and haycocks dry,
No whit less still and lonely fair
Than the high cloudlets in the sky.

And for that minute a blackbird sang
Close by, and round him, mistier,
Farther and farther, all the birds
Of Oxfordshire and Gloucestershire.

Tempted by his friendship with Robert Frost to move to the United
States well before that country had joined the war, Thomas eventu-
ally enlisted, despite fierce arguments with other members of his
family whose hatred of Germany he couldn't share. He wrote the
following poem on Boxing Day 1915, when he was home in London
on leave:

This is no case of petty right or wrong
That politicians or philosophers
Can judge. I hate not Germans, nor grow hot
With love of Englishmen, to please newspapers.
Beside my hate for one fat patriot
My hatred of the Kaiser is love true:–
A kind of god he is, banging a gong.
But I have not to choose between the two,

Or between justice and injustice. Dinned
With war and argument I read no more
Than in the storm smoking along the wind
Athwart the wood. Two witches' cauldrons roar.
From one the weather shall rise clear and gay;
Out of the other an England beautiful
And like her mother that died yesterday.
Little I know or care if, being dull,
I shall miss something that historians
Can rake out of the ashes when perchance
The phoenix broods serene above their ken.
But with the best and meanest Englishmen
I am one in crying, God save England, lest
We lose what never slaves and cattle blessed.
The ages made her that made us from dust:
She is all we know and live by, and we trust
She is good and must endure, loving her so:
And as we love ourselves we hate her foe.

Thomas addresses the war in many poems, but rarely confronts directly the grubby and terrifying reality of the trenches. He knew it, but he was more interested in holding in his mind a love of country rooted in rural realities. He begins 'Liberty', a poem of 1915, by brilliantly smashing together these two kinds of truth:

The last light has gone out of the world, except
This moonlight lying on the grass like frost
Beyond the brink of the tall elm's shadow.

And his best war poems are barely war poems at all, more the reflections of a genuine English patriot confronting death, as in the magnificent 'Rain':

Rain, midnight rain, nothing but the wild rain
On this bleak hut, and solitude, and me
Remembering again that I shall die
And neither hear the rain nor give it thanks
For washing me cleaner than I have been
Since I was born into this solitude.
Blessed are the dead that the rain rains upon:
But here I pray that none whom once I loved
Is dying to-night or lying still awake
Solitary, listening to the rain,
Either in pain or thus in sympathy
Helpless among the living and the dead,
Like a cold water among broken reeds,
Myriads of broken reeds all still and stiff,
Like me who have no love which this wild rain
Has not dissolved except the love of death,
If love it be towards what is perfect and
Cannot, the tempest tells me, disappoint.

If Edward Thomas and Charles Sorley show that our popular idea
of the 'war poets' is a limited one, the work of women poets during
1914–18 should unfamiliarise us further. For educated, thoughtful
women, the war brought both frustration and great opportunity:
they had to stand aside while their husbands, brothers and lovers
went to fight, and yet at the same time they had the chance – even
the obligation – to do things they would never have been allowed to
do in peacetime Edwardian Britain: to drive lorries and buses, to
administer offices, to go to France to nurse the wounded, to work in
the fields, and to labour in munitions factories. In the years just
before the war, militant suffragism had reached its zenith. Now
women took up smoking, and learned an independence they would
not surrender lightly; when they wrote their tone could be as blindly
patriotic as any retired colonel. Jessie Pope was a popular journalist
and writer, who discovered the manuscript of Robert Tressell's
socialist novel *The Ragged-Trousered Philanthropists*. When the war

came, the jingoism of her writing for popular newspapers infuriated the likes of Wilfred Owen, who ironically dedicated his 'Dulce et Decorum Est' to Pope and her like. But for all its jaunty tone, her poem 'War Girls' tells us a lot about the mood on the home front:

There's the girl who clips your ticket for the train,
And the girl who speeds the lift from floor to floor,
There's the girl who does a milk-round in the rain,
And the girl who calls for orders at your door.
Strong, sensible and fit,
They're out to show their grit
And tackle jobs with energy and knack ...

There's the motor girl who drives a heavy van,
There's the butcher girl who brings your joint of meat,
There's the girl who cries, 'All fares, please!' like a man,
And the girl who whistles taxis up the street.

For working-class girls in particular, all this new work brought cash prosperity undreamed-of before the war. Very little is known about Madeline Ida Bedford, though she was presumably a munitions worker, and has left a spirited short poem, 'Munition Wages', on that subject. She supports the argument made in this book that so-called occasional verse can act as a time capsule, preserving the rhythms and phrases of everyday speech:

Earning high wages?
Yus, Five quid a week.
A woman, too, mind you,
I calls it dim sweet.

Ye'are asking some questions –
But bless yer, here goes:
I spends the whole racket
On good times and clothes.

Me saving? Elijah!
Yer do think I'm mad.
I'm acting the lady,
But — I ain't living bad.

I'm having life's good times.
See 'ere, it's like this:
The 'oof come o' danger,
A touch-and-go bizz.

We're all here today, mate,
Tomorrow — perhaps dead,
If Fate tumbles on us
And blows up our shed.

Afraid! Are yer kidding?
With money to spend!
Years back I wore tatters,
Now — silk stockings, mi friend!

I've bracelets and jewellery,
Rings envied by friends;
A sergeant to swank with,
And something to lend.

I drive out in taxis,
Do theatres in style.
And this is mi verdict —
It is jolly worth while.

Worth while, for tomorrow
If I'm blown to the sky,
I'll have repaid mi wages
In death — and pass by.

It's a poem which, to the modern ear, sounds distinctly too celebratory for the period; but there were other women poets who, as they shaped the shells and munitions that would rip flesh apart, were agonising about what they were doing. This is by Mary Gabrielle Collins, and is called 'Women at Munition Making':

Their hands should minister unto the flame of life,
Their fingers guide
The rosy teat, swelling with milk,
To the eager mouth of the suckling babe
Or smooth with tenderness,
Softly and soothingly,
The heated brow of the ailing child.
Or stray among the curls
Of the boy or girl, thrilling to mother love.
But now,
Their hands, their fingers
Are coarsened in munition factories.
Their thoughts, which should fly
Like bees among the sweetest mind flowers
Gaining nourishment for the thoughts to be,
Are bruised against the law,
'Kill, kill.'
They must take part in defacing and destroying the natural
    body
Which, certainly during this dispensation
Is the shrine of the spirit.
O God!
Throughout the ages we have seen,
Again and again
Men by Thee created
Cancelling each other.
And we have marvelled at the seeming annihilation
Of Thy work.
But this goes further,

Taints the fountain head,
Mounts like a poison to the Creator's very heart.
O God!
Must It anew be sacrificed on earth?

Ezra Pound famously complained that during the war almost everybody seemed to be writing poetry – and there was a flood of mainly patriotic verse in all the printed media. But Charlotte Mew was a much more substantial literary figure than the other women quoted here, a poet greatly admired by Thomas Hardy, whose poem looking forward to peace from the perspective of 1915 confronts the growing war-exhaustion at home:

Let us remember Spring will come again
To the scorched, blackened woods, where all the wounded
    trees
Wait, with their old wise patience for the heavenly rain,
Sure of the sky: sure of the sea to send its healing breeze,
Sure of the sun. And even as to these
Surely the Spring, when God shall please
Will come again like a divine surprise
To those who sit to-day with their great Dead, hands in
    their hands, eyes in their eyes,
At one with Love, at one with Grief: blind to the scattered
    things and changing skies.

And yet when peace eventually came, the sheer weight of bereavement and loss, the sense of social dislocation and turmoil, meant that it didn't feel like a 'proper' peace. Eleanor Farjeon came from a family of novelists, musicians and theatre people. She's remembered mostly today for her children's stories and much-loved hymn:

Morning has broken,
Like the first morning,
Blackbird has spoken

Like the first bird;
Praise for the singing,
Praise for the morning,
Praise for them springing
Fresh from the Word.

But Farjeon was a woman of many moods and surprises – she was
a great friend of both Robert Frost and his friend Edward Thomas,
and at the war's end produced a surprising and essentially feminist
poem called 'Peace':

I
I am as awful as my brother War,
I am the sudden silence after clamour.
I am the face that shows the seamy scar
When blood and frenzy has lost its glamour.
Men in my pause shall know the cost at last
That is not to be paid in triumphs or tears,
Men will begin to judge the thing that's past
As men will judge it in a hundred years.

Nations! whose ravenous engines must be fed
Endlessly with the father and the son,
My naked light upon your darkness, dread! –
By which ye shall behold what ye have done:
Whereon, more like a vulture than a dove,
Ye set my seal in hatred, not in love.

II
Let no man call me good. I am not blest.
My single virtue is the end of crimes,
I only am the period of unrest,
The ceasing of horrors of the times;
My good is but the negative of ill,
Such ill as bends the spirit with despair,

Such ill as makes the nations' soul stand still
And freeze to stone beneath a Gorgon glare.

Be blunt, and say that peace is but a state
Wherein the active soul is free to move,
And nations only show as mean or great
According to the spirit then they prove. –
O which of ye whose battle-cry is Hate
Will first in peace dare shout the name of Love?

For the best-known and most substantial group of war poets, the great sin was that battle-cry of hate. Most of them went into the war as enthusiasts and left as cynics, and while there is more to the record than that, the group comprising Robert Graves, Siegfried Sassoon, Wilfred Owen, Isaac Rosenberg and Ivor Gurney richly deserve their place in the story of British poetry. In their way, and mostly against their will, they are as important and influential as the Romantics or the Elizabethan sonneteers.

Of all of them, the one whose reputation depends least on his war poetry is the same man who first turned to realistic descriptions of trench warfare. Robert Graves was the son of an Irish Gaelic scholar and a German aristocrat – he was related to the famous German nationalist historian Leopold von Ranke. Neither this, nor a long history of childhood illness, stopped him from joining up at the beginning of the war, with the Royal Welch Fusiliers. He was badly injured in the Battle of the Somme, but recovered and is now remembered for novels such as *I, Claudius* and his later writing on myths. His war poetry mostly lacks the seething anger of that by his friend Siegfried Sassoon, but it has the freshness and immediacy of good reportage. This is called simply '1915':

I've watched the Seasons passing slow, so slow,
In the fields between La Bassée and Bethune;
Primroses and the first warm day of Spring,
Red poppy floods of June,

August, and yellowing Autumn, so
To Winter nights knee-deep in mud or snow,
And you've been everything.

Dear, you've been everything that I most lack
In these soul-deadening trenches – pictures, books,
Music, the quiet of an English wood,
Beautiful comrade-looks,
The narrow, bouldered mountain-track,
The broad, full-bosomed ocean, green and black,
And Peace, and all that's good.

But as the war went on, Graves's tone hardened. In 'The Dead Boche' he turns on jingos at home with all the venom of Sassoon or Owen:

To you who'd read my songs of War
And only hear of blood and fame,
I'll say (you've heard it said before)
'War's Hell!' and if you doubt the same,
Today I found in Mametz Wood
A certain cure for lust of blood:

Where, propped against a shattered trunk,
In a great mess of things unclean,
Sat a dead Boche; he scowled and stunk
With clothes and face a sodden green,
Big-bellied, spectacled, crop-haired,
Dribbling black blood from nose and beard.

From his name you might assume that Siegfried Sassoon had German blood like Graves. Not so: the 'Siegfried' came from his mother, who was an Anglo-Catholic devoted to the operas of Wagner. His father, however, was Jewish, and despite his good looks, courage and huge talents, it seems that Sassoon always felt slightly out of place in English high society. His poems are among the angriest of all on the subject of the war, and in 1917 he went far enough to call publicly for negotiations with the Germans and an armistice, something which at the time was considered treasonable and might have led to him being shot, had he not been sent, through the influence of friends, to a mental asylum in Edinburgh instead. There, famously, he met Wilfred Owen. Sassoon was as brave physically as he was mentally. His poems have the virtue of being instantly comprehensible, but tend to be angry satires rather than deeper reflections. Here are three well-known examples – the first is called 'Base Details':

If I were fierce, and bald, and short of breath
I'd live with scarlet Majors at the Base,
And speed glum heroes up the line to death.
You'd see me with my puffy petulant face,
Guzzling and gulping in the best hotel,
Reading the Roll of Honour. 'Poor young chap,'
I'd say – 'I used to know his father well;
Yes, we've lost heavily in this last scrap.'
And when the war is done and youth stone dead,
I'd toddle safely home and die – in bed.

The second is 'Does it Matter?':

Does it matter? – losing your legs?
For people will always be kind,
And you need not show that you mind
When others come in after hunting
To gobble their muffins and eggs.
Does it matter? – losing your sight?
There's such splendid work for the blind;
And people will always be kind,
As you sit on the terrace remembering
And turning your face to the light.

Do they matter – those dreams in the pit?
You can drink and forget and be glad,
And people won't say that you're mad;
For they know that you've fought for your country,
And no one will worry a bit.

And finally, 'Attack':

At dawn the ridge emerges massed and dun
In the wild purple of the glow'ring sun,
Smouldering through spouts of drifting smoke that shroud
The menacing scarred slope; and, one by one,
Tanks creep and topple forward to the wire.
The barrage roars and lifts. Then, clumsily bowed
With bombs and guns and shovels and battle-gear,
Men jostle and climb to meet the bristling fire.
Lines of grey, muttering faces, masked with fear,
They leave their trenches, going over the top,
While time ticks blank and busy on their wrists,
And hope, with furtive eyes and grappling fists,
Flounders in mud. O Jesus, make it stop!

Siegfried Sassoon is such a heavily anthologised poet, with so many wonderful things to his name, that I will stop there. But I hope it's clear already what the experience of war did to English poetry in hands such as his: it cauterised all the loose, merely musical diction; it slashed away at the dryads and the damozels; and in its urgency it replaced the exhausted decadence of art for art's sake with clear, modern, descriptive language. In short, 1915 dragged English poetry from 1852 to about 1950 in one angry, impatient lurch. The war changed almost everything about Britain, and that included its relationship to poetry.

Many of the war poets were in a tight circle. Robert Graves, after arguing brutally with Siegfried Sassoon about his war protest, helped to get him sent to the Edinburgh mental home, and thus to save his life. There, Sassoon – posh, flashy, confident – met the much poorer and less self-confident, though probably equally homosexual, Wilfred Owen. Both men eventually returned to fight: Owen was less lucky than Sassoon, and died in the final week of the war. Then, almost nobody knew about his poetry, while Sassoon was a national figure. But slowly, decade by decade, Wilfred Owen has come to be seen as the ultimate First World War poet, in whose shadow the rest of them stand. He was mainly brought up in Birkenhead and Shrewsbury, the son of a station master. Without much money, he nevertheless gained the kind of rich education that was still possible in Edwardian Britain for the less well-off – he was saturated in the English Romantic poets and, as an evangelical Anglican, in the Bible. All sorts of literary cadences recur in his war poetry as a result, giving it a heft and resonance even Sassoon struggles to achieve:

> What passing-bells for these who die as cattle?
> Only the monstrous anger of the guns.
> Only the stuttering rifles' rapid rattle
> Can patter out their hasty orisons.
> No mockeries now for them; no prayers nor bells;
> Nor any voice of mourning save the choirs,
> The shrill, demented choirs of wailing shells;
> And bugles calling for them from sad shires.
> What candles may be held to speed them all?
> Not in the hands of boys, but in their eyes
> Shall shine the holy glimmers of good-byes.
> The pallor of girls' brows shall be their pall;
> Their flowers the tenderness of patient minds,
> And each slow dusk a drawing-down of blinds.

His greatest poem, 'Strange Meeting', is entirely modern in its tone and rhythms, yet reverberates with lessons learned from Keats and Milton – and its third line would have made Coleridge sick with envy.

413

It seemed that out of battle I escaped
Down some profound dull tunnel, long since scooped
Through granites which Titanic wars had groined.
Yet also there encumbered sleepers groaned,
Too fast in thought or death to be bestirred.
Then, as I probed them, one sprang up, and stared
With piteous recognition in fixed eyes,
Lifting distressful hands as if to bless.
And by his smile, I knew that sullen hall;
By his dead smile I knew we stood in Hell.
With a thousand fears that vision's face was grained;
Yet no blood reached there from the upper ground,
And no guns thumped, or down the flues made moan.
'Strange friend,' I said, 'Here is no cause to mourn.'
'None,' said the other, 'Save the undone years,
The hopelessness. Whatever hope is yours,
Was my life also; I went hunting wild
After the wildest beauty in the world,
Which lies not calm in eyes, or braided hair,
But mocks the steady running of the hour,
And if it grieves, grieves richlier than here.
For by my glee might many men have laughed,
And of my weeping something had been left,
Which must die now. I mean the truth untold,
The pity of war, the pity war distilled.
Now men will go content with what we spoiled.
Or, discontent, boil bloody, and be spilled.
They will be swift with swiftness of the tigress,
None will break ranks, though nations trek from progress.
Courage was mine, and I had mystery;
Wisdom was mine, and I had mastery;
To miss the march of this retreating world
Into vain citadels that are not walled.
Then, when much blood had clogged their chariot-wheels
I would go up and wash them from sweet wells,

Even with truths that lie too deep for taint.
I would have poured my spirit without stint
But not through wounds; not on the cess of war.
Foreheads of men have bled where no wounds were.
I am the enemy you killed, my friend.
I knew you in this dark; for so you frowned
Yesterday through me as you jabbed and killed.
I parried; but my hands were loath and cold.
Let us sleep now ...'

Finally, no book which purports to tell the story of the British experience through poetry can miss out Owen's most famous short poem, 'Dulce et Decorum Est' – words which would have been picked out in gold paint in almost every school in Britain at the time:

Bent double, like old beggars under sacks,
Knock-kneed, coughing like hags, we cursed through
    sludge,
Till on the haunting flares we turned our backs,
And towards our distant rest began to trudge.
Men marched asleep. Many had lost their boots,
But limped on, blood-shod. All went lame, all blind;
Drunk with fatigue; deaf even to the hoots
Of gas-shells dropping softly behind.

Gas! GAS! Quick, boys! – An ecstasy of fumbling
Fitting the clumsy helmets just in time,
But someone still was yelling out and stumbling
And flound'ring like a man in fire or lime. –
Dim through the misty panes and thick green light,
As under a green sea, I saw him drowning.
In all my dreams before my helpless sight
He plunges at me, guttering, choking, drowning.
If in some smothering dreams, you too could pace

Behind the wagon that we flung him in,
And watch the white eyes writhing in his face,
His hanging face, like a devil's sick of sin,
If you could hear, at every jolt, the blood
Come gargling from the froth-corrupted lungs
Bitter as the cud
Of vile, incurable sores on innocent tongues, –
My friend, you would not tell with such high zest
To children ardent for some desperate glory,

The old Lie: Dulce et decorum est
Pro patria mori.

For most people, I suspect, those flatly accusatory final few words represent the essential message of the British war poets. But as I've tried to show, there's much more to them than that. In 1985 a memorial slab to the war poets of 1914–18 was unveiled in Poets' Corner, Westminster Abbey, and sixteen names were included on it. Of those, there are two who have pushed themselves high up the public consciousness but whom I haven't mentioned yet. Both, like Wilfred Owen, were essentially working-class. Isaac Rosenberg, killed in the war, came from a Latvian-Jewish immigrant family and spent most of his upbringing in the intensely Jewish East End of London. Apprenticed to an engraver at the age of fourteen, Rosenberg got himself to the Slade Institute of Fine Arts, where he met many of the leading Modernist painters of the day. He could well have been famous as an artist, but a couple of years before the war he was already writing poetry. His nightmarish 'A Ballad of Whitechapel', in which he encounters a young girl in the street, perhaps a prostitute, and walks with her, shows how he had already moved beyond the pallid late Romanticism of the day, and how his Judaism infused his sharp, reporterly eye. It reminds me of William Blake. This is an extract only:

The traffic rolled,
A gliding chaos populous of din,
A steaming wail at doom the Lord had scrawled
For perilous loads of sin.

And my soul thought:
'What fearful land have my steps wandered to?
God's love is everywhere, but here is naught
Save love His anger slew.'

And as I stood
Lost in promiscuous bewilderment,
Which to my 'mazed soul was wonder-food,
A girl in garments rent

Peered 'neath lids shamed
And spoke to me and murmured to my blood.
My soul stopped dead, and all my horror named
At her forgot of God.

Her hungered eyes,
Craving and yet so sadly spiritual,
Shone like the unsmirched corner of a jewel
Where else foul blemish lies.

I walked with her
Because my heart thought, 'Here the soul is clean,
The fragrance of the frankincense and myrrh
Is lost in odours mean.'

She told me how
The shadow of black death had newly come
And touched her father, mother, even now
Grim-hovering in her home,

Where fevered lay
Her wasting brother in a cold, bleak room,
Which theirs would be no longer than a day,
And then – the streets and doom.

Rosenberg suffered from tuberculosis, and emigrated briefly to South Africa to try to cure himself. There, as he narrates in a poem, he heard that war had been declared. There is not a shred of patriotic enthusiasm, only foresightful dread. The world was going to hell:

Snow is a strange white word.
No ice or frost
Has asked of bud or bird
For Winter's cost.

Yet ice and frost and snow
From earth to sky
This Summer land doth know.
No man knows why.

In all men's hearts it is.
Some spirit old
Hath turned with malign kiss
Our lives to mould.

Red fangs have torn His face.
God's blood is shed.
He mourns from His lone place
His children dead.

O! ancient crimson curse!
Corrode, consume.
Give back this universe
Its pristine bloom.

His war poetry is tough, sardonic, and somehow that of an outsider, very far from the public school references of Rupert Brooke or Siegfried Sassoon. This, one of his best-known war poems, is called 'Break of Day in the Trenches':

The darkness crumbles away
It is the same old druid Time as ever,
Only a live thing leaps my hand,
A queer sardonic rat,
As I pull the parapet's poppy
To stick behind my ear.
Droll rat, they would shoot you if they knew
Your cosmopolitan sympathies,
Now you have touched this English hand
You will do the same to a German
Soon, no doubt, if it be your pleasure
To cross the sleeping green between.
It seems you inwardly grin as you pass
Strong eyes, fine limbs, haughty athletes,
Less chanced than you for life,
Bonds to the whims of murder,
Sprawled in the bowels of the earth,
The torn fields of France.
What do you see in our eyes
At the shrieking iron and flame
Hurled through still heavens?
What quaver – what heart aghast?
Poppies whose roots are in men's veins
Drop, and are ever dropping;
But mine in my ear is safe,
Just a little white with the dust.

Which, if nothing else, goes to prove that the poppies of Flanders' fields were not later fiction to encourage donations. A poem which is much less well-known, but I think even better, describes another feature of trench life ignored by most other war poets – the ubiquity of lice and the need for 'Louse Hunting':

Nudes – stark and glistening,
Yelling in lurid glee. Grinning faces
And raging limbs
Whirl over the floor one fire.
For a shirt verminously busy
Yon soldier tore from his throat, with oaths
Godhead might shrink at, but not the lice.
And soon the shirt was aflare
Over the candle he'd lit while we lay.

Then we all sprang up and stript
To hunt the verminous brood.
Soon like a demons' pantomine
The place was raging.
See the silhouettes agape,
See the glibbering shadows
Mixed with the battled arms on the wall.
See gargantuan hooked fingers
Pluck in supreme flesh
To smutch the supreme littleness.
See the merry limbs in hot Highland fling
Because some wizard vermin
Charmed from the quiet this revel
When our ears were half lulled
By the dark music
Blown from Sleep's trumpet.

As early as the late-Victorian period, Russian and Polish pogroms against the Jews had hugely swollen what had been a relatively small Jewish population in Britain – mainly in London and Manchester. Just as in Germany, British Jews felt particularly impelled to prove their patriotism by signing up for the war. When Siegfried Sassoon issued his public call for negotiations with Germany, part of his torment was the inevitable anti-Semitic reaction. Rosenberg, who had been much more marinated in the Jewish culture of the East End, was both less tormented and more defiant. This short poem, written in France, is called simply 'The Jew':

Moses, from whose loins I sprung,
Lit by a lamp in his blood
Ten immutable rules, a moon
For mutable lampless men.

The blonde, the bronze, the ruddy,
With the same heaving blood,
Keep tide to the moon of Moses.
Then why do they sneer at me?

Ivor Gurney was also an outsider, though in a very different way. Like Rosenberg he was multiply talented, though in music rather than the fine arts, and he is remembered today almost as much as a composer as a poet. A tailor's son from Gloucester, he showed early musical talent and became a chorister before reaching the Royal College of Music on a scholarship at almost exactly the same time as Rosenberg made it to the Slade. Almost all his life he suffered from mood swings and periodic breakdowns: he probably had bipolar disorder. Like Rosenberg he served in the trenches as a private, not an officer, in his case in the Gloucestershire Regiment, from where he began sending poems home. Perhaps properly, as a musician, Gurney's poems have a rhythmic music all their own which reminds me slightly of Gerard Manley Hopkins. This is 'On Somme':

Suddenly into the still air burst thudding
And thudding and cold fear possessed me all,
On the grey slopes there, where Winter in sullen brooding
Hung between height and depth of the ugly fall

Of Heaven to earth; and the thudding was illness' own.
But still a hope I kept that were we there going over
I; in the line, I should not fail, but take recover
From others' courage, and not as coward be known.
No flame we saw, the noise and the dread alone
Was battle to us; men were enduring there such
And such things, in wire tangled, to shatters blown.
Courage kept, but ready to vanish at first touch.
Fear, but just held. Poets were luckier once
In the hot fray swallowed and some magnificence.

The distinctive Gurney rhythm was well suited to the surreal chaos, clatter and mess of military life in France. Here is part of a poem called 'Crucifix Corner', which seems a perfect verbal equivalent to the best drawings and paintings of trench life:

There was a water dump there, and regimental
Carts came every day to line up and fill full
Those rolling tanks with chlorinated clear mixture;
And curse the mud with vain veritable vexture.
Aveluy across the valley, billets, shacks, ruins,
With time and time a crump there to mark doings.
On New Year's Eve the marsh glowed tremulous
With rosy mist still holding late marvellous
Sun-glow, the air smelt home; the time breathed home.
Noel not put away; new term not yet come,
All things said 'Severn', the air was full of those calm
    meadows;
Transport rattled somewhere in the southern shadows;
Stars that were not strange ruled the most quiet high
Arch of soft sky, starred and most grave to see, most high.
What should break that but gun-noise or last Trump?
But neither came. At sudden, with light jump
Clarinet sang into 'Hundred Pipers and A',
Aveluy's Scottish answered with pipers' true call

'Happy we've been a'together.' When nothing
Stayed of war-weariness or winter's loathing,
Crackers with Christmas stockings hung in the heavens …

Gurney was also unusual in the insistence with which he thought about what would happen after the war was over. He was no more forgiving of jingoism at home than were Owen or Sassoon, but he was if anything more political. He called this poem, provocatively, 'To the Prussians of England':

When I remember plain heroic strength
And shining virtue shown by Ypres pools,
Then read the blither written by knaves for fools
In praise of English soldiers lying at length,
Who purely dream what England shall be made
Gloriously new, free of the old stains
By us, who pay the price that must be paid,
Will freeze all winter over Ypres plains.
Our silly dreams of peace you put aside
And Brotherhood of man, for you will see
An armed Mistress, braggart of the tide
Her children slaves, under your mastery.
We'll have a word there too, and forge a knife,
Will cut the cancer threatens England's life.

Gurney survived the war, and went back to his first love, composing, though nothing was the same for him again. Far from being a militant figure, after being gassed and an unhappy love affair he succumbed once more to mental illness, and eventually died, after many years in a mental hospital, in 1937. In a very short trench poem dedicated to Bach, he seems almost to know what's coming:

Watching the dark my spirit rose in flood
On that most dearest Prelude of my delight.
The low-lying mist lifted its hood,
The October stars showed nobly in clear night.

When I return, and to real music-making,
And play that Prelude, how will it happen then?
Shall I feel as I felt, a sentry hardly waking,
With a dull sense of No Man's Land again?

But Gurney's eeriest poem of premonition, 'The Three Spectres', reminds us that after the war the majority, who were neither killed nor badly mutilated, had somehow to pick up their lives and start again in a country horribly traumatised:

As I went up by Ovillers
In mud and water cold to the knee,
There went three jeering, fleeing spectres,
That walked abreast and talked of me.

The first said, 'Here's a right brave soldier
That walks the dark unfearingly;
Soon he'll come back on a fine stretcher,
And laughing for a nice Blighty.'

The second, 'Read his face, old comrade,
No kind of lucky chance I see;
One day he'll freeze in mud to the marrow,
Then look his last on Picardie.'

Though bitter the word of these first twain
Curses the third spat venomously;
'He'll stay untouched till the war's last dawning
Then live one hour of agony.'

Liars the first two were. Behold me
At sloping arms by one – two – three;
Waiting the time I shall discover
Whether the third spake verity.

Although it was almost twenty years of agony rather than an hour, the third spectre had indeed spoken truthfully of Gurney's fate.

There is one final war poet writing at his best during this period, but not mentioned on the Westminster Abbey slab, no doubt because his war wasn't the same one as the rest of them. William Butler Yeats, mentioned already, may well be the greatest English-language poet of the entire twentieth century. On the eve of the First World War, one reason for some confidence in Berlin about Britain's lack of readiness to fight was the imminence of an Irish civil war. Rebellion in Ulster over government plans for Irish Home Rule had split British public opinion. Urged on by Kipling, a friend of his, the Ulster lawyer Edward Carson, one-time prosecutor of Oscar Wilde, had formed his Ulster Volunteer Force, which was arming and drilling. So, in England, were sympathisers. On the other side, Irish nationalists had formed the Irish Republican Brotherhood, and looked to the Kaiser's Germany for support in their planned uprising against the British.

Yeats, who had made his name in London literary circles, fell helplessly in love with Maud Gonne, an Irish nationalist heiress, who rejected him repeatedly and married the militant Irish nationalist Major John MacBride. Torn between respectability and his deep romantic feelings for Ireland, Yeats himself joined the Irish Republican Brotherhood as a young man, and knew many of those who rebelled in the 1916 Easter Rising. However, by 1912 he was no longer a Fenian revolutionary. He wrote extraordinary poetry about the uprising and yet, characteristically, didn't publish it at the time when it would have been particularly incendiary, waiting until 1920. Nonetheless, it is war poetry, and as the Irish situation degenerated into civil war in the early 1920s, Yeats bore witness to those horrors too. I've argued that the seismic shock of Flanders gave

English poetry a shake which brought it alive again, and something of the same is true of the poetry of Yeats. Confronting intractable and painful political choices, heroic sacrifice and betrayal, Yeats hammered out sentimentality and languor from his verse-making. He began to make poems that are so hard-edged, unflinching and classical they seem to stand outside time.

From 1914 onwards the great debate for patriotic Irishmen was whether to join the British forces, and wait for victory over Germany before trying to settle Ireland's future; or to conclude that England's misfortune was Ireland's chance. Following John Redmond, the moderate Irish nationalist leader, some 40,000 mainly Catholic Irishmen from the south enlisted in the British Army in 1914 and swore allegiance to King George V. Many more followed, right up to the moment of the Easter Rising in 1916. One such conflicted Irishman was Major Robert Gregory, the son of Yeats's great friend Lady Gregory. A famous sportsman and a talented artist – like Rosenberg he was at the Slade – he joined up in 1915 and transferred to the Royal Flying Corps in 1916. Aged thirty-seven, he was killed in his aircraft when an Italian pilot shot him down by accident. Yeats's first great war poem, 'An Irish Airman Foresees His Death', was published just after the war ended – and reading it, it isn't hard to see why:

I know that I shall meet my fate
Somewhere among the clouds above;
Those that I fight I do not hate,
Those that I guard I do not love;
My county is Kiltartan Cross,
My countrymen Kiltartan's poor,
No likely end could bring them loss
Or leave them happier than before.
Nor law, nor duty bade me fight,
Nor public men, nor cheering crowds,
A lonely impulse of delight
Drove to this tumult in the clouds;

I balanced all, brought all to mind,
The years to come seemed waste of breath,
A waste of breath the years behind
In balance with this life, this death.

The themes of this poem – the heroism of self-sacrifice, and the disgust for 'public men' and 'cheering crowds' – are subtly modulated in Yeats's greatest and most famous poem about the uprising, 'Easter 1916'. Thomas MacDonagh, a schoolteacher and playwright; Patrick Pearse, the leader of the Gaelic revival and nationalist hero; James Connolly, the socialist Irish leader; and John MacBride, the nationalist who had taken Maud Gonne from Yeats, and who he hated, were among the sixteen Irish rebels executed by the British after the rebellion failed. With impressive foresight, Yeats suggests that their killings would change everything. Indeed they did: the brutal suppression of what had been, numerically, quite a small-scale uprising in 1916 provoked a far greater surge of Irish nationalism, leading to the foundation of the modern republic in 1922.

I have met them at close of day
Coming with vivid faces
From counter or desk among grey
Eighteenth-century houses.
I have passed with a nod of the head
Or polite meaningless words,
Or have lingered awhile and said
Polite meaningless words,
And thought before I had done
Of a mocking tale or a gibe
To please a companion
Around the fire at the club,
Being certain that they and I
But lived where motley is worn:
All changed, changed utterly:
A terrible beauty is born.

That woman's days were spent
In ignorant good-will,
Her nights in argument
Until her voice grew shrill.
What voice more sweet than hers
When, young and beautiful,
She rode to harriers?
This man had kept a school
And rode our winged horse;
This other his helper and friend
Was coming into his force;
He might have won fame in the end,
So sensitive his nature seemed,
So daring and sweet his thought.
This other man I had dreamed
A drunken, vainglorious lout.
He had done most bitter wrong
To some who are near my heart,
Yet I number him in the song;
He, too, has resigned his part
In the casual comedy;
He, too, has been changed in his turn,
Transformed utterly:
A terrible beauty is born.

Hearts with one purpose alone
Through summer and winter seem
Enchanted to a stone
To trouble the living stream.
The horse that comes from the road.
The rider, the birds that range
From cloud to tumbling cloud,
Minute by minute they change;
A shadow of cloud on the stream
Changes minute by minute;

A horse-hoof slides on the brim,
And a horse plashes within it;
The long-legged moor-hens dive,
And hens to moor-cocks call;
Minute by minute they live:
The stone's in the midst of all.

Too long a sacrifice
Can make a stone of the heart.
O when may it suffice?
That is Heaven's part, our part
To murmur name upon name,
As a mother names her child
When sleep at last has come
On limbs that had run wild.
What is it but nightfall?
No, no, not night but death;
Was it needless death after all?
For England may keep faith
For all that is done and said.
We know their dream; enough
To know they dreamed and are dead;
And what if excess of love
Bewildered them till they died?
I write it out in a verse –
MacDonagh and MacBride
And Connolly and Pearse
Now and in time to be,
Wherever green is worn,
Are changed, changed utterly:
A terrible beauty is born.

Although it's the first stanza and the last seven lines of the poem that are best known, the whole thing is worth rereading because it underlines so strongly the aristocratic strain in Yeats – for him, a well-doing Protestant, the ideal people are not Catholic peasants or the urban working class, but horsemen and horsewomen, noble country people of fine education.

Patrick Pearse's own poetry had been simpler, rawer – effective propaganda poetry – and if there had ever been a rebellion of poets, this was it:

I am come of the seed of the people, the people that
    sorrow,
That have no treasure but hope,
No riches laid up but a memory
Of an Ancient glory.
My mother bore me in bondage, in bondage my mother
    was born,
I am of the blood of serfs;
The children with whom I have played, the men and
    women with whom I have eaten,
Have had masters over them, have been under the lash of
    masters,
And, though gentle, have served churls;
The hands that have touched mine, the dear hands whose
    touch is familiar to me,
Have worn shameful manacles, have been bitten at the
    wrist by manacles,
Have grown hard with the manacles and the task-work of
    strangers,
I am flesh of the flesh of these lowly, I am bone of their
    bone,
I that have never submitted;
I that have a soul greater than the souls of my people's
    masters,
I that have vision and prophecy and the gift of fiery
    speech,
I that have spoken with God on the top of His holy hill.
And because I am of the people, I understand the people,

I am sorrowful with their sorrow, I am hungry with their
    desire:
My heart has been heavy with the grief of mothers,
My eyes have been wet with the tears of children,
I have yearned with old wistful men,
And laughed or cursed with young men;
Their shame is my shame, and I have reddened for it,
Reddened for that they have served, they who should be
    free,
Reddened for that they have gone in want, while others
    have been full,
Reddened for that they have walked in fear of lawyers and
    of their jailors
With their writs of summons and their handcuffs,
Men mean and cruel!
I could have borne stripes on my body rather than this
    shame of my people.
And now I speak, being full of vision;
I speak to my people, and I speak in my people's name to
    the masters of my people.
I say to my people that they are holy, that they are august,
    despite their chains,
That they are greater than those that hold them, and
    stronger and purer,
That they have but need of courage, and to call on the
    name of their God,
God the unforgetting, the dear God that loves the peoples
For whom He died naked, suffering shame.
And I say to my people's masters: Beware,
Beware of the thing that is coming, beware of the risen
    people,
Who shall take what ye would not give.
Did ye think to conquer the people,
Or that Law is stronger than life and than men's desire to
    be free?

We will try it out with you, ye that have harried and held,
Ye that have bullied and bribed, tyrants, hypocrites, liars!

After the Rising, political life proved less heroic. Who, precisely, were 'my people'? As time went on, a conflict between Yeats's hauteur (he'd have made a convincing English squire) and the Catholic social revolution of the new Ireland became increasingly painful. There was the terrible beauty of violent revolution; but there was also the frail, sinking bark of elite Western culture. In his devastating poem 'The Second Coming', written in 1919, Yeats gives vent to his increasingly desolate view of politics. For him, and as we will see for many others, there was a real sense that civilisation as previously understood was going under. All that needs to be known about the poem is that 'gyre' refers to a two-thousand-year historical cycle which had become important to the poet's thinking; and that the nightmarish images of the second stanza take us back to Blake and Shelley:

Turning and turning in the widening gyre
The falcon cannot hear the falconer;
Things fall apart; the centre cannot hold;
Mere anarchy is loosed upon the world,
The blood-dimmed tide is loosed, and everywhere
The ceremony of innocence is drowned;
The best lack all conviction, while the worst
Are full of passionate intensity.
Surely some revelation is at hand;
Surely the Second Coming is at hand.

The Second Coming! Hardly are those words out
When a vast image out of Spiritus Mundi
Troubles my sight: somewhere in sands of the desert
A shape with lion body and the head of a man,
A gaze blank and pitiless as the sun,
Is moving its slow thighs, while all about it

Reel shadows of the indignant desert birds.
The darkness drops again; but now I know
That twenty centuries of stony sleep
Were vexed to nightmare by a rocking cradle,
And what rough beast, its hour come round at last,
Slouches towards Bethlehem to be born?

That this is not a one-off bout of splenetic despair is shown by
another great poem of the same year, this time entitled 'Nineteen
Hundred and Nineteen', a lament for the passing of civilisation
itself. Here's how it begins:

Many ingenious lovely things are gone
That seemed sheer miracle to the multitude,
Protected from the circle of the moon
That pitches common things about. There stood
Amid the ornamental bronze and stone
An ancient image made of olive wood –
And gone are Phidias' famous ivories
And all the golden grasshoppers and bees.
We too had many pretty toys when young:
A law indifferent to blame or praise,
To bribe or threat; habits that made old wrong
Melt down, as it were wax in the sun's rays;
Public opinion ripening for so long
We thought it would outlive all future days.
O what fine thought we had because we thought
That the worst rogues and rascals had died out.
All teeth were drawn, all ancient tricks unlearned,
And a great army but a showy thing;
What matter that no cannon had been turned
Into a ploughshare? Parliament and king
Thought that unless a little powder burned
The trumpeters might burst with trumpeting
And yet it lack all glory; and perchance

The guardsmen's drowsy chargers would not prance.
Now days are dragon-ridden, the nightmare
Rides upon sleep: a drunken soldiery
Can leave the mother, murdered at her door,
To crawl in her own blood, and go scot-free;
The night can sweat with terror as before
We pieced our thoughts into philosophy,
And planned to bring the world under a rule,
Who are but weasels fighting in a hole.

Lenin was in the Kremlin. The Kaiser's Germany was in ruins. Britain, bled dry, was riven by strikes and civil dissension. Ireland was on its way to an incredibly bitter civil war. A general sense of disillusion in the old political order that had been brought down by the World War led many at this stage to look for new and extreme answers, including fascism. In his dotage Yeats was intrigued by fascism, but before then he was more interested in analysing the gap between the old culture he associated himself with, and whatever was coming.

In his 'Meditations in Time of Civil War', written in 1922 when he was effectively cut off from the rest of the world in his old stone tower of Thoor Ballylee in Galway, Yeats toys with imagery familiar from the tradition of the English country house poem:

Surely among a rich man's flowering lawns,
Amid the rustle of his planted hills,
Life overflows without ambitious pains;
And rains down life until the basin spills,
And mounts more dizzy high the more it rains
As though to choose whatever shape it wills
And never stoop to a mechanical
Or servile shape, at others' beck and call.
Mere dreams, mere dreams!

The purpose of the poem, however, is to challenge, not to reinforce or repeat the easy assumptions of authority characteristic of the Protestant Ascendancy:

> What if the glory of escutcheoned doors,
> And buildings that a haughtier age designed,
> The pacing to and fro on polished floors
> Amid great chambers and long galleries, lined
> With famous portraits of our ancestors;
> What if those things the greatest of mankind
> Consider most to magnify, or to bless,
> But take our greatness with our bitterness?

At any rate, into the poet's bucolic fastness, the rude reality of civil war intrudes (and indeed, the blowing up of a nearby bridge flooded the tower's lower floor):

> An affable Irregular,
> A heavily-built Falstaffian man,
> Comes cracking jokes of civil war
> As though to die by gunshot were
> The finest play under the sun.
> A brown Lieutenant and his men,
> Half dressed in national uniform,
> Stand at my door, and I complain
> Of the foul weather, hail and rain,
> A pear-tree broken by the storm.

Yeats's good-humoured self-mockery turns darker in the next section of the poem, 'The Stare's Nest by My Window' – 'stare' is an archaic word for starling. The poet contemplates the end of his world:

The bees build in the crevices
Of loosening masonry, and there
The mother birds bring grubs and flies.
My wall is loosening; honey-bees,
Come build in the empty house of the stare.
We are closed in, and the key is turned
On our uncertainty; somewhere
A man is killed, or a house burned,
Yet no clear fact to be discerned:
Come build in the empty house of the stare.
A barricade of stone or of wood;
Some fourteen days of civil war;
Last night they trundled down the road
That dead young soldier in his blood:
Come build in the empty house of the stare.
We had fed the heart on fantasies,
The heart's grown brutal from the fare;
More Substance in our enmities
Than in our love; O honey-bees,
Come build in the empty house of the stare.

Until, in the end:

I see Phantoms of Hatred and of the Heart's Fullness and
    of the Coming Emptiness

I climb to the tower-top and lean upon broken stone,
A mist that is like blown snow is sweeping over all …

Now, a civil war is a different thing from a war between nations. In terms of the sheer number of dead, and the misery of the dying, the Irish one was a much lesser war than the European conflict of 1914–18, but it had a peculiar intimate savagery all its own. What is, I hope, obvious is that William Butler Yeats is responding to the shaking of everything he knows by trying to build new structures of his own – in essence, new myths for a new age. He wasn't alone in that: the story of poetry in England and Scotland in the 1920s and 30s is in part about creating new verbal worlds to keep at bay new, unsettling realities.

14

How Modern Were the Modernists?

Modernism. It's one of those grand, strutting terms that sound exciting but, when stopped in the street and questioned, aren't quite what you'd hoped. But it's useful and established; and it does describe something real. Around the time of the First World War there was a widespread rethinking across Europe and America of many of the old truths and artistic habits. In Britain we had, apart from the loss of so many people killed and wounded in the war: the Irish civil war; mass strikes and unemployment; a political class which, from David Lloyd George down, seemed corrupt, old and incompetent; and the social turbulence caused by assaults on old attitudes to marriage and the proper place of women. Some or all of these aspects of crisis and malaise are described in British poetry of the time. Almost all of the important poets eventually responded politically – veering off to communism, fascism or nationalism. The nature of British poetry changed. Whether it's the American imports Ezra Pound and T.S. Eliot, or Yeats in his late maturity, or Scotland's Hugh MacDiarmid, many of the poems written at this time look and sound like nothing that came before. They don't, apparently, hark back to the Edwardians, or the Victorians, or the Romantics.

Why is that? We come back to that slippery customer, Modernism. It has many faces – it's more urban than previous movements, it's less religious and moralistic, it's more difficult. Essentially, however, it tries to answer the following question: if the times have changed so much, if there is a revolution in the air and the old order seems to be tottering, shouldn't the arts change dramatically too? Shouldn't there be a new verbal order for these new times?

Easier said than done. It was clear that many old forms were exhausted – finely made, delicate oil paintings of well-manicured countryside; lush and soothing concertos; metrical, musical poems about the problems of love, or the troops of the Empire. To the Modernists, young and angry, these all seemed merely the higher ornamentation. The old world of amorous shepherds, hearty verses and morally uplifting Poet Laureates had to be swept from the mantelpiece in one violent, angry gesture, till it was all smashed: Ezra Pound ordered his followers to 'Make it new.'

The problem was this: the old ways included tactics and techniques, from poetic metre to naturalistic brushstrokes, which had been painfully evolved over centuries, and which by and large did their job well in conveying meaning. Get rid of them, and what did you have left to get your message over with?

Make it new – but how, and with what? And here's the odd answer that Modernism provides: you go back, you are deeply reactionary, and you delve into stories and forms much older than the ones you are reacting against. Thus, in Paris, Picasso starts drawing bathing women caricatured from classical times, and sketches like Ingres. In Moscow the Modernist and Bolshevist Kasimir Malevich turns to the oldest Russian icons of all, with their stark, geometric forms, for his inspiration. In Dublin and Paris, James Joyce remakes the novel by using the story of Ulysses as his structuring device. And it's the same in poetry. Ezra Pound himself turns to the poetry of the Provençal troubadours, the Anglo-Saxons and the classical Chinese to find new ways of writing. Yeats uses images from Byzantium and Irish mythology. T.S. Eliot becomes fascinated by the metaphysical poets, Dante and early Christian verse, as he manipulates his new poetry of many voices. Hugh MacDiarmid launches a Scottish literary renaissance by turning back to the great medieval poets, under the slogan 'Not Burns, but Dunbar!'

Put together, their work is successful in its first aim. It does disconcert and unsettle the middle-class audience that was traditionally available for poetry. We can see this in the flood of newspaper and magazine jokes, cartoons and irate editorials mocking the 'incomprehensible' and foreign-seeming painters and poets of the 1920s. As we'll see, this kind of Modernist revolution doesn't last long, and in poetry in particular there was a major backlash already evident by the end of the decade. But its early energy is impressive and, even now, a kind of tonic.

In Britain, two important aspects of Modernism were sex and Europe. The theories of Sigmund Freud and, more generally, a growing belief that sexual urges were deeper than morality, underpin much of the writing of this period – above all, of course, that of D.H. Lawrence. Also, in the period just before, and certainly just after the First World War, British culture was more open to European influences than it had been for a long time: Virginia Woolf, Vanessa Bell and the Bloomsbury group looked to Paris, to Gertrude Stein, Picasso, Matisse, Stravinsky and others for leadership. James Joyce found he could only get published in Paris. Key exhibitions of Continental Post-Impressionist painting, championed by Roger Fry in London, completely changed the way a new generation of British painters worked. Pound's horror of the war was triggered by the death of his friend Henri Gaudier-Brzeska, the French-Polish sculptor. Pound and Wyndham Lewis, that wicked and brilliant figure, learned much of their 'Vorticism' from Italians such as Marinetti.

So a good place to start, when considering British Modernism, is Mina Loy. Born in London in 1882 to an English mother and a Hungarian-Jewish father, she had made her way to Munich in her late teens and absorbed a lot of the new European thinking – Freud and Friedrich Nietzsche – before returning to study painting. Like a number of the poets we've been discussing, she was a painter before she was a writer. In 1903 she moved to Paris, and then to Florence. Her circle included Gertrude Stein, Apollinaire and Picasso, and she had a love affair with the leader of Futurism,

Filippo Marinetti. During the war she worked as a nurse, publishing poetry and a feminist manifesto. From 1916 onwards she bounced between Manhattan and Europe, always at the centre of a group of radical Modernists. You could argue that Mina Loy was barely British at all; but that's part of the point. This is a period when 'cosmopolitan culture' spreads networks across European capitals, including London, and becomes virtually dominant. And if you're talking cosmopolitan, Mina Loy is as good as it gets. T.S. Eliot admired her, and looking at her Futurist-inspired poem 'Human Cylinders', one can see why:

The human cylinders
Revolving in the enervating dusk
That wraps each closer in the mystery
Of singularity
Among the litter of a sunless afternoon
Having eaten without tasting
Talked without communion
And at least two of us
Loved a very little
Without seeking
To know if our two miseries
In the lucid rush-together of automatons
Could form one opulent wellbeing

Simplifications of men
In the enervating dusk
Your indistinctness
Serves me the core of the kernel of you
When in the frenzied reaching out of intellect to intellect
Leaning brow to brow communicative
Over the abyss of the potential
Concordance of respiration
Shames
Absence of corresponding between the verbal sensory

And reciprocity
Of conception
And expression
Where each extrudes beyond the tangible
One thin pale trail of speculation
From among us we have sent out
Into the enervating dusk
One little whining beast
Whose longing
Is to slink back to antediluvian burrow
And one elastic tentacle of intuition
To quiver among the stars ...

It's new. It's what Ezra Pound had called for. And yet it's only partially successful – all those jabbing, hectoring polysyllables, and free verse that feels loose rather than taut and inevitable. Pound directly confronted the problem of how to write in these lines from 'Hugh Selwyn Mauberley':

For three years, out of key with his time,
He strove to resuscitate the dead art
Of poetry; to maintain 'the sublime'
In the old scene. Wrong from the start –

No, hardly, but seeing he had been born
In a half-savage country, out of date ...

Turning to classical Latin, French and Chinese stories for his answer, Pound took the dramatic monologue form pioneered by Robert Browning, trying to create something fresh and pure which could stand by itself. Here's an extract from 'Homage to Sextus Propertius' which captures Pound's curious blend of the Yankee and the fusty:

There will be a crowd of young women doing homage to
    my palaver,
Though my house is not propped up by Taenarian
columns from Laconia (associated with Neptune and
    Cerberus),
Though it is not stretched upon gilded beams;
My orchards do not lie level and wide
as the forests of Phaecia,
the luxurious and Ionian,
Nor are my caverns stuffed stiff with a Marcian vintage,
My cellar does not date from Numa Pompilius,
Nor bristle with wine jars,
Nor is it equipped with a frigidaire patent;
Yet the companions of the Muses
will keep their collective nose in my books,
And weary with historical data, they will turn to my dance
    tune.
Happy who are mentioned in my pamphlets,
the songs shall be a fine tomb-stone over their beauty.

Does Ezra Pound belong here at all? Apart from the Anglo-Saxons, he wasn't a huge enthusiast for the British traditions of poetry. An American, he spent a long time in Paris before throwing in his lot with Mussolini's Italy, for which he was a willing propagandist. After serving time in a mental asylum after the Second World War, he holed up once more in Venice. Yet he is part of the British story. He cut his teeth with British poets in London, and his great project was to change English verse forever. Further, his great trauma, which provoked his increasingly obsessive hatred of the financial system, and then of the Jews, and his anti-Semitic fascism, was the First World War and its 'old men's lies':

These fought in any case,
and some believing
pro domo, in any case ...

Died some, pro patria,
walked eye-deep in hell
believing in old men's lies, then unbelieving
came home, home to a lie,
home to many deceits,
home to old lies and new infamy;
usury age-old and age-thick
and liars in public places.

Daring as never before, wastage as never before.
Young blood and high blood,
fair cheeks, and fine bodies;
fortitude as never before

frankness as never before,
disillusions as never told in the old days,
hysterias, trench confessions,
laughter out of dead bellies.

That's the same anger and despair that drove Hugh MacDiarmid into the arms of Lenin and Stalin, and provoked a general air of hysteria in the poetry of the 1920s. Pound's great lifelong work, full of beautiful things but marred by his vicious anti-Semitism and his generally batty politics, is *The Cantos*. This is from 'Canto XIII', dealing with Confucius, and therefore the proper ordering of society, is distinctly un-mad. Also, to my ear at least, it still sounds fresh, crisp and modern:

Kung walked
by the dynastic temple
and into the cedar grove,
and then out by the lower river,
And with him Khieu Tchi
and Tian the low speaking
And 'we are unknown,' said Kung,

'You will take up charioteering?
'Then you will become known,
'Or perhaps I should take up charioteering, or archery?
'Or the practice of public speaking?'
And Tseu-lou said, 'I would put the defences in order,'
And Khieu said, 'If I were lord of a province
'I would put it in better order than this is.'
And Tchi said, 'I would prefer a small mountain temple,
'With order in the observances,
with a suitable performance of the ritual,'
And Tian said, with his hand on the strings of his lute
The low sounds continuing
after his hand left the strings,
And the sound went up like smoke, under the leaves,
And he looked after the sound:
'The old swimming hole,
'And the boys flopping off the planks,
'Or sitting in the underbrush playing mandolins.'
And Kung smiled upon all of them equally.
And Thseng-sie desired to know:
'Which had answered correctly?'
And Kung said, 'They have all answered correctly,
'That is to say, each in his nature.'
And Kung raised his cane against Yuan Jang,
Yuan Jang being his elder,
For Yuan Jang sat by the roadside pretending to
be receiving wisdom.
And Kung said
'You old fool, come out of it,
'Get up and do something useful.'

T.S. Eliot, who regarded Pound as the greater poet, at least techni-
cally, was another American immigrant, but he took a very different
path, ending up more English than most of the English. As Pound
turned to fascism, Eliot, who had anti-Semitic skeletons of his own,

turned to the Church of England and the great traditions of English poetry for salvation. The former banker ended up as a rather grand figure, writing religious dramas; but his earlier Modernist work was shocking at the time, and still puzzles first-time readers greatly. 'The Love Song of J. Alfred Prufrock', published in 1915, is perhaps the key text for early British Modernism. In it, Eliot immediately establishes his unmistakable tone, somehow both conversationally relaxed and classical, as his anti-hero – useless or unnecessary men were a staple of the Modernist worldview – wanders through a recognisably Edwardian London:

Let us go then, you and I,
When the evening is spread out against the sky
Like a patient etherized upon a table;
Let us go, through certain half-deserted streets,
The muttering retreats
Of restless nights in one-night cheap hotels
And sawdust restaurants with oyster-shells:
Streets that follow like a tedious argument
Of insidious intent
To lead you to an overwhelming question ...
Oh, do not ask, 'What is it?'

Let us go and make our visit.
In the room the women come and go
Talking of Michelangelo.

The yellow fog that rubs its back upon the window-panes,
The yellow smoke that rubs its muzzle on the window-panes,
Licked its tongue into the corners of the evening,
Lingered upon the pools that stand in drains,
Let fall upon its back the soot that falls from chimneys,
Slipped by the terrace, made a sudden leap,
And seeing that it was a soft October night,
Curled once about the house, and fell asleep.

And indeed there will be time
To wonder, 'Do I dare?' and, 'Do I dare?'
Time to turn back and descend the stair,
With a bald spot in the middle of my hair –
(They will say: 'How his hair is growing thin!')
My morning coat, my collar mounting firmly to the chin,
My necktie rich and modest, but asserted by a simple pin –
(They will say: 'But how his arms and legs are thin!')
Do I dare
Disturb the universe?
In a minute there is time
For decisions and revisions which a minute will reverse.

'Prufrock' is not a particularly difficult poem. It shows Eliot's great versatility and metrical skill, which allowed him to be such an excellent writer of light verse in later life – *Old Possum's Book of Practical Cats* being the deathless example. But it caused outrage at the time. It was just so ... different. Eliot followed with further salvos, tightly rhymed and rhythmic poetry that continued to shock with its subject matter. But the big event, part of the reason 1922 is such an important year in the story of art and Modernism, was *The Waste Land*, a titanic poem which changed British poetry as radically as had Wordsworth and Coleridge's *Lyrical Ballads*. Modernist artists such as Picasso, Braque and Kurt Schwitters had long used collage – scraps of newspaper, torn fragments of advertisements, commercial products of all kinds – to rough up the surfaces of their paintings. Now Eliot did the same thing with poetry, crashing together overheard fragments of conversations, monologues suddenly broken off and eerie choruses apparently full of ancient wisdom. The overall theme of the poem is the deadly aridity of Western culture, and the search for some new way forward, which is only tentatively offered right at the end, and appears to be semi-Christian. It doesn't sound like a lot of fun. Yet the poet's verbal exuberance, his deep understanding of the history of English verse and his uncanny gift for rhythm keep us reading and transfixed. This is from part of the first section, 'The Burial of the Dead', in which Eliot, working for Lloyds Bank in the City, confronts contemporary London:

Under the brown fog of a winter dawn,
A crowd flowed over London Bridge, so many,
I had not thought death had undone so many.
Sighs, short and infrequent, were exhaled,
And each man fixed his eyes before his feet.
Flowed up the hill and down King William Street,
To where Saint Mary Woolnoth kept the hours
With a dead sound on the final stroke of nine.
There I saw one I knew, and stopped him, crying: 'Stetson!
'You who were with me in the ships at Mylae
'That corpse you planted last year in your garden,
'Has it begun to sprout? Will it bloom this year?
'Or has the sudden frost disturbed its bed?
'O keep the Dog far hence, that's friend to men,
'Or with his nails he'll dig it up again!
'You! hypocrite lecteur! – mon semblable, – mon frère!'

The poem really demands to be read in full, but it's too long to reprint here. The second section, 'A Game of Chess', provides my next extract. In it Eliot collides the disembodied, warning chorus, fragments of conversation, jazz music and the plight of working-class women waiting for their demobilised husbands – oh yes, and a pub on the edge of closing.

'My nerves are bad to-night. Yes, bad. Stay with me.
'Speak to me. Why do you never speak? Speak.
'What are you thinking of? What thinking? What?
'I never know what you are thinking. Think.'

I think we are in rats' alley
Where the dead men lost their bones.

'What is that noise?'
The wind under the door.
'What is that noise now? What is the wind doing?'
Nothing again nothing.
                                           'Do
You know nothing? Do you see nothing? Do you
    remember
Nothing?'
            I remember
Those pearls that were his eyes.
'Are you alive, or not? Is there nothing in your head?'
                                                    But
O O O O that Shakespeherian Rag –
It's so elegant
So intelligent
'What shall I do now? What shall I do?
I shall rush out as I am, walk the street
With my hair down, so. What shall we do to-morrow?
What shall we ever do?'
                        The hot water at ten.
And if it rains, a closed car at four.
And we shall play a game of chess,
Pressing lidless eyes and waiting for a knock upon the
    door.

When Lil's husband got demobbed, I said –
I didn't mince my words, I said to her myself,
HURRY UP PLEASE ITS TIME
Now Albert's coming back, make yourself a bit smart.
He'll want to know what you done with that money he
    gave you
To get yourself some teeth. He did, I was there.
You have them all out, Lil, and get a nice set,
He said, I swear, I can't bear to look at you.
And no more can't I, I said, and think of poor Albert,

He's been in the army for four years, he wants a good time
And if you don't give it him, there's others will, I said.
Oh is there, she said. Something o' that, I said.
Then I'll know who to thank, she said, and give me a
    straight look.
HURRY UP PLEASE ITS TIME

This is almost completely successful Modernist poetry: its underlying menace and despair reflect a Britain rocked and shaken by the past decade; it seems to describe the voices of real Londoners in 1922, and their preoccupations; and there is something sinister which fits well with a Britain whose prime minister was deeply corrupt, and conniving with the conman and possible murderer Maundy Gregory to sell honours. Eliot, even if his heart was still in Boston, 'gets' the Britain of the day better than any native. For contrast, a final excerpt from this remarkable poem comprises the fourth section, 'Death by Water'. Earlier, I pointed out how, searching for a stronger pulse, Modernists turned radically backwards. Here is a particularly beautiful example, with its echoes of Shakespeare's *The Tempest*.

Phlebas the Phoenician, a fortnight dead,
Forgot the cry of gulls, and the deep sea swell
And the profit and loss.
A current under sea
Picked his bones in whispers. As he rose and fell
He passed the stages of his age and youth
Entering the whirlpool.
Gentile or Jew
O you who turn the wheel and look to windward,
Consider Phlebas, who was once handsome and tall as
    you.

We will return to Eliot later. His work was so powerful and so influential that old anthologies of British poetry from the 1920s and 30s are cluttered with bad mimicry of him by lesser poets. Because Modernism was a break with so much, requiring real bravery, in order to be interesting every Modernist had to do it differently. There is nothing more boring than a derivative literary revolutionary.

If he understood nothing else, Hugh MacDiarmid understood that. The name is a *nom de plume*, or rather a *nom de guerre*, for a working-class postman's son, Christopher Murray Grieve, who was born in the Scottish Borders and served in the First World War, during which he closely observed the tension between Scottish and Irish soldiers and their English, public-schooled officers. Grieve went on to become a journalist and polemicist, whose overwhelming belief was that Scotland had to free itself from the British Empire and adopt radical socialism. Notoriously, he was thrown out of the Scottish National Party for his communism, and then thrown out of the Communist Party for his Scottish nationalism. He promised to be always 'where extremes meet', a promise he largely kept.

While T.S. Eliot looked back to earlier Christian poetry as a foundation for his Modernism, and Pound turned to Chinese, Provençal and Anglo-Saxon writing, MacDiarmid was determined to smash up literary English itself, and replace it with a Scots which he pillaged from old dictionaries. His idea was that the old, lost words of the Scottish dialect contained within them different ways of thinking and seeing the world which needed to be recaptured and re-presented to a modern Scottish audience. As with so many radical Modernist ideas, it seems completely impossible – even barking mad – and yet, for much of the time, MacDiarmid gets away with it triumphantly. He certainly writes the best Scottish poetry since Robert Burns. More than that, he provoked and inspired a whole movement of poets who followed his lead, while writing very different poetry themselves, so that Scotland became a centre for poetry in a way it hadn't been since the late 1400s. Here's his early poem 'The Watergaw', or rainbow. To translate it is to lose its music, but it's tough, so my very rough version would go as follows: 'One wet evening on a cold July day ["yow-trummle" is ewe-tremble – the sheared sheep are shivering], I saw an eerie sight – a rainbow with its shivering light beyond the approaching storm. And I thought of the last wild look you gave before you died. There was no smoke in the nightingale's house that night, and none in mine [in other words, perhaps, no flood of poetic inspiration], but I have thought ever since of that strange light, and I think that perhaps at last I understand what your look meant then.' Now, here's the real thing:

> Ae weet forenicht i' the yow-trummle
> I saw yon antrin thing,
> A watergaw wi' its chitterin' licht
> Ayont the on-ding;
> An' I thocht o' the last wild look ye gied
> Afore ye deed!
>
> There was nae reek i' the laverock's hoose
> That nicht – an' nane i' mine;
> But I hae thocht o' that foolish licht
> Ever sin' syne;
> An' I think that mebbe at last I ken
> What your look meant then.

There are many short poems by MacDiarmid which are at least as good as that, if not better. He was doing, in his way, what W.B. Yeats was trying to do in the Irish literary revival of the 1890s – but far more successfully. T.S. Eliot, who as a conservative Anglo-Catholic can have agreed with almost nothing that Hugh MacDiarmid stood for, nonetheless got the point and championed his work, so that his great early long poem 'A Drunk Man Looks at the Thistle' was successfully published in 1926. It's a meditation on the state of Scotland by a boozed-up amateur philosopher, adrift after a session in the pub and worried about what his wife is going to say when he gets home. MacDiarmid's view of Scottish culture was as bleak as Eliot's of English culture a few years earlier, and chimes with what Yeats felt about the newly independent Ireland at much the same time. 'A Drunk Man' rambles from topic to topic, embracing philosophy, bitter political satire and self-hatred. It can be shocking in places, and then very funny. The opening stanzas introduce the exhausted speaker, whose elbow, shoulder and throat can no longer cope with the fast whisky-drinking his friends expect. Anyway, it's probably not *real* whisky these days – just as the country called Scotland isn't the real Scotland:

I amna' fou sae muckle as tired – deid dune
It's gey and hard wark coupin' gless for gless
Wi' Cruvie and Gilsanquar and the like,
And I'm no juist as bauld as aince I wes.

The elbuck fankles in the coorse o' time,
The sheckle's no' sae souple, and the thrapple
Grows deef and dour: nae langer up and doun
Gleg as a squirrel speils the Adam's apple.

Forbye, the stuffie's no' the real MacKay.
The sun's sel' aince, as sune as ye began it,
Riz in your vera saul: but what keeks in
Noo is in truth the vilest 'saxpenny planet'.

And as the worth's gane doun the cost has risen.
Yin canna thow the cockles o yin's hert
Wi-oot haen cauld feet noo, jalousin what
The wife'll say [I dinna blame her fur't].

It's robbin Peter to pey Paul at least ...
And aa that's Scotch aboot it is the name,
Like aa thing else caad Scottish nooadays
– Aa destitute o speerit juist the same.

Unlike many other Modernists, MacDiarmid had two cracks at reshaping the language. Influenced by John Davidson's use of science in his poetry, and a lifelong enthusiast for the new perspectives twentieth-century science was opening up, he went on from his use of Scots to a kind of scientific English which is, to most people, at first sight completely incomprehensible, but which has a glorious music of its own – and if you take the trouble to translate it, makes perfect sense. As with the Scottish poetry, it couldn't really have been written any other way – the meanings are encoded in the unfamiliar words. This is the opening to 'On a Raised Beach', MacDiarmid's poem of stoical defiance written in the 1930s when he was destitute, living on a remote Shetland island, and under surveillance as a dangerous radical by MI5:

All is lithogenesis – or lochia,
Carpolite fruit of the forbidden tree,
Stones blacker than any in the Caaba,
Cream-coloured caen-stone, chatoyant pieces,
Celadon and corbeau, bistre and beige,
Glaucous, hoar, enfouldered, cyathiform,
Making mere faculae of the sun and moon,
I study you glout and gloss, but have
No cadrans to adjust you with, and turn again
From optik to haptik and like a blind man run
My fingers over you, arris by arris, burr by burr,
Slickensides, truité, rugas, foveoles,
Bringing my aesthesis in vain to bear,
An angle-titch to all your corrugations and coigns,
Hatched foraminous cavo-rilievo of the world,
Deictic, fiducial stones. Chiliad by chiliad
What bricole piled you here, stupendous cairn?
What artist poses the Earth écorché thus,
Pillar of creation engouled in me?
What eburnation augments you with men's bones,
Every energumen an Endymion yet?

All the other stones are in this haecceity it seems,
But where is the Christophanic rock that moved?
What Cabirian song from this catasta comes?

Phew. But try reading it out loud. After all that comes something
which sounds almost like an apology:

Deep conviction or preference can seldom
Find direct terms in which to express itself.

At different times of his life, MacDiarmid would indeed find direct
terms, writing immediately comprehensible, almost propagandistic
poetry about the condition of Scotland, the rise of fascism, and so
on. He found Modernism was not appropriate to every situation as,
during the 1930s, the world looked increasingly dark and danger-
ous. As we shall see, he was hardly alone in that.

Before we leave the Modernists there's one other poet, very
unlike MacDiarmid, we can't ignore. David Herbert Lawrence was
also a working-class boy, in his case from a Nottinghamshire
mining family. Best known these days for his novels, he was also a
fine poet and a less fine painter. Formally, as a novelist and a
painter, he can barely be called Modernist: while James Joyce is
breaking down and reshaping the language and Virginia Woolf is
experimenting with stream of consciousness, D.H. Lawrence's
novels are sturdily and traditionally made, no more radical in form,
really, than those of Thomas Hardy. His paintings, likewise, are
traditionally representative, if somewhat clumsily so. What makes
his work modern is its subject: the frankness about sex in the
novels, and the sexual nudity in the paintings. The new sexual and
moral world revealed by Freud and his followers isn't really central
to Eliot, Pound or MacDiarmid – they are all more political – but
it is for Lawrence.

He too felt the post-war culture was rotten and corrupt, but
instead of looking outwards for religious or political answers he
turned inward, searching for an emotional, sexual authenticity that

might liberate him. His poetry is, to this extent, at one with his novels and paintings, though it's more intense than the former, and generally less explicit than the latter. A Modernist poet doesn't have to be Modernist about everything – Hugh MacDiarmid's 'Drunk Man' uses traditional rhymes and quatrains; its Modernism is in its language and ideas. Linguistically, Lawrence's poems are highly conventional, though he uses something like free verse much of the time. What's unconventional about them is the subject matter. The tone is less sexual, and certainly less pornographic, than earthily sensual. In particular he identifies with the plant and animal world, in ways that are new in English poetry. 'Bavarian Gentians' is one of his best-loved poems. Without poems like this, it's hard to imagine the poetry of Ted Hughes or indeed Sylvia Plath. Lawrence is celebrating a sensuality that earlier generations of Britons would have regarded as something to be ashamed of:

Not every man has gentians in his house
in Soft September, at slow, Sad Michaelmas.
Bavarian gentians, big and dark, only dark
darkening the daytime torchlike with the smoking
    blueness of Pluto's gloom,
ribbed and torchlike, with their blaze of darkness spread
    blue
down flattening into points, flattened under the sweep of
    white day
torch-flower of the blue-smoking darkness, Pluto's dark-
    blue daze,
black lamps from the halls of Dis, burning dark blue,
giving off darkness, blue darkness, as Demeter's pale lamps
    give off light,
lead me then, lead me the way.
Reach me a gentian, give me a torch!
Let me guide myself with the blue, forked torch of a flower
down the darker and darker stairs, where blue is darkened
    on blueness

down the way Persephone goes, just now, in first-frosted
    September
to the sightless realm where darkness is married to
    dark
and Persephone herself is but a voice, as a bride
a gloom invisible enfolded in the deeper dark
of the arms of Pluto as he ravishes her once again
and pierces her once more with his passion of the utter
    dark
among the splendour of black-blue torches, shedding
fathomless darkness on the nuptials.

Bavarian gentians, tall and dark, but dark
darkening the daytime torch-like with the smoking
    blueness of Pluto's gloom,
ribbed hellish flowers erect, with their blaze of darkness
    spread blue,
blown flat into points, by the heavy white draught of the
    day.

It's classical. It's about some blueish flowers. But it's ravishing – and
it's about ravishing. Another of his famous poems, 'Snake', has much
more explicit sexual imagery running through it. Again, people in
England may have thought this way before, but they had never
written this way. It's an almost matter-of-fact encounter between
the poet and a thirsty snake, but Lawrence challenges the reader to
engage fully with it; to acknowledge truths we all share but rarely
talk about:

A snake came to my water-trough
On a hot, hot day, and I in pyjamas for the heat,
To drink there.
In the deep, strange-scented shade of the great dark
    carob-tree
I came down the steps with my pitcher

And must wait, must stand and wait, for there he was at
    the trough before
me.

He reached down from a fissure in the earth-wall in the
    gloom
And trailed his yellow-brown slackness soft-bellied down,
    over the edge of
the stone trough
And rested his throat upon the stone bottom,
And where the water had dripped from the tap, in a small
    clearness,
He sipped with his straight mouth,
Softly drank through his straight gums, into his slack long
    body,
Silently.

Someone was before me at my water-trough,
And I, like a second comer, waiting.

He lifted his head from his drinking, as cattle do,
And looked at me vaguely, as drinking cattle do,
And flickered his two-forked tongue from his lips, and
    mused a moment,
And stooped and drank a little more,
Being earth-brown, earth-golden from the burning bowels
    of the earth
On the day of Sicilian July, with Etna smoking.
The voice of my education said to me
He must be killed,
For in Sicily the black, black snakes are innocent, the gold
    are venomous.

And voices in me said, If you were a man
You would take a stick and break him now, and finish him
    off.

But must I confess how I liked him,
How glad I was he had come like a guest in quiet, to drink
    at my water-trough
And depart peaceful, pacified, and thankless,
Into the burning bowels of this earth?

Was it cowardice, that I dared not kill him?
Was it perversity, that I longed to talk to him?
Was it humility, to feel so honoured?
I felt so honoured.

And yet those voices:
If you were not afraid, you would kill him!

And truly I was afraid, I was most afraid,
But even so, honoured still more
That he should seek my hospitality
From out the dark door of the secret earth.

He drank enough
And lifted his head, dreamily, as one who has drunken,
And flickered his tongue like a forked night on the air, so
    black,
Seeming to lick his lips,
And looked around like a god, unseeing, into the air,
And slowly turned his head,
And slowly, very slowly, as if thrice adream,
Proceeded to draw his slow length curving round
And climb again the broken bank of my wall-face.

And as he put his head into that dreadful hole,
And as he slowly drew up, snake-easing his shoulders, and
    entered farther,
A sort of horror, a sort of protest against his withdrawing
    into that horrid black hole,
Deliberately going into the blackness, and slowly drawing
    himself after,
Overcame me now his back was turned.

I looked round, I put down my pitcher,
I picked up a clumsy log
And threw it at the water-trough with a clatter.

I think it did not hit him,
But suddenly that part of him that was left behind
    convulsed in undignified haste.
Writhed like lightning, and was gone
Into the black hole, the earth-lipped fissure in the
    wall-front,
At which, in the intense still noon, I stared with
    fascination.

And immediately I regretted it.
I thought how paltry, how vulgar, what a mean act!
I despised myself and the voices of my accursed human
    education.

And I thought of the albatross
And I wished he would come back, my snake.

For he seemed to me again like a king,
Like a king in exile, uncrowned in the underworld,
Now due to be crowned again.

And so, I missed my chance with one of the lords
Of life.
And I have something to expiate:
A pettiness.

None of the poets I have discussed in this chapter, apart from Hugh MacDiarmid, actually saw action in the First World War, but they were changed by it, and its demoralising effect on Western civilisation. They all dealt with their despair differently. T.S. Eliot virtually ignored the war, and embraced both Englishness and Anglicanism with fervour – not that he did fervour very convincingly – while Pound, Loy and Lawrence all sought exile, to fascist Italy, New Mexico, Manhattan, anywhere but Britain. MacDiarmid alone stayed and tried to build a political response. That wasn't a Modernist thing to do, but it became the most popular response of the next generation, the political poets of the 1930s, to whom we turn now.

15

Lefties and Righties: Outrage and Laughter in Britain Between the Wars

The Modernists continued to recruit, and inspire – Basil Bunting, the Northumbrian poet, was writing substantial Modernist verse well into the 1960s – but for most poets in Britain between the two world wars, they weren't inspiring enough. Eliot and Pound might be two huge alpine peaks, admired by intellectuals and noticed by many more; but below them there was almost nothing, a void where a serious readership might have been found. Very crudely, two things replaced Modernism. The first was socialist political poetry of protest, culminating in the poets of the Spanish Civil War. The second was observational verse by largely conservative writers, who began to scoop up the large audience difficult Modernists had lost.

There was, for the leftist poets, a derisive compendium name: 'MacSpaunday' – that is, Louis MacNeice, Stephen Spender, W.H. Auden and Cecil Day-Lewis. Then and now, Auden overshadowed the rest, and remains one of the English poets of the mid-century certain still to be read a hundred years from now. But MacSpaunday is a recognisable figure – baggy serge trousers, tweed jacket, open-necked shirt, big flop of hair, public schoolboy, educated at Cambridge, joined the Communist Party, almost certainly gay. He's loud, self-assured, and if he isn't very careful (though mostly he is) he's going to get himself killed fighting for the republicans in Spain.

John Cornford was the first of this mould, born in Cambridge and educated there too. A great-grandson of Charles Darwin, he joined the Communist Party when he was still an undergraduate, and fell desperately in love with another young communist student, Margot Heinemann. Impossibly handsome and dashing – for some, communism was as romantic then as revolutionary French republicanism had been to the original Romantics – he went to Spain, joined the Marxist but anti-Stalin POUM, and was duly killed in action. His most famous poem, artfully enough constructed to make one wonder what he might have written had he survived, was a love letter from the Spanish front to Heinemann:

Heart of the heartless world,
Dear heart, the thought of you
Is the pain at my side,
The shadow that chills my view.

The wind rises in the evening,
Reminds that autumn's near.
I am afraid to lose you,
I am afraid of my fear.

On the last mile to Huesca,
The last fence for our pride,
Think so kindly, dear, that I
Sense you at my side.

And if bad luck should lay my strength
Into the shallow grave,
Remember all the good you can;
Don't forget my love.

Not much in that reveals the Marxist or even the volunteer soldier; but Cornford could be a sharp war poet, as in the following poem, meant as a rallying cry to all those left at home:

This is a quiet sector of a quiet front.

We buried Ruiz in a new pine coffin,
But the shroud was too small and his washed feet stuck
    out.
The stink of his corpse came through the clean pine
    boards
And some of the bearers wrapped handkerchiefs round
    their faces.
Death was not dignified.
We hacked a ragged grave in the unfriendly earth
And fired a ragged volley over the grave.

You could tell from our listlessness, no one much missed
    him.

This is a quiet sector of a quiet front.
There is no poison gas and no H.E.

But when they shelled the other end of the village
And the streets were choked with dust
Women came screaming out of the crumbling houses,
Clutched under one arm the naked rump of an infant.
I thought: how ugly fear is.

This is a quiet sector of a quiet front.
Our nerves are steady; we all sleep soundly.

In the clean hospital bed, my eyes were so heavy
Sleep easily blotted out one ugly picture,
A wounded militiaman moaning on a stretcher,
Now out of danger, but still crying for water,
Strong against death, but unprepared for such pain.

This on a quiet front.

But when I shook hands to leave, an Anarchist worker
Said: 'Tell the workers of England
This was a war not of our own making
We did not seek it.
But if ever the Fascists again rule Barcelona
It will be as a heap of ruins with us workers beneath it.'

To many modern readers the heroic tone probably sounds ridiculous, but that was the mood of the times: there was an almost hysterical (and after all, soundly based) fear of Continental fascism, combined with a naïve enthusiasm for a communist revolution which depended upon not knowing, or in some cases wanting to know, much about what was actually happening in Stalin's Russia. 'Full Moon at Tierz' is Cornford's most explicitly Marxist poem, and captures very well the belief that all of history was now at a turning point:

The past, a glacier, gripped the mountain wall,
And time was inches, dark was all.
But here it scales the end of the range,
The dialectic's point of change,
Crashes in light and minutes to its fall.

Time present is a cataract whose force
Breaks down the banks even at its source
And history forming in our hands
Not plasticine but roaring sands,
Yet we must swing it to its final course.

The intersecting lines that cross both ways,
Time future, has no image in space,
Crooked as the road that we must tread,
Straight as our bullets fly ahead.
We are the future. The last fight let us face.

Wystan Hugh Auden was a much greater talent as a poet than Cornford, and later in life he would come to repudiate his communist poetry and turn, rather as T.S. Eliot did, to Christianity. But for a period he was as hot and passionate as Cornford, and, charismatic as he was, he brought a lot of others in his wake. There is a vast amount of his early verse which could be quoted here, much of it, including gay love songs, well known in British culture still. But it's his poem 'Spain' that really deserves to be quoted at length. In it, he picks up Cornford's sense that this was a crucial moment in human history: a global revolution is on the way which will change everything. What makes Auden Auden is mostly all here: the thoughtful mingling of the contemporary and the ancient, the urgency of rhythm, and, particularly in the second half of the poem, the almost hectoring self-confidence. Here is how it is: this is how you must behave. Later, after he had fled Britain in 1939 for the United States, and observed from afar the titanic struggle against Hitler, and learned more about the horrors of Stalinist Russia, Auden came to dislike this poem, and tried to censor it. In particular, the casual line about 'the necessary murder' was one the older man found made him sick. Rightly so; but the original poem is a historical document, which tells us a great deal about how some of the cleverest people in Britain were thinking in the 1930s:

> Yesterday all the past. The language of size
> Spreading to China along the trade-routes; the diffusion
> Of the counting-frame and the cromlech;
> Yesterday the shadow-reckoning in the sunny climates.
>
> Yesterday the assessment of insurance by cards,
> The divination of water; yesterday the invention
> Of cartwheels and clocks, the taming of
> Horses. Yesterday the bustling world of the navigators.
>
> Yesterday the abolition of fairies and giants,
> The fortress like a motionless eagle eyeing the valley,

The chapel built in the forest;
Yesterday the carving of angels and alarming gargoyles;

The trial of heretics among the columns of stone;
Yesterday the theological feuds in the taverns
And the miraculous cure at the fountain;
Yesterday the Sabbath of witches; but to-day the struggle.

Yesterday the installation of dynamos and turbines,
The construction of railways in the colonial desert;
Yesterday the classic lecture
On the origin of Mankind. But to-day the struggle.

Yesterday the belief in the absolute value of Greek,
The fall of the curtain upon the death of a hero;
Yesterday the prayer to the sunset
And the adoration of madmen. But to-day the struggle.

As the poet whispers, startled among the pines,
Or where the loose waterfall sings compact, or upright
On the crag by the leaning tower:
'O my vision. O send me the luck of the sailor.'

And the investigator peers through his instruments
At the inhuman provinces, the virile bacillus
Or enormous Jupiter finished:
'But the lives of my friends. I inquire. I inquire.'

And the poor in their fireless lodgings, dropping the
    sheets
Of the evening paper: 'Our day is our loss. O show us
History the operator, the
Organiser. Time the refreshing river.'

And the nations combine each cry, invoking the life
That shapes the individual belly and orders
The private nocturnal terror:
'Did you not found the city state of the sponge,

'Raise the vast military empires of the shark
And the tiger, establish the robin's plucky canton?
Intervene. O descend as a dove or
A furious papa or a mild engineer, but descend.'

And the life, if it answers at all, replied from the heart
And the eyes and the lungs, from the shops and squares of
    the city
'O no, I am not the mover;
Not to-day; not to you. To you, I'm the

'Yes-man, the bar-companion, the easily-duped;
I am whatever you do. I am your vow to be
Good, your humorous story.
I am your business voice. I am your marriage.

'What's your proposal? To build the just city? I will.
I agree. Or is it the suicide pact, the romantic
Death? Very well, I accept, for
I am your choice, your decision. Yes, I am Spain.'

Many have heard it on remote peninsulas,
On sleepy plains, in the aberrant fishermen's islands
Or the corrupt heart of the city.
Have heard and migrated like gulls or the seeds of a
    flower.

They clung like burrs to the long expresses that lurch
Through the unjust lands, through the night, through the
    alpine tunnel;

They floated over the oceans;
They walked the passes. All presented their lives.

On that arid square, that fragment nipped off from hot
Africa, soldered so crudely to inventive Europe;
On that tableland scored by rivers,
Our thoughts have bodies; the menacing shapes of our
    fever

Are precise and alive. For the fears which made us respond
To the medicine ad, and the brochure of winter cruises
Have become invading battalions;
And our faces, the institute-face, the chain-store, the ruin

Are projecting their greed as the firing squad and the
    bomb.
Madrid is the heart. Our moments of tenderness blossom
As the ambulance and the sandbag;
Our hours of friendship into a people's army.

To-morrow, perhaps the future. The research on fatigue
And the movements of packers; the gradual exploring of
    all the
Octaves of radiation;
To-morrow the enlarging of consciousness by diet and
    breathing.

To-morrow the rediscovery of romantic love,
the photographing of ravens; all the fun under
Liberty's masterful shadow;
To-morrow the hour of the pageant-master and the
    musician,

The beautiful roar of the chorus under the dome;
To-morrow the exchanging of tips on the breeding of terriers,

The eager election of chairmen
By the sudden forest of hands. But to-day the struggle.

To-morrow for the young the poets exploding like bombs,
The walks by the lake, the weeks of perfect communion;
    Auden's to-day
To-morrow the bicycle races
Through the suburbs on summer evenings. But to-day the
    struggle.

To-day the deliberate increase in the chances of death,
The conscious acceptance of guilt in the necessary murder;
To-day the expending of powers
On the flat ephemeral pamphlet and the boring meeting.

To-day the makeshift consolations: the shared cigarette,
The cards in the candlelit barn, and the scraping concert,
The masculine jokes; to-day the
Fumbled and unsatisfactory embrace before hurting.

The stars are dead. The animals will not look.
We are left alone with our day, and the time is short, and
History to the defeated
May say Alas but cannot help nor pardon.

Auden's today never came, at least in Britain, and most of us can be
thankful for that. Yet his extraordinary ability to reach out into
different parts of twentieth-century and historic experience, and
pull them tightly together, synthesising them in a single argument,
is an extraordinary achievement. And alongside the naïve revolu-
tionary tub-thumping, Auden can be eerily prescient and a wonder-
ful observer. His 'Epitaph on a Tyrant' is brisk, exact, and completely
relevant in the twenty-first century, alas:

Perfection, of a kind, was what he was after,
And the poetry he invented was easy to understand;
He knew human folly like the back of his hand,
And was greatly interested in armies and fleets;
When he laughed, respectable senators burst with
    laughter,
And when he cried the little children died in the streets.

Auden's reputation in Britain has never completely recovered from his departure in 1939, but once he was in Manhattan he did give us the most remarkable poem about the mood of dread not just in the UK but across the world, just before Hitler's war began. At his best, Auden can be incantatory, appearing to speak for an era. The hyper-clever Yorkshire boy, fascinated by geology and the classics, religion and politics, eventually matured into a gravelly authority which, once heard, cannot be forgotten. The first three stanzas of 'September 1, 1939' are – well – perfect.

I sit in one of the dives
On Fifty-second Street
Uncertain and afraid
As the clever hopes expire
Of a low dishonest decade:
Waves of anger and fear
Circulate over the bright
And darkened lands of the earth,
Obsessing our private lives;
The unmentionable odour of death
Offends the September night.

Accurate scholarship can
Unearth the whole offence
From Luther until now
That has driven a culture mad,
Find what occurred at Linz,

What huge imago made
A psychopathic god:
I and the public know
What all schoolchildren learn,
Those to whom evil is done
Do evil in return.

Exiled Thucydides knew
All that a speech can say
About Democracy,
And what dictators do,
The elderly rubbish they talk
To an apathetic grave;
Analysed all in his book,
The enlightenment driven away,
The habit-forming pain,
Mismanagement and grief:
We must suffer them all again.

Cecil Day-Lewis, Louis MacNeice and Stephen Spender have all been rather overshadowed by Auden, but all three were fine observers and recorders of mid-century Britain – in some ways closer to the ground than the Master. Day-Lewis, Irish-born and Oxford-educated, gives his group's definitive response to the lack of war poetry in the Second World War, after the collapse of leftist dreams:

They who in folly or mere greed
Enslaved religion, markets, laws,
Borrow our language now and bid
Us speak up in freedom's cause.

It is the logic of our times,
No subject for immortal verse –
That we who live by honest dreams
Defend the bad against the worse.

But of all the group, it's the Belfast-born Louis MacNeice that I have grown to love particularly. He was never much of a propaganda poet, but was a wonderful describer of the world around him. 'Bagpipe Music', deservedly famous, has a romping energy and an addictive rhythm which shows that even in the 1930s, social commentary didn't have to be ponderous:

> It's no go the merry-go-round, it's no go the rickshaw,
> All we want is a limousine and a ticket for the peepshow.
> Their knickers are made of crepe-de-chine, their shoes are
>   made of python,
> Their halls are lined with tiger rugs and their walls with
>   head of bison.
>
> John MacDonald found a corpse, put it under the sofa,
> Waited till it came to life and hit it with a poker,
> Sold its eyes for souvenirs, sold its blood for whiskey,
> Kept its bones for dumbbells to use when he was fifty.
>
> It's no go the Yogi-man, it's no go Blavatsky,
> All we want is a bank balance and a bit of skirt in a taxi.
>
> Annie MacDougall went to milk, caught her foot in the
>   heather,
> Woke to hear a dance record playing of Old Vienna.
> It's no go your maidenheads, it's no go your culture,
> All we want is a Dunlop tyre and the devil mend the
>   puncture.

Under the amusement, there's plenty of sharp social satire going on: this isn't the culture the idealistic young leftists at Cambridge were hoping for. Yet again, the real working classes, with their aspirations for a better life, were letting down the intellectuals. But Louis MacNeice doesn't sound too upset:

It's no go the Herring Board, it's no go the Bible,
All we want is a packet of fags when our hands are idle.

It's no go the picture palace, it's no go the stadium,
It's no go the country cot with a pot of pink geraniums,
It's no go the Government grants, it's no go the elections,
Sit on your arse for fifty years and hang your hat on a
   pension.

After the Depression, and admittedly in the south more than the
north, the 1930s became a decade of English hedonism, the first
real explosion of consumer culture, with Butlin's holidays, relatively
cheap cars and ubiquitous cinemas. MacNeice's 'Autumn Journal' is
a long, loose, compulsively readable reflection on Britain before the
Second World War. In this passage, characteristically, we find him
right in the middle of things, caught between

   the passing of the Morning Post and of life's climacteric
   And the growth of vulgarity, cars that pass the gate-lodge
   And crowds undressing on the beach
   And the hiking cockney lovers with thoughts directed
   Neither to God nor Nation but each to each.
   But the home is still a sanctum under the pelmets,
   All quiet on the Family Front,
   Farmyard noises across the fields at evening
   While the trucks of the Southern Railway dawdle shunt
   Into poppy sidings for the night – night which knows no
      passion
   No assault of hands or tongue
   For all is old as flint or chalk or pine-needles
   And the rebels and the young
   Have taken the train to town or the two-seater
   Unravelling rails or road,
   Losing the thread deliberately behind them –
   Autumnal palinode.

And I am in the train too now and summer is going
South as I go north
Bound for the dead leaves falling, the burning bonfire,
The dying that brings forth
The harder life, revealing the trees' girders,
The frost that kills the germs of laissez-faire;
West Meon, Tisted, Farnham, Woking, Weybridge,
Then London's packed and stale and pregnant air.
My dog, a symbol of the abandoned order,
Lies on the carriage floor,
Her eyes inept and glamorous as a film star's,
Who wants to live, i.e. wants more
Presents, jewellery, furs, gadgets, solicitations
As if to live were not
Following the curve of a planet or controlled water
But a leap in the dark, a tangent, a stray shot.
It is this we learn after so many failures,
The building of castles in sand, of queens in snow,
That we cannot make any corner in life or in life's beauty,
That no river is a river which does not flow.
Surbiton, and a woman gets in, painted
With dyed hair but a ladder in her stocking and eyes
Patient beneath the calculated lashes,
Inured for ever to surprise …

It would be wrong, however, an absolute dereliction of duty, to leave
Louis MacNeice without quoting his finest short poem. In 'Snow'
he demonstrates that a poet can discover, in the most humdrum of
moments, new and useful things to say. If you take one single poem
away from the 1930s, as a kind of consolation, these be the verses:

The room was suddenly rich and the great bay-window was
Spawning snow and pink roses against it
Soundlessly collateral and incompatible:
World is suddener than we fancy it.

World is crazier and more of it than we think,
Incorrigibly plural. I peel and portion
A tangerine and spit the pips and feel
The drunkenness of things being various.

And the fire flames with a bubbling sound for world
Is more spiteful and gay than one supposes –
On the tongue on the eyes on the ears in the palms of your
   hands –
There is more than glass between the snow and the huge
   roses.

Up to now it has looked as if the 'political' poets of the 1930s were
men of the left. Most of them were. But not all. The man who coined
the term 'MacSpaunday' was a fiery right-winger, Roy Campbell,
who went to fight with the fascists against the socialists in Spain. A
hard-drinking horseman and fisherman, born in South Africa, he
fell into the hard-drinking Bohemian world of Oxford and London,
but turned entirely against the Freudianism and Marxism that was
fashionable at the time. A lesbian relationship between his wife and
Vita Sackville-West, lover of Virginia Woolf, provoked a break-up
in his old friendships with the Bloomsbury group. Later, he savagely
satirised them. Campbell emigrated to Spain, where he witnessed
the slaughter of monks and nuns by communists; he became a
supporter of the fascist dictator Franco, though at the beginning of
the Second World War he turned his back on Nazism and returned
to serve in the British Army.

   His extreme politics, and his equally extreme satire, have lowered
his reputation. Hugh MacDiarmid expended an entire and lengthy
poem attacking him. But in his day Roy Campbell was compared
to T.S. Eliot, and later became a close friend and colleague of Dylan
Thomas. 'We are Like Worlds' combines the sense of history on the
march that the left felt, with the egotism and imagery of D.H.
Lawrence:

We bear to future times the secret news
That first was whispered to the new-made earth:
We are like worlds with nations in our thews,
Shaped for delight, and primed for endless birth.
We never kiss but vaster shapes possess
Our bodies: towering up into the skies,
We wear the night and thunder for our dress,
While, vaster than imagination, rise
Two giant forms, like cobras flexed to sting,
Bending their spines in one tremendous ring
With all the starlight burning through their eyes,
Fire in their loins, and on their lips the hiss
Of breath indrawn above some steep abyss.
When, like the sun, our heavenly desire
Has turned this flesh into a cloud of fire
Through which our nerves their strenuous lightning fork
Eternity has blossomed in an hour
And as we gaze upon that wondrous flower
We think the world a beetle on its stalk.

Campbell also wrote substantial religious verse, but at his best he was a razor-sharp satirist. His best quatrain is an attack on some South African novelists:

You praise the firm restraint with which they write –
I'm with you there, of course:
They use the snaffle and the curb all right,
But where's the bloody horse?

Away from the intelligentsia, and from extreme politics of left and right, British poetry between the wars threw up an interesting group of largely conservative and mostly humorous poets – not a group in the Auden sense, but more of an alignment, or attitude.

I start with two men born in the 1870s, who worked throughout the first half of the twentieth century but became best known between the wars. Both were Catholic and anti-Semitic; neither was most celebrated for his adult poetry. George Bernard Shaw conflated the two of them, rather like MacSpaunday, calling them 'the Chesterbelloc'. Hilaire Belloc was half French, a tough-looking and pugnacious man, remembered by millions for his *Cautionary Tales for Children*. A Liberal MP for five years before the First World War, Belloc's political and social thinking were conditioned by his fervent Roman Catholicism. He believed that the decline of religion left Europe vulnerable to Islam. His poetry is rarely angrily political or overtly serious; but his satires on political life, generally very funny, reflect an age in which the Houses of Parliament had lost much of their old authority, and were seen by the inter-war generation as a boarding house for the corrupt and the senile. Here is the second part of his 'Lord Lundy'. I fail to see why Dryden's political satire is regarded as great poetry, and Belloc's is seen as trivia.

It happened to Lord Lundy then,
As happens to so many men:
Towards the age of twenty-six,
They shoved him into politics;
In which profession he commanded
The Income that his rank demanded
In turn as Secretary for
India, the Colonies, and War.
But very soon his friends began
To doubt if he were quite the man:
Thus if a member rose to say
(As members do from day to day),
'Arising out of that reply ...!'
Lord Lundy would begin to cry.
A Hint at harmless little jobs
Would shake him with convulsive sobs.
While as for Revelations, these
Would simply bring him to his knees,
And leave him whimpering like a child.

It drove his colleagues raving wild!
They let him sink from Post to Post,
From fifteen hundred at the most
To eight, and barely six – and then
To be Curator of Big Ben! ...
And finally there came a Threat
To oust him from the Cabinet!

The Duke – his aged grand-sire – bore
The shame till he could bear no more.
He rallied his declining powers,
Summoned the youth to Brackley Towers,
And bitterly addressed him thus –
'Sir! you have disappointed us!
We had intended you to be
The next Prime Minister but three:
The stocks were sold; the Press was squared:
The Middle Class was quite prepared.
But as it is! ... My language fails!
Go out and govern New South Wales!'

The Aged Patriot groaned and died:
And gracious! how Lord Lundy cried!

But Belloc's best lines on British parliamentary governance, applicable when he wrote them in 1923, with the reformist Labour Party struggling against stodgily unimaginative Tories and discredited Liberals, have sadly never quite gone out of date. The four lines are simply called 'On a General Election':

The accursed power which stands on Privilege
(And goes with Women, and Champagne, and Bridge)
Broke – and Democracy resumed her reign:
(Which goes with Bridge, and Women, and Champagne.)

The other half of the monstrous Chesterbelloc, Gilbert Keith Chesterton, was a London boy. He was yet another student of the fine arts at the Slade, who dabbled in occult mysteries, as did W.B. Yeats and almost anybody else with artistic pretensions in the final years of the nineteenth century. He could draw beautifully and wrote copiously in almost every field, though these days he is probably best-known for his Father Brown stories. Chesterton was undoubtably an anti-Semite, though it should be said that he was also an early and ferocious opponent of Nazi Germany and its race theories. Because we tend to see politics still in terms of left and right, we often forget that in the 1920s and 30s very many people rejected both fascism and communism, and looked for a different way forward. One of the ways that was briefly popular was the Catholic social teaching known as Distributism – essentially a belief in private property and a relatively weak state in which property is distributed as widely as possible, rather than being accumulated by capitalists. Both Belloc and Chesterton were prominent and passionate advocates of Distributism, which at least allowed them to stand outside the warring tribes of the age. Chesterton's poetry is like the man himself, large and baggy. Hugely fat, he was rarely to be seen without a black cape, broad-brimmed hat, cigar and a sword stick. His best-known poem is a tribute to the lack of order and organisation in English history and culture: 'The Rolling English Road' is the kind of thing that Kipling might have written, had he had a better sense of humour. But it's not trivial. It has a real message, highly applicable to the British in the age of dictators:

Before the Roman came to Rye or out to Severn strode,
The rolling English drunkard made the rolling English
    road.
A reeling road, a rolling road, that rambles round the
    shire,
And after him the parson ran, the sexton and the squire;
A merry road, a mazy road, and such as we did tread

The night we went to Birmingham by way of Beachy
    Head.

I knew no harm of Bonaparte and plenty of the
    Squire,
And for to fight the Frenchman I did not much desire;
But I did bash their baggonets because they came arrayed
To straighten out the crooked road an English drunkard
    made,
Where you and I went down the lane with ale-mugs in our
    hands,
The night we went to Glastonbury by way of Goodwin
    Sands.

His sins they were forgiven him; or why do flowers run
Behind him; and the hedges all strengthening in the sun?
The wild thing went from left to right and knew not which
    was which,
But the wild rose was above him when they found him in
    the ditch.
God pardon us, nor harden us; we did not see so clear
The night we went to Bannockburn by way of Brighton
    Pier.

My friends, we will not go again or ape an ancient rage,
Or stretch the folly of our youth to be the shame of age,
But walk with clearer eyes and ears this path that
    wandereth,
And see undrugged in evening light the decent inn of
    death;
For there is good news yet to hear and fine things to be
    seen,
Before we go to Paradise by way of Kensal Green.

Chesterton's other major political poem, 'The Secret People of England', is much quoted by English nationalists and others who feel excluded from the political system, even today. It has an entirely deliberate hint of populist menace, but it starts, as we expect with Chesterton, in a genial tone:

> Smile at us, pay us, pass us; but do not quite forget;
> For we are the people of England, that never have spoken
> yet.
> There is many a fat farmer that drinks less cheerfully,
> There is many a free French peasant who is richer and
> sadder than we.
> There are no folk in the whole world so helpless or so
> wise.
> There is hunger in our bellies, there is laughter in our eyes;
> You laugh at us and love us, both mugs and eyes are wet:
> Only you do not know us. For we have not spoken yet.
>
> The fine French kings came over in a flutter of flags and
> dames.
> We liked their smiles and battles, but we never could say
> their names.

The poem carries on with a distinctively Catholic view of English history, savaging the Tudors for the Reformation and mocking of the reformers of the Age of Enlightenment, before turning to the rise of capitalists and capitalist-farmers in the nineteenth century. And here the tone becomes decidedly less genial:

> Our patch of glory ended; we never heard guns again.
> But the squire seemed struck in the saddle; he was foolish,
> as if in pain,
> He leaned on a staggering lawyer, he clutched a cringing
> Jew,

He was stricken; it may be, after all, he was stricken at
　Waterloo.
Or perhaps the shades of the shaven men, whose spoil is
　in his house,
Come back in shining shapes at last to spoil his last
　carouse:
We only know the last sad squires rode slowly towards the
　sea,
And a new people takes the land: and still it is not we.

They have given us into the hand of new unhappy lords,
Lords without anger or honour, who dare not carry their
　swords.
They fight by shuffling papers; they have bright dead alien
　eyes;
They look at our labour and laughter as a tired man looks
　at flies.
And the load of their loveless pity is worse than the
　ancient wrongs,
Their doors are shut in the evening; and they know no
　songs.

We hear men speaking for us of new laws strong and
　sweet,
Yet is there no man speaketh as we speak in the street.
It may be we shall rise the last as Frenchmen rose the first,
Our wrath come after Russia's wrath and our wrath be the
　worst.
It may be we are meant to mark with our riot and our rest
God's scorn for all men governing. It may be beer is best.
But we are the people of England; and we have not spoken
　yet.
Smile at us, pay us, pass us. But do not quite forget.

So if, dear reader, you are inclined to quote parts of that poem – and my goodness, it's quotable – do not quite forget that what Chesterton actually seems to be advocating is an English revolution that will be worse in its bloodshed than the Russian one, which killed so many millions.

A much gentler figure than either Belloc or Chesterton was the last of the major non-leftist poets and humorists to begin to publish between the wars. Many modern poets deny that John Betjeman was really even a poet at all, rather a crowd-pleasing verse-maker of conventional and sentimental views. That's not entirely fair. But it's not entirely unfair, either. Born in 1909 to a north London family of Dutch descent, Betjeman was a contemporary of Louis MacNeice's. Like Belloc and Chesterton he was a committed Christian, although in his case not a Roman Catholic but a high Anglican. An academic failure at Oxford, as a young man he knew Auden and Spender, and scratched a living as a schoolteacher and journalist. It's the journalist in him which makes his poetry of the 1930s still so much worth reading – he was an acute observer of middle-class snobberies and fads, like MacNeice but lighter and funnier. His poems are studded with references to contemporary brands and gadgets – again, if you want to know what slices of 1930s English life were like to live through, Betjeman shouldn't be underestimated. And he can do shabby just as well as Auden: here is his 'Death in Leamington':

She died in the upstairs bedroom
By the light of the ev'ning star
That shone through the plate glass window
From over Leamington Spa.

Beside her the lonely crochet
Lay patiently and unstirred,
But the fingers that would have work'd it
Were dead as the spoken word.

And Nurse came in with the tea-things
Breast high 'mid the stands and chairs —
But Nurse was alone with her own little soul,
And the things were alone with theirs.

She bolted the big round window,
She let the blinds unroll,
She set a match to the mantle,
She covered the fire with coal.

And 'Tea!' she said in a tiny voice,
'Wake up! It's nearly five'
Oh! Chintzy, chintzy cheeriness,
Half dead and half alive.

Do you know that the stucco is peeling?
Do you know that the heart will stop?
From those yellow Italianate arches
Do you hear the plaster drop?

Nurse looked at the silent bedstead,
At the grey, decaying face,
As the calm of a Leamington ev'ning
Drifted into the place.

She moved the table of bottles
Away from the bed to the wall;
And tiptoeing gently over the stairs
Turned down the gas in the hall.

That's uncharacteristically melancholy, at least for early Betjeman.
Of all his earlier poems, 'A Subaltern's Love Song' has been the most
enduringly popular. Written shortly after the war had started, it's
the essence of the English suburban paradise:

Miss J. Hunter Dunn, Miss J. Hunter Dunn,
Furnish'd and burnish'd by Aldershot sun,
What strenuous singles we played after tea,
We in the tournament – you against me!

Love-thirty, love-forty, oh! weakness of joy,
The speed of a swallow, the grace of a boy,
With carefullest carelessness, gaily you won,
I am weak from your loveliness, Joan Hunter Dunn.

Miss Joan Hunter Dunn, Miss Joan Hunter Dunn,
How mad I am, sad I am, glad that you won,
The warm-handled racket is back in its press,
But my shock-headed victor, she loves me no less.

Her father's euonymus shines as we walk,
And swing past the summer-house, buried in talk,
And cool the verandah that welcomes us in
To the six-o'clock news and a lime-juice and gin.

The scent of the conifers, sound of the bath,
The view from my bedroom of moss-dappled path,
As I struggle with double-end evening tie,
For we dance at the Golf Club, my victor and I.

On the floor of her bedroom lie blazer and shorts,
And the cream-coloured walls are be-trophied with sports,
And westering, questioning settles the sun,
On your low-leaded window, Miss Joan Hunter Dunn.

The Hillman is waiting, the light's in the hall,
The pictures of Egypt are bright on the wall,
My sweet, I am standing beside the oak stair
And there on the landing's the light on your hair.

By roads 'not adopted', by woodlanded ways,
She drove to the club in the late summer haze,
Into nine-o'clock Camberley, heavy with bells
And mushroomy, pine-woody, evergreen smells.

That poem, enjoyable as it is, suggests why Betjeman isn't, in the end, a poet of the first rank. He is soppy, and he is twee. In later life he would be made Poet Laureate, and do this country great service by campaigning for the preservation of many beautiful Victorian buildings. And after all, among the things Britain was fighting for in 1939 was, presumably, the right to be soppy and twee. Over the Channel, worse failings were becoming visible.

16

Revolt Against the Metropolis: Britain in the 1940s and 50s

Why didn't the Second World War produce a generation of poets as famous and important as the first one had? There are some obvious answers. First, although there was bitter hand-to-hand fighting in North Africa, Italy, the Far East and Europe itself, there was nothing like the wholesale human confrontation of 1914 to 1918 – this was a more scattered and in some ways less intense conflict. Second, despite the best efforts of W.H. Auden and his followers – some of them now in America – poetry simply seemed to matter less than it had in Edwardian times. The new war produced films, novels, documentaries and memoirs alongside the poetry. Finally, when it comes to the pity of war, some things don't need saying twice; and anyway, to most British people the war against Hitler seemed almost self-evidently morally right, compared to the more morally ambiguous war against the Kaiser.

Nevertheless, 1939–45 did produce interesting and memorable poetry, and one of the first things we notice is that it tends to be coming from poets far away from the old Oxbridge–London metropolitan nexus. Yorkshire voices, Scottish voices and Welsh voices; and this is a trend that will continue long after the war. It's as if, now that poetry is beginning to seem rather more marginal to the British experience, there's more space for the rest of Britain, the vast expanses and cities ignored by the metropolitan elite, to speak out. Whatever the reason, it's an unmistakable trend.

The best poet of the Second World War is the now relatively little-known Henry Reed. Born in Birmingham in 1914, he knew both W.H. Auden and Louis MacNeice. He was called up to the British Army in 1941, though he spent most of the conflict, rather unhappily, as a translator of Japanese. Post-war he became a play-wright and broadcaster, and survived until 1986. Much military experience, of course, has nothing to do with terror and killing, but is pure boredom and stupidity. Henry Reed wrote his best-known poetry about military basic training. 'Naming of Parts' is a wry and lovely poem about learning to use firearms; there is something of the impatience with traditional authority in this which carried over into 1945 and the election of Britain's first socialist government.

To-day we have naming of parts. Yesterday,
We had daily cleaning. And to-morrow morning,
We shall have what to do after firing. But to-day,
To-day we have naming of parts. Japonica
Glistens like coral in all of the neighbouring gardens,
And to-day we have naming of parts.

This is the lower sling swivel. And this
Is the upper sling swivel, whose use you will see,
When you are given your slings. And this is the piling swivel,
Which in your case you have not got. The branches
Hold in the gardens their silent, eloquent gestures,
Which in our case we have not got.

This is the safety-catch, which is always released
With an easy flick of the thumb. And please do not let me
See anyone using his finger. You can do it quite easy
If you have any strength in your thumb. The blossoms
Are fragile and motionless, never letting anyone see
Any of them using their finger.

And this you can see is the bolt. The purpose of this
Is to open the breech, as you see. We can slide it
Rapidly backwards and forwards: we call this
Easing the spring. And rapidly backwards and forwards
The early bees are assaulting and fumbling the flowers:
They call it easing the Spring.

They call it easing the Spring: it is perfectly easy
If you have any strength in your thumb: like the bolt,
And the breech, and the cocking-piece, and the point of
    balance,
Which in our case we have not got; and the
    almond-blossom
Silent in all of the gardens and the bees going backwards
    and forwards,
For to-day we have naming of parts.

Henry Reed wasn't a one-poem wonder – 'Judging Distances' is
closely related to 'Naming of Parts', and just as good, but its message
is too similar for it to be reproduced here.

Keith Douglas, a boy from an unhappy and a rackety Kent family
whose pre-war verses were admired by T.S. Eliot, is widely regarded
as Britain's best Second World War poet who was actually involved
in the fighting. He served with the Northamptonshire Yeomanry in
North Africa – he was at el Alamein – before being killed shortly
after the D-Day landings. Some find his poems rather cold and
heartless; but they have a directness and an unsparing attitude to
the business of war which sets them apart. This one is called simply
'How to Kill' – it describes the hand grenade and the sniper's rifle,
though Douglas himself would in fact be killed by a German
mortar.

Under the parabola of a ball,
a child turning into a man,
I looked into the air too long.

The ball fell in my hand, it sang
in the closed fist: Open Open
Behold a gift designed to kill.

Now in my dial of glass appears
the soldier who is going to die.
He smiles, and moves about in ways
his mother knows, habits of his.
The wires touch his face: I cry
NOW. Death, like a familiar, hears

And look, has made a man of dust
of a man of flesh. This sorcery
I do. Being damned, I am amused
to see the centre of love diffused
and the wave of love travel into vacancy.
How easy it is to make a ghost.

The weightless mosquito touches
her tiny shadow on the stone,
and with how like, how infinite
a lightness, man and shadow meet.
They fuse. A shadow is a man
when the mosquito death approaches

Of all the Scottish poets associated with the literary renaissance begun by Hugh MacDiarmid, none has had more influence on modern Scottish culture than Hamish Henderson. Born in Blairgowrie, Perthshire, he moved to London as a child and later became involved in the anti-Nazi resistance, helping rescue Jews from Hitler's Germany. Always on the left, and at the beginning of the war a pacifist, Henderson ended up as an intelligence officer with the 51st Highland Division, and became a leading voice of the Eighth Army. His 'Elegies for the Dead in Cyrenaica' are, alongside the works of Keith Douglas, the most complete and satisfying

British war poetry of the conflict. Henderson mingles a defiant contempt for Nazi Germany with humane compassion for the German soldiers who fell in the desert. 'Mak siccar' means 'make sure', a phrase attributed to one of Robert the Bruce's companions after a notorious murder – one final knife in the dying body:

> We'll mak siccar!
> Against the bashing cudgel
> against the contemptuous triumphs of the big battalions
>   ... mak siccar
> against the executioner
> against the tyrannous myth and the real terror
> mak siccar ...

But what of the soldiers?

> No blah about their sacrifice: rather tears or reviling
> of the time that took them, than an insult so outrageous.
> All barriers are down: in the criss-crossed enclosures
> where most lie now assembled in their aching solitude
> those others lie too – who were also the sacrificed
> of history's great rains, of the destructive transitions.
> This one beach where high seas have disgorged them like
>   flotsam
> reveals in its nakedness their ultimate alliance.

And, asks Henderson, who became a communist, what is the point of it all, this killing? In the end, his answer is human internationalism:

> So the words that I have looked for, and must go on
>   looking for,
> Are words of whole love, which can slowly gain the power
> To reconcile and heal. Other words would be pointless.

As a boy in Perthshire, Henderson had grown up with Gypsy ballads. From the first he had a strong sense of the popular folk tradition, and his greatest contribution to Scotland would come after the war, when he trailed around the country with a primitive tape recorder, collecting the old songs and stories before they finally disappeared. Thanks to him Edinburgh University founded its School of Scottish Studies, and a great flowering of folk music and ballad writing continued, and continues, in the Scottish nation. As for Henderson's own ballads, he was only partly responsible for the famous 'Song of the D-Day Dodgers', which vents the anger of Eighth Army men fighting in Italy after a speech by Lady Astor in which she implied that in some way soldiers in other theatres of war were evading or dodging the D-Day beaches. If you want to hear the authentic sound of British troops during this war, it's a good place to start:

We're the D-Day Dodgers out in Italy –
Always on the vino, always on the spree.
Eighth Army scroungers and their tanks
We live in Rome – among the Yanks.
We are the D-Day Dodgers, over here in Italy.

We landed at Salerno, a holiday with pay,
Jerry brought the band down to cheer us on our way
Showed us the sights and gave us tea,
We all sang songs, the beer was free.
We are the D-Day Dodgers, way out in Italy.

The Volturno and Cassino were taken in our stride
We didn't have to fight there. We just went for the ride.
Anzio and Sangro were all forlorn.
We did not do a thing from dusk to dawn
For we are the D-Day Dodgers, over here in Italy.

On our way to Florence we had a lovely time.
We ran a bus to Rimini right through the Gothic Line.
On to Bologna we did go.
Then we went bathing in the Po.
For we are the D-Day Dodgers, over here in Italy.

Once we had a blue light that we were going home
Back to dear old Blighty, never more to roam.
Then somebody said in France you'll fight.
We said never mind, we'll just sit tight,
The windy D-Day Dodgers, out in Sunny Italy.

Now Lady Astor, get a load of this.
Don't stand up on a platform and talk a load of piss.
You're the nation's sweetheart, the nation's pride
We think your mouth's too bloody wide.
We are the D-Day Dodgers, in Sunny Italy.

When you look 'round the mountains, through the mud
    and rain
You'll find the crosses, some which bear no name.
Heartbreak, and toil and suffering gone
The boys beneath them slumber on
They were the D-Day Dodgers, who'll stay in Italy.

So listen all you people, over land and foam
Even though we've parted, our hearts are close to home.
When we return we hope you'll say
'You did your little bit, though far away
All of the D-Day Dodgers, way out there in Italy.'

The first version of this hugely popular song, which kept changing,
was written by Lance Sergeant Harry Pynn of the Tank Rescue
Section, in the 78th Infantry Division. It should be recorded that
Lady Astor's speech in the House of Commons didn't actually use

the phrase, so far as we can tell; but the bitterness of an army that felt its contribution was being downplayed was very real. Henderson exemplifies all of those British servicemen who felt on the one hand that the future was with internationalism and the brotherhood of man, but on the other that this was one 'good war' well worth fighting. Although he can never have made a good communist – he was far too rebellious and individualistic – Henderson's most influential poem was socialist, a ballad of apology for Scottish imperialism, sung at the opening of the Scottish Parliament and now almost an alternative national anthem for the Scots.

It's called 'Freedom Come-All-Ye'. It's in Scots, so here is my very rough translation, with many apologies to Hamish Henderson: 'Dawn, and the wild wind is blowing the clouds helter-skelter over the bay; but there's more than a wild wind blowing through the great glen of the world today. It's a thought for all the rats, the swaggering rogues – time for them to find somewhere else for their evil tricks. Never again will bold and fearless men march to war, while braggarts boast at home, or children from coal mines and cottages mourn the ships we sent down the Clyde. No more will families we have harried curse Scotland the Brave. Black and white, married to one another, will empty the vile barracks of their masters. So, come on, all you who love freedom, and never mind the warnings of the carrion crows: in your house, all God's children can get whisky, food and shelter. When John MacLean [the Glasgow Revolutionary] meets his friends from [working-class] Springburn, all the roses and the wild cherries will bloom, and a black boy from beyond Nyanga [possibly a reference to Nelson Mandela] will smash all the gallows of the powerful down.' That précis, of course, has nothing of the urgent poetic force of the original Scots, which has to be heard sung to a pipe tune, 'The Bloody Fields of Flanders', for full effect:

Roch the wind in the clear day's dawin
Blaws the cloods heelster-gowdie ow'r the bay,
But there's mair nor a roch wind blawin
Through the great glen o' the warld the day.

It's a thocht that will gar oor rottans –
A' they rogues that gang gallus, fresh and gay –
Tak the road, and seek ither loanins
For their ill ploys, tae sport and play.

Nae mair will the bonnie callants
Mairch tae war when oor braggarts crously craw,
Nor wee weans frae pit-heid and clachan
Mourn the ships sailin' doon the Broomielaw.

Broken faimlies in lands we've herriet,
Will curse Scotland the Brave nae mair, nae mair;
Black and white, ane til ither mairriet,
Mak the vile barracks o' their maisters bare.

So come all ye at hame wi' Freedom,
Never heed whit the hoodies croak for doom.
In your hoose a' the bairns o' Adam
Can find breid, barley-bree and painted room.

When MacLean meets wi's freens in Springburn
A' the roses and geans will turn tae bloom,
And a black boy frae yont Nyanga
Dings the fell gallows o' the burghers doon.

Though Hamish Henderson's career lasted well into the 1970s, and that poem comes from the anti-Polaris guided-missile protest movement of the 1960s, the 1940s were a very important decade in Scottish poetry. A large cluster of poets emerged from MacDiarmid's shadow, some writing in Scots, some in English, and Sorley MacLean in Gaelic. Of the Scots group, Robert Garioch was the most talented. A painter's son from Edinburgh, he was conscripted into the Royal Signals and spent three years as a German prisoner of war. His most characteristic poems are wry satires on Edinburgh life, written in Scots after the war. He was also a splendid translator into Scots of the scurrilous Italian sonnets of the Roman poet Giuseppe Belli. Here is his beautiful poem in English, 'Letter from Italy', a simple love letter back home from a poet caught in North Africa:

From large red bugs, a refugee,
I make my bed beneath the sky,
safe from the crawling enemy
though not secure from nimbler flea.
Late summer darkness comes, and now
I see again the homely Plough
and wonder: do you also see
the seven stars as well as I?
And it is good to find a tie
of seven stars from you to me.
Lying on deck, on friendly seas,
I used to watch, with no delight,
new unsuggestive stars that light
the tedious Antipodes.
Now in a hostile land I lie,
but share with you these
ancient high familiar named divinities.
Perimeters have bounded me,
sad rims of desert and of sea,
the famous one around Tobruk,
and now barbed wire, which way I look,
except above – the Pléiades.

Another Garioch war poem, 'Property', reflects on how war can strip a man down to the bare essentials and shake to pieces his original ideas about what matters:

Our man should have no thought for property,
he said, and drank down his pint.
Mirage is found in the desert and elsewhere.

Later, in Libya (sand & scrub,
the Sun two weeks to Midsummer)
he carried all his property over the sand:
socks, knife and spoon, a dixie,
toilet kit, the Works of Shakespeare,
blanket, groundsheet, greatcoat,
and a water bottle holding no more water ...

The soldier and other 'scorched men' walk on through the desert –
one gets the impression that they are prisoners of war – until a hot,
dry wind rises:

... Suffusing the sand in the air,
the sun burned in darkness.
No man now whistled, only the sandy wind.
The greatcoat first, then blanket discarded
and the other property lay absurd on the Desert,
but he kept his water-bottle.
In February, in a cold wet climate,
he has permanent damp in his bones
for the lack of that groundsheet.
He has a different notion of the values of things.

Bare, unsentimental and unself-pitying, that poem brings a truth
out of war that nobody else quite gets to. But the classic Garioch is
Scots-English and satirical. This sonnet is called 'Glisk [i.e. glimpse]
of the Great'. Translations? The N.B. Grill was for many years a
famously posh restaurant in Edinburgh's Princes Street. 'Creashy' is
a wonderfully expressive word for greasy, a 'bawr' is a joke, and
'bailies' are magistrates. Finally, a 'heid-yin' is a grandee, particularly
a pompous grandee. The rest, I think, is pretty self-explanatory, and
even for English-only readers, well worth it:

I saw him comin out the N.B. Grill
Creashy and winey, wi his famous voice

Crackin some comic bawr to please three choice
Notorious bailies, lauchan fit to kill.

Syne thae fowre crousie cronies clam intill
A muckle big municipal Rolls-Royce,
And disappeared, aye lauchan, wi a noise
That droont the traffic, towards the Calton Hill.

As they rade by, it seemed the sun was shinin
Brichter nor usual roun thae cantie three
That wi thon weill-kent Heid-yin had been dinin.

Nou that's the kinna thing I like to see;
Tho ye and I look on an canna jyn in,
It gies our toun some tone, ye'll aa agree.

It's not a poem that Hugh MacDiarmid could have written – it's too gently amused, too quiet – but it shows that as a result of the Scottish literary renaissance, a spirit and tone in poetry that seemed to have been lost since the death of Robert Fergusson, or perhaps since those of Dunbar and Henryson in late medieval times, had magically revived in the twentieth century.

And it wasn't only Scotland. At the same time that Garioch and other Scots were hitting their stride, a remarkable young Welsh poet, Dylan Thomas, was hitting his. Hard drinking, surrealist in spirit and with an extraordinary mellifluous gift, he's not normally thought of as a war poet. But he spent much of his short life in London, including during the Blitz, and produced some vividly memorable images of the war as it affected civilians, including this tribute to a centenarian, killed in a dawn raid by German bombers:

When the morning was waking over the war
He put on his clothes and stepped out and he died,
The locks yawned loose and a blast blew them wide,

He dropped where he had loved on the burst pavement
   stone
And the funeral grains of the slaughtered floor.
Tell his street on its back he stopped a sun
And the craters of his eyes grew springshoots and fire
When all the keys shot from the locks, and rang.
Dig no more for the chains of his grey-haired heart.
The heavenly ambulance drawn by a wound
Assembling waits for the spade's ring on the cage.
O keep his bones away from that common cart,
The morning is flying on the wings of his age
And a hundred storks perch on the sun's right hand.

Like many artists, Dylan Thomas was in some part of his mind a
raging extremist; he entitled the following poem 'A Refusal to
Mourn the Death, by Fire, of a Child in London'. In some of his
verse Thomas tips over into babbling self-indulgence – words and
sounds and symbols almost for their own sake, late Romanticism
which became quite marked in Britain in the 1940s. Here, however,
he holds it together and achieves a grandeur we associate more with
religious poets of the seventeenth century:

Never until the mankind making
Bird beast and flower
Fathering and all humbling darkness
Tells with silence the last light breaking
And the still hour
Is come of the sea tumbling in harness

And I must enter again the round
Zion of the water bead
And the synagogue of the ear of corn
Shall I let pray the shadow of a sound
Or sow my salt seed
In the least valley of sackcloth to mourn

The majesty and burning of the child's death.
I shall not murder
The mankind of her going with a grave truth
Nor blaspheme down the stations of the breath
With any further
Elegy of innocence and youth.

Deep with the first dead lies London's daughter,
Robed in the long friends,
The grains beyond age, the dark veins of her mother,
Secret by the unmourning water
Of the riding Thames.
After the first death, there is no other.

Before his London years, Thomas had enjoyed an intermittently idyllic Welsh rural childhood. The romanticism of the 1940s, no doubt a reaction against the political poetry and the Modernism of the previous decade, can seem extremely tiresome – there are lots of consciously archaic paintings and drawings, wispy and prancing poetry too – but Thomas at his best achieves a lush freshness that still takes the breath away. Here's the opening of his 'Fern Hill':

Now as I was young and easy under the apple boughs
About the lilting house and happy as the grass was green,
The night above the dingle starry,
Time let me hail and climb
Golden in the heydays of his eyes,
And honoured among wagons I was prince of the apple
  towns
And once below a time I lordly had the trees and leaves
Trail with daisies and barley
Down the rivers of the windfall light.

And as I was green and carefree, famous among the barns
About the happy yard and singing as the farm was home,

In the sun that is young once only,
Time let me play and be
Golden in the mercy of his means,
And green and golden I was huntsman and herdsman, the
    calves
Sang to my horn, the foxes on the hills barked clear and
    cold,
And the sabbath rang slowly
In the pebbles of the holy streams.

At the other end of the British Isles, another small boy enjoyed an Eden-like childhood in an area which seemed for a long time to have been left behind by the twentieth century. Edwin Muir was born in 1887 on the Orkney Islands, into a world of oral stories, farming and fishing, and almost no mechanical implements at all. In 1901 the family moved to Glasgow and Eden vanished, a trauma from which he never really recovered. A friend, and then an enemy, of Hugh MacDiarmid, Muir turned his back on Scottish national-ism. He was a highly internationalist figure, who translated and introduced Franz Kafka to a British audience. He lived long enough to become horrified by the possibilities of nuclear war, the dimly-seen background to one of his most beautiful poems, 'Horses', contrasting the Orkney of his childhood with what happened in the twentieth century.

Those lumbering horses in the steady plough,
On the bare field – I wonder, why, just now,
They seemed terrible, so wild and strange,
Like magic power on the stony grange.

Perhaps some childish hour has come again,
When I watched fearful, through the blackening rain,
Their hooves like pistons in an ancient mill
Move up and down, yet seem as standing still.

Their conquering hooves which trod the stubble down
Were ritual that turned the field to brown,
And their great hulks were seraphims of gold,
Or mute ecstatic monsters on the mould.

And oh the rapture, when, one furrow done,
They marched broad-breasted to the sinking sun!
The light flowed off their bossy sides in flakes;
The furrows rolled behind like struggling snakes.

But when at dusk with steaming nostrils home
They came, they seemed gigantic in the gloam,
And warm and glowing with mysterious fire
That lit their smouldering bodies in the mire.

Their eyes as brilliant and as wide as night
Gleamed with a cruel apocalyptic light,
Their manes the leaping ire of the wind
Lifted with rage invisible and blind.

Ah, now it fades! It fades! And I must pine
Again for the dread country crystalline,
Where the blank field and the still-standing tree
Were bright and fearful presences to me.

Another poem, confusingly with almost the same title, 'The Horses,'
written after the war, is more explicit about the looming global
threat. This might seem the wrong place to include it, and it might
seem self-indulgent to have two poems by the same poet on almost
the same theme. However, for very many writers – and Edwin Muir
can speak for them here – the horrors of the Second World War
and the Nazi death camps prefigured a world that seemed simply
more evil and dangerous than it had ever been. The nuclear threat,
coming soon afterwards, merely reinforced this sense that mankind
had left Eden and walked straight into hell. If that seems melo-

dramatic, to many writers of the 1940s, it didn't. So here is the opening of that second poem, which reintroduces those mysterious gigantic horses of the previous one:

Barely a twelvemonth after
The seven days war that put the world to sleep,
Late in the evening the strange horses came.
By then we had made our covenant with silence,
But in the first few days it was so still
We listened to our breathing and were afraid.
On the second day
The radios failed; we turned the knobs; no answer.
On the third day a warship passed us, heading north,
Dead bodies piled on the deck. On the sixth day
A plane plunged over us into the sea. Thereafter
Nothing. The radios dumb ...

The poem then expands into a meditation on the failure of the industrial world. The farmers now abandon their tractors, which

... Lie about our fields; at evening
They look like dank sea-monsters crouched and waiting.
We leave them where they are and let them rust:
'They'll moulder away and be like other loam'.
We make our oxen drag our rusty ploughs,
Long laid aside. We have gone back
Far past our fathers' land.
And then, that evening
Late in the summer the strange horses came.
We heard a distant tapping on the road,
A deepening drumming; it stopped, went on again
And at the corner changed to hollow thunder.
We saw the heads
Like a wild wave charging ...

As we enter the middle part of the twentieth century, the poetry of Edwin Muir is encouraging because it shows that, without excessive artifice or artificial cleverness, it's possible to write gripping, emotionally grown-up poetry about the world as it is. At times from the Edwardian era onwards it has seemed that British poetry is growing effete and bloodless, casting around wearily for new subjects. Muir shows unequivocally that there is plenty to write about, even if it can't be easily uncovered from London or the grander universities.

Except, with the right sensibility, it can. Florence Margaret Smith, universally known as Stevie Smith, was born in Hull but brought up in Palmers Green, north London, in a house composed almost entirely of women – her feckless father had deserted the family early, and was rarely in touch. Stevie Smith spent most of her life working in publishing, as a secretary, and suffered from lifelong illness; but inside this unpromising biographical envelope, an entirely original mind was developing. Although she was also a novelist, Stevie Smith is best known for her poems, which are uneasily balanced between childlike comedy and a dark, generally pessimistic adult awareness of death and disappointment. She's important partly because she set a tone which has stayed popular – the tone of the unsettling, beady-eyed child telling truths to the heedless adult world. She's not 'like' anyone, but she reminds me of Christopher Smart, another childlike intellect adrift in a painful world. Here's her 'Alone in the Woods':

Alone in the woods I felt
The bitter hostility of the sky and the trees
Nature has taught her creatures to hate
Man that fusses and fumes
Unquiet man
As the sap rises in the trees
As the sap paints the trees a violent green
So rises the wrath of Nature's creatures
At man

So paints the face of Nature a violent green.
Nature is sick at man
Sick at his fuss and fume
Sick at his agonies
Sick at his gaudy mind
That drives his body
Ever more quickly
More and more
In the wrong direction.

In her matter-of-factness, her rejection of grand political state-ments and her directness, so unlike the Modernists, Stevie Smith is an underrated influence on the next generation of poets in Britain, the so-called 'Movement' of the 1950s – Philip Larkin, Kingsley Amis, Elizabeth Jennings, Donald Davie and the rest. She wrote for a long time, breaking through before the Second World War and still producing original poetry in the 1970s. She was an expert at taking the apparently small, and making an unforgettably large statement out of it. Most famous of all, of course, is her 'Not Waving but Drowning'. It's not quite free verse, and it's a technical triumph – a masterclass in getting to the action fast, no messing about, and then getting out quickly.

But still he lay moaning:
I was much further out than you thought
And not waving but drowning.

Poor chap, he always loved larking
And now he's dead
It must have been too cold for him his heart gave way,
They said.

Oh, no no no, it was too cold always
(Still the dead one lay moaning)

I was much too far out all my life
And not waving but drowning.

Perhaps because of her nickname, picked up from a jockey in child-
hood, it's very easy to see Stevie Smith as somehow essentially
unserious. That would be a great mistake. She was a highly moral
and judgemental writer. Long before the social and sexual revolu-
tion of the 1960s, Britain in the 1940s was being morally and
culturally shaken up, both by the social dislocation caused by the
war – many couples divided, families split up, and so forth – and
by the Americanisation caused, particularly in the cities, by the
arrival of so many GIs, bringing new words, new customs and
looser morals. It's not surprising that there was a turn back to the
reassurances of tradition. Stevie Smith was certainly part of this. In
her poem 'Valuable', based on reading two newspaper paragraphs,
one about rising illegitimacy rates and one about a panther which
briefly escaped from a Paris zoo, she writes:

All these illegitimate babies …
Oh girls, girls,
Silly little cheap things,
Why do you not put some value on yourselves,
Learn to say, No?
Did nobody teach you?
Nobody teaches anybody to say No nowadays,
People should teach people to say No …

… Oh these illegitimate babies!
Oh girls, girls,
Silly little valuable things,
You should have said, No, I am valuable,
And again, It is because I am valuable
I say, No.
Nobody teaches anybody they are valuable nowadays.

Stevie Smith's traditionalism achieves spiritual depth at times, unusual in modern British poetry. I think she is still badly underrated. Here is one final example of Smith, yet another poet apparently coming from the edges of mainstream poetic culture, on fiery form. 'All things hurry to be eaten or eat' – she had quite a cutting edge.

Away, melancholy,
Away with it, let it go.

Are not the trees green,
The earth as green?
Does not the wind blow,
Fire leap and the rivers flow?
Away melancholy.

The ant is busy
He carrieth his meat,
All things hurry
To be eaten or eat.
Away, melancholy.

Man, too, hurries,
Eats, couples, buries,
He is an animal also
With a hey ho melancholy,
Away with it, let it go.

Man of all creatures
Is superlative
(Away melancholy)
He of all creatures alone
Raiseth a stone
(Away melancholy)
Into the stone, the god

Pours what he knows of good
Calling, good, God.
Away melancholy, let it go.

Speak not to me of tears,
Tyranny, pox, wars,
Saying, Can God
Stone of man's thoughts, be good?
Say rather it is enough
That the stuffed
Stone of man's good, growing,
By man's called God.
Away, melancholy, let it go.

Man aspires
To good,
To love
Sighs;

Beaten, corrupted, dying
In his own blood lying
Yet heaves up an eye above
Cries, Love, love.
It is his virtue needs explaining,
Not his failing.

Away, melancholy,
Away with it, let it go.

One of the difficulties of a project like this, matching poetry with
changing social attitudes, is that some poets go on for such a long
time, changing as they go – where should they be placed? A case in
point is Basil Bunting, that great Northumbrian Modernist, who
carried on unabashed well into the 1970s. But the following poem,
'What the Chairman told Tom', sits well with another theme of the

1940s, which is a growing lack of confidence in the very craft of poetry writing itself. What's it for? Does it really still matter in the age of radio, and then television? W.H. Auden confronted this subject, as we will see shortly, but Bunting's witty account of a job interview is a gem:

Poetry? It's a hobby.
I run model trains.
Mr Shaw there breeds pigeons.

It's not work. You dont sweat.
Nobody pays for it.
You could advertise soap.

Art, that's opera; or repertory —
The Desert Song.
Nancy was in the chorus.

But to ask for twelve pounds a week —
married, aren't you? —
you've got a nerve.

How could I look a bus conductor
in the face
if I paid you twelve pounds?

Who says it's poetry, anyhow?
My ten year old
can do it and rhyme.

I get three thousand and expenses,
a car, vouchers,
but I'm an accountant.

They do what I tell them,
my company.
What do you do?

Nasty little words, nasty long words,
it's unhealthy.
I want to wash when I meet a poet.

They're Reds, addicts,
all delinquents.
What you write is rot.

Mr Hines says so, and he's a schoolteacher,
he ought to know.
Go and find work.

During the war years, two of the great titans of pre-war poetry were still close to top form: the Englishman Auden, writing in America; and the American T.S. Eliot, writing in England. Neither of them inclined to address world affairs directly, but they were both, like Stevie Smith, agonised about what was happening to the wider culture. In his *Four Quartets*, published during the war on grainy paper, as economy pamphlets, Eliot meditates on subjects as varied as the nature of time and memory, and the strength of English literary culture. The fourth and last of the poems, 'Little Gidding', delayed in the writing because of the London Blitz, is for me the greatest of Eliot's poetry. It focuses on the Northamptonshire religious community that entranced George Herbert. The poem, much concerned with religious fire, and containing Eliot's response to the Luftwaffe raids, is also a spiritual journey which becomes his tribute to England at the time of her maximum peril:

If you came this way,
Taking the route you would be likely to take
From the place you would be likely to come from,

If you came this way in may time, you would find the
    hedges
White again, in May, with voluptuary sweetness.
It would be the same at the end of the journey,
If you came at night like a broken king,
If you came by day not knowing what you came for,
It would be the same, when you leave the rough road
And turn behind the pig-sty to the dull facade
And the tombstone. And what you thought you came for
Is only a shell, a husk of meaning
From which the purpose breaks only when it is fulfilled
If at all. Either you had no purpose
Or the purpose is beyond the end you figured
And is altered in fulfilment. There are other places
Which also are the world's end, some at the sea jaws,
Or over a dark lake, in a desert or a city –
But this is the nearest, in place and time,
Now and in England.

If you came this way,
Taking any route, starting from anywhere,
At any time or at any season,
It would always be the same: you would have to put off
Sense and notion. You are not here to verify,
Instruct yourself, or inform curiosity
Or carry report. You are here to kneel
Where prayer has been valid. And prayer is more
Than an order of words, the conscious occupation
Of the praying mind, or the sound of the voice praying.
And what the dead had no speech for, when living,
They can tell you, being dead: the communication
Of the dead is tongued with fire beyond the language of
    the living.
Here, the intersection of the timeless moment
Is England and nowhere. Never and always.

Switching then to the rhyme scheme used by Dante describing purgatory and hell, Eliot confronts the effect of aerial warfare, the shuddering, dusty shells it leaves behind, with the regeneration and rebuilding barely glimpsed:

Ash on an old man's sleeve
Is all the ash the burnt roses leave.
Dust in the air suspended
Marks the place where a story ended.
Dust inbreathed was a house –
The walls, the wainscot and the mouse,
The death of hope and despair,
This is the death of air.

There are flood and drouth
Over the eyes and in the mouth,
Dead water and dead sand
Contending for the upper hand.
The parched eviscerate soil
Gapes at the vanity of toil,
Laughs without mirth.
This is the death of earth.

Water and fire succeed
The town, the pasture and the weed.
Water and fire deride
The sacrifice that we denied.
Water and fire shall rot
The marred foundations we forgot,
Of sanctuary and choir.
This is the death of water and fire.

W.H. Auden never experienced the Blitz, of course, since he was living in Manhattan through the war and only returned to Britain for substantial periods in the 1950s. Nevertheless, in parallel with

Stevie Smith and T.S. Eliot, the war turned Auden to religious reflections, and in 1941 he rejoined the Anglican Church. His greatest poem of the period uses the death of W.B. Yeats to reflect on the collapse of Western civilisation itself, and to challenge the validity of poetry in the modern world. It isn't a consoling poem, but it's a very fine one. Here are the first two passages:

I
He disappeared in the dead of winter:
The brooks were frozen, the airports almost deserted,
The snow disfigured the public statues;
The mercury sank in the mouth of the dying day.
What instruments we have agree
The day of his death was a dark cold day.

Far from his illness
The wolves ran on through the evergreen forests,
The peasant river was untempted by the fashionable
    quays;
By mourning tongues
The death of the poet was kept from his poems.

But for him it was his last afternoon as himself,
An afternoon of nurses and rumours;
The provinces of his body revolted,
The squares of his mind were empty,
Silence invaded the suburbs,
The current of his feeling failed; he became his admirers.

Now he is scattered among a hundred cities
And wholly given over to unfamiliar affections,
To find his happiness in another kind of wood
And be punished under a foreign code of conscience.
The words of a dead man
Are modified in the guts of the living.

But in the importance and noise of to-morrow
When the brokers are roaring like beasts on the floor of
    the Bourse,
And the poor have the sufferings to which they are fairly
    accustomed,
And each in the cell of himself is almost convinced of his
    freedom,
A few thousand will think of this day
As one thinks of a day when one did something slightly
    unusual.
What instruments we have agree
The day of his death was a dark cold day.

II
You were silly like us; your gift survived it all:
The parish of rich women, physical decay,
Yourself. Mad Ireland hurt you into poetry.
Now Ireland has her madness and her weather still,
For poetry makes nothing happen: it survives
In the valley of its making where executives
Would never want to tamper, flows on south
From ranches of isolation and the busy griefs,
Raw towns that we believe and die in; it survives,
a way of happening, a mouth.

Poetry survives, but as it were in a capsule, inside society but no longer a living or dynamic part of civilisation. This is a pessimistic message to the poets of the post-war generation. Luckily, few of them would accept it.

17

The Age
of Larkin

Although I haven't talked much so far about the other main arts –
painting, sculpture, architecture and so forth – right up to the
1950s, it's possible to see clear parallels between them and what was
happening in British poetry. The cooler, conversational poets of the
eighteenth century are matched by conversation-piece oil paintings,
and the rough stuff by the art of Hogarth and the caricaturists.
There is Romantic landscape painting, focusing on Welsh moun-
tains, the Lake District and rushing Highland streams, which
roughly corresponds to Romantic poetry and its interests. The
Decadents in poetry are closely matched by the painters – Whistler,
Aubrey Beardsley and so on. Even up to the 1940s the new
Romanticism and Surrealism of poets such as Dylan Thomas and
David Gascoyne finds its equivalent in John Piper, Paul Nash and
Stanley Spencer. David Jones is both poet and artist.

But after the Second World War, this correspondence seems to
break down completely. It's a very exciting period in the plastic arts,
with the arrival of Abstract Expressionism and then later Pop Art.
Architects, armed with reinforced concrete, create the 'new brutal-
ism' and cold, clean lines of housing and municipal buildings never
seen before. Very little of this seems to be reflected in poetry, which
remains traditional and just 'very English'. There is comparatively
little interest in what the Americans or the Europeans are up to.
There are no dramatic technical innovations of the scale of abstract

painting. At first sight, it's as if poets, confronted by the clatter and consumerism of modern society, have indeed retreated into the quiet, calm, conservative-minded ghetto Auden was worried about. Luckily, as we prod down a bit, the story is more complicated and more interesting.

It starts with English Surrealism, a movement more distinguished in paintings than in poetry. David Gascoyne, who spent much time in Paris during the 1930s getting to know the great French and Spanish Surrealists, was a leading figure of the British movement – a sometime communist who returned to France after the war. Surrealism, rooted in Freud and purporting to uncover psychological and mythic truths behind the façade of modern life, was (and is) a serious and substantial project. But something quickly goes wrong with the poetry. Here is Gascoyne's 'The Cubicle Domes' – or rather, the beginning of it: it doesn't get any better:

Indeed indeed it is growing very sultry
The indian feather pots are scrambling out of the room
The slow voice of the tobacconist is like a circle
Drawn on the floor in chalk and containing ants
And indeed there is a shoe upon the table
And indeed it is as regular as clockwork
Demonstrating the variability of the weather
Or denying the existence of man altogether
For after all why should love resemble a cushion
Why should the stumbling-block float up towards the
    ceiling
And in our attic it is always said
That this is a sombre country the wettest place on earth
And then there is the problem of living to be considered
With its vast pink parachutes full of underdone mutton
Its tableaux of the archbishops dressed in their underwear

To which one might respond – that's quite enough of that, thank you, David. And, broadly speaking, that was the point of the 'Movement' poets of the 1950s. No more splishy-splashy Dylan Thomas-y incontinence; fewer archbishops dressed in their underwear.'Verbal obscurity, metaphysical pretentiousness and romantic rhapsodising' were, according to the novelist David Lodge, the main villains of the Movement, which culminated during 1955–56. Reading collections of 1940s Surrealist verse, it is impossible not to sympathise.

Elizabeth Jennings was born in Lincolnshire but spent most of her life in Oxford, a devout Roman Catholic who suffered periods of mental illness. Her poetry is traditional in style, tough-minded and spare, all prized Movement qualities. Her short poem 'Answers' could almost be a manifesto, or better still, an anti-manifesto:

I kept my answers small and kept them near;
Big questions bruised my mind but still I let
Small answers be a bulwark to my fear.

The huge abstractions I kept from the light;
Small things I handled and caressed and loved.
I let the stars assume the whole of night.

But the big answers clamoured to be moved
Into my life. Their great audacity
Shouted to be acknowledged and believed.

Even when all small answers build up to
Protection of the spirit, still I hear
Big answers striving for their overthrow

And all the great conclusions coming near.

In a world that had been rocked by the big answers of fascism, and was still being rocked by the dangerously great conclusions of

Marxism, one can understand this English retreat or withdrawal. Somehow it contains the essence of a besieged feeling in England after the war. Elizabeth Jennings was a knowing poet and understood how this restraint might seem, to younger people, old-fashioned and timid, as she says in 'The Young Ones', a poem about the newly fashionable 'generation gap':

> They slip on to the bus, hair piled up high.
> New styles each month, it seems to me. I look,
> Not wanting to be seen, casting my eye
> Above the unread pages of a book.
>
> They are fifteen or so. When I was thus,
> I huddled in school coats, my satchel hung
> Lop-sided on my shoulder. Without fuss
> These enter adolescence; being young
>
> Seems good to them, a state we cannot reach,
> No talk of 'awkward ages' now. I see
> How childish gazes staring out of each
> Unfinished face prove me incredibly
>
> Old-fashioned. Yet at least I have the chance
> to size up several stages – young yet old,
> doing the twist, mocking an 'old-time' dance:
> so many ways to be unsure or bold.

Robert Conquest, an Anglo-American historian who led the academic charge against Stalinism and its Western defenders, was a friend of Elizabeth Jennings and a leading figure in the Movement. Here's a poem of his from the 1950s about guided missiles, though very much without the political moralising of the anti-nuclear movement of the time:

Soft sounds and odours brim up through the night
A wealth below the level of the eye;
Out of a black, an almost violet sky
Abundance flowers into points of light.

Till from the south-west, as their low scream mars
And halts this warm hypnosis of the dark,
Three black automata cut swift and stark,
Shaped clearly by the backward flow of stars.

Stronger than lives, by empty purpose blinded,
The only thought their circuits can endure is
The target-hunting rigour of their flight;

And by that loveless haste I am reminded
Of Aeschylus' description of the Furies:
'O barren daughters of the fruitful night.'

Conquest was not merely an opponent of the socialism of post-war
Britain, and its propensity to whitewash the crimes of communism;
he was an enemy as well of all extremism and posturing in poetry,
as his witty 'Epistemology of Poetry' makes dryly clear:

Across the long-curved bight or bay
The waves move clear beneath the day
And, rolling in obliquely, each
Unwinds its white torque up the beach.

Beneath the full semantic sun
The twisting currents race and run.
Words and evaluations start.
And yet the verse should play its part.

Below a certain threshold light
Is insufficient to excite
Those mechanisms which the eye
Constructs its daytime objects by:

A different system wakes behind
The dark, wide pupils till the mind
Accepts an image of this sea
As clear, but in an altered key.

Now darkness falls. And poems attempt
Light reconciling done and dreamt.
I do not find it in the rash
Disruption of the lightning flash.

Those vivid rigours stun the verse
And neural structure still prefers
The moon beneath whose moderate light
The great seas glitter in the bight.

This is the response of the wary and the in-control-of-themselves, and thus very much in tune with the Britain of the late 1950s, which had turned its back on the radical socialism of Clement Attlee's 1945 Labour government. British power might be in decline, but it didn't feel that way to most Britons. The country was still essentially a military nation, with national service in operation from 1947 to 1963, bringing more than two million British men into the forces. Much of the Empire was still being held on to. Britain was a military and commercial nation; the royal family was almost universally adored, while former colonies such as Australia, New Zealand and South Africa were being promoted as a kind of alternative British California. After the 1953 coronation of Queen Elizabeth II there was much talk of a new Elizabethan age, but also a growing impatience with the stuffiness of British culture – the social hierarchies, the puritanism, the rationing, the lack of fun.

Kingsley Amis, novelist and poet, right-wing polemicist, jazz enthusiast and professional shocker, was a child of this period. With his close university friend Philip Larkin he was also the dominant voice of the Movement and, frankly, the reason it's still remembered now. There is a certain coarseness, a brutality, about Amis's verse, at its best the puncturing anger of the young and frustrated. In the late 1950s an anti-morning-sickness drug called Thalidomide began to be marketed and sold in Britain. Within a few years, children with birth defects, including being born without arms or legs or both, were being noticed by doctors. A long legal and political campaign against the drug's manufacturers followed. Amis's 'To a Baby Born Without Limbs' well summarises his tone of voice:

This is just to show you who's boss around here.
It'll keep you on your toes, so to speak,
Make you put your best foot forward, so to speak,
And give you something to turn your hand to, so to speak.
You can face up to it like a man,
Or snivel and blubber like a baby.
That's up to you. Nothing to do with Me.
If you take it in the right spirit,
You can have a bloody marvellous life,
With the great rewards courage brings,
And the beauty of accepting your LOT.
And think how much good it'll do your Mum and Dad,
And your Grans and Gramps and the rest of the shower,
To be stopped being complacent.
Make sure they baptise you, though,
In case some murdering bastard
Decides to put you away quick,
Which would send you straight to LIMB-O, ha ha ha.
But just a word in your ear, if you've got one.
Mind you DO take this in the right spirit,
And keep a civil tongue in your head about Me.

Because if you DON'T,
I've got plenty of other stuff up My sleeve,
Such as leukemia and polio,
(Which incidentally you're welcome to any time,
Whatever spirit you take this in.)
I've given you one love-pat, right?
You don't want another.
So watch it, Jack.

It's a brutal satire of the brusque, 'common-sense' attitude of an old establishment, now tottering on its feet.

Amis's friend Philip Larkin, while in some respects an unpleasant personality, was undoubtably the greatest English poet of the post-war period. From early on, he was able to combine critical admiration with genuine popularity. If there's one British poet since Auden and Eliot to whom everybody who loves poetry still turns with a shiver of pleasure, it's Larkin. Gangling, bespectacled, he looked uncannily like the comedian Eric Morecambe after a crash diet, and spent most of his life working as the university librarian at Hull. His slim volumes of verse began in 1945 and followed at, roughly speaking, ten-year intervals until 1974. Like Amis, he embraced aspects of lower-brow, Americanised mass culture, such as jazz music and science fiction, as well as being an unapologetic enthusiast for pulp pornography. Appropriately for a man who came to be seen as the spokesman for the declining Britain of his times, Larkin was a pessimist, albeit a very sharp and funny one. He once said that deprivation was for him what daffodils were for Wordsworth. Accused of being a solitary fellow, he responded: I have no enemies, but my friends don't like me. Attacked by critics for being racist and misogynistic, in 2008 he was nevertheless voted Britain's greatest post-war writer. His breakthrough collection, *The Less Deceived* came out in 1955; it wouldn't be unreasonable to describe the period from then until the 1970s as the age of Larkin.

Like Thomas Hardy, another great English eccentric and pessimist, who strongly influenced him, Larkin delighted in complex structures and had no problem about addressing some of the issues of his time. 'This Be the Verse' was his ironic title for one of his rudest and most characteristic poems. It takes pessimism as far as it can go – and then pushes it off a cliff. Note, however, that the whole poem is inside inverted commas; we are not to assume that this is actually Larkin talking.

> They fuck you up, your mum and dad.
> They may not mean to, but they do.
> They fill you with the faults they had
> And add some extra, just for you.
>
> But they were fucked up in their turn
> By fools in old-style hats and coats,
> Who half the time were soppy-stern
> And half at one another's throats.
>
> Man hands on misery to man.
> It deepens like a coastal shelf.
> Get out as early as you can,
> And don't have any kids yourself.

When he came to edit *The Oxford Book of Twentieth-Century English Verse*, Larkin did not put in nearly enough of his own poems, and that was one of the ones he left out. But he did include his almost equally famous poem protesting at the grind of daily work, 'Toads':

> Why should I let the toad *work*
> Squat on my life?
> Can't I use my wit as a pitchfork
> And drive the brute off?

Six days of the week it soils
With its sickening poison –
Just for paying a few bills!
That's out of proportion.

Lots of folk live on their wits:
Lecturers, lispers,
Losels, loblolly-men, louts –
They don't end up as paupers;

Lots of folk live up lanes
With fires in a bucket,
Eat windfalls and tinned sardines –
They seem to like it.

Their nippers have got bare feet,
Their unspeakable wives
Are skinny as whippets – and yet
No one actually *starves*.

Ah, were I courageous enough
To shout *Stuff your pension!*
But I know, all too well, that's the stuff
That dreams are made on:

For something sufficiently toad-like
Squats in me, too;
Its hunkers are heavy as hard luck,
And cold as snow,

And will never allow me to blarney
My way to getting
The fame and the girl and the money
All at one sitting.

I don't say, one bodies the other
One's spiritual truth;
But I do say it's hard to lose either
When you have both.

In the end it's more than the protest of the salaryman against the
modern world; it's a poem of self-disgust as well. To me at least the
final stanza isn't entirely convincing, given the anger that had been
building up before. Perhaps this, from Larkin's *Letters to Monica*, is
more authentic on the subject:

Morning, noon & bloody night,
Seven sodding days a week,
I slave at filthy WORK, that might
Be done by any book-drunk freak.
This goes on until I kick the bucket.
FUCK IT FUCK IT FUCK IT FUCK IT

Well, that's Philip Larkin in his most demotic form. But he's a much
subtler poet when he wants to be, and captures quite a lot of the
modern British experience that nobody else seems to notice, as for
instance in this lovely poem about loneliness – a state endured by
many millions, and written about by almost nobody. It makes me
think of William Cowper:

When I was a child, I thought,
Casually, that solitude
Never needed to be sought.
Something everybody had,
Like nakedness, it lay at hand,
Not specially right or specially wrong,
A plentiful and obvious thing
Not at all hard to understand.

Then, after twenty, it became
At once more difficult to get
And more desired – though all the same
More undesirable; for what
You are alone has, to achieve
The rank of fact, to be expressed
In terms of others, or it's just
A compensating make-believe.

Much better stay in company!
To love you must have someone else,
Giving requires a legatee,
Good neighbours need whole parishfuls
Of folk to do it on – in short,
Our virtues are all social; if,
Deprived of solitude, you chafe,
It's clear you're not the virtuous sort.

Viciously, then, I lock my door.
The gas-fire breathes. The wind outside
Ushers in evening rain. Once more
Uncontradicting solitude
Supports me on its giant palm;
And like a sea-anemone
Or simple snail, there cautiously
Unfolds, emerges, what I am.

The English have always been a solitary people of fences and hedges and blinds and double locks, an accumulation of privacies. And yet Larkin, as I have indicated, is also a public poet. Here, he writes sadly and angrily about Britain's decline in the world; written during the Labour government of Harold Wilson in 1969, 'Homage to a Government' appears to be a poem about a decolonisation, but is rather one about a collapse of responsibility. In its quiet way, it's as angry and stinging as anything by Shelley:

Next year we are to bring the soldiers home
For lack of money, and it is all right.
Places they guarded, or kept orderly,
Must guard themselves, and keep themselves orderly.
We want the money for ourselves at home
Instead of working. And this is all right.

It's hard to say who wanted it to happen,
But now it's been decided nobody minds.
The places are a long way off, not here,
Which is all right, and from what we hear
The soldiers there only made trouble happen.
Next year we shall be easier in our minds.

Next year we shall be living in a country
That brought its soldiers home for lack of money.
The statues will be standing in the same
Tree-muffled squares, and look nearly the same.
Our children will not know it's a different country.
All we can hope to leave them now is money.

Many people would say that that's the story of the British in the second half of the twentieth century, reduced to three stanzas but leaving out nothing essential. Philip Larkin didn't always write so seriously. In his 'Annus Mirabilis', he transposes Dryden's year of miracles from 1666 to 1963. Larkin may have had his old-fogeyish views, but in his enthusiasm for, and frankness about, sex he was more a child of the 1960s than of the 1940s.

Sexual intercourse began
In nineteen sixty-three
(Which was rather late for me) –
Between the end of the *Chatterley* ban
And the Beatles' first LP.

Up till then there'd only been
A sort of bargaining,
A wrangle for a ring,
A shame that started at sixteen
And spread to everything.

Then all at once the quarrel sank:
Everyone felt the same,
And every life became
A brilliant breaking of the bank,
A quite unlosable game.

So life was never better than
In nineteen sixty-three
(Though just too late for me) –
Between the end of the *Chatterley* ban
And the Beatles' first LP.

There are perhaps another hundred or so poems by Philip Larkin that demand to be included in this book. Obviously that's impossible, so I close this section on the Movement with the finest short poem he wrote. 'As Bad as a Mile' is about failure, and the collapse of all our early hopes, and therefore a lament for lost naïvety. It shows that in the year 1960 the great traditions of English poetry were still alive and well. John Donne, had he been able to, would have admired it:

Watching the shied core
Striking the basket, skidding across the floor,
Shows less and less of luck, and more and more
Of failure spreading back up the arm
Earlier and earlier, the unraised hand calm,
The apple unbitten in the palm.

The group of poets who came after the Movement called themselves, with flat precision, the 'Group'. They included many memorable poets, and a handful of seriously good ones; but the hero of this hour isn't really known for his poetry. Philip Hobsbaum, brought up in Yorkshire in a Polish-Jewish family, did write, but more criticism than poetry. What he really did, however, was to assemble clusters of eager younger poets together – in Cambridge, where he was educated, and in London, and in Belfast and Glasgow as well. Under his watchful but friendly eye the workmanlike ethos of the Movement extended itself all around the UK. Of all the poets who came under his influence, it was the Australian Peter Porter who made the most colourful mark. Larkin had been alert to the fast-changing culture, but Porter immersed himself in the new 'swinging' Britain, as his poem of the very early 1960s addressed to the Elizabethan playwright John Marston demonstrates:

All the boys are howling to take the girls to bed.
Our betters say it's a seedy world. The critics say
Think of them as an Elizabethan Chelsea set.
Then they've never listened to our lot – no talk
Could be less like – but the bodies are the same:
Those bums and sweaters of the King's Road
Would fit Marston's stage. What's in a name,
If Cheapside and the Marshalsea mean Eng. Lit.
And the Fantasie, Sa Tortuga, Grisbi, Bongi-Bo
Mean life? A cliché? What hurts dies on paper,
Fades to classic pain. Love goes as the MG goes.
The colonel's daughter in black stockings, hair
Like sash cords, face iced-white, studies art,
Goes home once a month. She won't marry the men
She sleeps with, she'll revert to type – it's part
Of the side-show: Mummy and Daddy in the wings,
The bongos fading on the road to Haslemere
Where inheritors are inheriting still.
Marston's Malheureux found his whore too dear;

Today some Jazz Club girl on the social make
Would put him through his paces, the aphrodisiac cruel.
His friends would be the smoothies of our Elizabethan age –
The Rally Men, Grantchester Breakfast Men, Public
   School
Personal Assistants and the fragrant PROs,
Cavalry-twilled tame publishers praising Logue,
Classics Honours Men promoting Jazzetry,
Market Researchers married into *Vogue*.
It's a Condé Nast world and so Marston's was.
His had a real gibbet – our death's out of sight.
The same thin richness of these worlds remains –
The flesh-packed jeans, the car-stung appetite
Volley on his stage, the cage of discontent.

In the 1950s there was a major effort to persuade British people, worn down by the war and privation, to contemplate emigration, above all to Australia and New Zealand. But quite soon there was a much smaller, more culturally significant, migration in the other direction, as ambitious, cultured Aussies and Kiwis came to London and helped to change it: Clive James, the poet, critic and television presenter, Germaine Greer, pioneering feminist, and Peter Porter himself were among them. Associated with the Group was another migrant, the New Zealander Fleur Adcock. Like James and Porter, she brought a new eye to what was beginning to seem a slightly tired poetic scene. Here's her 'Happy Ending', a lovely, sharply observed and distinctly female take on the something that happens every day of every year, an unsuccessful attempt at lovemaking:

After they had not made love
she pulled the sheet up over her eyes
until he was buttoning his shirt:
not shyness for their bodies – those
they had willingly displayed – but a frail
endeavour to apologise.

Later, though, drawn together by
a distaste for such 'untidy ends'
they agreed to meet again; whereupon
they giggled, reminisced, held hands
as though what they had made was love –
and not that happier outcome – friends.

Isn't that beautiful? I'd like to say that it marks a growing maturity in sex relations in the Britain of the second part of the twentieth century. But I have no evidence for that whatever. Still, to show that Fleur Adcock can do this kind of thing again and again, here's her equally well-observed short poem about youth and age, 'Kissing':

The young are walking on the riverbank
arms around each other's waist and shoulders,
pretending to be looking at the waterlilies
and what might be a nest of some kind, over
there, which two who are clamped together
mouth to mouth have forgotten about.
The others, making courteous detours
around them, talk, stop talking, kiss.
They can see no one older than themselves.
It's their river. They've got all day.
Seeing's not everything. At this very
moment the middle-aged are kissing
in the backs of taxis, on the way
to airports and stations. Their mouths and tongues
are soft and powerful and as moist as ever.
Their hands are not inside each other's clothes
(because of the driver) but locked so tightly
together that it hurts: it may leave marks
on their not of course youthful skin, which they won't
notice. They too may have futures.

John Wain and Thom Gunn are two other poets associated with the Movement, and the movements that came after the Movement, who deserve to be remembered here. Gunn was the son of a well-known Fleet Street journalist, born in Gravesend in Kent, and one of the first poetic voices of the modern gay liberation movement. His poetry dealt frankly, rather than explicitly, with sex and drugs, and he ended up living in California, where he died. Nobody else in British poetry in the second half of the century sounds anything like him, partly because of his chosen subject matter. This is from his motorbike poem, 'On the Move'. With emptier roads, and car ownership still not quite booming, the 1950s and early 1960s was a golden age for bikers. The speed freaks of the 'ton-up club' and the competing tribes of Mods and Rockers were only part of it: for hundreds of thousands of young men, two wheels and an engine signalled a freedom that had been unimaginable for their parents. The final line of Gunn's poem could almost be one of the decade's mottoes:

On motorcycles, up the road, they come:
Small, black, as flies hanging in the heat, the boys.
Until the distance throws them forth, their hum
Bulges to thunder held by calf and thigh.
In goggles, donned impersonality,
In gleaming jackets trophied with the dust,
They strap in doubt – by hiding it, robust –
And almost hear a meaning in their noise.

Exact conclusion of their hardiness
Has no shape yet, but from known whereabouts
They ride, direction where the tyres press.
They scare a flight of birds across the field:
Much that is natural, to the will must yield.
Mainly manufacture both machine and soul,
And use what they imperfectly control
To dare a future from the taken routes …

A minute holds them, who have come to go:
The self-defined, astride the created will
They burst away; the towns they travel through
Are home for neither bird nor holiness,
For birds and saints complete their purposes.
At worst, one is in motion; and at best,
Reaching no absolute, in which to rest,
One is always nearer by not keeping still.

Although Thom Gunn and John Wain both pursued academic careers, they could hardly have been more different. Wain immersed himself in the Oxford circles of J.R.R. Tolkien, of *Lord of the Rings*, and C.S. Lewis of *Narnia*. The social observation in his early novels led him to be labelled, along with Amis and Larkin, as one of the 'angry young men', but he was more genial and academic than that suggests, and combined novels with excellent literary biographies. This was the period of maximum paranoia about a looming nuclear war and the end of civilisation. In 1958 Wain came across a news report in a Sunday paper which claimed that Major Claude Eatherly, the pilot of one of the planes on the USAF raid that dropped the atomic bomb on Hiroshima in 1945, was suffering nightmares, and had refused to touch his pension because he regarded it as a premium for murder. He became a petty thief instead, and ended up in prison. This is from Wain's 'song' about the major:

Good news. It seems he loved them after all.
His orders were to fry their bones to ash.
He carried up the bomb and let it fall.
And then his orders were to take the cash,

A hero's pension. But he let it lie.
It was in vain to ask him for the cause.
Simply that if he touched it he would die.
He fought his own, and not his country's wars.

His orders told him he was not a man:
An instrument, fine-tempered, clear of stain,
All fears and passions closed up like a fan:
No more volition than his aeroplane.

But now he fought to win his manhood back.
Steep from the sunset of his pain he flew
Against the darkness in that last attack.
It was for love he fought, to make that true.

This seems to me to have the spirit of Siegfried Sassoon. The poem widens out into a meditation on how killing destroys the killer, whether the victims are Japanese civilians or foxes caught in a trap. Then, in its third section, Wain ups the ante further, so that we are reminded of a great puritanical religious sermon:

Hell is a furnace, so the wise men taught.
The punishment for sin is to be broiled.
A glowing coal for every sinful thought.

The heat of God's great furnace ate up sin,
Which whispered up in smoke or fell in ash:
So that each hour a new hour could begin.

So fire was holy, though it tortured souls,
The sinners' anguish never ceased, but still
Their sin was burnt from them by shining coals.

Hell fried the criminal but burnt the crime,
Purged where it punished, healed where it destroyed:
It was a stove that warmed the rooms of time.

No man begrudged the flames their appetite.
All were afraid of fire, yet none rebelled.
The wise men taught that hell was just and right ...

We will come upon more political and anti-nuclear poets in the next chapter; but I hope we have read enough here to deal with the myth that British poetry after the war became limp and bloodless, or cut off from the rest of the British experience in a time of tumbling, dazzling, disorientating change.

18

Fresh Freshness

And then, with no movement, and no group, from all corners of the British Isles, there breaks yet another loud wave of new poetry. In Orkney, Wales, Yorkshire, there emerged harder-edged poets of nature, all of them still read and loved today; from Liverpool and London there came new political poets and comic poets who insisted on reading their verses aloud. It would be too much to say that during the 1960s and 70s there was a successful move to democratise poetry, to wrest it away from the academic reading groups and small elite readerships; but there was at least a determined attempt to do this, which changed our relationship with poetry in subtle, important ways. This period threw up some extraordinary characters. Bill Griffiths was an Essex-born poet and student of Anglo-Saxon who spent some of his early years as a Hell's Angel, and went briefly to Brixton prison. He ended up in County Durham, as a collector and promoter of Northumbrian and pit-dialect writing. England sometimes seems like a country whose main fusebox is in London, with all the main cables leading to and from the capital. It isn't so: Griffiths' connections between Essex and the north-east are an example. Like many of the new poets, he lived his life and died his death in poverty.

Welcome to the village, he sez.

It's a quiet life around here, you know.

A wooden kirk,
a few simple rules

There are trees (evergreens of course)

Altho' it is very quiet,
sheep there are, safely grazing

A widow could safely walk (sez Bede)
but there is not much room

in fact it is a strictly average windowsill

with models
models of things

all homes
are moulded

around a station, a farm, a church

The thing from the churchyard
that was found with its hand missing
in the excavation
undertook on the north side
called
several times
wanted converse
about your assumptions
regarding exotic irrational exocultures
and the Taliban.

It held a copy of *The Guardian*
and pointed excitedly to the bit
in 1962 about repatriating Rastas from Jamaica.
It seemed angry.
Somehow grander and grander they march banners
    maroon and patterned with wheat, passing stars,
    passion, peace.
Will call back.

Michael Horovitz was a very different character, but just as much an enthusiast for breaking the old barriers of poetry. Born in Frankfurt to a large Jewish family who escaped Hitler's Germany for London, he studied at Oxford in the late 1950s, where he founded *New Departures*, a magazine quite closely in league with the American beat poets. He went on to develop and promote his own jazz-poetry, performed with the help (if help is the right word) of a buzzing, squeaking kazoo. In 1969 he edited *Children of Albion*, an anthology of underground poetry published by Penguin which became a kind of rallying ground for the new poets. Like Bill Griffiths, he published a great deal while managing not to make much money. His surreal imagination is reminiscent of Edward Lear. This is part of his poem 'Look Ahead':

Our toes are ahead of us – they have grown out of us
Our nails are ahead of our toes – we can't reach to cut them
Our hammers are ahead of our nails – they strike
    like underpaid lightning
Our sickles are ahead of our hammers – shape
    of our hammer toes
Our televisions are ahead of our cinemas – our films are
    because we don't use good toothpaste
Our commercials are ahead of our patrons
    all is peddled

Our cycles are ahead of our tricycles and our trickles are
    our fashionable works of art
    trickled   by cyclists   on paint ...

Our piledriver toes hammer furiously on motorcycles
    but the hammers are sliced by sickles
Struck hard by our frames our nails catch up with our toes
    till at last we're in   we find our teeth
    fully grown

    footballers

The new pop poets piggybacked to a certain extent on the achieve-
ments of pop music. If the guitar bands of the 1960s could find and
hold new audiences, why couldn't poets? The question seemed an
urgent one in Liverpool, home of the Merseybeat sound, including
the Beatles and many more. From there, in particular, came the
modern troubadours, men like Roger McGough, Brian Patten and
Adrian Henri. Shoulder to shoulder with them was the great and
highly political performance poet, playwright and voice of the anti-nu-
clear movement, Adrian Mitchell. Their poetry sold well on the page,
and in pamphlets, but above all they wanted to return poetry to
younger audiences and public spaces, from the Albert Hall to rooms
above pubs. Mitchell is characteristic, in that you really had to hear
him and see him to get the full effect of his charismatic personality.

There is no 'characteristic' Adrian Mitchell poem, and most of
them are greatly improved if you've had the luck to hear him live,
and to internalise his cadences. But 'Saw it in the Papers', one of his
performance favourites, is a good introduction. Mitchell begins by
relating the true but terrible story of a young mother who went out
drinking, leaving her baby in a pram and forgetting it, so that it died
of hunger. She pleaded guilty to manslaughter and was sent to
prison for four years. Mitchell explains that she had been deserted
by the man she loved, and that her character had changed. He asks:

Is there any love in prisons?

She must have been in great pain.

There is love in prisons.
There is great love in prisons.
A man in Gloucester prison told me:
'Some of us care for each other.
Some of us don't.
Some of us are gentle,
some are brutal.
All kinds.'

I said: 'just the same as people outside.'
He nodded twice,
and stared me in the eyes.

What she did to him was terrible.
There was no evidence of mental instability.
What was done to her was terrible.
There is no evidence of mental instability.

Millions of children starve, but not in England.
What we do not do for them is terrible.

Is England's love locked up in England?
There is no evidence of mental instability.

Only love can unlock locked up love.

Unlock all of your love.
You have enough for this woman.
Unlock all of your love.
You have enough to feed all those millions of children.

Cry if you like.
Do something if you can. You can.

That's Adrian Mitchell at his angriest; but he was a poet who wrote about his love of music, his love of sex, his love of dogs, and his belief that poetry could still change the world. Alongside all of that, he was a very fine nearly-nonsense poet. Here is his satire on English meanness, 'Ten Ways to Avoid Lending Your Wheelbarrow to Anybody':

1. Patriotic
May I borrow your wheelbarrow?
I didn't lay down my life in World War II
so that you could borrow my wheelbarrow.

2. Snobbish
May I borrow your wheelbarrow?
Unfortunately Samuel Beckett is using it.

3. Overweening
May I borrow your wheelbarrow?
It is too mighty a conveyance to be wielded
by any mortal save myself.

4. Pious
May I borrow your wheelbarrow?
My wheelbarrow is reserved for religious ceremonies.

5. Melodramatic
May I borrow your wheelbarrow?
I would sooner be broken on its wheel
and buried in its barrow.

6. Pathetic
May I borrow your wheelbarrow?
I am dying of schizophrenia
and all you can talk about is wheelbarrows.

7. Defensive
May I borrow your wheelbarrow?
Do you think I'm made of wheelbarrows?

8. Sinister
May I borrow your wheelbarrow?
It is full of blood.

9. Lecherous
May I borrow your wheelbarrow?
Only if I can fuck your wife in it.

10. Philosophical
May I borrow your wheelbarrow?
What is a wheelbarrow?

From this I hope it's obvious that in his quest for new audiences – he famously said, 'Most people ignore most poetry because most poetry ignores most people' – Adrian Mitchell was breaking open and rethinking what poetry is, and what it can be. He was artful, but never wanted the artfulness to get in the way of a clear, fresh message. Here is his poem about youthful sexuality, 'A Puppy Called Puberty':

It was like keeping a puppy in your underpants
A secret puppy you weren't allowed to show to anyone
Not even your best friend or your worst enemy

You wanted to pat him stroke him cuddle him
All the time but you weren't supposed to touch him

He only slept for five minutes at a time
Then he'd suddenly perk up his head
In the middle of school medical inspection
And always on bus rides
So you had to climb down from the upper deck
All bent double to smuggle the puppy off the bus
Without the buxom conductress spotting
Your wicked and ticketless stowaway.

Jumping up, wet-nosed, eagerly wagging –
He only stopped being a nuisance
When you were alone together
Pretending to be doing your homework
But really gazing at each other
Through hot and hazy daydreams

Of those beautiful schoolgirls on the bus
With kittens bouncing in their sweaters.

Paired with this, Mitchell wrote the mordant 'A Dog Called Elderly'
not long before his death in 2008:

And now I have a dog called Elderly
And all he ever wants to do
Is now and then be let out for a piss
But spend the rest of his lifetime
Sleeping on my lap in front of the fire.

We can't call Adrian Mitchell a Liverpool poet, except perhaps in
spirit – he was born near Hampstead Heath in London. Roger
McGough, however, was born on the outskirts of Liverpool.
Educated at Hull, he was influenced by Philip Larkin before return-
ing to Liverpool and immersing himself in the pop culture of the
city as it was going through its 1960s boom. He was a key member
of the band Scaffold, which had a hit song, 'Lily the Pink', and made

his poetic breakthrough in 1967 with the publication of the *Mersey Sound* anthology. Like Mitchell, he was a great believer in music and performance as a way of bringing poetry to new audiences. His 'Youngman's Death' is a good example of the McGough talent for wordplay and a kind of wiry whimsy:

Let me die a youngman's death
not a clean and inbetween
the sheets holywater death
not a famous-last-words
peaceful out of breath death

When I'm 73
and in constant good tumour
may I be mown down at dawn
by a bright red sports car
on my way home
from an allnight party

Or when I'm 91
with silver hair
and sitting in a barber's chair
may rival gangsters
with hamfisted tommyguns burst in
and give me a short back and insides

Or when I'm 104
and banned from the Cavern
may my mistress
catching me in bed with her daughter
and fearing for her son
cut me up into little pieces
and throw away every piece but one

Let me die a youngman's death
not a free from sin tiptoe in
candle wax and waning death
not a curtains drawn by angels borne
'what a nice way to go' death

Like his friend Adrian Mitchell, who was bullied at school and
never forgot it, Roger McGough had vivid schoolday memories –
isn't it odd that poets only begin to write about their schooldays
(cricket apart) in the twentieth century?

A millionbillionwillion miles from home
Waiting for the bell to go. (To go where?)
Why are they all so big, other children?
So noisy? So much at home they
Must have been born in uniform
Lived all their lives in playgrounds
Spent the years inventing games
That don't let me in. Games
That are rough, that swallow you up.

And the railings.
All around, the railings.
Are they to keep out wolves and monsters?
Things that carry off and eat children?
Things you don't take sweets from?
Perhaps they're to stop us getting out
Running away from the lessins. Lessin.
What does a lessin look like?
Sounds small and slimy.
They keep them in the glassrooms.
Whole rooms made out of glass. Imagine.

I wish I could remember my name
Mummy said it would come in useful.

Like wellies. When there's puddles.
Yellowwellies. I wish she was here.
I think my name is sewn on somewhere
Perhaps the teacher will read it for me.
Tea-cher. The one who makes the tea.

Brian Patten left his school at fifteen to become a music journalist, but soon turned to full-time poetry. Even Roger McGough's most enthusiastic admirers wouldn't say he was the most handsome poet of the twentieth century; but Patten arrived looking like the pop star Marc Bolan, with a great tangle of black hair and boyish good looks. Perhaps not surprisingly, his early love poems were particularly popular. They tend to be clear, limpid even, and wistful in tone. This was written for a lover who was normally late, but not always:

I was sitting thinking of our future
And of how friendship had overcome
So many nights bloated with pain;

I was sitting in a room that looked out on to a garden
And a stillness filled me,
Bitterness drifted from me,

I was as near paradise as I am likely to get again.

I was sitting thinking of the chaos
We had caused in one another
And was amazed we had survived it.

I was thinking of our future
And of what we would do together,
And where we would go and of how,

When night came, burying me bit by bit,
And you entered the room,
Trembling, solemn-faced,

On time for once.

Because we tend to group poets together, and to assume that different kinds of poets dislike one another, it's interesting to note that Philip Larkin not only admired and helped Roger McGough, but felt the same about Brian Patten. All of them, in their different ways, shared a distaste for the idea that poetry should be difficult, or elitist, or just for certain kinds of people. Here, Patten takes head-on the question 'If You Had to Hazard a Guess Who Would You Say Your Poetry is For?':

For people who have nowhere to go in the afternoons,
For people who the evening banishes to small rooms,
For good people, people huge as the world.
For people who give themselves away forgetting
What it is they are giving,
And who are never reminded.
For people who cannot help being kind
To the hand bunched in pain against them.
For inarticulate people,
People who invent their own ugliness,
Who invent pain, terrified of blankness;
For people who stand forever at the same junction
Waiting for the chances that have passed.
And for those who lie in ambush for themselves,
Who invent toughness as a kind of disguise,
Who, lost in self-defeating worlds,
Carry remorse inside them like a plague;
And for the self-seeking self lost among them
I hazard a poem.

The third of the Liverpool poets was Adrian Henri, a very talented painter as well as a poet; and a boisterous rock performer as well as a painter. Like others of his generation, he was hugely influenced by the American beat poets such as Allen Ginsberg, and he went further than the others in mingling music and performance poetry. And like Adrian Mitchell he was also influenced by William Blake; Albion, as an ideal vision of England, was in his mind when he wrote this, about Albion's daughters, who turn out to be contemporary, sassy Scouse girls:

The daughters of Albion
Arriving by underground at Central Station
Eating hot ecclescakes at the Pierhead
Writing 'Billy Blake is fab' on a wall in Mathew St
Taking off their navyblue schooldrawers and
Putting on nylon panties ready for the night

The daughters of Albion
See the moonlight beating down on them in Bebington
Throw away their chewinggum ready for the goodnight
 kiss
Sleep in the dinnertime sunlight with old men
Looking up their skirts in St Johns Gardens
Comb their darkblonde hair in suburban bedrooms
Powder their delicate little nipples/wondering if tonight
 will be the night
Their bodies pressed into dresses or sweaters
Lavender at the Cavern or pink at the Sink

The daughters of Albion wondering how to explain why
 they didn't go home

The daughters of Albion
Taking the dawn ferry to tomorrow
Worrying about what happened
Lacing up blue sneakers over brown ankles
Fastening up brown stockings to blue suspenderbelts

Beautiful boys with bright red guitars
In the spaces between the stars

Reelin' an' a-rockin'
Wishin' an' a-hopin'
Kissin' an'-prayin'
Lovin' an' a-layin'

Mrs Albion you've got a lovely daughter.

In general, the performance poets of the 1960s, although they did also write what could be described as 'nature poems', were urban artists. Their freshness embraced the youth culture of Britain's cities during a time of transformation. But this period also saw the arrival of some extraordinary new poets of the countryside, who sounded like nobody had done before. Chief among them were Yorkshire's Ted Hughes and, from Northern Ireland, Seamus Heaney. They remain examples of poets who broke away from any limited or elite status to reach a comparatively huge public, in schools and more generally.

Ted Hughes's life has been completely overshadowed by his tragic marriage to Sylvia Plath, the disturbed American poet who gassed herself in 1963. Like one of the hunted wild animals in his own poems, Hughes became the quarry of feminist critics who believed that, through an infidelity, he had killed one of the unique female voices of the century. It was a fate which, with weird masochism, he almost seemed to embrace. He had been brought up in the real countryside – the working Yorkshire countryside of farmers, gamekeepers, fishermen and poachers. During the Second

World War his duties allowed him to lounge around for weeks at a time memorising Shakespeare and Yeats by heart before studying English at Cambridge University. Few poets have been as well prepared in their immersion in rural England, and the English poetic tradition. Hughes knocked around doing various odd jobs, but he was always destined to be a poet; for a few years, at least, his relationship with Sylvia Plath, herself a powerful and unsettling voice, was mutually beneficial. Later in life, after her death and the suicide of a later lover – he was, at the very least, unlucky – Hughes became a friend of the royal family, the Poet Laureate who succeeded John Betjeman, and increasingly oracular.

His early poetry fizzes with the lethal drama of the natural world; it's anti-romantic countryside poetry. Hughes deploys grinding, crushing clusters of consonants and metrical tricks which are reminiscent not of Wordsworth or Keats or Tennyson, but of the unknown Anglo-Saxon poets we began with. Here is his relatively early 'Hawk Roosting'. As with the medieval *The Owl and the Nightingale*, it's the poem of a countryman who knows his birds:

I sit in the top of the wood, my eyes closed.
Inaction, no falsifying dream
Between my hooked head and hooked feet:
Or in sleep rehearse perfect kills and eat.

The convenience of the high trees!
The air's buoyancy and the sun's ray
Are of advantage to me;
And the earth's face upward for my inspection.

My feet are locked upon the rough bark.
It took the whole of Creation
To produce my foot, my each feather:
Now I hold Creation in my foot

Or fly up, and revolve it all slowly –
I kill where I please because it is all mine.
There is no sophistry in my body:
My manners are tearing off heads –

The allotment of death.
For the one path of my flight is direct
Through the bones of the living.
No arguments assert my right:

The sun is behind me.
Nothing has changed since I began.
My eye has permitted no change.
I am going to keep things like this.

His *Crow* poems became particularly famous – there was something about the dark, murderous bird which became associated with the poet himself, saturnine and beaky. They were much satirised: *Private Eye* parodied them mercilessly. But they have a genuine, unsettling force. It's interesting that Hughes had trouble finishing the *Crow* sequence after Sylvia Plath's death. This is called 'Crow's Nerve Fails':

Crow, feeling his brain slip,
Finds his every feather the fossil of a murder.

Who murdered all these?
These living dead, that root in his nerves and his blood
Till he is visibly black?

How can he fly from his feathers?
And why have they homed on him?

Is he the archive of their accusations?
Or their ghostly purpose, their pining vengeance?
Or their unforgiven prisoner?

He cannot be forgiven.

His prison is the earth. Clothed in his conviction,
Trying to remember his crimes

Heavily he flies.

For many years it was assumed that Ted Hughes had never written, and would never write, on that central tragedy of his life, the suicide of Sylvia Plath, and the relationship that preceded it. He became more and more concerned with myth, primal energy and esoteric subjects, and willingly turned his hand, as Poet Laureate, to poems celebrating the royal family – the kind of verse-making which had become hugely unpopular and was not much regarded by most of his peers. Then, in 1998, just a few months before he died, he published a big collection of poems, *The Birthday Letters*, brimming with passionate memories of his life with Plath. He recounts their first meeting, their first kisses, how good they were for one another's poetry, his clumsy awkwardness, his growing understanding of the depth of her madness, and her deeply dysfunctional family. The poems can be painful and difficult to read. Sometimes it feels as if we are pruriently eavesdropping on deep private grief. It's probably too early to say whether the book will be remembered as among his greatest poetry – the story was too sensational – but it is certainly poetry that will be read a hundred years from now. In one of the poems, 'The Blue Flannel Suit', he addresses an ugly outfit Plath had bought for her first teaching class in college, using it as a metaphor for her life:

I had let it all grow. I had supposed
It was all okay. Your life

Was a liner I voyaged in.
Costly education had fitted you out.
Financiers and committees and consultants
Effaced themselves in the gleam of your finish.
You trembled with the new life of those engines.

That first morning,
Before your first class at College, you sat there
Sipping coffee …
… I watched
The strange dummy stiffness, the misery,
Of your blue flannel suit, its straitjacket, ugly
Half-approximation to your idea
Of the proprieties that you hoped to ease into,
And your horror in it. And the tanned
Almost green undertinge of your face
Shrunk to its wick, your scar lumpish, your plaited
Head pathetically tiny.
You waited,
Knowing yourself helpless in the tweezers
Of the life that judged you, and I saw
The flayed nerve, the unhealable face-wound
Which was all you had for courage.
I saw that what gripped you, as you sipped,
Were terrors that had killed you once already.
Now, I see, I saw, sitting, the lonely
Girl who was going to die.
That blue suit,
A mad, execution uniform,
Survived your sentence. But then I sat, stilled,
Unable to fathom what stilled you
As I looked at you, as I am stilled
Permanently now, permanently
Bending so briefly at your open coffin.

No. No, there is no doubt, is there? That's a magnificent poem, absolutely honest and saying all that ever needed to be, or needs to be, said.

And what of Sylvia Plath herself? Many would say that she isn't a British writer in any sense. The college where she was teaching was in America; her family, and therefore the roots of her disturbance, were all American. But there are other ways of looking at this. Her poetry contains some fine landscape verse, rooted in England; she was hugely influenced by Hughes, who was as English as we can find; her greatest poems were written in a burst during the freezing London winter of 1962, after Hughes had left her, following his affair with Assia Wevill. As important as any of that, she's seen as a pioneering feminist voice, in Britain just as much as in the United States. This is from her poem 'Wuthering Heights', a tribute to the upland Brontë country, shot through with her death obsession:

There is no life higher than the grasstops
Or the hearts of sheep, and the wind
Pours by like destiny, bending
Everything in one direction.
I can feel it trying
To funnel my heat away.
If I pay the roots of the heather
Too close attention, they will invite me
To whiten my bones among them.

The sheep know where they are,
Browsing in their dirty wool-clouds,
Gray as the weather.
The black slots of their pupils take me in.
It is like being mailed into space,
A thin, silly message.
They stand about in grandmotherly disguise,
All wig curls and yellow teeth
And hard, marbly baas.

I come to wheel ruts, and water
Limpid as the solitudes
That flee through my fingers.
Hollow doorsteps go from grass to grass;
Lintel and sill have unhinged themselves
Of people and the air only
Remembers a few odd syllables.
It rehearses them moaningly:
Black stone, black stone.

The sky leans on me, me, the one upright
Among all horizontals.
The grass is beating its head distractedly.
It is too delicate
For a life in such company;
Darkness terrifies it.
Now, in valleys narrow
And black as purses, the house lights
Gleam like small change.

That is very Yorkshire, plainly stated and closely observed; but it
has something in it of Ted Hughes – and for the full force of Plath
in her madness and fury we have to turn to those 1962 poems,
collected in *Ariel*, one of the most sensation-causing poetry books
published in the twentieth century. This is, in full, the terrifying
'Lady Lazarus':

I have done it again.
One year in every ten
I manage it –

A sort of walking miracle, my skin
Bright as a Nazi lampshade,
My right foot

A paperweight,
My face a featureless, fine
Jew linen.

Peel off the napkin
O my enemy.
Do I terrify? –

The nose, the eye pits, the full set of teeth?
The sour breath
Will vanish in a day.

Soon, soon the flesh
The grave cave ate will be
At home on me

And I a smiling woman.
I am only thirty.
And like the cat I have nine times to die.

This is Number Three.
What a trash
To annihilate each decade.

What a million filaments.
The peanut-crunching crowd
Shoves in to see

Them unwrap me hand and foot
The big strip tease.
Gentlemen, ladies

These are my hands
My knees.
I may be skin and bone,

Nevertheless, I am the same, identical woman.
The first time it happened I was ten.
It was an accident.

The second time I meant
To last it out and not come back at all.
I rocked shut

As a seashell.
They had to call and call
And pick the worms off me like sticky pearls.

Dying
Is an art, like everything else,
I do it exceptionally well.

I do it so it feels like hell.
I do it so it feels real.
I guess you could say I've a call.

It's easy enough to do it in a cell.
It's easy enough to do it and stay put.
It's the theatrical

Comeback in broad day
To the same place, the same face, the same brute
Amused shout:

'A miracle!'
That knocks me out.
There is a charge

For the eyeing of my scars, there is a charge
For the hearing of my heart —
It really goes.

And there is a charge, a very large charge
For a word or a touch
Or a bit of blood

Or a piece of my hair or my clothes.
So, so, Herr Doktor.
So, Herr Enemy.

I am your opus,
I am your valuable,
The pure gold baby

That melts to a shriek.
I turn and burn.
Do not think I underestimate your great concern.

Ash, ash –
You poke and stir.
Flesh, bone, there is nothing there –

A cake of soap,
A wedding ring,
A gold filling.

Herr God, Herr Lucifer
Beware
Beware.

Out of the ash
I rise with my red hair
And I eat men like air.

The Hughes–Plath story transfixed Britain. It was a ghastly private
tragedy, but in its way it showed that in the 1960s poetry was still
part of mainstream culture; and poets were regarded as important

truth-tellers. Ted Hughes, in a long public career, continued to be the public face of British poetry for many people. But, inevitably, the melodrama of this story overshadowed many poets, some of whom were as important.

Geoffrey Hill, the Worcestershire-born poet and academic, beat Michael Horovitz in the election for the Chair of Poetry at Oxford in 2010. His work is always described as dense, allusive and steeped in English history; it is much admired around the world. His critics find him too difficult, and perhaps too right-wing, though it would be more accurate to say that he is an anti-materialistic radical. As with some of Ted Hughes's writing, religion and myth play an important part in Hill's poetry, and he continues to be a big influence on poets today. Readers may feel that he's just too chewy, too clumpy, to be included in a chapter called 'Fresh Freshness', but Hill's arrival on the scene with *King Log* in 1968 introduced a profoundly original English voice, which has kept sounding original for decades. His best-known collection is his 1971 *Mercian Hymns*, mingling the great King Offa from the eighth century with the contemporary west Midlands of his own upbringing. Laid out as prose, there's something immediately energising and exciting about them:

> King of the perennial holly-groves, the riven sandstone: overlord of the M5: architect of the historic rampart and ditch, the citadel at Tamworth, the summer hermitage in Holy Cross: guardian of the Welsh Bridge and the Iron Bridge: contractor to the desirable new estates: saltmaster: moneychanger: commissioner for oaths: martyrologist: the friend of Charlemagne.
> 'I liked that,' said Offa, 'sing it again.'

No modern English poet – not even Ted Hughes – engaged in the country's strange, haunted history with the imaginative vigour of Geoffrey Hill. He reminds me of a poetic version of the great twentieth-century Welsh novelist John Cowper Powys – and that's meant as a high compliment. Here's some more, parts five and six, from *Mercian Hymns*:

So much for the elves' wergild, the true governance of England, the gaunt warrior-gospel armoured in engraved stone. I wormed my way heavenward for ages amid barbaric ivy, scrollwork of fern.

Exile or pilgrim set me once more upon that ground: my rich and desolate childhood. Dreamy, smug-faced, sick on outings – I who was taken to be a king of some kind, a prodigy, a maimed one.

The princes of Mercia were badger and raven. Thrall to their freedom, I dug and hoarded. Orchards fruited above clefts. I drank from honeycombs of chill sandstone.

'A boy at odds in the house, lonely among brothers.' But I, who had none, fostered a strangeness; gave myself to unattainable toys.

Candles of gnarled resin, apple-branches, the tacky mistletoe. 'Look' they said and again 'look.' But I ran slowly; the landscape flowed away, back to its source.

In the schoolyard, in the cloakrooms, the children boasted their scars of dried snot; wrists and knees garnished with impetigo.

By now the attentive reader (if you're still there) may be worried about three things in my modern selection. First, where are the Scots and the Irish? Second, Sylvia Plath apart, aren't there more women poets worth focusing on? Third, we are a multicultural nation now, aren't we? Are there no black poets, no Asian poets, in this patchwork quilt of British verse? Oh, for goodness' sake: where do you think we are going next?

19

Celts, Britons and Their Friends: Modern British Poetry Furth of England

Both Scotland and Northern Ireland experienced major political shake-ups in the latter part of the twentieth century and the opening decades of the twenty-first. Wales experienced a smaller shift. But in all of the geographically lesser partners of the United Kingdom there was a rising nationalist sensibility, reflected in vigorous and sometimes very fine poetry, from the 1950s right through to the current day.

After the bloody civil war known as 'the Troubles', which killed more than 3,500 people between 1969 and 2001, John Major's Conservative administration eventually repealed the Government of Ireland Act. The 1993 Downing Street Declaration stated that Britain had no 'selfish economic or strategic interest' in Northern Ireland. Early the following year, the IRA responded by announcing a temporary ceasefire, and complex negotiations began, covering issues such as the decommissioning of weapons, the status of the largely Protestant Royal Ulster Constabulary, and the practice of marching into rival communities in a mixture of celebration and provocation. It was a tortuous process, nearly derailed by further terrorist atrocities, rows over prisoners and the mutual distrust of unionist and republican leaders. Yet, shepherded by the American Senator George Mitchell, agreement was finally reached on Good Friday 1998, during the premiership of Tony Blair. It was then overwhelmingly ratified in a referendum, and Northern Ireland got a new devolved assembly, bringing in previously excluded Catholic republicans, including former gunmen, alongside Ulster Protestant unionists. In 2005 the IRA officially announced an end to hostilities and the decommissioning of its weapons.

In Scotland, the struggle for home rule had gone on through most of the twentieth century, though largely at the margins of politics. By the 1970s and 80s pressure had grown, and eventually, in 1998, again under Tony Blair's government, a referendum was held which overwhelmingly endorsed the idea of a Scottish parliament with substantial powers of its own, but working under the overall authority of Westminster. Far from quelling Scottish Nationalism, however, devolution appeared to drive it forwards. The Scottish National Party won power in Edinburgh in 2007, and swiftly renamed the Scottish executive the Scottish government. Support north of the border for both the Conservative and Labour parties crumbled. In 2014 the Scots voted in a referendum on independence, and for a few heady weeks it seemed as if they were about to choose to leave the United Kingdom. In the end the vote was firmly against independence, by 55 to 45 per cent.

And yet, as I write this in early 2015, it is clear that these matters are far from over. SNP support, and support for Scottish independence – they're not always the same thing – have risen substantially since the referendum. The general election story has centred on the almost explosive rise of the SNP, virtually wiping out Scottish Labour, and there must be a substantial chance that Scotland and England will divorce at some point over the next decade. If that happened, it would start a cascade of change elsewhere in Britain. The Northern Irish settlement is probably not forever: the number of Catholics with republican sympathies is growing, and Scottish independence might well have a big knock-on effect, encouraging a revival of Irish nationalism. Wales, with its own devolved assembly, is looking on attentively. So for the first time in more than two hundred years, the question of Britishness – What is it? Does it really exist? – is alive again.

In this collection I have tried to show that the people of the British Isles, whatever their governance, share a lot in terms of their history, landscapes, religious prejudices and experience of social change. But if poetry tells us important truths about how people actually feel, we would expect Irish and Scottish poetry of modern times to reflect profound changes in attitudes to identity. And they do.

Seamus Heaney was born on a farm in County Londonderry on the eve of the Second World War, the son of a farmer and cattle dealer. His mother's side of the family worked in the local linen mill, and all were Catholics. He went on to study English at Queen's College, Belfast, where he discovered the poetry of Ted Hughes. Later he was talent-spotted by the same Philip Hobsbaum who had formed the Group. By the mid-1960s he was regularly publishing poetry. His breakthrough collection, *Death of a Naturalist*, came out in 1966, and from then on he was a star in the world of verse. He spent much of his life in the United States and in Dublin, accumulating so many awards and prizes that even before he won the Nobel Prize for Literature in 1995 he was known jocularly at home as 'famous Seamus'. By the time he died in 2013 he was probably the best-known poet in the world.

Why? At first sight, many of his poems are humble accounts of rural life and the people he knew, close to the earth and close to the commonplace. He very rarely writes about the great events, the bloodshed and treachery, the idealistic hopes and messy political compromises, that overwhelmed the Northern Ireland of his time. As a famous Catholic voice, Heaney was under great pressure to speak out for 'his people' – to become a propaganda mouthpiece, in effect, for the IRA. While himself no admirer of the British state, Heaney stubbornly refused to take on that role. Like many Ulstermen, he was dry, shy and occasionally sly. He rooted his politics in the land and the people he knew, and their human value. He did, at the worst moments, directly address what was happening, but always in his own way, as in the lovely poem 'Casualty', as fine as the political poetry of W.B. Yeats, written in the immediate after-

math of 'Bloody Sunday' in January 1972, when British para-
troopers shot thirteen protesters dead in Londonderry (a four-
teenth would die later of his wounds). It appears to be about a
fisherman Heaney knew in the pub – a real man, as it happens –
and the poem reveals its true subject with gentle but deadly delib-
eration, like a line being cast out:

I
He would drink by himself
And raise a weathered thumb
Towards the high shelf,
Calling another rum
And blackcurrant, without
Having to raise his voice,
Or order a quick stout
By a lifting of the eyes
And a discreet dumb-show
Of pulling off the top;
At closing time would go
In waders and peaked cap
Into the showery dark,
A dole-kept breadwinner
But a natural for work.
I loved his whole manner,
Sure-footed but too sly,
His deadpan sidling tact,
His fisherman's quick eye
And turned observant back.

Incomprehensible
To him, my other life.
Sometimes on the high stool,
Too busy with his knife
At a tobacco plug
And not meeting my eye,

In the pause after a slug
He mentioned poetry.
We would be on our own
And, always politic
And shy of condescension,
I would manage by some trick
To switch the talk to eels
Or lore of the horse and cart
Or the Provisionals.

But my tentative art
His turned back watches too:
He was blown to bits
Out drinking in a curfew
Others obeyed, three nights
After they shot dead
The thirteen men in Derry.
PARAS THIRTEEN, the walls said,
BOGSIDE NIL. That Wednesday
Everyone held
His breath and trembled.

II
It was a day of cold
Raw silence, wind-blown
Surplice and soutane:
Rained-on, flower-laden
Coffin after coffin
Seemed to float from the door
Of the packed cathedral
Like blossoms on slow water.
The common funeral
Unrolled its swaddling band,
Lapping, tightening

Till we were braced and bound
Like brothers in a ring.

But he would not be held
At home by his own crowd
Whatever threats were phoned,
Whatever black flags waved.
I see him as he turned
In that bombed offending place,
Remorse fused with terror
In his still knowable face,
His cornered outfaced stare
Blinding in the flash.

He had gone miles away
For he drank like a fish
Nightly, naturally
Swimming towards the lure
Of warm lit-up places,
The blurred mesh and murmur
Drifting among glasses
In the gregarious smoke.
How culpable was he
That last night when he broke
Our tribe's complicity?
'Now, you're supposed to be
An educated man,'
I hear him say. 'Puzzle me
The right answer to that one.'

III
I missed his funeral,
Those quiet walkers
And sideways talkers

Shoaling out of his lane
To the respectable
Purring of the hearse …
They move in equal pace
With the habitual
Slow consolation
Of a dawdling engine,
The line lifted, hand
Over fist, cold sunshine
On the water, the land
Banked under fog: that morning
I was taken in his boat,
The screw purling, turning
Indolent fathoms white,
I tasted freedom with him.
To get out early, haul
Steadily off the bottom,
Dispraise the catch, and smile
As you find a rhythm
Working you, slow mile by mile,
Into your proper haunt
Somewhere, well out, beyond …

Dawn-sniffing revenant,
Plodder through midnight rain,
Question me again.

He could be more direct. In 'The Frontier of Writing' from 1987, Heaney reflects on what had become a completely routine event in Northern Ireland, stopping at a military checkpoint. But if you want to know how it felt, that sense of all-round mild paranoia and unfreedom, here's the answer:

The tightness and the nilness round that space
when the car stops in the road, the troops inspect
its make and number and, as one bends his face

towards your window, you catch sight of more
on a hill beyond, eyeing with intent
down cradled guns that hold you under cover

and everything is pure interrogation
until a rifle motions and you move
with guarded unconcerned acceleration –

a little emptier, a little spent
as always by that quiver in the self,
subjugated, yes, and obedient.

So you drive on to the frontier of writing
where it happens again. The guns on tripods;
the sergeant with his on-off mike repeating

data about you, waiting for the squawk
of clearance; the marksman training down
out of the sun upon you like a hawk.

And suddenly you're through, arraigned yet freed,
as if you'd passed from behind a waterfall
on the black current of a tarmac road

past armour-plated vehicles, out between
the posted soldiers flowing and receding
like tree shadows into the polished windscreen.

Apart from being a great poet – he made words and their sounds
mimic the natural universe and mankind's engagement with in it as
nobody had done for centuries – and a fine essayist and critic,

Seamus Heaney was one of the greatest translators of the late twentieth century, from Anglo-Saxon to ancient Greek. And it was in *The Cure at Troy*, a translation of Sophocles' play *Philoctetes*, that Heaney gave his definitive verdict on the peace process, one pithy and memorable enough to catch the ear of Bill Clinton in 1995:

History says, Don't hope
On this side of the grave,
But then, once in a lifetime
The longed-for tidal wave
Of justice can rise up,
And hope and history rhyme.

Heaney is such a fine poet, speaking from a rural Catholic tradition outside the mainstream of British poetry, that it's tempting just to carry on quoting him. That would be very unfair, however, to the other Irish poets of recent times. It would be unfair in particular to Patrick Kavanagh, an older poet who hugely influenced Heaney. Kavanagh grew up not so far away from Heaney's family, but on the southern side of the border, in the county of Monaghan. Born in 1904, he worked as a farm labourer and a shoemaker until his late twenties. He eventually moved to Dublin, and literary circles there, working as a journalist and barman, publishing novels and poetry. Had it not been for Heaney, he would probably be the best-known Irish poet after W.B. Yeats – a very different man, a genuine son of the soil, who suffered almost as much misfortune in his life as that other great Irishman Jonathan Swift. He was taken ill at the first performance of a play adapted from his novel *Tarry Flynn*, and died in 1967. It isn't hard to see what Heaney learned from him, not least the belief that the big truths are rooted in ordinary soil and common people's lives, not in the abstractions or academies. But to say that Kavanagh doesn't romanticise rural life is something of an understatement. This poem is called 'Having to Live in the Country':

Back once again in wild, wet Monaghan
Exiled from thought and feeling,
A mean brutality reigns:
It is really a horrible position to be in
And I equate myself with Dante
And all who have lived outside civilization.
It isn't a question of place but of people;
Wordsworth and Coleridge lived apart from the common
    man,
Their friends called on them regularly.
Swift is in a somewhat different category
He was a genuine exile and his heavy heart
Weighed him down in Dublin.
Yet even he had compensations for in the Deanery
He received many interesting friends
And it was the eighteenth century.

I suppose that having to live
Among men whose rages
Are for small wet hills full of stones
When one man buys a patch and pays a high price for it
That is not the end of his paying.
'Go home and have another bastard' shout the children,
Cousin of the underbidder, to the young wife of the
    purchaser.
The first child was born after six months of marriage,
Desperate people, desperate animals.
What must happen the poor priest
Somewhat educated who has to believe that these people
    have souls
As bright as a poet's – though I don't, mind, speak for
    myself.

For an essentially urban people – and the Irish have become almost as urban as the English and Scots – it's all too easy to look back softly at the lost Arcadia of rural life; which is why poets like Patrick Kavanagh, who actually lived it, are so important. This is a kind of ballad of hate to the 'Stony Grey Soil' of Monaghan where the poet spent so much of his life:

O stony grey soil of Monaghan
The laugh from my love you thieved;
You took the gay child of my passion
And gave me your clod-conceived.

You clogged the feet of my boyhood
And I believed that my stumble
Had the poise and stride of Apollo
And his voice my thick tongued mumble.

You told me the plough was immortal!
O green-life conquering plough!
The mandril stained, your coulter blunted
In the smooth lea-field of my brow.

You sang on steaming dunghills
A song of cowards' brood,
You perfumed my clothes with weasel itch,
You fed me on swinish food.

You flung a ditch on my vision
Of beauty, love and truth.
O stony grey soil of Monaghan
You burgled my bank of youth!

But you would hope, wouldn't you, that there was more to Patrick Kavanagh's story than that – that all those years of rackety behaviour in Dublin and elsewhere would have produced more bounce, more money in the bank of youth; and his best-loved poem, 'On Raglan Road', is indeed full of bounce and zest, as well as regret. It reminds me of Swinburne – or it would, had Swinburne had much to say beyond the music.

On Raglan Road on an autumn day I met her first and
 knew
That her dark hair would weave a snare that I might one
 day rue;
I saw the danger, yet I walked along the enchanted way,
And I said, let grief be a fallen leaf at the dawning of the
 day.

On Grafton Street in November we tripped lightly along
 the ledge
Of the deep ravine where can be seen the worth of
 passion's pledge,
The Queen of Hearts still making tarts and I not making
 hay –
O I loved too much and by such and such is happiness
 thrown away.

I gave her gifts of the mind I gave her the secret sign that's
 known
To the artists who have known the true gods of sound and
 stone
And word and tint. I did not stint for I gave her poems to
 say.
With her own name there and her own dark hair like
 clouds over fields of May

On a quiet street where old ghosts meet I see her walking
 now
Away from me so hurriedly my reason must allow
That I had wooed not as I should a creature made of clay –

When the angel woos the clay he'd lose his wings at the
    dawn of day.

Closer in time to Seamus Heaney, and a friend who shared the
experience of the Troubles, is the Belfast poet Michael Longley.
Nobody, including Heaney, has written better about the violence of
the time, bringing consolation to the bereaved. This is a short poem
about the murder of an ice-cream seller by the IRA:

Rum and raisin, vanilla, butterscotch, walnut, peach:
You would rhyme off the flavours. That was before
They murdered the ice-cream man on the Lisburn Road
And you bought carnations to lay outside his shop.
I named for you all the wild flowers of the Burren
I had seen in one day: thyme, valerian, loosestrife,
Meadowsweet, tway blade, crowfoot, ling, angelica,
Herb robert, marjoram, cow parsley, sundew, vetch,
Mountain avens, wood sage, ragged robin, stitchwort,
Yarrow, lady's bedstraw, bindweed, bog pimpernel.

Longley was both classically trained, fascinated by Ovid and
Homer, and a disgusted observer of Northern Irish sectarianism.
In the following poem, 'The Butchers', he brings the two together:

When he had made sure there were no survivors in his
    house
And that all the suitors were dead, heaped in blood and
    dust
Like fish that fishermen with fine-meshed nets have
    hauled
Up gasping for salt water, evaporating in the sunshine,
Odysseus, spattered with muck and like a lion dripping
    blood
From his chest and cheeks after devouring a farmer's
    bullock,

Ordered the disloyal housemaids to sponge down the
  armchairs
And tables, while Telemachos, the oxherd and the
  swineherd
Scraped the foor with shovels, and then between the
  portico
And the roundhouse stretched a hawser and hanged the
  women
So none touched the ground with her toes, like long-
  winged thrushes
Or doves trapped in a mist-net across the thicket where
  they roost,
Their heads bobbing in a row, their feet twitching but not
  for long,
And when they had dragged Melanthios's corpse into the
  haggard
And cut off his nose and ears and cock and balls, a dog's
  dinner,
Odysseus, seeing the need for whitewash and disinfectant,
Fumigated the house and the outhouses, so that
  Hermes
Like a clergyman might wave the supernatural baton
With which he resurrects or hypnotises those he chooses,
And waken and round up the suitors' souls, and the
  housemaids',
Like bats gibbering in the nooks of their mysterious cave
When out of the clusters that dangle from the rocky
  ceiling
One of them drops and squeaks, so their souls were
  bat-squeaks
As they fittered after Hermes, their deliverer, who led
  them
Along the clammy sheughs, then past the oceanic streams
And the white rock, the sun's gatepost in that dreamy
  region,

Until they came to a bog-meadow full of bog-asphodels
Where the residents are ghosts or images of the dead.

Longley is himself an agnostic, but comes from the Protestant side
of the Northern Irish divide, born in 1939 to parents who had
arrived from England. He clearly loathed the IRA, but had no more
time for the bigotry of the loyalist tradition. Here's his 'Wounds' of
1972, another poem which conflates the then and the now:

Here are two pictures from my father's head —
I have kept them like secrets until now:
First, the Ulster Division at the Somme
Going over the top with 'Fuck the Pope!'
'No Surrender!': a boy about to die,
Screaming 'Give 'em one for the Shankill!'
'Wilder than Gurkhas' were my father's words
Of admiration and bewilderment.
Next comes the London-Scottish padre
Resettling kilts with his swagger-stick,
With a stylish backhand and a prayer.
Over a landscape of dead buttocks
My father followed him for fifty years.
At last, a belated casualty,
He said — lead traces flaring till they hurt —
'I am dying for King and Country, slowly.'
I touched his hand, his thin head I touched.
Now, with military honours of a kind,
With his badges, his medals like rainbows,
His spinning compass, I bury beside him
Three teenage soldiers, bellies full of
Bullets and Irish beer, their flies undone.
A packet of Woodbines I throw in,
A lucifer, the Sacred Heart of Jesus
Paralysed as heavy guns put out
The night-light in a nursery for ever;

Also a bus-conductor's uniform –
He collapsed beside his carpet-slippers
Without a murmur, shot through the head
By a shivering boy who wandered in
Before they could turn the television down
Or tidy away the supper dishes.
To the children, to a bewildered wife,
I think 'Sorry Missus' was what he said.

After all this horror, what hope remains? And yet the story of
Northern Ireland is of a stumbling but determined and courageous
attempt to find some form of reconciliation, a journey that can be
followed in Michael Longley's poetry: his 'Ceasefire' is, characteris-
tically, half-rooted in Homer:

I
Put in mind of his own father and moved to tears
Achilles took him by the hand and pushed the old king
Gently away, but Priam curled up at his feet and
Wept with him until their sadness filled the building.

II
Taking Hector's corpse into his own hands Achilles
Made sure it was washed and, for the old king's sake,
Laid out in uniform, ready for Priam to carry
Wrapped like a present home to Troy at daybreak.

III
When they had eaten together, it pleased them both
To stare at each other's beauty as lovers might,
Achilles built like a god, Priam good-looking still
And full of conversation, who earlier had sighed:

IV

'I get down on my knees and do what must be done
And kiss Achilles' hand, the killer of my son.'

Perhaps the greatest achievement of Seamus Heaney was to bring new generations to adore the meat and muscle of poetic language – those blunt-nosed, square-fingered, hard and slippery words he specialised in. Like all major poets, Heaney subtly changed the trade itself.

Harri Webb's poem for St David's Day is a relatively rare example of Welsh nationalist poetry from before the 1970s. Wales, sharply divided between the Welsh-speaking north and west and the industrialised, English-speaking south and east, did not provoke the kind of constitutional crises facing Scotland and Ireland. But there was, from the 1960s onwards, a growing Welsh nationalist movement, arsonist in its extreme wing but for the most part much more focused on culture and poetry. Webb was a working-class boy from Swansea who was educated at Oxford before joining the British forces in the Second World War. He was demobilised to Scotland, where he met Hugh MacDiarmid and was converted to militant nationalism:

On the first day of March we remember
St. David the pride of our land,
Who taught us the stern path of duty
And for freedom and truth made a stand.

So here's to the sons of St. David,
Those youngsters so loyal and keen
Who'll haul down the red, white and blue, lads,
And hoist up the red, white and green.

In the dark gloomy days of December
We mourn for Llywellyn with pride

Who fell in defence of his country
With eighteen brave men by his side.

So here's to the sons of Llywellyn,
The heirs of that valiant eighteen
Who'll haul down the red, white and blue, lads,
And hoist up the red, white and green.

In the warm, golden days of September,
Great Owain Glyndwr took the field,
For fifteen long years did he struggle
And never the dragon did yield.

So here's to the sons of Great Owain,
Who'll show the proud Sais what we mean
When we haul down the red, white and blue, lads,
And hoist up the red, white and green.

There are many more names to remember
And some that will never be known
Who were loyal to Wales and the gwerin*
And defied all the might of the throne.

So here's to the sons of the gwerin
Who care not for the prince or for queen,
Who'll haul down the red, white and blue, lads,
And hoist up the red, white and green!

Scotland was spared the bloodshed of Northern Ireland, and enjoyed a more complete cultural revolution than Wales; but it too became increasingly uneasy inside the United Kingdom during the second half of the twentieth century. We've already met two of the supreme Scottish poets of the century, the fiercely nationalist and

---

* The people of Wales.

Marxist Hugh MacDiarmid, and the un-fierce Edwin Muir. Discussing the Second World War, we met the wonderful Robert Garioch, one of the supreme Edinburgh poets of the period: many of the Scots who became well known in the 1950s and 60s had been war poets, either serving or observing; war is a terrible thing, but it got many Scots out, forcing them to look at Europe and the wider world around them as never before.

Sydney Goodsir Smith was one of the most colourful and convivial figures of the Scottish poetry scene, a host whose Edinburgh flat was crammed at night with whisky-drinking and argumentative bards, and whose own work in Scots is unique. Although he was born in New Zealand, nobody, except possibly MacDiarmid himself, was so saturated in and captivated by earlier Scottish poetry – the medieval bards Dunbar and Henryson, and then Fergusson and Burns, all of whom we met earlier. But Smith, the son of a professor of forensic medicine and himself a medical student for a while, had a delight in wordplay and an interest in Modernist experimentation which also found him compared frequently to James Joyce and Dylan Thomas. Relatively late in his career, in 1965 – he died at the early age of fifty-eight in 1975 – he wrote a political poem about Edinburgh, then without a parliament or assembly of any kind, called 'Kynd Kittock's Land'. It deals with exactly the self-hatred and cultural insecurity we somtimes find in Wales. The Scots, in this case, isn't very difficult, but to help English readers, the first stanza means something like: 'This disreputable, wretched city, deflated from its old importance, half of it smug and complacent but having lost all its pride in race or spirit, and the other half as wild and rough as ever it was in its secret heart, has also lost all of its gumption. The independently minded man now sits on Edinburgh's craggy spine, begging cap in hand, enduring the wind and the rain that has always watered the city's genius.' The rest is obvious, or at least not difficult.

This rortie wretched city
Sair come doun frae its auld hiechts

The hauf o't smug, complacent,
Lost til all pride of race or spirit,
The tither wild and rouch as ever
In its secret hairt
But lost alsweill, the smeddum tane,
The man o' independent mind has cap in hand the day
Sits on its craggy spine
And drees the wind and rain
That nourished all its genius
Weary wi centuries
This empty capital snorts like a great beast
Caged in its sleep, dreaming of freedom
But with nae belief,
Indulging an auld ritual
Whase meaning's been forgot owre lang,
A mere habit of words – when the drink's in –
And signifying naething.

This rortie wretched city
Built on history
Built of history
Born of feud and enmity
Suckled on bluid and treachery
Its lullabies the clash of steel
And shouted slogan, sits here in her lichtit cage,
A beast wi the soul o' an auld wrukled whure ...

That's just the opening of a much longer poem which, for anyone prepared to search it out, remains well worth reading, full of warmth and oomph; but that introductory tirade against modern Scotland reflects a political and cultural despair common at this period. Maurice Lindsay, from Dunbartonshire, wrote in English and in a more jocular vein, and adored Goodsir Smith:

Dear Goodsir Smith, who sang of drink and women,
a connoisseur of laughter, wit and art;
of Scotland's writers warmly the most human,
moneyed and monocled to play the part ...

That tribute comes from 'A Net to Catch the Winds', Lindsay's autobiographical reflection (not unlike John Betjeman in tone) on a musical childhood and a career spent in journalism and television. In the course of it, he too grumbles about Scotland's post-war status:

A shadow that has lost its substance, feeling
as well supported as a verbless clause,
the Scottish spirit's been too long congealing
in banknotes, sour religion and thinned laws,
while roundabout, the busy world is dealing
in purposes that were a living cause.
Though Scots pretend they long for devolution,
they vote unchanged the London Constitution.

That frees them from the burden of decision,
allowing them complain when things go wrong ...

... One must stay positive, though Scotland's slipping
beyond retrieval to provincial status;
for what will not return it's no use weeping.
Mankind's long march goes on. It should elate us
that slowly fairer values are out stripping
those with which privilege could still negate us
if democratic rule became dictation,
to tyrants' or Trade Unions' subjugation.

It was, perhaps, as wild a piece of dreaming
to visualise of virile Scotland, free
to make its choices, as the thought that scheming

among the globe-trotting statesmen could decree
a peaceful balance for the world's redeeming,
the universal, equal vis-à-vis.
Since history is the sum of spent confusion,
all human life must end in disillusion.

In a pithier mood, Maurice Lindsay responded to the 1978 devolution referendum, when Scots voted narrowly for a devolved assembly – but too narrowly for it to come about. *Scotland the What?* was a popular comedy revue at the time – and is the name of the poem. For the uninitiated, the tawse is a heavy leather strap traditionally used to punish Scottish schoolchildren; and to girn is to whinge, or complain. This poem demonstrates that worries about Scotland's place in the UK were not confined to the left:

Is Scotland a nation, or not?
Is a question that troubles the Scot,
since our banknote and laws,
our religion and tawse
don't add up to self-confident thought.

Where's the What for which Scots keep on yearning?
We strike when we ought to be earning;
An Assembly! we shout
then vote the thing out
and get back to the business of girning.

Yet no matter how deeply one delves
through what history is stocked on our shelves,
at least we still joke
of the pig in the poke
we buy when we treat with ourselves.

A much more substantial poet was Edwin Morgan, one of the big figures of the Scottish literary renaissance. Born in Glasgow in

1920, he became the city's first Poet Laureate in 1999, and five years later was named the first Scottish equivalent of the Poet Laureate, the Scots Makar. A conscientious objector who served in the Royal Army Medical Corps during World War II, and a gay man in Scotland when that was a difficult thing to be, Morgan was first associated with the radical performance poetry and experimentation of the 1960s. He would go on to write highly political poems and be a major influence in Scotland during its transition and the devolution years; 'The Coin', one of his meditations in *Sonnets for Scotland*, imagines an entirely different republican history:

> We brushed the dirt off, held it to the light.
> The obverse showed us Scotland, and the head
> of a red deer; the antler-glint had fled
> but the fine cut could still be felt. All right:
> we turned it over, read easily One Pound,
> but then the shock of Latin, like a gloss,
> Respublica Scotorum, sent across
> such ages as we guessed but never found
> at the worn edge where once the date had been
> and where as many fingers had gripped hard
> as hopes their silent race had lost or gained.
> The marshy scurf crept up to our machine,
> sucked at our boots. Yet nothing seemed ill-starred.
> And least of all the realm the coin contained.

The bulk of Morgan's poetry was playful and experimental, mining science fiction and sound effects, and commenting more on the big social changes going on in twentieth-century Scotland than on constitutional questions. A good example of his earlier poetry is 'The Loch Ness Monster's Song', one for everyone to try at home:

> Sssnnnwhuffffll?
> Hnwhuffl hhnnwfl hnfl hfl?

Gdroblboblhobngbl gbl gl g g g g glbgl.
Drublhaflablhaflubhafgabhaflhafl fl fl –
gm grawwwww grf grawf awfgm graw gm.
Hovoplodok – doplodovok – plovodokot-doplodokosh?
Splgraw fok fok splgrafhatchgabrlgabrl fok splfok!
Zgra kra gka fok! Grof grawff gahf?
Gombl mbl bl – blm plm, blm plm, blm plm, blp.

What distinguished Morgan from most of the other Scottish poets mentioned here was that he was always distinctively and proudly Glaswegian, rooted in the industrial west. He wrote a lot about Glasgow in its industrial decline and revolutionary fervour. Generally a taut, formal poet, here is his sonnet 'Clydegrad':

It was so fine we lingered there for hours.
The long broad streets shone strongly after rain.
Sunset blinded the tremble of the crane
we watched from, dazed the heliport-towers.
The mile-high buildings flashed, flushed, greyed, went
    dark,
greyed, flushed, flashed, chameleons under flak
of cloud and sun. The last far thunder-sack
ripped and spilled its grumble. Ziggurat-stark,
a power-house reflected in the lead
of the old twilight river leapt alive
lit up at every window, and a boat
of students rowed past, slid from black to red
into the blaze. But where will they arrive
with all, boat, city, earth, like them, afloat?

Scottish home rule and nationalist politics have become so charged and controversial recently that I can't resist including Edwin Morgan's optimistic poem written for the opening of the new Scottish Parliament on 9 October 2004. The building itself was radical, expensive and controversial. Morgan's poem is a celebration of democracy and what it can achieve, and a stern injunction to the new generation of Scottish politicians to be brave and bold. To my ear, it is public poetry of a very high order:

> Open the doors! Light of the day, shine in; light of the
> mind, shine out!
> We have a building which is more than a building.
> There is a commerce between inner and outer, between
> brightness and shadow, between the world and those
> who think about the world.
> Is it not a mystery? The parts cohere, they come together
> like petals of a flower, yet they also send their tongues
> outward to feel and taste the teeming earth.
> Did you want classic columns and predictable pediments?
> A growl of old Gothic grandeur? A blissfully boring
> box?
> Not here, no thanks! No icon, no IKEA, no iceberg, but
> curves and caverns, nooks and niches, huddles and
> heavens, syncopations and surprises. Leave symmetry to
> the cemetery.
> But bring together slate and stainless steel, black granite
> and grey granite, seasoned oak and sycamore, concrete
> blond and smooth as silk – the mix is almost alive – it
> breathes and beckons – imperial marble it is not!

> Come down the Mile, into the heart of the city, past the
> kirk of St Giles and the closes and wynds of the noted
> ghosts of history who drank their claret and fell down
> the steep tenement stairs into the arms of link-boys but
> who wrote and talked the starry Enlightenment of their
> days –
> And before them the auld makars who tickled a Scottish
> king's ear with melody
> and ribaldry and frank advice –

And when you are there, down there, in the midst of
   things, not set upon an hill with your nose in the air,
   This is where you know your parliament should be
And this is where it is, just here.

What do the people want of the place? They want it to be
   filled with thinking persons as open and adventurous as
   its architecture.
A nest of fearties is what they do not want.
A symposium of procrastinators is what they do not want.
A phalanx of forelock-tuggers is what they do not want.
And perhaps above all the droopy mantra of 'it wizny me'
   is what they do not want.
Dear friends, dear lawgivers, dear parliamentarians, you
   are picking up a thread of pride and self-esteem that has
   been almost but not quite, oh no not quite, not ever
   broken or forgotten.
When you convene you will be reconvening, with a sense
   of not wholly the power, not yet wholly the power, but a
   good sense of what was once in the honour of your
   grasp.
All right. Forget, or don't forget, the past. Trumpets and
   robes are fine, but in the present and the future you will
   need something more.
What is it? We, the people, cannot tell you yet, but you
   will know about it when we do tell you.
We give you our consent to govern, don't pocket it and
   ride away.
We give you our deepest dearest wish to govern well, don't
   say we have no mandate to be bold.
We give you this great building, don't let your work and
   hope be other than great when you enter and begin.
So now begin. Open the doors and begin.

Liz Lochhead is another Glasgow poet, who succeeded Edwin Morgan as the country's national poet or Makar. Though much younger, she too emerged with the new wave of 1960s poets – Adrian Mitchell was a lifelong friend. An excellent performance poet, who still likes to read her poems to public audiences, Lochhead is first and foremost Scotland's leading woman poet. Funny, bawdy, theatrical and tender, she is at the opposite pole to the whisky-sodden, hectoring male certainties of the original Scottish Renaissance poets. She writes well and frankly about sex and relationships, but even more important, she records women's experiences in modern Scotland. This poem, 'For My Grandmother Knitting', deals with a woman who had moved from being a fisher girl, gutting the catch, to a knitter; it's really about, however, what has happened to the Scottish working classes, with their skill and their dexterity, in a world de-skilled and driven by shopping.

There is no need they say
but the needles still move
their rhythms in the working of your hands
as easily
as if your hands
were once again those sure and skilful hands
of the fisher-girl.

You are old now
and your grasp of things is not so good
but master of your moments then
deft and swift
you slit the still-ticking quick silver fish.
Hard work it was too
of necessity.

But now they say there is no need
as the needles move

in the working of your hands
once the hands of the bride
with the hand-span waist
once the hands of the miner's wife
who scrubbed his back
in a tin bath by the coal fire
once the hands of the mother
of six who made do and mended
scraped and slaved slapped sometimes
when necessary.

But now they say there is no need
the kids they say grandma
have too much already
more than they can wear
too many scarves and cardigans –
gran you do too much
there's no necessity …

At your window you wave
them goodbye Sunday.
With your painful hands
big on shrunken wrists.
Swollen-jointed. Red. Arthritic. Old.
But the needles still move
their rhythms in the working of your hands
easily
as if your hands remembered
of their own accord the patter
as if your hands had forgotten
how to stop.

Again and again, Lochhead writes poems that trip off the tongue and seem delightfully simple but which, again and again, are composed of layer upon layer of meaning. She is a poet who knows the Scottish tradition inside out. In this wonderful poem, she imagines the mouse in Burns's famous verse talking back to her in her own kitchen. Using Burns's own favourite stanza, Standard Habbie, Lochhead manages to make a poem about environmental degradation and animal rights, Scottish male chauvinism and the joys of Robert Burns. It's full of details any modern Scot will enjoy, from Daphne Broon, the hapless unmarried girl in a famous Scottish cartoon strip, to the contemporary obsession with the national poet's virile member. It starts with a short explanation:

The present author being, from her mother's milk, a lover of the poetic effusions of Mr Robert Burns and all creatures therein (whether mouse, louse, yowe, dug or grey mare Meg) was nonetheless appalled to find, in her slattern's kitchen, sitting up washing its face in her wok, the following phenomenon:

It's me. The eponymous the moose
The To a Mouse that – were I in your hoose,
A bit o dust ablow the bed thon dodd o' oose
That, quick, turns tail,
Is – eek! – a livin creature on the loose,
Wad gar you wail.

Aye, I've heard you fairly scraich, you seem
Gey phobic 'boot Mice in Real Life yet dream
Aboot Man-Mouse Amity? Ye'll rhyme a ream!
Yet, wi skirt wrapt roon,
I've seen ye staun up oan a chair an scream
Like Daphne Broon.

But I'm adored – on paper! – ever since
First ye got me at the schule, at yince
Enchantit – wha'd aye thocht poetry was mince
Till ye met Rabbie,
My poor, earth-born companion, an the prince
O Standard Habbie.

For yon is what they cry the form he wrote in
An' you recite. Gey easy, as you ken, to quote in
Because it sticks. I will allow it's stoatin,
This nifty stanza
He could go to sicc lengths wi, say sicc a lot in
Largs to Lochranza,

Plockton to Peebles, Dumfries to Dundee,
If a wean kens ony poem aff by hert, it's Me!
Will greet ower ma plough-torn nest, no see
The bit o' a gap
Atween the fause Warld o' Poetry
An baited trap.

Get Rentokil! Get real! Wha you love
'S the ploughman in the poem, keen to prove
Saut tears, sigh, sympathy – he's sensitive.
Wee sermon:
Mice, men, schemes agley, Himsel' above
Cryin me Vermin.
Ploughman? That will be right! Heaven-taught?
He drank deep o The Bard, and Gray, and Pope – the lot.
I, faur frae the spontaneous outburst you thought,
Am an artifact.
For Man's Dominion he was truly sorry?
Not! 'T was all an act.

Burns, baith man and poet, liked to dominate.
His reputation wi the lassies wasna great.
They still dinna ken whether they love to hate,
Or hate to love.
He was 'an awfy man!' He left them tae their fate,
Push came to shove.

Couldnae keep it in his breeks? Hell's bells, damnation,
I wad be the vera last to gie a peroration
On the daft obsession o this prurient Nation,
His amatory antics.
He was – beating them tae it by a generation –
First o th' Romantics.

Arguably I am a poem wha, prescient, did presage
Your Twentyfirst Century Global Distress Age.
I'm a female mouse though, he didna give a sausage
For ma sparklin een! As for Mother Nature?
Whether yez get the message Remains to be seen.

Thus far we've been describing urban poets, and that's right, because modern Scotland is an overwhelmingly urban country, most of whose people speak an urban, demotic Scots, used by most of Scotland's poets. Before we leave this kind of poetry, there's one final poet who needs to be quoted, because he deploys that gritty, plosive, hard-edged language more enthusiastically than anyone else. Tom Leonard comes from a solidly working-class Glasgow family – his father was an Irish train driver who moved to the city, and his mother worked in a dynamite factory. Part of the same generation as Liz Lochhead, he burst onto the poetry scene in 1969, and is particularly famous in Scotland for his satirical attack on the English voices of BBC newsreaders (such as, I suppose, the current writer). It's very funny, and if you can't follow a word of it, you are part of the joke.

this is thi
six a clock
news thi
man said n
thi reason
a talk wia

BBC accent
iz coz yi
widny wahnt
mi ti talk
aboot thi
trooth wia
voice lik
wanna yoo
scruff. if
a toktaboot
thi trooth
lik wanna yoo
scruff yi
widny thingk
it wuz troo.
jist wanna yoo
scruff tokn.
thirza right
way ti spell
ana right way
to tok it. this
is me tokn yir
right way a
spellin. this
is ma trooth.
yooz doant no
thi trooth
yirsellz cawz
yi canny talk
right. this is
the six a clock
nyooz. belt up.

The modern Scottish experience, however, isn't simply urban, and isn't all political. The country's best-loved poets include Gaelic speakers such as Sorley MacLean, and poets who focus on rural life, from the Orcadian George Mackay Brown to the arch proponent of what we might call Scottish Highland Zen, Norman MacCaig.

Sorley MacLean, or more properly Somhairle MacGill-Eain, was born on the island of Raasay, off Skye, in 1911. He went to Edinburgh University, and was writing fine poetry in Gaelic from the 1930s onwards, at which time he was, broadly speaking, a communist. He fought during the Second World War with the Eighth Army, and was badly wounded at the Battle of El Alamein; along with Hamish Henderson and Robert Garioch, he's one of the talented platoon of Scottish war poets. After the war, he returned to the Highlands and spent most of his life as a schoolteacher. His real significance is that, following a long period of relative quiet in Gaelic writing, he proved that it was possible to be a committed, thoroughly modern and serious poet writing in Gaelic rather than in English or Scots. To that extent he was a one-man cultural renaissance.

He translated most of his own poems into English, and it's the translations I will give here; when he was reading, it was his practice to read a poem in Gaelic first, and then in English. As someone who doesn't understand a word of Gaelic, I can say that the former sounded like wind coming over a hill, or the distant noise of breaking waves. And the translations, somehow, don't sound like the work of any English-speaking poet I know. Here, first, is 'Death Valley', one of his poems from the war in North Africa:

Some Nazi or other has said that the Fuehrer
had restored to German manhood the
'right and joy of dying in battle'.

Sitting dead in 'Death Valley'
below the Ruweisat Ridge,
a boy with his forelock down about his cheek
and his face slate-grey;

I thought of the right and the joy
that he got from his Fuehrer,
of falling in the field of slaughter
to rise no more;

of the pomp and the fame
that he had, not alone,
though he was the most piteous to see
in a valley gone to seed

with flies about grey corpses
on a dun sand
dirty yellow and full of the rubbish
and fragments of battle.

Was the boy of the band
who abused the Jews
and communists, or of the greater
band of those

led, from the beginning of generations,
unwillingly to the trial
and mad delirium of every war
for the sake of rulers?

Whatever his desire or mishap,
his innocence or malignity,
he showed no pleasure in his death
below the Ruweisat Ridge.

And here, by contrast, is the opening of 'Hallaig', a magnificent
lament for his people, the MacLeods, and by extension for all the
Gaels of north-west Scotland who were driven from their land and
culture not just by the Highland clearances of the eighteenth and
nineteenth centuries, but by the great economic shifts which made

subsistence agriculture on poor soil intolerable. Raasay's dozen townships were cleared during 1852–54 and its entire population, some ninety-four families, driven from their homes and forced into exile: Hallaig was the name of one of the deserted towns. Rich in symbols and music, this is the authentic verse of the Gaelic people, the poetry that W.B. Yeats tried to imagine into existence from English, largely unsuccessfully:

'Time, the deer, is in the wood of Hallaig'

The window is nailed and boarded
through which I saw the West
and my love is at the Burn of Hallaig,
a birch tree, and she has always been

between Inver and Milk Hollow,
here and there about Baile-Chuirn:
she is a birch, a hazel,
a straight, slender young rowan.

In Screapadal of my people
where Norman and Big Hector were,
their daughters and their sons are a wood
going up beside the stream.

Proud tonight the pine cocks
crowing on the top of Cnoc an Ra,
straight their backs in the moonlight –
they are not the wood I love.

I will wait for the birch wood
until it comes up by the cairn,
until the whole ridge from Beinn na Lice
will be under its shade.

If it does not, I will go down to Hallaig,
to the Sabbath of the dead,
where the people are frequenting,
every single generation gone.

They are still in Hallaig,
MacLeans and MacLeods,
all who were there in the time of Mac Gille Chaluim:
the dead have been seen alive.

The men lying on the green
at the end of every house that was,
the girls a wood of birches,
straight their backs, bent their heads.

Between the Leac and Fearns
the road is under mild moss
and the girls in silent bands
go to Clachan as in the beginning,

and return from Clachan,
from Suisnish and the land of the living;
each one young and light-stepping,
without the heartbreak of the tale.

From the Burn of Fearns to the raised beach
that is clear in the mystery of the hills,
there is only the congregation of the girls
keeping up the endless walk,

coming back to Hallaig in the evening,
in the dumb living twilight,
filling the steep slopes,
their laughter a mist in my ears,

and their beauty a film on my heart
before the dimness comes on the kyles,
and when the sun goes down behind Dun Cana
a vehement bullet will come from the gun of Love;

and will strike the deer that goes dizzily,
sniffing at the grass-grown ruined homes;
his eye will freeze in the wood,
his blood will not be traced while I live.

Hugh MacDiarmid told Sorley MacLean before his death that he considered the two of them the finest poets modern Scotland had produced. It's interesting that he didn't include his other friend and sometime drinking partner Norman MacCaig, even though MacCaig is probably more read by today's Scots than either of the others. Born in Edinburgh in 1910 and a conscientious objector during the war, MacCaig was, like MacLean, a teacher. He divided his life between Edinburgh and Assynt, in the north-west Highlands. A fanatical fisherman, he wrote poetry that is limpid, simple and often informed by a spiky mysticism: he called himself, only half jokingly, a Zen Presbyterian. MacDiarmid's caution about him may have been related to MacCaig's resolute lack of interest in mainstream politics or Scottish nationalism. Here is his short poem 'Patriot':

My only country
is six feet high
and whether I love it or not
I'll die
for its independence.

Like some other good poets, MacCaig takes the small and, by staring at it hard, unpacks the big within it. Here is his 1985 poem 'Small Boy':

He picked up a pebble
and threw it into the sea.

And another, and another.
He couldn't stop.

He wasn't trying to fill the sea.
He wasn't trying to empty the beach.

He was just throwing away,
nothing else but.

Like a kitten playing
he was practising for the future

when there'll be so many things
he'll want to throw away

if only his fingers will unclench
and let them go.

Though he also wrote a lot about Edinburgh, MacCaig was above all a nature poet, responding to the vast spaces and watery landscapes of the Scottish north-west Highlands. Here is a poem set on the north side of the great, mysterious mountain called Suilven:

The three-inch-wide streamlet
trickles over its own fingers
down the sandstone slabs
of my favourite mountain

Like the Amazon it'll reach the sea.
Like the Volga
it'll forget its own language there

its water goes down my throat
with glassy coldness,
like something suddenly remembered.

I drink
its freezing vocabulary
and half understand the purity
of all beginnings.

That's MacCaig, with his huge bony forehead and dark, challenging eyes. If you like that poem there are hundreds more, just as good.

What MacCaig didn't have, as an Edinburgh man, was an insider's understanding of the history and culture of the Scottish north. George Mackay Brown of Orkney was a different kettle of freshly caught fish. The Orcadians are like nobody else in the British Isles, except perhaps their near neighbours and rivals from Shetland. Their history isn't Gaelic, but Norse. The Earldom of Orkney was held for the Norwegian crown, and then the Danish crown, until the cluster of islands was passed to Scotland in 1468 as part of the marriage settlement between King James III and Princess Margaret of Denmark. Orkney has its own heroes, such as St Magnus, executed around 1115 after a Viking battle; and the Viking sagas were recounted over smoking peat fires for centuries. In modern times, without the oil boom that has transformed Shetland, Orkney remained a place almost cut off from modern history, islands of seafarers and subsistence crofters – or, as George Mackay Brown put it, fishermen with ploughs.

The son of an impoverished tailor, Mackay Brown spent most of his life in the small town of Stromness, though he visited Edinburgh frequently and was a friend of the other main figures in the Scottish literary renaissance, joining them on heroic Edinburgh pub crawls. He has influences – notably the other Orcadian poet we have met, Edwin Muir, and, after he was received into the Roman Catholic Church, Gerard Manley Hopkins – but his mature poetry, and indeed his novels and short stories, sound like no one else. They

almost feel as if they are standing outside time, in a quasi-medieval
space pinned out by rituals and the cycle of the seasons. Here is
'Hamnavoe Market', about a group of men who have, all too rarely,
a little money to spend in what passes for the metropolis:

They drove to the Market with ringing pockets.

Folster found a girl
Who put wounds on his face and throat,
Small and diagonal, like red doves.

Johnston stood beside the barrel.
All day he stood there.
He woke in a ditch, his mouth full of ashes.

Grieve bought a balloon and a goldfish.
He swung through the air.
He fired shotguns, rolled pennies,
ate sweet fog from a stick.

Heddle was at the Market also.
I know nothing of his activities.
He is and always was a quiet man.

Garson fought three rounds with a negro boxer,
And received thirty shillings,
Much applause, and an eye loaded with thunder.

Where did they find Flett?
They found him in a brazen circle,
All flame and blood, a new Salvationist.

A gypsy saw in the hand of Halcro
Great strolling herds, harvests, a proud woman.
He wintered in the poorhouse.

They drove home from the Market under the stars
Except for Johnston
Who lay in a ditch, his mouth full of dying fires.

Mackay Brown speaks to and for all those Britons who, well into
the twentieth century, were still living economically marginal lives,
on the very edges of modernity. Not everybody had a car and a
chequebook. Here is another of his poems, I think a very good one,
about a beachcomber:

Monday I found a boot —
Rust and salt leather.
I gave it back to the sea, to dance in.

Tuesday a spar of timber worth thirty bob.
Next winter
It will be a chair, a coffin, a bed.

Wednesday a half can of Swedish spirits.
I tilted my head.
The shore was cold with mermaids and angels.

Thursday I got nothing, seaweed,
A whale bone,
Wet feet and a loud cough.

Friday I held a seaman's skull,
Sand spilling from it
The way time is told on kirkyard stones.

Saturday a barrel of sodden oranges.
A Spanish ship
Was wrecked last month at The Kame.

Sunday, for fear of the elders,
I sit on my bum. What's heaven?
A sea chest with a thousand gold coins.

Like Seamus Heaney, Robin Robertson, brought up in the north-east of Scotland, is fascinated by the darkness, directness and bloody nature of the ancient tales. But he is as unlike a Victorian translator from the Greek as can be imagined – much sharper, considerably darker. Here is his version of the moment from the legend of Actaeon, described by Ovid, when the transgressive hunter has been turned into a stag, and is being ripped to pieces by his own hounds:

While they held down their prey,
the rest of the pack broke on him like surf,
dipping their teeth into his flesh
till there was no place left for further wounds,
and at every wound's mouth was the mouth of a dog.
Surge upon surge, the riptide crashed and turned,
battening on, and tearing away – maddened – in the red spume.
Actaeon groaned: a sound which wasn't human,
but which no stag could produce.
Falling to his knees, like a supplicant at prayer, he bowed
in silence as the angry sea crashed on him once again
and the dogs hid his body with their own ...

Robertson's poetry covers the gamut. He writes about sex, ageing, regret, great artists of the past, moving house and life-changing operations. In his poem 'Hammersmith Winter' he describes the urban loneliness which is for millions a central part of modern life:

It is so cold tonight; too cold for snow,
and yet it snows. Through the drawn curtain
shines the snowlight I remember as a boy,
sitting up at the window watching it fall.
But you are not here, now, to lead me back

to bed. None of you are. Look at the snow,
I said, to whoever might be near, I'm cold,
would you hold me. Hold me. Let me go.

Robertson can be very gentle and mild; but there's a blackness about him that returns again and again, a recurrence of ancient savagery. Here is his short poem 'Law of the Island':

They lashed him to old timbers
that would barely float,
with weights at the feet so
only his face was out of the water.
Over his mouth and eyes
they tied two live mackerel
with twine, and pushed him
out from the rocks.

They stood, then,
smoking cigarettes
and watching the sky,
waiting for a gannet
to read that flex of silver
from a hundred feet up,
close its wings
and plummet-dive.

The most unsettling thing, of course, about the poem is the cigarettes: we are still living, some of the time at least, in Ovid's world.

The twentieth century, and the opening years of this century, have been a fabulous time for Scottish poetry, the most exciting since late medieval times. All of the poets I've quoted have had an effect on yet another generation, the here-and-now poets of a Scotland that feels on the edge of reclaiming its political independence. We will meet them, and a whole host of other younger names, in the final section of this book.

20

Here Comes Everybody: The British and Poetry Now

It cannot quite be done: giving a fair account of contemporary British poetry is simply impossible. In the hot press and hubbub of so many talented poets of today, how could one possibly be fair? The brutal and remorseless winnowing of time and critical reputation hasn't happened yet, and won't for a long time to come: it's unclear who are the Christopher Smarts and Anne Askews of today; and who the mere Matthew Priors and Colley Cibbers. But there are useful questions to be asked, which can be probed.

First, we know that modern Britain is a more feminised society than it used to be. Compared to Scandinavia and some other European countries there is still a long way to go, but we have more female politicians and comedians, many more female novelists and women in the armed services, and there's even a growth in top-flight and properly paid female sport. So we'd expect poetry in Britain in the twenty-first century to include far more female poets, a new balance. Is that so?

Second, we are a much more mixed, multicultural society after the major Caribbean and Asian migrations of the middle of the twentieth century, and the more recent European ones. Is that reflected in the contemporary British poetry scene?

Third, if we are talking about the very biggest social changes, we would expect more poetry about ageing and old age, for we are a fast-ageing society in which, presumably, a much larger number of poetry readers are older people.

Then there are other questions which may give some clue as to the reasons for the vigour and significance of poetry today. We've had nearly one and a half thousand years of religious and nature poetry: has it now vanished? We know that most people get their news, of everything from world events to the doings of their friends, from online media: has poetry, on websites as well as in niche publishing, been able to hold its own in a multicoloured cascade of media and storytelling forms? For generations it's been one of the most important ways in which particularly clever, talented and sensitive people have described their own experiences, and looked around them at the events of their own times. Is all of that now withering, or is it still true?

I'm not going to begin to try to give a comprehensive account of poetry in contemporary Britain – I may be stupid, but I'm not that stupid. Instead, I'm going to try to answer some of these questions.

One of them, at least, is easy: it isn't simply that we are seeing more prominent women poets at the moment, it's that they have almost taken over. The current Poet Laureate, Carol Ann Duffy, one of the most popular and successful we have had for a very long time, is a gay woman whose breakthrough book was of love poetry. Wales now has a national poet of its own – Gillian Clarke. And, as I've mentioned, so does Scotland – Liz Lochhead. Of the most successful nature poets at the moment – all of them, broadly speaking, political as well – I can immediately think of three who can't be ignored: Kathleen Jamie from Scotland, Alice Oswald from the West Country, and Liz Berry from the Black Country. Wittiest popular poet? Wendy Cope, or is it Ursula (U.A.) Fanthorpe? And then there's Jackie Kay, and Ruth Padel, and … well, you get the picture.

Carol Ann Duffy was born in a working-class family in the Glasgow Gorbals, though they moved when she was young to Stafford in England. She came under the influence of Liverpool's Adrian Henri, discussed earlier, and was later in a relationship with the Scottish poet Jackie Kay. She's probably most admired for her love poetry, collected in the 2003 volume *Rapture*, one of the essential poetry books of recent years. In it, she portrays love as a process of constant and uncontrollable change. This poem is called 'Hand':

Away from you, I hold hands with the air,
you are imagined, untouchable hand. Not there,
your fingers braid with mine as I walk.
Far away in my heart, you start to talk.

I squeeze the air, kicking the auburn leaves,
everything suddenly gold. I half believe
your hand is holding mine, the way
it would if you were here. What do you say

in my heart? I bend my head to listen, then feel
your hand reach out and stroke my hair, as real
as the wind caressing the fretful trees above.
Now I can hear you clearly, speaking of love.

Since being appointed Poet Laureate in 2009, Carol Ann Duffy has flung herself with great vigour into the task of trying to prove that in the modern news-saturated and celebrity-addled age, public poetry can still find things to say that other forms can't. Her first poem as Laureate was a furious sonnet, published in the *Guardian* (but subsequently removed from its website), about the MPs' expenses scandal. She has also written about the footballer David Beckham and his achilles injury, about the erupting volcano in Iceland, about the Afghan war, about climate change and about gay rights. Indeed, it's hard to think of things her public poetry hasn't touched. The achievement is that, time and time again, she finds memorable and even useful words. Here is her response, for instance, to the Scottish independence referendum of September 2014, published on the morning after the vote. The Gaelic line at the beginning simply means 'I love you':

Tha gaol agam ort.
A thistle can draw blood,
so can a rose,
growing together
where the river flows, shared currency,
across a border it can never know;
where, somewhen, Rabbie Burns might swim,
or pilgrim Keats come walking
out of love for him.
Aye, here's to you,
cousins, sisters, brothers,
in your brave, bold, brilliant land:
the thistle jags our hearts,
take these roses
from our bloodied hands.

Nothing, it might be thought, is harder to write compelling poetry
about in the modern age than great state events. But in April 2011
Duffy had the job of writing a poem for the wedding of Kate
Middleton to the heir to the throne, Prince William, Duke of
Cambridge. It's pretty obvious that Duffy is a woman of the left, as
well as being gay. How would she deal with the challenge of avoid-
ing both schmaltz and toadying? Triumphantly, is the answer, in a
love poem centred on the image of the rings, and supposed to be
said by both bride and groom:

I might have raised your hand to the sky
to give you the ring surrounding the moon
or looked to twin the rings of your eyes
with mine
or added a ring to the rings of a tree
by forming a handheld circle with you, thee,
or walked with you
where a ring of church-bells
looped the fields,

or kissed a lipstick ring on your cheek,
a pressed flower,
or met with you
in the ring of an hour,
and another hour ...
I might
have opened your palm to the weather, turned, turned,
till your fingers were ringed in rain
or held you close,
they were playing our song,
in the ring of a slow dance
or carved our names
in the rough ring of a heart
or heard the ring of an owl's hoot
as we headed home in the dark,
or the ring, first thing,
of chorusing birds
waking the house,
or given the ring of a boat, rowing the lake,
or the ring of swans, monogamous, two,
or the watery rings made by the fish
as they leaped and splashed
or the ring of the sun's reflection there ...
I might have tied
a blade of grass,
a green ring for your finger,
or told you the ring of a sonnet by heart,
or brought you a lichen ring
found on a warm wall,
or given a ring of ice in winter
or in the snow,
sung with you the five gold rings of a carol,
or stolen a ring of your hair,
or whispered the word in your ear
that brought us here,

where nothing and no one is wrong,
and therefore I give you this ring.

One last example of public poetry still alive: in 2009 the two last British Army World War I veterans, Harry Patch and Henry Allingham, died. Britain has been obsessed by this war, in part thanks to its poets, for a very long time, and the BBC asked Duffy to compose a poem in response. She called it 'Last Post':

In all my dreams, before my helpless sight,
He plunges at me, guttering, choking, drowning.
If poetry could tell it backwards, true, begin
that moment shrapnel scythed you to the stinking mud ...
but you get up, amazed, watch bled bad blood
run upwards from the slime into its wounds;
see lines and lines of British boys rewind
back to their trenches, kiss the photographs from home –
mothers, sweethearts, sisters, younger brothers
not entering the story now
to die and die and die.
Dulce – No – Decorum – No – Pro patria mori.
You walk away.
You walk away; drop your gun (fixed bayonet)
like all your mates do too –
Harry, Tommy, Wilfred, Edward, Bert –
and light a cigarette.
There's coffee in the square,
warm French bread
and all those thousands dead
are shaking dried mud from their hair
and queuing up for home. Freshly alive,
a lad plays Tipperary to the crowd, released
from History; the glistening, healthy horses fit for heroes,
    kings.
You lean against a wall,

your several million lives still possible
and crammed with love, work, children, talent, English
    beer, good food.
You see the poet tuck away his pocket-book and smile.
If poetry could truly tell it backwards,
then it would.

If she carries on like this, there's every chance that Carol Ann Duffy, spreading her work through popular newspapers and broadcasters, will have something of the impact on the more liberal, feminised Britain of the early twenty-first century that Rudyard Kipling had on the Britain of Empire's zenith.

In the previous chapter we saw examples of equally good public poetry being made in Scotland. In Wales, Gillian Clarke, the national poet there, produces raw and sensuous verse about rural life. Clarke is a woman of her times: like Duffy, she has been addressing one of the great anxieties of the new century, climate change. Here, the challenge is to write poetry that doesn't shrink from what's happening, but isn't so apocalyptic or loaded with science that it puts readers off. Her poem about a polar bear is one example of her response:

Snowlight and sunlight, the lake glacial.
Too bright to open my eyes
in the dazzle and doze
of a distant January afternoon.
It's long ago and the house naps in the plush silence
of a house asleep, like absence,
I'm dreaming on the white bear's shoulder,
paddling the slow hours, my fingers in his fur.
His eyes are glass, each hair a needle of light.
He's pegged by his claws to the floor like a shirt on the
    line.
He is a soul. He is what death is. He is transparency,
a loosening floe on the sea.

But I want him alive.
I want him fierce
with belly and breath and growl and beating heart,
I want him dangerous,
I want to follow him over the snows
between the immaculate earth and now,
between the silence and the shot that rang
over the ice at the top of the globe,
when the map of the earth was something we knew by
   heart,
and they had not shot the bear,
had not loosed the ice,
had not, had not …

Reading a cross-section of contemporary British poetry, one of the things that distinguishes it from, say, journalism or broadcasting is that the different tones and even words of different parts of these islands persist into this century. Poetry is simply less homogeneous, less pasteurised, than other ways of writing. Liz Berry is a young poet from the Black Country, now working in Birmingham, who freely uses the distinctive language of her region. The following poem, 'Birmingham Roller', is concerned with the local obsession with tumbling pigeons. The following glossary may help: 'wench' is an affectionately meant name for a woman; 'yowm' means 'you are'; 'tranklement' is bits and bobs, or ornaments; 'onds' are hands; 'jimmucking' is shaking; and 'donny' means hand:

Wench, yowm the colour of ower town:
concrete, steel, oily rainbow of the cut.

Ower streets am in yer wings,
ower factory chimdeys plumes on yer chest,

yer heart's the china ower owd girls dust
in their tranklement cabinets.

Bred to dazzlin in backyards by men
whose onds grew soft as feathers

just to touch you, cradle you from egg
through each jeth-defying tumble.

Little acrobat of the terraces,
we'm winged when we gaze at you

jimmucking the breeze, somersaulting through
the white breathed prayer of January

and rolling back up like a babby's yo-yo
caught by the open donny of the clouds.

Alice Oswald's poetry is rooted in the West Country: she lives at
Dartington in Devon. Trained in the classics at Oxford, and then
as a gardener, she seems influenced by Geoffrey Hill among others.
There is a richness and a squelching intensity about her poems,
which include the very long 'Dart' from 2002, an account of walking
the length of the Devon river, told through a medley of voices and
characters – in this extract, a lonely walker, not far from the river's
source:

What I love is one foot in front of another. South south
    west and down the contours.
I go slipping between Black Ridge and White Horse Hill
    into a bowl of the moor where echoes can't get out.

Listen, a lark spinning around one note splitting and
    mending it

and I find you in the reeds, a trickle coming out of a bank,
    a foal of a river

one step-width water
of linked stones
trills in the stones
glides in the trills
eels in the glides
in each eel a fingerwidth of sea

in walking boots, with twenty pounds on my back: spare
    socks, compass, map, water purifier so I
can drink from streams, seeing the cold floating spread out
    above the morning,

tent, torch, chocolate not much else.

Which'll make it longish, almost unbearable between my
    evening meal and sleeping,
when I've got as far as stopping, sitting in the tent door
    with no book, no saucepan, not so much as a stick
to support the loneliness

he sits clasping his knees, holding his face low down
    between them,
he watches black slugs,
he makes a little den of his smells and small thoughts
he thinks up a figure far away on the tors
waving, so if something does happen,
if night comes down and he has to leave the path
then we've seen each other, somebody knows where we are.

In the English tradition – I'm thinking of Herbert, Henry Vaughan, Shakespeare and Ted Hughes – poetry about nature tends to be also poetry about haunted landscapes, with stories of the spirit in them. A short poem by Alice Oswald from 2005, addressed to the moon, suggests that this tradition remains alive: even now, modern Britain isn't all sodium streetlights and easy explanations.

I will give you one glimpse
a glimpse of the moon's grievance
whose appearance is all pocks and points
that look like frost-glints

I will wave my hand to her
in her first quarter
when the whole world is against her
shadowy exposure of her centre

o the moon loves to wander
I will go clockwise and stare
when she is huge when she is half elsewhere
half naked, in struggle with the air

and growing rounder and rounder
a pert peering creature
I love her sidling and awkward
when she's not quite circular

o criminal and ingrown
skinned animal o moon
carrying inside yourself your own
death's head, your dark one

why do you chop yourself away
piece by piece, to that final trace
of an outline of ice
on a cupful of space?

In Scotland, Kathleen Jamie made her reputation as a poet concerned with living inside a natural world which has its own spiritual reality and can constantly startle. She writes in both English and Scots. This is a poem called, with admirable Scots economy, 'Poem':

I walk at the land's edge,
turning in my mind
a private predicament.
Today the sea is indigo.
Thirty years an adult
same mind, same
ridiculous quandaries
but every time the sea
appears differently: today
a tumultuous dream,
flinging its waves ashore —

Nothing resolved,
I tread back over the moor —
but every time the moor
appears differently: this evening,
tufts of bog-cotton
unbutton themselves in the wind —
and then comes the road
so wearily familiar
the old shining road
that leads everywhere

Scottish politics in recent years have been more turbulent, and drawn in far more people, than in England; you would expect Scottish poets therefore to be more political, and you'd be right. Kathleen Jamie has made two interesting interventions in the current debate about Scottish independence. 2014 marked not only the Scottish referendum but the seven hundredth anniversary of the epic battle of Bannockburn, in which Robert the Bruce defeated a much larger English army and secured Scottish independence for centuries. The site of the battle is being renovated for tourists, and was the scene of a large celebration. There was a competition for a poem to be inscribed on a rotunda in the middle of the battlefield. Would it be Anglophobic? Would it be tub-thumpingly patriotic, with a swagger in its kilt? It would not: Jamie produced a short and very beautiful poem about love of country which is inclusive, not exclusive – read those last two lines carefully:

Here lies our land: every airt
Beneath swift clouds, glad glints of sun,
Belonging to none but itself.
We are mere transients, who sing
Its westlin' winds and fernie braes,
Northern lights and siller tides,
Small folk playing our part.
'Come all ye', the country says.
You win me, who take me most to heart.

Jamie has also written national reflections, such as her famous 'Mr and Mrs Scotland are Dead', which, taking its start from letters found on an old rubbish dump, dryly laments the cosy Unionist Scotland of the 1960s – 'fair but cool, showery but nevertheless …' which now seems so far away. In jollier mood, her 1987 poem 'The Way We Live' confronts the slippy speed and variousness of modern life:

Pass the tambourine, let me bash out praises
to the Lord God of movement, to Absolute
non-friction, flight, and the scary side:
death by avalanche, birth by failed contraception.
Of chicken tandoori and reggae, loud, from tenements,
commitment, driving fast and unswerving
friendship. Of tee-shirts on pulleys, giros and Bombay,
barmen, dreaming waitresses with many fake-gold
bangles. Of airports, impulse, and waking to uncertainty,
to strip-lights, motorways, or that pantheon –
the mountains. To overdrafts and grafting
and the fit slow pulse of wipers as you're
creeping over Rannoch, while the God of moorland

walks abroad with his entourage of freezing fog,
his bodyguard of snow.
Of endless gloaming in the North, of Asiatic swelter,
to launderettes, anecdotes, passions and exhaustion,
Final Demands and dead men, the skeletal grip
of government. To misery and elation; mixed,
the sod and caprice of landlords.
To the way it fits, the way it is, the way it seems
to be: let me bash out praises – pass the tambourine

So far, and not for reasons of political correctness, this has been a chapter of women poets, but it's time to introduce a male voice. Because the Scottish question, and therefore the future of the United Kingdom, remains so live, I want to include a couple of the Scottish academic and poet Robert Crawford's reflections from the pro-independence side of the argument. The first, 'Declaration', demonstrates that to be in favour of independence doesn't mean that you see your country through rose-tinted spectacles – or indeed thistle-tinted spectacles:

My name is Scotland. I am an alcoholic.
Sexism runs through me as through a stick of rock.
For all my blotchy pinkness, I am determined
To be less prim about my gene-pool, more airily
    cosmopolitan;
To love my inner Mary, my Floral Clock and John Thou
    Shalt Knox.
I can live fine without nuclear subs.
I've built far too many warships.
All I want now is my dignity back,
To stand on my own unsteady feet,
Sobered up, but not too sober, to renew
My auld alliance with this tipsy planet,
My dependence
And my independence.

Crawford remains an optimist about Scotland, however, as this poem, 'The Scottish Constitution', from his 2014 collection *Testament* shows:

> It must contain silver sands. It must hold water
> In the shape of lochans, hydro dams, and firths.
>
> It must be just, in the sense both of perjink*
> And even-handed, shaking hands with all.
>
> It must be old, with the wisdom of the rookie,
> It needs to know its onions, has to laugh
>
> And dance at weddings, all recriminations,
> Selkie stories, fiscal memoranda.
>
> It must be shy, tongue-tied, then eloquent,
> Catching your eye and holding it for ever,
>
> However far you go, to whatever shores,
> Atolls or cities, it must hold you fast.

I don't know about you, but that's a place I wouldn't mind living. Does Robert Crawford actually want Scotland to become independent, however? He does: this is his short poem 'Reveille':

> Wake up, new nation,
> Stretch yourself. It's time
> To fling the covers back, and sing,
> Alarm-clock loud, a sharpened trill of song
> Greeting the daylight now that Dawn has broken,
> You who have slept so long – too long –
> With one eye open.

---

* Neat, precise.

Well, we will see. Politics does matter: its failure spreads a generalised depression while possible successes offer us all new ways ahead. The Scottish question is an unusual one in that it engages the entrails and stomach, as well as the mind. There has been noticeably little poetry written about the politics of the EU, or indeed austerity. Perhaps that's partly because satire is done so differently now.

If political satire in poetry seems to be tottering, however, more generalised satire isn't. Wendy Cope was born in Kent, and spent the first part of her adult life as a teacher before moving into publishing and journalism. Her breakthrough collection of poetry, *Making Cocoa for Kingsley Amis*, came out in 1986, and in 1998 she topped a poll as the popular favourite to replace Ted Hughes as Poet Laureate. There's a tradition of what we might call the higher light verse in Britain, including Hilaire Belloc, G.K. Chesterton, T.S. Eliot and, in some of his moods, Kingsley Amis himself. 'Light' need not mean unserious: in some respects the false-naïve style of Stevie Smith could be called 'light', yet she was one of the most deadly serious poets of the 1950s. Cope can often sound like Smith, although she's a happier soul:

Bloody men are like bloody buses –
You wait for about a year
And as soon as one approaches your stop
Two or three others appear.

You look at them flashing their indicators,
Offering you a ride.
You're trying to read the destinations,
You haven't much time to decide.

If you make a mistake, there is no turning back.
Jump off, and you'll stand there and gaze
While the cars and the taxis and lorries go by
And the minutes, the hours, the days.

Cope writes a lot about love and its idiocies – and about modern poetry too, including this small gem about the kind of poetry reading many of us, arriving with hope in our hearts, have endured:

Everybody in this room is bored.
The poems drag, the voice and gestures irk.
He can't be interrupted or ignored.

Poor fools, we came here of our own accord
And some of us have paid to hear this jerk.
Everybody in the room is bored.

The silent cry goes up, 'How long, O Lord?'
But nobody will scream or go berserk.
He won't be interrupted or ignored.

Or hit by eggs, or savaged by a horde
Of desperate people maddened by his work.
Everybody in the room is bored,

Except the poet. We are his reward,
Pretending to indulge his every quirk.
He won't be interrupted or ignored.

At last it's over. How we all applaud!
The poet thanks us with a modest smirk.
Everybody in the room was bored.
He wasn't interrupted or ignored.

So Cope, whose books sell by the barrowload, is mainly a poet who hopes to entertain and amuse us – isn't she?

Write to amuse? What an appalling suggestion!
I write to make people anxious and miserable and to
worsen their indigestion.

Ursula Askham Fanthorpe, always 'U.A.', who died in 2009, was born, like Cope, in Kent, and also spent much of her working life as a teacher, in her case at the very posh Cheltenham Ladies' College. It was only after changing careers, and becoming a receptionist at a Bristol hospital, that she began to write poetry seriously. Once she'd started, she found she could hardly stop – book after book came out, delighting an ever-widening circle of readers. Fanthorpe is famous for taking an odd angle on the world, and is also a great celebrant of England and Englishness, as in this short extract from her early poem 'Earthed':

> But earthed for all that, in the chalky
> Kent mud, thin sharp ridges between wheel-tracks, in
> Surrey's wild gravel,
>
> In serious Cotswold uplands, where
> Limestone confines the verges like yellow teeth,
> And trees look sideways.

She has a sense of history as strong as Thomas Hardy's, and some-times as mordant, as in her poem about, as it were, the year zero – when BC became AD:

> This was the moment when Before
> Turned into After, and the future's
> Uninvented timekeepers presented arms.
> This was the moment when nothing
> Happened. Only dull peace
> Sprawled boringly over the earth.
> This was the moment when even energetic Romans
> Could find nothing better to do
> Than counting heads in remote provinces.
> And this was the moment
> When a few farm workers and three
> Members of an obscure Persian sect

Walked haphazard by starlight straight
Into the kingdom of heaven.

That's beautiful, precise, and casts an angled, unfamiliar light on a
very familiar story; but it doesn't, perhaps, explain quite why U.A.
Fanthorpe inspires fanatical devotion. On the other hand, the
following poem, 'Atlas', from her 1995 collection *Safe as Houses*,
does. It's about the kind of love almost no other poets describe, and
which, however, keeps the world going.

There is a kind of love called maintenance
Which stores the WD40 and knows when to use it;

Which checks the insurance, and doesn't forget
The milkman; which remembers to plant bulbs;

Which answers letters; which knows the way
The money goes; which deals with dentists

And Road Fund Tax and meeting trains,
And postcards to the lonely; which upholds

The permanently rickety elaborate
Structures of living, which is Atlas.

And maintenance is the sensible side of love,
Which knows what time and weather are doing
To my brickwork; insulates my faulty wiring;
Laughs at my dryrotten jokes; remembers
My need for gloss and grouting; which keeps
My suspect edifice upright in air,
As Atlas did the sky.

Formidably cultured, a lesbian at times and in places when that was awkward, and a Quaker, Fanthorpe speaks for an Englishness which is reserved yet passionate, still on the surface yet boiling underneath. She reminds me, above all, of William Cowper, though she dodged his madness.

She is also sometimes compared to Craig Raine, the Oxford professor who with his friend Christopher Reid devised what has been called the 'Martian' school of poetry – poetry based on un-familiar second-takes, which disorientate and make the world seem fresh. Raine was born in County Durham. His father was a boxer who became a faith healer; his life was transformed by the English teacher at Barnard Castle school, a man who'd known W.H. Auden. Most of his adult life has been spent in academia, rather like a latter-day Matthew Arnold, periodically coming out for literary boxing matches and the publication of poetry.

The Raine angle – like Fanthorpe, acute, glancing, meant to make the mundane surprising – can be illustrated by his poem about a gardener from his 1978 book *The Onion, Memory*:

Up and down the lawn he walks with cycling hands
that tremble on the mower's stethoscope.

Creases blink behind his knees.
He stares at a promise of spray

and wrestles with Leviathan alone. Victorious,
he bangs the grass box empty like clog …

The shears are a Y that wants to be an X –
he holds them like a water diviner,

and hangs them upside down, a wish-bone.
His hands row gently on the plunger

and detonate the Earth. He smacks the clods
and dandles weeds on trembling prongs.

They lie, a heap of dusters softly shaken out.
At night he plays a pattering hose, fanned

like a drummer's brush. His aim is to grow
the Kremlin – the roses' tight pink cupolas

ring bells ... For this he stands in weariness,
tired as a teapot, feeling the small of his back.

One of the challenges for modern poets, rather as for modern
painters, is how to find ways to make things new – after all those
predecessors, is there anything fresh to say, any fresh ways to say it?
I think it's fair to say that Craig Raine has found a new way to make
poetry. The danger is that it can seem academic, a trick of the light,
rather than an original worldview. It's a big risk, but time and again
Raine has demonstrated that he – if not his many imitators – can
still pull it off. A classic challenge for the poet (we've already had
William Cowper, John Davidson and Louis MacNeice) is to find
something new to say about that mundane miracle, snowfall. Here
is Raine's 'How Snow Falls':

Like the unshaven prickle
of a sharpened razor,
this new coldness in the air,
the pang
of something intangible.
Filling our eyes,
the sinusitis of perfume
without the perfume.
And then love's vertigo,
love's exactitude,
this snow, this transfiguration
we never quite get over.

By now it may seem that modern English poets don't tend to write very much about the biggest subjects – about war, or overseas, or the state of the world generally. James Fenton, born in Lincolnshire in 1949, has spent most of his working life as a journalist-cum-war reporter and commentator; but he is also considered by some shrewd judges to be the greatest poet in English of his generation. Part of the crowd of young writers that gathered around the *New Statesman* in the 1970s, he was the quiet, droll, modest one among Martin Amis, Christopher Hitchens and Julian Barnes. His unforgettable 'German Requiem', looking back at the prime horror of the twentieth century, begins like this:

> It is not what they built. It is what they knocked down.
> It is not the houses. It is the spaces in between the houses.
> It is not the streets that exist. It is the streets that no
>   longer exist.
> It is not your memories which haunt you.
> It is not what you have written down.
> It is what you have forgotten, what you must forget.
> What you must go on forgetting all your life.
> And with any luck oblivion should discover a ritual.
> You will find out that you are not alone in the enterprise.
> Yesterday the very furniture seemed to reproach you.
> Today you take your place in the Widow's Shuttle.
>
> The bus is waiting at the southern gate
> To take you to the city of your ancestors
> Which stands on the hill opposite, with gleaming
>   pediments,
> As vivid as this charming square, your home.
> Are you shy? You should be. It is almost like a wedding,
> The way you clasp your flowers and give a little tug at your
>   veil. Oh,
> The hideous bridesmaids, it is natural that you should
>   resent them

Just a little, on this first day.
But that will pass, and the cemetery is not far.
Here comes the driver, flicking a toothpick into the gutter,
His tongue still searching between his teeth.
See, he has not noticed you. No one has noticed you.
It will pass, young lady, it will pass.

How comforting it is, once or twice a year,
To get together and forget the old times.
As on those special days, ladies and gentlemen,
When the boiled shirts gather at the graveside
And a leering waistcoat approaches the rostrum.
It is like a solemn pact between the survivors.
The mayor has signed it on behalf of the freemasonry.
The priest has sealed it on behalf of all the rest.
Nothing more need be said, and it is better that way —

The better for the widow, that she should not live in fear
    of surprise,
The better for the young man, that he should move at
    liberty between the armchairs,
The better that these bent figures who flutter among the
    graves
Tending the nightlights and replacing the
    chrysanthemums
Are not ghosts,
That they shall go home.
The bus is waiting, and on the upper terraces
The workmen are dismantling the houses of the dead.

But when so many had died, so many and at such speed,
There were no cities waiting for the victims.
They unscrewed the name-plates from the shattered
    doorways
And carried them away with the coffins.

So the squares and parks were filled with the eloquence of
    young cemeteries:
The smell of fresh earth, the improvised crosses
And all the impossible directions in brass and enamel.

So, living among us today there are traditionally skilled, alert poets writing on a huge range of important subjects; and very many of them are women.

But another question I asked at the beginning of this chapter was whether poetry today represents the full multicultural and mixed nature of modern Britain, which has been very rapidly changed by immigration. And the flat answer is: no, it doesn't. Black British poetry does have a profile; the trouble is, it tends to have only one name attached to it, that of the Rastafarian poet Benjamin Zephaniah. Born to a Barbadian father and a Jamaican mother in Birmingham's Handsworth district, he left his approved school at the age of just thirteen, and illiterate. Yet, fired by Jamaican culture and street politics, he has clawed his way up to the point where he was offered an OBE; although, as a determined anti-imperialist – as well as a vegan, a campaigner for electoral reform and a long-term critic of the British justice system – he refused it. Zephaniah's poetry is well-known to children and adults. Here is his 'The British', a witty reflection on the melting pot that is Britain today:

Take some Picts, Celts and Silures
And let them settle,
Then overrun them with Roman conquerors.

Remove the Romans after approximately 400 years
Add lots of Norman French to some
Angles, Saxons, Jutes and Vikings, then stir vigorously.

Mix some hot Chileans, cool Jamaicans, Dominicans,
Trinidadians and Bajans with some Ethiopians, Chinese,
Vietnamese and Sudanese.

Then take a blend of Somalians, Sri Lankans, Nigerians
And Pakistanis,
Combine with some Guyanese
And turn up the heat.

Sprinkle some fresh Indians, Malaysians, Bosnians,
Iraqis and Bangladeshis together with some
Afghans, Spanish, Turkish, Kurdish, Japanese
And Palestinians
Then add to the melting pot.

Leave the ingredients to simmer.

As they mix and blend allow their languages to flourish
Binding them together with English.

Allow time to be cool.

Add some unity, understanding, and respect for the future,
Serve with justice
And enjoy.

Note: All the ingredients are equally important. Treating
one ingredient better than another will leave a bitter
unpleasant taste.

Warning: An unequal spread of justice will damage the
people and cause pain. Give justice and equality to all.

That is, in the end, an optimistic and even perhaps slightly cosy
poem. By way of contrast, here is Zephaniah's furious response to
the miscarriage of justice after the 1993 murder of the black
London teenager Stephen Lawrence:

We know who the killers are,
We have watched them strut before us
As proud as sick Mussolinis,
We have watched them strut before us
Compassionless and arrogant,
They paraded before us,
Like angels of death
Protected by the law.

It is now an open secret
Black people do not have
Chips on their shoulders,
They just have injustice on their backs
And justice on their minds,
And now we know that the road to liberty
Is as long as the road from slavery.

The death of Stephen Lawrence
Has taught us to love each other
And never to take the tedious task
Of waiting for a bus for granted.
Watching his parents watching the cover-up
Begs the question
What are the trading standards here?
Why are we paying for a police force
That will not work for us?

The death of Stephen Lawrence
Has taught us
That we cannot let the illusion of freedom
Endow us with a false sense of security as we walk the
    streets,
The whole world can now watch
The academics and the super cops
Struggling to define institutionalised racism

As we continue to die in custody
As we continue emptying our pockets on the pavements,
And we continue to ask ourselves
Why is it so official
That black people are so often killed
Without killers?

We are not talking about war or revenge
We are not talking about hypothetics or possibilities,
We are talking about where we are now
We are talking about how we live now
In dis state
Under dis flag, (God Save the Queen),
And God save all those black children who want to grow
    up
And God save all the brothers and sisters
Who like raving,
Because the death of Stephen Lawrence
Has taught us that racism is easy when
You have friends in high places.
And friends in high places
Have no use whatsoever
When they are not your friends.

Dear Mr Condon,
Pop out of Teletubby land,
And visit reality,
Come to an honest place
And get some advice from your neighbours,
Be enlightened by our community,
Neglect your well-paid ignorance
Because
We know who the killers are.

There are, of course, plenty of other British poets of substance and of colour; it's just that Benjamin Zephaniah has seemed to loom so large. Because this book is about Britain, this archipelago, I have with great sadness excluded Derek Walcott of Saint Lucia, who may well be the greatest English-language poet writing at the moment. John Agard is another rebel child of the old Empire, but although he was born in Guyana in South America in 1949, he arrived in Britain in the 1970s and has lived here since. He has been a great proponent of poetry in schools, and is a hugely powerful performer, of the Adrian Mitchell school. With a Portuguese mother, he's had to put up with being called 'half-caste'; one of his strongest poems is his droll response:

Excuse me
standing on one leg
I'm half-caste.

Explain yuself
wha yu mean
when yu say half-caste
yu mean when Picasso
mix red an green
is a half-caste canvas?
explain yuself
wha yu mean
when yu say half-caste
yu mean when light an shadow
mix in de sky
is a half-caste weather?
well in dat case
england weather
nearly always half-caste
in fact some o dem cloud
half-caste till dem overcast
so spiteful dem don't want de sun pass

ah rass?
explain yuself
wha yu mean
when yu say half-caste
yu mean tchaikovsky
sit down at dah piano
an mix a black key
wid a white key
is a half-caste symphony?

Explain yuself
wha yu mean
Ah listening to yu wid de keen
half of mih ear
Ah looking at yu wid de keen
half of mih eye
an when I'm introduced to yu
I'm sure you'll understand
why I offer yu half-a-hand
an when I sleep at night
I close half-a-eye
consequently when I dream
I dream half-a-dream
an when moon begin to glow
I half-caste human being
cast half-a-shadow
but yu must come back tomorrow
wid de whole of yu eye
an de whole of yu ear
an de whole of yu mind.

an I will tell yu
de other half
of my story.

Jackie Kay is a Scottish poet, really: that's what she sounds like, and that's how she writes. She was born in Edinburgh in 1961 to a Scottish mother and a Nigerian father, and then adopted as a baby by a family of communists from Glasgow. She is black, however, and has recently made a pilgrimage to find her original family. Here's a short poem, 'George Square', after the place in Glasgow where protest marches traditionally end up, a tribute to her adoptive parents, lifelong peaceniks:

> My seventy-seven-year-old father
> put his reading glasses on
> to help my mother do the buttons
> on the back of her dress.
> 'What a pair the two of us are!'
> my mother said, 'Me with my sore wrist,
> you with your bad eyes, your soft thumbs!'
>
> And off they went, my two parents
> to march against the war in Iraq,
> him with his plastic hips. Her with her arthritis,
> waved at each other like old friends, flapping,
> where they'd met for so many marches over their years,
> for peace on earth, for pity's sake, for peace, for peace.

As that poem reminds us, apart from being more feminised and more ethnically mixed than in the past, modern Britain is also just much older. So we'd expect poetry to grapple with old age, death and bereavement as it affects us in the new century, rather than as it did in Tudor or Victorian times. Sure enough, we have 'oldie' poets writing about this relatively new subject in a fresh way. Clive James, who has been writing superb verse since the 1970s, would squirm and protest at being included in this group. Yet he himself has said that the imminence of death has given him a wonderful new subject: poets always need something challenging to write about, and fate has certainly dealt James an interesting hand lately.

Most of us, one way or another, will end up in a hospital, being assaulted by drugs and tubes, and deeply disorientated. Few of us, sadly, have the competence to reply, as James does, to 'My Latest Fever':

> My latest fever clad me in cold sweat
> And there I was, in hospital again,
> Drenched, and expecting an attack of bugs
> As devastating as the first few hours
> Of Barbarossa, with the Russian air force
> Caught on the ground and soldiers by the thousand
> Herded away to starve, while Stalin still
> Believed it couldn't happen. But instead
> The assault turned out to be as deadly dull
> As a bunch of ancient members of the Garrick
> Emerging from their hutch below the stairs
> To bore me from all angles as I prayed
> For sleep, which only came in fits and starts.
> Night after night was like that. Every day
> Was like the night before, a hit parade
> Of jazzed-up sequences from action movies.
> While liquid drugs were pumped into my wrist,
> My temperature stayed sky high. On the screen
> Deep in my head, heroes repaired themselves.
> In Rambo First Blood, Sly Stallone sewed up
> His own arm. Then Mark Wahlberg, star of Shooter,
> Assisted by Kate Mara, operated
> To dig the bullets from his body. Teeth
> Were gritted in both cases. No-one grits
> Like Sly: it looks like a piano sneering.
> Better, however, to be proof against
> All damage, as in Salt, where Angelina
> Jumps from a bridge onto a speeding truck
> And then from that truck to another truck.
> In North Korea, tortured for years on end,

She comes out with a split lip. All this mayhem
Raged in my brain with not a cliché scamped.
I saw the heroes march in line towards me
In slow-mo, with a wall of flame behind them,
And thought, as I have often thought, 'This is
The pits. How can I make it stop?' It stopped.
On the eleventh day, my temperature
Dived off the bridge like Catherine Zeta Jones
From the Petronas towers in Kuala Lumpur.
I had no vision of the final battle.
The drugs, in pill form now, drove back the bugs
Into the holes from which they had attacked.
It might have been a scene from Starship Troopers:
But no, I had returned to the real world.
They sent me home to sleep in a dry bed
Where I felt better than I had for months.
No need to make a drama of my rescue:
Having been saved was like a lease of life,
The thing itself, undimmed by images –
A thrill a minute simply for being so.

But the James poem about illness and old age that has established itself as an instant classic is his reflection on mortality while looking at a flame-coloured Japanese maple tree in the small back garden of his Cambridge house. It is a splendid example of how poetry, in the year 2015, can still speak to us freshly, and even shockingly, about what is all, and forever, around:

Your death, near now, is of an easy sort.
So slow a fading out brings no real pain.
Breath growing short
Is just uncomfortable. You feel the drain
Of energy, but thought and sight remain:

Enhanced, in fact. When did you ever see
So much sweet beauty as when fine rain falls
On that small tree
And saturates your brick back garden walls,
So many Amber Rooms and mirror halls?

Ever more lavish as the dusk descends
This glistening illuminates the air.
It never ends.
Whenever the rain comes it will be there,
Beyond my time, but now I take my share.

My daughter's choice, the maple tree is new.
Come autumn and its leaves will turn to flame.
What I must do
Is live to see that. That will end the game
For me, though life continues all the same:

Filling the double doors to bathe my eyes,
A final flood of colours will live on
As my mind dies,
Burned by my vision of a world that shone
So brightly at the last, and then was gone.

A similar kind of poem by the magnificent Scottish poet Douglas
Dunn was part of a sequence written after his wife's death in 1981:
again, it describes something that has become absolutely familiar in
contemporary Britain. It is called 'Second Opinion':

We came to Leeds for a second opinion.
After her name was called,
I waited among the apparently well
And those with bandaged eyes and dark spectacles.

A heavy mother shuffled with bad feet
And a stick, a pad over one eye,
Leaving her children warned in their seats.
The minutes went by like a winter.

They called me in. What moment worse
Than that young doctor trying to explain?
'It's large and growing.' 'What is?' 'Malignancy.'
'Why there? She's an artist!'

He shrugged and said, 'Nobody knows.'
He warned me that it might spread. 'Spread?'
My body ached to suffer like her twin
and touch the cure with lips and healing sesames.

No image, no straw to support me – nothing
To see or hear. No leaves rustling in sunlight.
Only the mind sliding against events
And the antiseptic whiff of destiny.

Professional anxiety –
His hand on my shoulder
Showing me the door, a scent of soap,
Medical fingers, and his wedding ring.

Approaching the end of this book – and I hope you've enjoyed some of it as much as I've enjoyed compiling all of it – there's a danger we are getting too gloomy, albeit on the gravest subject of all. I'm going to end, therefore, with some James Michie. A classicist, like so many of the best poets, best known for his translations of Horace's odes, he spent much of his life as a publisher, bringing out among other things Sylvia Plath's key books. He died of throat cancer in 2007, but not before delighting the readers of the *Oldie* magazine with his reflections on a modern old age. His poem 'Heigh-ho!', expressing his refusal to worry about the great causes, reminds me of Arthur Hugh Clough:

My days of global worrying are long gone.
I'm now a joker callused by the years.
When people badger me to comment on
Aids, clones, the owners only, nuclear fears ...
I simply wag my great big furry ears.

Deplorable, I know, but there you are.
As the arrival of the unthinkable nears –
Atomic chaos, a colliding star,
Calamitous climatic change – my dears,
I simply wag my great big furry ears.

I'm a part of it, so I can sympathise
With the world drenched in blood and sweat and tears,
And yet I somehow lack the enterprise
To act: I watch, reach for the glass that cheers –
And simply wag my great big furry ears.

A former conscientious objector, Michie was in fact a brave man,
with an understated British stoicism about what is, ultimately,
intolerable. Here is 'Hospital Joke':

Shelley had his little whine
the 'superincumbent hours' –
Mine is life without weather and wine,
Nothing but slops and flowers.

The moral of this verse is:
However dire one's ills,
Be thankful for small nurses
And blue remembered pills.

Short, and stoic: but not as short and stoic as his last poem, 'Cancer,
or the Biter Bit':

I used to fancy crabmeat as a treat:
Now Crab's the epicure, and I'm the meat.

I entitled this last chapter 'Here Comes Everybody', but I have signally and shamefully failed to deliver on that promise. What, no Christopher Logue? No George Macbeth, R.S. Thomas or Derek Mahon? No Andrew Motion or Christopher Reid? I know, I know, I know – many lovers of many fine poets will be shaking their fists, or at least gnashing their teeth. And I'm sorry. The trouble is that modern British poetry is such a crowded field that there isn't room to herd all of the prize beasts into a book this size. But I hope I've answered the real question, the final question: does poetry still matter to our society? If it's reporting well on our hopes and fears, the world around us, and who we feel we currently are, then poetry is doing its old job, the job it has always done. What a poet looks like has changed – a poet is now more likely to have a uterus, for a start. Poems don't look the same, either. They flash up on our screens, surrounded by irritating adverts; or they are printed safely towards the back of posh newspapers and magazines; sometimes they suddenly display themselves on hoardings, or in the London Underground. Poetry books are more beautifully designed than I can ever remember, yet they are still relatively unpopular; their sales declined by 25 per cent from 2009 to 2013. In that year, one of the feistiest and most adventurous independent poetry publishers, Salt, announced that it was no longer viable to produce single-author volumes.

And yet ... Well-chosen anthologies are doing very well; poetry prizes still make headlines; poets such as Liz Lochhead and Carol Ann Duffy remain 'news'. And crucially, what poems are, what poems do – that hasn't changed. They are still bringing us the freshest of fresh news, packets of thought at full tilt, straight from the front line of being alive. Ever since Caedmon amused and impressed a bunch of rain-sodden monks with his alliteration and metre, poetry has been central to all our cultures on these islands. It still is.

Acknowledgements

'Happy Ending' and 'Kissing' by Fleur Adcock. © Fleur Adcock. Reproduced by kind permission of Bloodaxe Books.

'Half Caste' by John Agard. Copyright ©1996 by John Agard. Reproduced by kind permission of John Agard c/o Caroline Sheldon Literary Agency Ltd.

'To Be a Baby Born Without Limbs' by Kingsley Amis. © The Estate of Kingsley Amis.

'The Death of King Arthur' by Simon Armitage. © Simon Armitage. Reproduced by kind permission of Faber & Faber Ltd.

'Epitaph on a Tyrant', 'September 1, 1939' and 'Spain' by W.H. Auden. © The Estate of W.H. Auden. Reproduced with permission of Curtis Brown Group Ltd, London.

'Munition Wages' by Madeline Ida Bedford. © The Estate of Madeline Ida Bedford.

'Lord Lundy' by Hilaire Belloc. From *Cautionary Tales for Children*. Reproduced by permission of Peters Fraser & Dunlop (www.petersfraserdunlop.com) on behalf of the Estate of Hilaire Belloc.

'Birmingham Roller' by Liz Berry. From *Black Country*. Published by Chatto & Windus. Reproduced by permission of The Random House Group Ltd.

ACKNOWLEDGEMENTS

'Death in Leamington' and 'A Subaltern's Love Song' by John
  Betjeman. From *Collected Poems*. © The Estate of John
  Betjeman 1955, 1958, 1962, 1964, 1968, 1970, 1979, 1981,
  1982, 2001. Reproduced by permission of John Murray Press,
  an imprint of Hodder and Stoughton Limited.
'Beachcomber' and 'Hamnavoe Market' by George Mackay
  Brown. Copyright © 2005 The Estate of George Mackay
  Brown. Reproduced by permission of John Murray Press, an
  imprint of Hodder and Stoughton Limited.
'What the Chairman told Tom' by Basil Bunting. © The Estate of
  Basil Bunting. Reproduced by kind permission of Bloodaxe
  Books.
'On a General Election', 'On Some South African Novelists' and
  'We Are Like Worlds' by Roy Campbell. © The Estate of Roy
  Campbell.
'Polar' by Gillian Clarke. © Gillian Clarke. Reproduced by kind
  permission of Carcanet Press.
'Women at Munition Making' by Mary Gabrielle Collins. © The
  Estate of Mary Gabrielle Collins.
'Epistemology of Poetry' and 'Guided Missiles Experimental
  Range' by Robert Conquest. Reproduced with permission of
  Curtis Brown Group Ltd, London, on behalf of Robert
  Conquest. Copyright © 1956.
'Bloody Men', 'A Reading' and 'Serious Concerns' by Wendy Cope.
  © Wendy Cope. Reproduced by kind permission of Faber &
  Faber Ltd.
'Stately Homes of England' by Noël Coward. Copyright ©
  NC Aventales AG 1937 by permission of Alan Brodie
  Representation Ltd. (www.alanbrodie.com)
'Declaration', 'Reveille' and 'The Scottish Constitution' by Robert
  Crawford. © James Crawford. Reproduced by permission of
  The Random House Group Ltd.
'They Who in Folly or Mere Greed' by Cecil Day-Lewis. From
  Complete Poems. Published by Sinclair Stevenson. Reproduced
  by permission of The Random House Group Ltd.

642

'Hand', 'Last Post', 'Rings' and 'September 2014' by Carol Ann
     Duffy. Licensed by Rogers, Coleridge and White on behalf of
     Carol Ann Duffy.
'Second Opinion' by Douglas Dunn. © Douglas Dunn.
     Reproduced by kind permission of United Agents LLP.
'The Waste Land', 'The Love Song of J. Alfred Prufrock' and 'Little
     Gidding' by T.S. Eliot. © The Estate of T.S. Eliot. Reproduced
     by kind permission of Faber & Faber Ltd.
'Atlas', 'BC:AD' and 'Earthed' by U.A. Fanthorpe. From *New and
     Collected Poems* (Enitharmon Press, 2010).
'Morning has Broken' and 'Peace' by Eleanor Farjeon. 'Morning
     has Broken' is taken from *Blackbird Has Spoken*, published by
     Macmillan.
'German Requiem' by James Fenton. © James Fenton.
     Reproduced by kind permission of Faber & Faber Ltd.
'Glisk of the Great', 'Letter from Italy' and 'Property' by Robert
     Garioch. © The Estate of Robert Garioch.
'The Cubical Domes' by David Gascoyne. From *New Collected
     Poems* (Enitharmon, 2014).
'1915' and 'The Dead Boche' by Robert Graves. © Robert Graves.
     Reproduced by kind permission of Carcanet Press.
'Decorating and Insurance Factors' by Bill Griffiths. First published in
     Durham & Other Sequences (Sheffield: West House Books, 2002).
'On the Move' by Thom Gunn. © The Estate of Thom Gunn.
     Reproduced by kind permission of Faber & Faber Ltd.
'Casualty', 'Cure at Troy' and 'From the Frontier of Writing' by
     Seamus Heaney. © The Estate of Seamus Heaney. Reproduced
     by kind permission of Faber & Faber Ltd.
'Elegies for the Dead' and 'Freedom Come All Ye' by Hamish
     Henderson. 'Song of the D-Day Dodgers' by Hamish
     Henderson and Harry Pym. Reproduced by permission of the
     Estate of Hamish Henderson.
'Mrs Albion You've Got a Lovely Daughter' by Adrian Henri.
     Licensed by Rogers, Coleridge and White on behalf of the
     Estate of the late Adrian Henri.

'Look Ahead' by Michael Horovitz. Copyright © Michael
   Horovitz 2015. The poem first appeared in *Growing Up:
   Selected Poems & Pictures 1951–'79* (Allison & Busby, 1979).
'Blue Flannel Suit', 'Crow's Nerve Fails' and 'Hawk Rooting' by
   Ted Hughes. © The Estate of Ted Hughes. Reproduced by
   kind permission of Faber & Faber Ltd.
'Japanese Maple' and 'My Latest Fever' by Clive James. © Clive
   James.
'Poem', 'Here Lies our Land' and 'The Way We Live' by Kathleen
   Jamie. © Kathleen Jamie. Reproduced by kind permission of
   Enitharmon Press and Bloodaxe Books.
'Answers' and 'The Young Ones' by Elizabeth Jennings. From *The
   Collected Poems*, published by Carcanet Press. Reproduced by
   kind permission of Penguin Classics.
'Having to Live in the Country', 'On Raglan Road' and 'Stony Grey
   Soil' by Patrick Kavanagh. © The Estate of Patrick Kavanagh.
'George Square' by Jackie Kay. © Jackie Kay. Reproduced by kind
   permission of Bloodaxe Books.
'Annus Mirabilis', 'As Bad as a Mile', 'Best Society', 'Homage to
   Government', 'Letters to Monica', 'This Be the Verse' and 'Toads'
   by Philip Larkin. © The Estate of Philip Larkin. Reproduced
   by kind permission of Faber & Faber Ltd.
'Unrelated Incidents – No.3' by Tom Leonard. From *Outside the
   Narrative* (Etruscan Books/WordPower, 2010).
'A Net to Catch the Winds' and 'Scotland the What?' by Maurice
   Lindsay. © The Estate of Maurice Lindsay.
'For My Grandmother Knitting' and 'From a Mouse' by Liz
   Lochhead. © Liz Lochhead.
'The Butchers', 'Ceasefire', 'The Ice Cream Man' and 'Wounds' by
   Michael Longley. © Michael Longley 2007.
'Human Cylinders' by Mina Loy. © The Estate of Mina Loy.
'Patriot' and 'Small Boy' by Norman MacCaig. © The Estate of
   Norman MacCaig.
'A Drunk Man Looks at a Thistle', 'On a Raised Beach' and 'The
   Watergaw' by Hugh MacDiarmid. © The Estate of Hugh

MacDiarmid. Reproduced by kind permission of Carcanet Press.

'Death Valley' and 'Hallaig' by Sorley MacLean. © The Estate of Sorley MacLean. Reproduced by kind permission of Carcanet Press.

'Autumn Journal', 'Bagpipe Music' and 'Snow' by Louis MacNeice. From *Collected Poems*, published by Faber & Faber.

'First Day at School' and 'Youngman's Death' by Roger McGough. © Roger McGough.

'Cancer, or the Biter Bit', 'Heigh-ho!' and 'Hospital Joke' by James Michie. From *Collected Poems*. Published by Sinclair Stevenson. Reproduced by permission of The Random House Group Ltd.

'A Puppy Called Puberty', 'A Dog Called Elderly', 'Saw it in the Papers' and 'Ten Ways to Avoid Lending Your Wheelbarrow to Anybody' by Adrian Mitchell. Licensed by United Agents on behalf of the Estate of the late Adrian Mitchell.

'Clydegrad', 'The Coin', 'Open the Doors' and 'Loch Ness Monster's Song' by Edwin Morgan. © The Estate of Edwin Morgan. Reproduced by kind permission of Carcanet Press.

'Horses' by Edwin Muir. © The Estate of Edwin Muir. Reproduced by kind permission of Faber & Faber Ltd.

'Dart' and 'Moon Hymn' by Alice Oswald. © Alice Oswald. Reproduced by kind permission of Faber & Faber Ltd.

'If You Had To Hazard A Guess Who Would You Say Your Poetry Is For?' and 'On Time for Once' by Brian Patten. Licensed by Rogers, Coleridge and White on behalf of Brian Patten.

'John Martson Advises Anger' by Peter Porter. Licensed by Rogers, Coleridge and White on behalf of the Estate of the late Peter Porter.

'Canto XIII', 'Homage to Sextus Propertius' and 'Hugh Selwyn Mauberley' by Ezra Pound. © The Estate of Ezra Pound. Reproduced by kind permission of Faber & Faber Ltd.

'Gardener' and 'How Snow Falls' by Craig Raine. 'Gardener' copyright © Craig Raine, 1978. 'How Snow Falls' copyright © Craig Raine, 2010.

'Naming of Parts' by Henry Reed. © The Estate of Henry Reed. Reproduced by kind permission of Carcanet Press.

'The Death of Actaeon', 'Hammersmith Winter' and 'Law of the Island' by Robin Robertson. Licensed by Rogers, Coleridge and White on behalf of Robin Robertson.

'Base Details' by Siegfried Sassoon. Copyright © Siegfried Sassoon by kind permission of the Estate of George Sassoon.

'All Things Hurry', 'Alone in the Woods', 'Not Waving but Drowning' and 'Valuable' by Stevie Smith. © The Estate of Stevie Smith. Reproduced by kind permission of Faber & Faber Ltd.

'Kynd Kittock's Land' by Sydney Goodsir Smith. © The Estate of Sydney Goodsir Smith. Reproduced by kind permission of Alma Books.

'Among Those Killed In The Dawn Raid Was A Man Aged A Hundred', 'A Refusal to Mourn the Death, by Fire, of a Child in London' and 'Fern Hill' by Dylan Thomas. From *The Collected Poems of Dylan Thomas: The New Centenary Edition* (Orion). Reproduced with the permission of The Trustees for the Copyrights of Dylan Thomas.

'A Song about Major Eatherly' by John Wain. Copyright © The Estate of John Wain 2015.

'The Red, White and Green' by Harri Webb. Licensed with permission of Dr Meic Stephens.

'The British' and 'What Stephen Lawrence Has Taught Us' by Benjamin Zephaniah. 'The British' taken from WICKED WORLD (Puffin, 2000). Text copyright © Benjamin Zephaniah, 2000 Illustrations copyright © Sarah Symonds, 2000; 'What Stephen Lawrence Has Taught Us' © Benjamin Zephaniah. Reproduced by kind permission of United Agents LLP.

Index of Poets

Poems by unknown or anonymous
    authors are listed by title.
Entries in **bold** indicate pages on
    which a poem, or a poet's work,
    is quoted.

Adcock, Fleur **531–2**
Agard, John **632–3**
Alcock, Mary 257, **258–9**
Amis, Kingsley 506, **522–3**, 534,
    620
Armitage, Simon **25–6**
Arnold, Matthew **325–6**, 624
Askew, Anne 63, **64–8**, 92, 605
Auden, W.H. 462, **466–72**, 477,
    484, 488–9, 510, 511, 513,
    514–15, 517, 523, 624

Bale, John 82, **83–4**, 95
Barber, Mary **226–8**
Barbour, John **43–4**
Bedford, Madeline Ida **404–5**
Behn, Aphra 171, **176–8**, 179
Belloc, Hilaire **478–9**, 480, 484,
    620
Beowulf 6

Berry, Liz 606, **612–13**
Betjeman, John **484–7**, 551, 582
'Bevis of Hampton' 22
Bisset, James 256, **257–8**
Blake, William 161, 171, 234, 245,
    246–51, 253, 256, 259, 278,
    281, 376, 416, 432, 549
Bradstreet, Anne **164–7**
Brooke, Rupert **390–5**, 397–8, 419
Browning, Elizabeth Barrett 342,
    343–9
Browning, Robert 314, 336, **341–2**,
    343, 442
Bunting, Basil 462, 509, **510–11**
Burns, Robert xi, 180, 229, 259,
    260–7, 268, 278, 286, 439, 451,
    580, 590, 608
Byron, George Gordon, Lord 271,
    278, 302, **303–9**

Caedmon **1–2**, 3–7, 12, 640
Campbell, Roy 476, **477**
Carroll, Lewis (Charles Lutwidge
    Dodgson) 333, **334–6**
Cavendish, Margaret, Duchess of
    Newcastle 178, **179–82**

Chapman, George 296
Chaucer, Geoffrey 21, 22, 31, 35–6, **37–42**, 43–5, 48, 54, 112, 240, 278, 296
Chesterton, G.K. **480–3**, 484, 620
Cibber, Colley 605
Clancy, Thomas Owen **14–15**
Clare, John 259, **268–71**, 272, 276, **277**, 278, 280, 286, 298, **300**, 400
Clarke, Gillian 606, **611–12**
Clough, Arthur Hugh 319, **320–5**, 638
Coleridge, Samuel Taylor 278–9, 284, **290–5**, 296, 302–3, 358, 413, 447
Collins, Mary Gabrielle **406–7**
Conquest, Robert 519, **520–1**
Cope, Wendy 606, **620–1**, 622
Cornford, John **463–5**, 466
Cotton, Charles **182–4**
Coward, Noël 316, **317–18**
Cowley, Abraham 154, **155–6**
Cowper, William 184, 234, **235–41**, 242, 526, 624, 625
Crabbe, George 271, **272–6**, 277
Crawford, Robert **618–19**

Davidson, John 373, **374–9**, 454, 625
Davie, Donald 506
Day-Lewis, Cecil 462, **472**
Donne, John 69, 70, 119, **125–9**, 133, 149, 165, 202, 278, 281, 331, 529
Douglas, Gavin xii, 45
Douglas, Keith **490–1**
'Dream of the Rood, The' **6–7**
Dryden, John 171, **184–95**, 211, 302, 478, 528

Duffy, Carol Ann 606, **607–11**, 640
Dunbar, William xi, **48–54**, 56, 58, 60, 112, 133, 439, 499, 580
Dunn, Douglas **637–8**

Eliot, T.S. 130, 331, 362, 438–9, 441, 445, **446–50**, 451–2, 455, 461, 462, 466, 476, 490, **511–13**, 514, 523, 620

Fanthorpe, U.A. 606, **622–3**, 624
Farjeon, Eleanor **407–9**
Fenton, James **626–8**
Fergusson, Robert xii, **229–30**, 499, 580
FitzGerald, Edward 314
Frost, Robert 400, 401, 408

Garioch, Robert 496, **497–9**, 580, 594
Gascoyne, David 516, **517**, 518
Gawain and the Green Knight 22–3, **27–31**, 32, 36
Gay, John **215–18**
Ginsberg, Allen 549
Gower, John 35, 37
Graves, Robert **409–10**, 412
Gray, Thomas 197, 211, **212–14**, 591
Griffiths, Bill 537, **538–9**
Gunn, Thom **533–4**
Gurney, Ivor 409, **421–5**
'Guy of Warwick' 22

Hardy, Thomas 351, **379–85**, 386, 407, 455, 523, 622
Heaney, Seamus 6, 550, 564, **565–70**, 574, 578, 603
Hemans, Felicia **315–19**

Henderson, Hamish 491, **492–6**, 594

Henri, Adrian 540, **549–50**, 606

Henryson, Robert xi, 45, **46–7**, 48, 54, 499, 580

Herbert, George 133, **134–9**, 149, 171, 198, 231, 245, 278, 331, 511, 614

Herrick, Robert **147–8**

Heywood, John 77, **78–82**, 83

Hill, Geoffrey **560–1**, 613

Hobsbaum, Philip 530, 564

Hopkins, Gerard Manley **331–3**, 421, 600

'Horn' 22

Horovitz, Michael **539–40**, 560

Housman, A.E. 351, **385–8**

Hughes, Ted 456, 550, **551–4**, 555–6, 559–60, 564, 614, 620

James, Clive 531, 634, **635–37**

James I, King (of Scotland) **44–5**

Jamie, Kathleen 606, 615, **616–18**

Jennings, Elizabeth 506, **518–19**

Jones, David 516

Jonson, Ben 88, 89, 119, **120–5**, 133, **147**, 148, 152

Kavanagh, Patrick 570, **571–4**, 579

Kay, Jackie 606–7, **634**

Keats, John 245, 259, 276, 278–9, 296, **297–301**, 302, 309, 355, 413, 551, 608

Kennedy, Walter 52, 54

Kipling, Rudyard 320, 350, 361, **362–73**, 374, 377, 388, 397, 425, 480, 611

Langland, William **32–5**, 36

Lanier, Aemilia **149–52**, 154

Larkin, Philip 506, 522, 523, **524–9**, 530, 534, 544, 548

Lawrence, D.H. 440, 455, **456–61**, 476

Lear, Edward 336, 539

Leonard, Tom **592–3**

Lindsay, Maurice **581–3**

Lochhead, Liz **588–92**, 606, 640

Logue, Christopher 640

Longley, Michael **574–8**

Lovelace, Richard **146**

Loy, Mina 440, **441–2**, 461

Lydgate, John 35

Macbeth, George 640

MacCaig, Norman 594, **598–600**

MacDiarmid, Hugh (Christopher Murray Grieve) xii, 377, 438–9, 444, 451, **452–5**, 456, 461, 476, 491, 496, 499, 502, 578, 580, 598

McGough, Roger 540, 544, **545–7**, 548

Mackay Brown, George 594, 600, **601–3**

MacLean, Sorley (Somhairle MacGill-Eain) 496, **594–8**

MacNeice, Louis 462, 472, **473–6**, 484, 489, 625

Mahon, Derek 640

Marvell, Andrew 143, **144–5**, 149, **156–8**, 167, **168–9**, 184

Mather, Joseph **253–5**

Medwall, Henry **75–7**

Meredith, George **329–30**

Mew, Charlotte **410**

Michie, James 638, **639–40**

Middleton, Thomas 88, 129–30, **131**

Milton, John 149, 158, 161, **162–4**, 167, 184, 187, 207, 245–6, 248, 296, 307, 338, 413

Mitchell, Adrian 240, 540, **541–4**, 545–6, 549, 588, 632

Morgan, Edwin 583, **584–7**, 588

Morris, William **354–5**

Morte Arthure 24, **25–6**

Motion, Andrew 640

Muir, Edwin **502–4**, 580, 600

Nashe, Thomas **131–3**

Newbolt, Henry 388, **389–90**, 397

Newton, John 234

Oswald, Alice 606, **613–14**

Owen, Wilfred 397, 404, 409–11, **413–16**, 423

Owl and the Nightingale, The 17, **18–21**, 551

Pack, Richardson 219, **220**

Padel, Ruth 606

Patmore, Coventry **327–9**, 331, 336

Patten, Brian 540, **547–8**

Pearse, Patrick 427, 429, **430–2**

Plath, Sylvia 456, 550–3, **555–9**, 561, 638

Pomfret, John **198–200**

Pope, Alexander, 171, 196–8, 205–6, **206–11**, 215, 224, 236–7, 302, 591

Pope, Jessie 403, **404**

Porter, Peter **530–1**

Pound, Ezra **8–9**, 342, 381, 407, 438–40, **442–5**, 451, 455, 461, 462

Prior, Matthew 605

Pynn, Harry 494

Raine, Craig **624–5**

Raleigh, Walter 112, 114, **115–17**, 119

Ramsay, Allan 228

Reed, Henry **489–90**

Reid, Christopher 624, 640

Robertson, Robin **603–4**

Rochester, Earl of, *see* Wilmot, John

Rosenberg, Isaac 409, 416, **417–21**, 426

Rossetti, Christina 352, **353**

Rossetti, Dante Gabriel **351–2**

Sassoon, Siegfried 397, 409–10, **411–12**, 413, 419, 420, 423, 535

Scott, Walter xii, 271

'Sea Chaplain's Petition …, A' 222–3, **223–4**

'Seafarer, The' **8–9**, 12

Shadwell, Thomas 185

Shakespeare, William xi, 22, 51, 56, 61, 70, 73–5, 77–8, 81, 85, 88–94, **95–103**, 104, **105–111**, 112, 117–18, 120, 122–3, 129–30, 133, 142, 149, 152, 207, 208, 213, 278, 450, 498, 551, 591, 614

Shelley, Percy Bysshe 245, 278, 287, **288**, 296, 302, **309–13**, 315, 432, 527

Shenstone, William 224, **225–6**

Skelton, John **57–60**

Smart, Christopher **231–3**, 234, 278, 505, 605

Smith, Stevie (Florence Margaret Smith) **506–9**, 511, 514, 620

Smith, Sydney Goodsir **580–1**, 582

Smollett, Tobias 219, **221–2**, 260

Somervile, William **218–19**, 220

Sorley, Charles Hamilton 397, **398–400**, 403
Southey, Robert 286, 303
Southwell, Robert **94–5**
Spender, Stephen 462, 472, 484
Spenser, Edmund 74, 112, **113–14**, 162, 224, 296
Still, John 84, **85–7**
Suckling, Sir John **145–6**
'Sumer is icumen in' 17
Swift, Jonathan xii, **200–5**, 206, 210, 219, 224, 226, 228, 278, 574
Swinburne, Algernon Charles **355–6**, 573
Symons, Arthur **356–7**, 360

Taylor, John **118–19**
Tennyson, Alfred, Lord 314, **336–41**, 343, 551
Thomas, Dylan xii, 476, **499–502**, 516, 518, 580
Thomas, Edward 351, 400, **401–3**, 408
Thomas, R.S. 640
Thomson, James 197

Udall, Nicholas **84–5**

Vaughan, Henry **139–42**, 171, 281, 331, 614

Wain, John 533, **534–5**
Walcott, Derek 632
'Wanderer, The' **9**
Watts, Isaac 230
Webb, Harri **578–9**
Webster, John **129–30**
Wesley, Charles 231
Whitney, Isabella **69–72**, 78, 89
Wilde, Oscar 350, **357–9**, 360, 387, 425
Wilmot, John, Earl of Rochester 171, **172–6**, 185, 188, 302, 325
Winstanley, Gerrard 158, **159–61**
Wolcot, John ('Peter Pindar') **251–3**
Woodhouse, James 255, **256–7**
Wordsworth, William 245, 259, 272, 276, 278, **279–90**, 291–3, 296, 302–4, 315, 336, 447, 523, 551
Wroth, Mary 152, **153–4**
Wyatt, Thomas 60, **61–2**, 63, 112

Y Goddodin 3, 24
Yeats, W.B. xii, **360–1**, 390, 425, **426–9**, **432–6**, 438–9, 452–3, 480, 514, 551, 564, 570, 596

Zephaniah, Benjamin **628–31**, 632